Basics of
Career Counseling

LEE E. ISAACSON
Purdue University

ALLYN AND BACON, INC.
Boston   London   Sydney   Toronto

To Larry and Stephen, sons who make a father proud

Library of Congress Cataloging in Publication Data

Isaacson, Lee E.
  Basics of career counseling.

  Includes index.
  1. Vocational guidance. I. Title.
HF5381.I67 1985   371.4'25'02373   84–21607
ISBN 0–205–08326–9

Series Editor: Jeffery W. Johnston
Production Coordinator: Helyn Pultz
Production Services: Bywater Production Services

Printed in the United States of America

10 9 8 7   90

Contents

Preface

In career counseling, like counseling in general, the counselor must identify and respond appropriately to attitudes, behaviors, feelings, and thoughts expressed by clients. Further, career counselors assist clients in acquiring, processing, and applying information about the self and the world of work that is needed for effective decision making, planning, and subsequent implementation of plans.

In other words, there are three broad areas in which effective career counselors must have knowledge and competence. First, they must have the skills required of all counselors—the ability to hear what a client is expressing and to help the client understand what he or she is feeling, thinking, or acting out. Second, career counselors must understand the structure of the occupational world, what is required to enter, survive, and advance in it, and what impact it has on all of us. Third, and most important, career counselors must be able to help clients develop accurate, objective understanding of themselves including abilities, ambitions, interests, motivations, and values, and help them relate these personal attributes to the characteristics essential to success in various occupations, so that through the use of logical decision-making procedures, appropriate career choices and plans are made and implemented by clients.

This book is an attempt to help individuals planning to become counselors to understand the close relationship of those three areas and to integrate them into an effective career counseling style. Counseling theory and techniques are basic components in every counselor preparation program; and individual assessment and career information similarly are almost universally required. Only rarely, however, is an attempt made to help counselors-in-training to combine the theory and application of these three areas into a system that helps them to deal with clients. This volume has been written to bridge that gap.

The first four chapters provide a theoretical and philosophical foundation for career counseling. After looking at the impact that work has on everyone's life, we consider the major theories of career development and then the ways these theories expand or limit the activities of career counselors. Chapters 5 and 6 emphasize the relationship between career counseling and counseling in general, and particularly underscore what is sometimes misunderstood or not recognized—that career counseling is a special application of counseling requiring special skills and knowledge. For example, a client who seeks counseling because of a problem or concern, as counseling progresses, may realize the counseling that will be most helpful is career counseling. Some clients seek career counseling hoping it will alleviate or resolve other problems they face. Chapter 6 has been written with the assumption that those clients must be helped with their interfering concerns before they are able to pursue career planning in an effective, self-fulfilling manner.

Chapters 7 and 8 summarize important concepts in the areas of individual appraisal and the general structure of the world of work. Chapter 9 includes a careful consideration of a crucial aspect of career counseling—how the counselor can help clients understand the occupational relevance of their uniquely personal attributes. Many counselors, especially neophytes, encounter difficulty in helping clients to expand their occupational horizons and see the wide range of options available to them. This chapter describes an array of resources the counselor can employ in this expanding process. The second part of Chapter 9 discusses how this panorama of options can be selectively narrowed as the decision-making process continues. Chapter 10 focuses on some factors that influence the development of plans after a tentative choice has been made.

Chapter 11 discusses the role now being played by computer assisted career guidance systems and considers the use of these programs in expanding the professional services of career counselors. The final chapter, Chapter 12, considers additional problems involved in career counseling with special population groups such as those who are entering the occupational world later than most, those who are making or considering midstream changes, and those who have special physical, economical, or educational needs.

We live in a time when the interactions of increasing technology, limited physical and natural resources, and wider recognition of world-wide human need and potential, converge on the relationships between humans and work. The career counselor can help that relationship be personally satisfying and socially beneficial.

A host of people deserve a special note of gratitude for their help in bringing this book into being. These include, among others, numerous graduate students whose questions motivated a search for better answers, colleagues who shared ideas and supplied encouragement, and authors of journals and books whose thoughts sometimes challenged and sometimes clarified hazy ideas. Many pages would be required to list each person separately.

Finally, there are a few individuals who must be recognized for their very special contributions. These include Barbara Krause, whose patience and skill in translating page after page of illegible long hand moved the manuscript into readable form; Richard Kinnier, John Dagley, and Robert Gibson, whose careful and thoughtful reviews helped refine and improve the manuscript; and my wife Ardis, whose unwavering support and help kept me at an almost endless task.

1

Work and contemporary life

Work is one of the basic ingredients of human activity. It is, and has been, a central aspect of life in all cultures from prehistoric times to modern civilizations. One recent study (*Work in America,* 1973, p. 1) reminds us that scientists see the presence of primitive tools as a clue to determining if relics found in archeological explorations are human or animal. Work is significant in the life of the individual and in the relationships between individual and family and between individual and society.

Earlier definitions of work usually equated the concept with paid employment. More recently, *Work in America* and other sources suggest that work is an activity that produces something valued by other people. Similarly, Hoyt (1975) proposes that work is a conscious effort, other than activities whose primary purpose is either coping or relaxation, aimed at producing benefits for oneself and others. These broader definitions extend the concept to include the efforts of homemakers, volunteers, and others who are engaged in productive activity but may receive no financial remuneration.

The concept of career has also undergone change in recent years. Early definitions tended to restrict the application of the word to those individuals who had pursued a single occupation over a very long period of time with great success. Thus, one might speak of the career of a famous statesman, an outstanding physician, or a renowned actress, but one would not likely use the term to refer to a craftsman, a teacher, a nurse, or a storekeeper. Recently, usage has broadened so that the word is appropriately applied to almost everyone. There now appears to be considerable consensus for equating the word to an individual's lifelong work pattern. Thus it encompasses the work history of each individual where the term *work* is used in the broad sense described above.

The concept that work is the chronological sequence of all work-related experiences for every individual has recently been reconfirmed by a committee of the National Vocational Guidance Association (Sears, 1982). Most individuals start their careers as students preparing for work, acquire some part-time paid and/or unpaid experience while students, then move on to a series of positions that may be full- or part-time, paid or unpaid, and continue for variable lengths of time. In other words, it includes all of one's sequence of work-related activities, starting at least as soon as one enters school and likely extending into postretirement years while one is engaged in producing benefits for self and others. It does not include other non-work-related aspects of life that belong to the roles of friend, neighbor, citizen, spouse, parent, and so forth.

In these introductory sections we will attempt to examine the place of work in the lives of individuals and its impact on human groups such as the family and society in general. Later in the chapter we will review changes that are occurring in the structure of work and how work relates to mental health.

WORK AND THE INDIVIDUAL

As the median age of our population gradually moves upward, increasing attention is being paid to adults in our society. Studies by psychologists, sociologists, and others, of development in infancy, childhood, and adolescence are now being supplemented by research on adult development. Examples of recent efforts include *The Seasons of a Man's Life* by Levinson et al. (1978) and *Transformations: Growth and Change in Adult Life* by Gould (1978). Both books emphasize the importance of work throughout adult life and both focus primarily on the early adulthood period covering ages seventeen to forty-five. The reader must keep in mind that both studies also included only adult men. Comparable studies of adult women or of both men and women have not yet found their way into the research literature. When such studies are completed we will know more about the relationship to work of both genders. These two studies are significant because they suggest a path for future research. It would be erroneous to assume either that they are sexist because the subjects are all men or that the results apply equally well to women.

The Levinson study consists of the analysis of extended interviews over several years with a group of forty men, including four single occupational subgroups of ten men employed as biologists, executives, novelists, and factory workers. The authors conclude that the major components of adult life are the following:

Occupation
Marriage/family
Friendships/peers
Ethnicity
Religion
Leisure

Among the above components of life they identify the first two, occupation and marriage/family, as usually the most central aspects. Additionally, the authors state that a man's work is the primary base for his life in society. They consider the developmental patterns of life to be established on a combined biological, psychological, and social foundation. Further, they view individual life structure as consisting of a sequence of alternating developmental periods. A relatively stable, structure-building period is followed by a transitional, structure-changing period, replaced in turn by another stable period.

The developmental periods reported for their subjects include the following, with estimated ages:

1.	Childhood and adolescence	0–22
2.	Early adulthood	17–45
	Early adult transition	17–22
	Entering the adult world	23–28
	Age thirty transition	28–33
	Settling down	33–40
3.	Middle adulthood	40–65
	Midlife transition	40–45
	Entering middle adulthood	45–50
	Age fifty transition	50–55
	Culmination of middle adulthood	55–60
4.	Late adulthood	60–

Although the age clusters covered by the various periods and subcycles are not specific, the Levinson group believes there is more rigidity in the pattern than previously thought because their sample experienced these cycles within a year or so of the indicated ages. The almost clocklike transition from one cycle to the next appeared to be unaffected by other aspects of the subjects' lives.

According to this study, one of four major tasks faced during the early adulthood period (ages 17–45) is that of forming an occupation. Other tasks include forming a dream, goal, or purpose for life and incorporating it into one's life structure; forming a mentor relationship with an older adult who will become advisor, confidant, and sponsor; and forming love relationships, marriage, and family.

The task of forming an occupation is seen as extending across what is called the *novice phase* of early adulthood, including the periods of early adult transition (ages 17–22), entering the adult world (ages 23–28), the age thirty transition (ages 28–33), and sometimes even beyond this time. The Levinson group reports that their sample subjects made a first occupational choice between the ages of 17 and 29, and often subsequently changed to another choice. Those subjects who chose early often indicated that they later regretted the early choice, while those who delayed their choice reported they didn't have enough time to engage in what they considered to be enduring work. Levinson states that a man doesn't complete the preparatory phase of occupational development until he reaches the age thirty transition period, between ages 28 and 33.

The viewpoint expressed by the Levinson group that occupational formation occurs primarily in the decade of the twenties appears to conflict somewhat with the views of career development theorists, most of whom would suggest an earlier period. We will review these theoretical positions in a later chapter. The apparent discrepancy perhaps can be explained by the focus in the Levinson study on the events of adult life as recalled by adult subjects. Significance certainly can be attached to the evidence of occupational uncertainty, reconsideration, and modification extending throughout the twenties reported by this group. The implication of this longer period of uncertainty and self-doubt is very important for career counselors because this suggests the need for providing career counseling services—particularly focusing on support programs, clarification of values and self-understanding, and realignment of career goals—long beyond the choice and preparation periods usually associated with formal schooling.

The Levinson group (1978) further suggests important career-related aspects in the *settling down period* that extends across the years from ages 33 to 40. They report that men face two major tasks during these years: first, establishing a niche in society, and second, working toward advancement. These two tasks are usually accomplished in one of five typical patterns, labeled as follows:

A.   Advancement within a stable life structure.
B.   Serious failure or decline within a stable life structure.
C.   Breaking out: trying for a new life structure.
D.   Advancement which itself produces a change in life structure.
E.   Unstable life structure.

Over half of the men studied were identified as following the first sequence and the remainder were scattered across the other four options. For the larger group, this suggests they are progressing toward self-identified goals satisfactorily and they generally consider themselves to be successful rather than failures. Occupationally, they are most likely to continue on the path that they chose and defined earlier. Another 20 percent of the group were identified as following the second sequence. These men generally displayed satisfactory progress according to society's standards but failed to accomplish significant goals that they had set for themselves or that might provide the basis for important advancements in future years. This group, along with those identified with the other three patterns, were likely to make dramatic changes in their work or love relationships or both.

During their early forties, according to Levinson et al., men again find themselves in a period of transition. In this stage they review the past and begin to make new plans and choices for the years ahead. They also begin to deal with some basic philosophic issues in their lives that Levinson designates as *polarities*. Eighty percent of the subjects reported this to be a time of moderate or severe crisis affecting every part of their lives. The pattern followed in the previous settling down period influences the way this period is managed. Between the ages of 43 and 47, all of the men had entered the period labeled as *middle adulthood*. During this time, the nature of their work changed substantially. As we will see in Chapter 3, Super (1953) refers to this as the *maintenance stage* of career development.

Gould (1978) concentrates almost entirely on the age span from 16 to 45. Like Levinson, he divides this early adulthood period into four parts, with almost identical age groups: 16–22, 22–28, 28–34, 35–45. His description of these developmental sequences affirms many positions taken by Levinson. For example, Gould also states that the period from 28 to 34 is the time when career commitments deepen.

Both studies confirm that work remains one of the central aspects of adult life, as was suggested much earlier in the writings of Sigmund Freud, Carl Jung, and Erik Erikson. Work has great influence on identifying who the individual really is, what status is held in society, the material rewards received by the individual, and the psychological satisfactions realized.

Because both Levinson and Gould limited their research to adult men, we must wait for parallel studies of adult women. Although we cannot confirm the cyclic patterns identified in these two studies, we can infer that work and marriage/family hold positions of centrality in the lives of women as well. One significant event of the past decade has been the influx of women into work outside the home. As the proportion of adult women who are engaged in work for pay continues to increase, we can assume that they too will view work as a means of self-expression and self-actualization. Perhaps one of the significant transitions in contemporary life may be the full involvement of most women in the activities of paid employment.

WORK AND THE FAMILY

Long ago, when life was simpler (or more likely, only in American mythology), the idea often arose that the concepts of work and of family were two distinctly different areas. In fact, Kanter (1977) describes this view in these words:

> In a modern industrial society work life and family life constitute two separate and nonoverlapping worlds, with their own function, territories, and behavioral rules. Each operates by its own laws and can be studied independently. (p. 8)

Many authors have demonstrated quite emphatically that even in those simpler times work exerted a heavy impact on family life. In a study of the Victorian period in England, Banks (1954) points out that so-called middle-class men often found it necessary to postpone marriage until their incomes had reached a level that would permit setting up a household commensurate with their social class. Further, as the costs of educating children increased for this middle-class group, family size was more restrictively controlled. Similarly, Rowntree (1922), studying working-class families in England at the turn of the century, notes that such individuals encountered a life cycle of five periods: starting with poverty during their childhood, then some relief as they or their siblings added to family income, succeeded by poverty as they started their own families, followed by some ease as the children's earnings augmented family income, and finally a return to poverty during older, declining years. During the period studied, Rowntree found that the average income for an unskilled worker was always a little less than that needed to support a family of moderate size at the minimal level.

Focusing on more recent events, Oppenheimer (1982) studied Public Use Samples from 1960 and 1970 Decennial Census Data of the United States in order to compare differences, according to male age level, in family data for eight occupational groups (professional, managerial, sales, clerical, craft, operative, service, and labor), further divided by income level. She particularly examined the interaction of family and career cycles with special attention given to three periods of economic stress produced by this interaction. She labeled these stress periods as *life-cycle squeezes* and concluded that most modern families face three such squeezes: the first at the time they are attempting to establish an independent household; the second when children reach the costliest period of maintenance, usually during adolescence; and the third in the postretirement period.

Oppenheimer identified nine adaptive behaviors used by families to promote the replacement of the family over generations at the same or a higher socioeconomic level. These strategies are employed in various ways, often related to the occupational status of the family. They are applied by families to overcome or resolve the stress that can be expected to occur during one of the life-cycle squeezes identified above. These behavioral factors include the following:

1.   Nonmarriage of some adult children.
2.   Age at marriage.
3.   Age at birth of the first child.
4.   Spacing of subsequent children.
5.   Total number of children born.
6.   Economic role of children.
7.   Economic role of wives and its timing.
8.   Economic role of husbands and its timing.
9.   Migration of individuals or families.

For example, it has not been uncommon in previous generations for one child in a family to delay or forego marriage in order to remain in the home and provide care or financial support for elderly or disabled parents caught in the third life-cycle squeeze. Oppenheimer points out the significance of both husband's and wife's age at the time of the first child's birth. The husband's age is important because it predicts his position in the career cycle when child-rearing costs will be most expensive, and the wife's age may suggest both family size and the likelihood of her entry or return to paid employment. Both the spacing of births of children and the total number of children in the family influence whether or when the mother enters or returns to paid employment as well as the severity and duration of the second life-cycle squeeze.

The adaptive behaviors identified by Oppenheimer are subject to the influence of various constraints that families may encounter. These include the following:

1.   Prevailing mortality and morbidity conditions.
2.   Fertility control capabilities.
3.   Family standard of living.
4.   Cost of raising children.
5.   Structure of economic opportunities for earnings.
6.   Nonfamilial sources of income and their relationship to the life cycle.

The interaction of applicable constraints on the available adoptive behaviors leads the family to develop strategies that appear to be appropriate. Influential factors in determining the chosen strategies are the social and economic conditions of the family, largely related to the male's occupational status. Oppenheimer's data showed that the various occupational groups selected strategies according to the career trajectory or pattern that represented that occupational group. She describes three groups in particular:

high-income white-collar families, low-income blue-collar families, and low-income white-collar families. We will consider each group briefly.

High-income white-collar occupations (mostly professionals and managers) usually show a steeply rising income level with age and an aspiration for a high-level lifestyle. The families in these occupations are economically vulnerable early in their adult life because the first lifestyle squeeze is usually very stressful as a result of the high costs of establishing an independent household at a relatively high level of living. Children in these families contribute little or nothing to the economy of the family because they are involved in prolonged periods of education. The men in these occupations leave school later than the men in all other occupational groups. For example, Oppenheimer reports that her 1960 data showed that only 56 percent of these men (mainly the managers) had completed their education by age twenty-one compared to 97 percent of all other men. By 1970 the figures had become 40 percent of those men versus 90 percent of all other men. These men marry later, have children later, and tend to have fewer children than men in other groups. However, these postponements and restrictions are less likely to occur when funds from other sources are available to the couple and they are willing to function at a lower standard of living for a period. Outside sources of funds might include subsidized education, grants from parents, loan funds, subsidized student housing, and the like. Since the 1960 and 1970 census data were collected, significant changes have occurred in the employment of women. One can speculate that women's increased involvement in income producing work may also have a notable impact on the age of marriage for this occupational group, with the wife's earnings providing major support during the period the husband is completing professional training.

Except for one group of skilled craft workers whose income placed them in a higher income level, most blue-collar workers studied by Oppenheimer were in the two lower-income levels. The blue-collar group included craft workers, operatives, service workers, and laborers. These workers generally had lower earnings, a rather flat age-to-earnings profile with an early and low peak, and a modest lifestyle. Any sharp increase in earnings for this group was likely to occur in their early years of employment unless they were able to capitalize on upward occupational mobility. The more common pattern of a flat profile with an early low peak also included some decline in income in later years. These families in general are often caught in a difficult bind resulting from delaying the first squeeze because of lack of financial resources to establish a home. When this delay occurs, the second squeeze is likely to be particularly severe because the increased child-rearing costs of that period may take place after earnings have started to decline and become more uncertain.

Some changes in technology point to an increase in on-the-job training of blue-collar workers, resulting in more job security and some relief from the double-bind squeeze. However, the drastic changes in many industries such as steel and automobile manufacture in the early 1980's may also indicate the continued vulnerability of blue-collar workers who cannot sell skills readily in periods of technological restructure.

This blue-collar lower-income group showed a pattern of early marriage and early childbirth, with the number of children somewhat related to external factors such as infant mortality. Most families demonstrated some reliance on income contribution by adolescent and young adult children living in the home, and some of these young adult children sometimes delayed or abandoned plans for marriage in order to help the parents financially.

Families are often caught in a conflict between short-term and long-term goals related to the overall welfare of the family—if children go to work early to assist with family finances, they often limit their schooling and commit themselves to a lifelong lower-level income. Prevailing social pressures, as well as child labor laws and school-leaving-age laws, now generally restrict early employment of children and appear to resolve this conflict by protecting the children. For example, Oppenheimer reports significant increases in the school leaving age each decade of this century, with 53 percent of the husbands born in 1896–1905 reporting in 1960 that they had left school by age thirteen, and only 8 percent of the 1936–1945 birth group reporting in 1970 a similar experience; and while 71 percent of the first group had left school by age sixteen, only 24 percent of the second group had done so.

Oppenheimer speculates that many blue-collar families may adopt strategies of delaying marriage and childbirth because more women are engaged in premarital employment. If the number of children in each family is also reduced, the wives may resume employment in larger numbers and in this way replace the economic support previously supplied to families by older children. However, successful application of the strategy may depend upon the level of education acquired earlier by the wife.

Of the three larger groups described by Oppenheimer, the lower-income white-collar families are often caught in the most difficult economic squeeze. They generally expect their children to attain a socioeconomic position equal to or greater than that of the parents. This aspiration usually means a higher school leaving age than that of the parents in order to obtain enough education to maintain an option for employment at least at the parents' level. The longer educational period usually results in delay in both marriage and childbearing and thus children make little or no economic contribution to the family. Wives generally have a higher educational background and often significant premarital work experience, thus making it easier for them to return to work or to maintain a position in the world of work. One result of this is that the number of children in each family in this group tends to be smaller than among the blue-collar families.

Oppenheimer describes several implications of the data she studied. One of these is that the societal emphasis on longer schooling for all children has intensified the burden on all families during the second squeeze but has also increased the options for upward mobility for the children. While the pressure of the second squeeze has intensified, the economic security of middle-aged men has generally improved because of less demand for physical strength, increased job security, and better health care, thus partly offsetting the economic squeeze. Another factor of increasing importance has been the improved capability for more effectively controlling the number and timing of children. This factor exerts influence on the extent to which women can participate in work. This, in turn, requires changes in the way that women work—the kinds of jobs they hold, the access to training for work, the opportunity for advancement in work. If families develop plans based on greater work involvement by women, that planning will generally require more consistency in work and less intermittent involvement.

While Oppenheimer was studying census data to ascertain the impact of work on family life, Davis (1982) was engaged in an intensive study of a relatively small sample of families to study the same problem. Oppenheimer provides a picture of that influence on a broad scale and Davis looks at what might be called the "nitty-gritty" effect. She interviewed members of thirty couples, always talking with the wife and frequently with the husband. She used only families that included both husband and wife and at least one child under age eighteen. Half (53 percent) of the families consisted of four people, 20 percent consisted of three members, 17 percent were five-member families, and 10 percent had six or more members. Among the thirty husbands, four were students and twenty-six were employed full-time. Among the wives, eleven were employed full-time, four were employed part-time, two were full-time students, and thirteen were full-time housewives. All were white, lived in the San Francisco area, and were relatively highly educated, with 40 percent of the husbands holding advanced degrees and 33 percent of the wives holding bachelor degrees and 13 percent with advanced degrees. The husbands reported that they worked an average of 51.9 hours weekly and the full-time employed wives reported an average of 40 hours.

Davis particularly studied the day-in and day-out effect of work on the lives of the family members. She concluded that the rational, organized work world "out there" and the emotionally oriented family group "in here" cannot be kept separate but instead constantly interact with each other. Assuming the traditional view that housework is a full-time job conducted by the wife while the husband is engaged in full-time employment outside the home, she looked for changes in family life produced by changes in that traditional arrangement. One major concern was the change in family life brought about by the increased participation of women in employment—in other words, if the housewife isn't home during the day, who is doing the housework?

Davis points out that every link between a family member and any outside activity such as work, school, clubs or organizations, leisure activities, volunteer efforts, or whatever, places a constraint on that person and to some extent influences or even overrides family concerns. The most influential factors are those viewed as mandatory such as work and school. She clearly describes the problem faced by many wives thus:

> The whole situation becomes particularly complicated when the wife takes on important external commitments. A husband who works long hours outside the home can justify the neglect of his domestic duties by claiming that he is performing his chief function of breadwinning with extra zeal. This is not true for the wife. She is *supposed* to assign highest priority to family duties. This then is the modern woman's dilemma. If she goes out to work and consequently neglects her family, she is morally reprehensible. If she works but refuses to neglect her family, she probably never will progress very far with her career. If she does not go out to work, she denies herself the primary avenue in modern society for obtaining prestige, self-validation, and other important rewards. (p. 14)

In the traditional family, external commitments that might be considered optional, such as volunteer activities or involvement in organizations or clubs, still produce an impact on the family schedule and the time available for family matters. The employed wife is likely to have similar commitments plus the mandatory pressures that come with employment. If she is a dual-earner, a worker who works for income, or the satisfaction that accompanies work, or for social or other reasons, she may be able to limit or control some of the employment pressures. If, however, she is a dual-career person, a worker dedicated to the advancement of her career, she will face a myriad of work-related pressures similar to those encountered by the career-oriented husband. Mead (1982) reports that dual-earner and dual-career couples identify their most pressing problems to be related to time management, and traditional couples list first economic matters.

Davis describes many factors that influence family functions and the amount of housework that must be completed to maintain the family. For example, the more children in the family, and the younger their ages, the more hours of housework likely to be required. The size and nature of the living quarters is another factor, as is the presence of modern technology in the form of freezers, microwave ovens, laundry facilities, etc. Families who include production functions such as bread baking, food canning, and furniture and clothing making require more hours than families that engage only in maintenance activities such as superficial cleaning, tidying, and minor repair. Further influences include individual preferences and skills—some prefer elaborate dinners cooked from scratch while others choose hotdogs and TV dinners. Obviously, within the family, some housekeeping duties are clearly optional; however, even minimal maintenance of the family requires the mandatory commitment of some time to these functions.

Families with both husband and wife employed were more likely to organize housework than were one-earner families. Organization involves planning, setting schedules, and assigning tasks in ways very similar to the external workplace. Two-earner families were found to do most housework on the weekend while single-earner families followed the reverse pattern, with most housework hours occurring during the work week.

As more wives enter employment, a question arises regarding who does what housework. Gender roles have been recognized in family maintenance activities for many decades, with traditional families often assigning outdoors or time-controlled activities such as lawn-mowing, snow-shoveling, painting, and automobile care to the husband and daily care activities such as cooking, sweeping, dusting, picking up, laundry, and so forth to the wife. Scanzoni and Fox (1980) report that during the decade of the seventies some shift away from this traditional position was seen in terms of both attitude and behavior, although considerable distance appears to remain between present behavior and a more equitable future.

Studies of changing gender role seem to produce results according to the approach used in the study. According to Davis, studies asking about relative amounts of time spent on various household chores tend to show that husbands of employed wives do more housework than husbands of wives not employed, although in both cases the wife remains responsible for most of it. Studies that ask for reports of absolute amounts of time spent by keeping daily activity logs or time-budget studies show very little, if any, increased effect on husband's housework time as a result of the wife's employment. In families with adolescent children, the major transfer of housework duties is to the children rather than to the husband.

Davis found in an earlier 1972 study that husbands contributed two and one-half minutes of housework for each hour the wife was employed outside the home. By 1976 the time had increased to five minutes for each hour of employment. The greatest change occurs in the amount of time spent by the wife: each hour of outside employment reduces her average time spent on housework by twenty-three minutes. Thus the wife who is employed for a typical eight-hour day will spend three hours less time per day on housework than will her nonemployed counterpart.

Davis found that traditionally minded couples felt that it was appropriate for a married woman to work outside the home provided that young children were not part of the family, and further provided that her work did not interfere in any way with her family duties. Also they felt it was appropriate for a husband to help the wife with housework if she were especially busy, but the helping should be viewed as a personal favor and not as a sharing of responsibility. Egalitarian families felt that families should be free to decide who does what task, even reversing earning roles if they desire. Davis found a third group with mixed viewpoints who generally expressed egalitarian beliefs but practiced rather traditional behavior. For example, some said that husband and wife should share household duties when both worked full-time, but ideally the husband should earn enough so that the wife didn't have to work. Within the thirty couples, almost all of the employed wives held either egalitarian or mixed views, and the nonemployed wives held traditional or mixed views. The husbands of employed wives were most likely to be egalitarian, and smaller but equal-sized groups were traditional or mixed. Husbands of nonemployed wives were more likely to hold a mixed view in contrast with their wives' traditional or mixed view. Actual behavior appeared to be more a product of practical pressures such as time limitations than of ideological view.

An implication seen in the evidence appears to be that greater time pressures on families as a result of more hours spent in employed status will lead to greater organization of family activity, especially attempting to increase efficiency and to make better choices of time usage. Further, it is clear that involvement in work does affect the domestic activities of family members—the functions performed, and when and how they are performed. Finally, in many families work tends to dominate family life.

One of the most significant changes in the labor force during the past decade has been the increase in the number of women engaged in full-time employment outside the home. It is clearly apparent that the pattern is no longer one of traditional premarriage or prechildbearing involvement, but instead reflects a much longer and more consistent participation. Some women will undoubtedly select a dual-earner role that will permit them to give primacy to spouse and family; many, however, will opt for a dual-career pattern wherein job responsibilities will require a heavy commitment of time and energy. Regardless of the type of involvement, either will require adjustments in attitudes and behaviors within the family. Levinson (1978), discussing the development of adult men, observed that one of the paradoxes of life is the fact that one is required to make choices and major decisions (referring to occupation and love relationship) before one is really prepared to make them. Starting one's occupational activity and also one's marriage when both members of a couple are engaged in employment requires cooperation, understanding, tolerance, and much flexibility.

Many strategies for solving the problems faced by two-worker families are already beginning to appear. These include job-sharing, in which two people divide the responsibilities of a single job, and the development of home-based work centers in which the individual, using technology such as computers, fulfills the job requirements at home rather than at the office. Other strategies include maternity and paternity leave, creation of child-care centers at places of work, year-round school programs, and flexible work schedules.

Another recent phenomenon has been the increase in single-parent families, largely produced by rising divorce rates. The relationship between work and family becomes even more complex in this situation since the one adult has total responsibility for both aspects. Work is usually an economic necessity, and family relationships are often strained and exacerbated by the absence of the missing family member. It is almost inevitable that problems and difficulties in one area will impinge on the other.

Our purpose in this section has been to explore the impact of work on family life. Whether one looks at data obtained with the breadth of the Decennial Census or the depth of intensive interviews, the conclusion is the same: work touches and influences every part of family life and every family member.

WORK AND SOCIETY

If we define work as the production of goods and services valued by others, and define society as the totality of social relationships among human beings, we see at once the intense and pervasive interdependence of these two concepts. Neither can be defined, explained, or understood without due consideration of the other. This interaction is also apparent when we look at branches of knowledge such as economics, politics, and sociology. Many writers in each of these fields point to the significant influence of the writings of Karl Marx, Max Weber, and Emile Durkheim in forming the basis for their academic discipline.

Salaman (1980) states that many early writers believed that the ways in which the means of production are owned and the nature of the relationship between employers and workers in production determine the social and political structure and process. Others, for example Kerr et al. (1973), propose that the way that work and technology are designed determines the social and political structure. They place primary emphasis on how workers are recruited and how the labor force is developed and maintained. Freidson (1982) contends that occupations, as organized forms of differentiated productive activity, can be only partially explained by using both organizational theory and class or social-structure theory. He points out that many occupations exist in complex organizations, some exist in the labor market outside of any organizational structure, and some exist in hybrid situations where they are seen within an organization but appear to be freestanding, self-directing suppliers of labor.

Salaman summarizes the well-known view of Marx, who pointed to the inherently political nature of the way work is designed under capitalism in order to maximize profitability, and to direct and control the activities of employees whose interests conflict with those of the employers. Salaman also recalls the views of Adam Ferguson and Adam Smith, whose writings suggest the social phenomenon of worker alienation—the idea that increasingly finer divisions of labor separate the worker from any sense of relationship to the product of his or her effort. Alienation or separation develop, according to Ferguson, not only between worker and product, but also between worker and self, and worker and community. Marx later applied the view developed by Ferguson and Smith in much of his own writing. For the past century and a half, concern with the relationship between the worker and work has been basic to much writing in economics, political science, and sociology. Today, this focus on the worker/work affinity is primary when one describes societies with adjectives such as advanced, agrarian, capitalist, communist, industrial, socialist, and the like.

Hamilton (1980) describes the sociological study of work as following one or the other of two basic approaches. Those who use a *structural model approach* see work as deriving from the structural characteristics of society and its major institutional areas. Most models that follow this approach build on the theoretical positions of Marx, Weber, and Durkheim. Others accept a *human-relations model,* which is mainly atheoretical and focuses on a managerial-type approach to improving the work situation. The latter view grew out of the famous Hawthorne Works studies conducted in the late 1920s, which revealed the heavy influence on worker production caused by informal work groups. This discovery of the impact of views of fellow workers on output conflicted with the earlier structural view that workers acted individually in self-interest.

It would probably be difficult to identify any society that represents a pure form of either of these two models. Most capitalist societies—where theory proposes that employers will control and dominate the workplace and the worker—have permitted or encouraged the expansion of regulation, interference by the government in economic activity, development of state or public ownership, and the creation of welfare systems, all to serve as counteracting forces to capitalistic pressures. Similarly, most socialistic and communistic societies have found that the lack of incentive and the growth of stifling bureaucracies have necessitated the use of some form of private enterprise. Salaman (1980) suggests that the impact of either political form on the worker may be quite similar. His position is clearly stated in the following paragraph:

> It is far from clear that work in a Russian car factory is substantially different from working for Ford. The technology is the same. The size of the organization and its conditions will be broadly similar. There may be some differences in levels of reward of manual work in the two countries, if not absolutely, at least relative to other work and occupational groups, but the hierarchical nature of the organization and the specialization, subdivision and nature of actual work tasks will be very similar. And while events and decisions in the Ford plant will be governed by the company's drive for profit, in the Russian case such decisions follow the organization's attempts to fulfill the levels of output, input and efficiency that had been set by the centralized planning departments. In neither case, it would seem, does the ordinary worker play much, if any, of a part in determining the nature of his work, or its objectives, nor does he work for himself in any meaningful sense, despite the fact that in the USSR he ostensibly owns the means of production. (p. 7)

Parsons (1960) has suggested that differences are found not between industrialized nations with differing political structures but rather between industrialized and nonindustrialized nations. These differences can be found, he believes, in social institutions, social roles, stratification systems, and their power structures. The differences are produced by the fact that the industrialized nations have become more complex.

In the following pages we will look briefly at some of the ways that work and society interact to influence the life of the worker. The topics considered here are simply representative of the many ways that this interrelationship occurs.

The concept of social class first appeared somewhere in antiquity, but the industrial revolution provided the basis for its rapid growth. As factories replaced cottage industries, ownership and pursuit of profit on a larger scale created a new group who joined the "landed gentry" to form an upper class. As factories expanded in size and proliferated in numbers, they provided the setting for the creation of a working class, drawn primarily from agrarian and cottage settings, to operate the factory machines. Very soon, the two groups reflected vast differences in lifestyle, values, and political views.

Between these two groups a third group developed consisting, for the most part, of the managerial and administrative staff of the factories. Affiliated with this middle group, but outside the owner-worker factory structure, were the small business owner-operators, the professionals (physicians, lawyers, teachers, and so on), and the skilled craftsmen who in a special way were business operators. The managers, for obvious reasons, developed political and social views compatible with those of the capital owners. Because the remainder of the middle class had a greater degree of independence, based primarily on the security provided by their business or personal skills, their political and social beliefs were more diverse but still tended to be more similar to those of the upper class than to those of the working class.

Although we profess to minimize or disregard class in present-day society, its residuals are still apparent in much of everyday life. Working-class members see work as a place where they can sell their labor. Even though worker organizations have brought some degree of affluence to production-line work, they have not been as successful in helping the worker to obtain greater control over the job and work life. Affluence has been gained at the cost of long hours, increasing division and simplification of tasks, and greater alienation. The worker, even though he or she may dislike the job, stays with it because of the pay. Middle-class workers usually have better working conditions, brighter promotion or advancement prospects, higher levels of job security, and are more likely to consider work as a potential source of satisfaction.

The influence of social class on occupational participation has been well documented by numerous sociological studies. One of the best known of these is Hollingshead's (1949) study which has been succeeded by at least two follow-up studies in more recent years. One significant finding reported in that early study showed that more than three-fourths of upper-middle-class youngsters hoped to attain professional or business careers while less than ten percent of lower-working-class youth held such goals. Of course, many factors other than so-called social class influence occupational goals; nevertheless, such overwhelming figures make it difficult to maintain an argument that social class has no influence. Blau et al. (1956) saw the influences of social and cultural structure on occupational choice having an effect due to their impact on the individual's personality development and on the economic and social conditions in which occupational choices are made.

Closely related to the influence of social-class membership are hereditary factors. Osipow (1983) has pointed to the fact that inheritance is most likely to be influential when the older generation has large capital investments to pass along to its offspring. Examples of this situation include family-owned businesses and farms. Osipow also proposes that inheritance may be more influential when families are subject to physical or psychological isolation. Examples of the first include occupations in farming, lumbering, or fishing. Examples of psychological isolation include medical, military, and religious occupations.

The American dream, typified by the famous Horatio Alger stories of earlier days, saw the poor boy rising to fame and fortune despite his lowly birth and innumerable hardships and obstacles. Further, our history records many cases where that is exactly what occurred. To assume, however, that those cases were typical is to stretch the evidence a bit far. Access to educational opportunity is often the crucial factor in those famous success stories. Very often access to education and the quality of that education are directly related to family occupational status, and thus are related to the social-class phenomenon.

Montagna (1977) distinguishes between social class and social status by suggesting that the first is related to the earlier concept of ownership versus worker role as discussed above, while status is primarily a measure of prestige derived from one's occupation and lifestyle. Occupational prestige has been studied extensively for nearly three-quarters of a century. The reported results show surprising consistency over time as well as across very diverse groups based on age, education, gender, and nationality.

Studies by Counts (1925), Deeg and Paterson (1947), and Hakel, Hollmann, and Dunnette (1968) show that, over a forty-two year period and with slightly different reporting groups, occupations tended to hold the same relative status position. In all three studies, the five highest prestige occupations included physician, lawyer, superintendent of schools, banker, and civil engineer. Similarly, all three studies showed the listed occupations with lowest prestige to be truck driver, coal miner, janitor, hod carrier, and ditch digger. Within the middle ranges some variability was apparent, but even here the changes in position were relatively modest.

Somewhat similar studies were reported by the National Opinion Research Center (1947) and by Hodge, Seigel, and Rossi (1964). The first study used a longer list of ninety occupations and a carefully selected sample of three thousand individuals picked according to region, size of city, age, sex, status, and race. The second study was a replication of the first, conducted approximately fifteen years later. The correlation between prestige scores on the two studies was reported as .99. The resulting scores were generally similar to those of the studies reported above.

Caplow (1954) has identified eight factors that influence occupational prestige. He includes the following items:

1. Extent of responsibility in the work.
2. Nature of the work.
3. Amount of formal education required.
4. Length of training.
5. Authority.
6. Social class attributes of the occupation.
7. Income, both amount and certainty.
8. Behavioral control. (pp. 52–57)

Caplow believes that the last item, the extent to which occupational members control their own work and the work of other occupations, correlates most closely with the order in which occupations are ranked. In other words, occupations that are not only self-directing but also control what other occupations do hold high prestige status, and those occupations that lack self-direction and also are controlled by other relatively low-status occupations hold low occupational status.

Most studies of occupational prestige are conducted by asking individuals either to rank occupations according to status or to classify the occupation according to a predetermined scale. As seen in the studies reported above, individuals respond in amazingly similar ways. Thus, we must conclude that society assigns to occupations a reputational level that is widely recognized, understood, and accepted. Further, changes in status can occur, but such changes are usually slow and modest.

The interaction between work and the individual and between work and the family described in the previous sections of this chapter obviously influence the relationship between work and society if we think of society as the larger collection of individuals and families. Perhaps the relationship between work and society can be summarized in the following generalizations:

1. Work and society are concepts that, in part, define each other. Society divides work into occupations, each consisting of a recognized body of skills, activities, and knowledge that is seen as providing an identity and often a set of values or attitudes. Work, by its degree of complexity and breadth or variety, identifies the nature of the society as agrarian or industrial and to a large extent determines the world status of the society.
2. Society establishes the structural model within which work is

organized—private versus public ownership or some combination of the two. The presence in the society of certain groups of workers with recognized, viable skills makes possible, perhaps requires, that those social divisions be made.

3. Society legitimizes certain occupations and repudiates others as illegal, immoral, or asocial. It may establish legal controls and regulations for occupations through licensure or certification, and it may establish a favored status through special acts or exemptions.
4. Society stratifies itself into loosely identified classes that appear to relate primarily to broad occupational membership, such as white-collar, blue-collar, service, and farm labor, with each group exhibiting some difference in lifestyle.
5. Occupations are accorded status or prestige by society on the basis of several work-related factors.
6. Individuals make occupational choices that partially reflect their relationship to society, and that choice in turn establishes their relationship to and status in the general society.

WORK AND ECONOMIC AND INDUSTRIAL CHANGE

An enigma associated with work is its reflection of both constancy and fluidity—while it appears to remain stable and uniform, it also appears to be adjusting and changing. Although both aspects seem always present, cyclical dominance shifts back and forth. The mid-1980s appear to be one of the periods in which change is on the ascendancy, with modification and revision of the world of work proceeding at a breath-taking pace.

Changes in the world of work can often be anticipated in advance of their arrival because these changing trends are caused by factors that are already evident. Other changes may be temporary in nature and are produced by transitory situations. Detailed discussion of causes of these long-term and short-term trends can be found elsewhere (Isaacson, 1977).

Typical causes of long-term trends are changes in the birth rate or death rate; availability of natural resources; technological progress, inventions, or discovery; patterns of capitalizing or financing occupational activities; the average age of workers in a particular field; and, finally, changes in the way of life of large segments of the population.

Short-term changes in work can be created by any of the following: wars or similar calamities; natural disasters such as earthquakes, epidemics, or floods; fads; seasonal variations; and short-range economic factors. The impact of short-term changes can be very severe and intense but, because of the brief time span, conditions soon return to approximately the same status that existed before the sudden change. Long-term trends, on the other hand, produce an influence that extends over several years or decades.

Currently used buzz words such as "automation," "high technology," "robotics," and "computers" elicit both fear of change and the thrill of new opportunities. The words and the concepts have been around for some time. The earliest effective computer, known as Univac, was developed during World War II. In spite of its immense size and ponderous behavior, often plagued by breakdowns and delays, it demonstrated new possibilities for change in the workplace. Early advocates of automation pointed to the chance to relieve men and women of monotonous and abasing tasks and providing them instead with lives of leisure and abundance. Those who viewed the development with concern pointed to the possibility of turning the few workers lucky enough to have jobs into "machines" and robbing most workers of independence and self-esteem.

The application of automation (the automatic, centralized control of an integrated production system) to industry in this country has usually met with resistance from workers and their representative organizations because of the fear of worker displacement. Nobel-prize-winning economist Wassily Leontief suggested in the early 1950s that industrially backward, undeveloped countries could expedite their national development by moving directly into automated manufacturing. Large quantities of manufactured goods, such as ready-to-wear clothing, made in developing countries like South Korea, Singapore, and Thailand are now available in American stores as a result of those countries' following the suggestion to skip directly to automated industry. Other highly industrialized countries like Japan and Germany rebuilt their war-destroyed industries with provisions for automation. Recent decline in American industries such as steel and automobile manufacture has shown the tremendous advantages to Japan and Germany resulting from their decisions.

Major economic and social change rarely occurs because of a single factor. The highest unemployment rates in over forty years cannot simply be assigned to changing technology. Other important contributing causes certainly include attempts to reduce inflation, continuing high interest rates, failure of industry to modernize, resistance by unions to new procedures, increasing competition from other countries, and other factors. Four significant developments that appear to be influencing American work have been described recently by Gillett (1983). We will consider each of his four items briefly.

First, Gillett suggests, an extensive "deindustrialization" of the American economy is occurring. Many large corporations have diverted capital (financial resources, plants, and equipment) from productive investment in national industries into unproductive speculation, mergers, and acquisition of other companies. Some companies have closed down obsolete or noncompetitive plants where low productivity, high labor costs, obsolete equipment, or inefficient management have been unable to meet the pressure of competition. Other companies have relocated plants that were efficient and productive to sites where labor costs are cheaper, sometimes in foreign countries. Still other companies have become affiliated with existing foreign competitors that can produce comparable products at lower costs and higher profit ratios.

The movement of one factory overseas not only displaces the workers who were previously employed in that factory, but also affects the jobs of workers who provided raw materials, subassemblies, and other components for that factory. Further, workers in unrelated fields providing goods and services to the workers in the first factory are also influenced by the loss of those jobs through reduced demand for the goods and services they provide. Frequently, the displaced workers are unable to obtain other jobs with equivalent income, and economic activity throughout the geographic area is depressed and dislocated.

A second change noted by Gillett, closely related to deindustrialization, is the product of rapid advancement in transportation and communication technologies. The use of large cargo aircraft simplifies the movement of supplies and equipment to and from widely dispersed factories and permits rapid relocation of entire factories. The use of word processors and computers joined by satellite communications systems brings control and operation of complex manufacturing processes across the world into the home office. As a result, many multinational companies doubled the amount of their overseas investments between 1960 and 1980 as they searched for higher profits, often through lower labor costs.

The greater use of new technology, especially computers and microelectronics, thus leading to greater automation is the third development identified by Gillett. As indicated earlier, the transition to automation started many years ago but progressed slowly until very recently. Technological developments, as well as competition from overseas, increase the pace at which movement to automation now occurs. Gillett quotes Harley Shaiken of MIT as stating that General Motors will computerize 90 percent of its machine tools within a decade, while another company will replace two-thirds of its production painters and half of its production welders with robots. If such changes occur as anticipated, at least a million additional workers will be displaced, further exacerbating heavy unemployment figures.

Finally, Gillett points to the continued "deskilling" of many jobs—the application of technology to simplify the work performed by the worker. Increasing specialization requires fewer skills from the worker and results in dehumanizing and alienating the worker.

Whether jobs are exported through the relocation of capital and factories or eliminated through the use of automation and robots, the impact on the factory worker produces the same devastating result. The loss of a regular job, especially one where the worker felt secure because of lengthy seniority or highly developed skills, often exacts deep and tragic costs. The costs are reflected not only in the financial expense of lost income but also in rising rates of alcoholism, mental illness, suicide, child abuse, wife-beating, and other personal and social problems.

New employment opportunities will develop for many displaced workers. Technological advancement in any field often creates a need for new products and new services. Abandoned factories and stores are often taken over by another company and reopened or converted to slightly different uses. However, the development of new industries or the conversion of old work-sites to new uses requires considerable time and often fails to coincide with the geographic location of displaced workers. This results in many workers being unable to transfer easily to equivalent work that will use their existing skills productively.

The options available to most workers in these circumstances are quite limited and almost all of them have tremendously disrupting consequences for the worker and his or her family. The simplest option (however, only very rarely possible) is for the worker to shift to a comparable position at another work-site within the same geographic area. If a worker has other salable skills, he or she can look locally for jobs that use those skills. If there is a demand for the given skills elsewhere, the worker can consider relocating. The reality of the situation usually is that, when technological advancement results in large worker redundancy, the worker skills are obsolete and no longer salable. The worker then may opt to acquire new skills that can be sold to existing or anticipated new local employers. The final option is to combine the acquisition of new skills with relocation.

The most frequent result of rapid technological change is the creation of a large number of underemployed workers. This situation occurs as many workers are replaced by robotics or other mechanized procedures. Possessing obsolete skills, displaced workers search for whatever lower-level jobs are available or else retrain for reentry into the work force, usually at a lower skill level than their previous employment. The presence of this group of job seekers increases the competition for any available jobs, so that new entrants, such as school and college graduates, returning homemakers, and others, are also more inclined to seize any available position even though it may be at a lower skill level than their preparation merits. Thus underemployment is compounded. Over an extended period, some of the underemployed will find an opportunity to move into positions appropriate to their skill level or will acquire new training that permits them to move up; however, most will remain trapped in a state of underemployment.

Resolving major displacements requires planning and coordination beyond the scope of individuals and even local governing units. Effective solutions can probably be managed only at regional, state, or federal levels because of the need for attracting and developing new businesses and industries, arranging capitalization or financing, establishing training programs, identifying potential participants, and so forth. Displaced workers are likely to need an array of social services to help with the many crises produced by unemployment, including counseling to maintain self-esteem and to develop new career plans.

Displaced workers who resolve their dilemma by seeking employment at a lower level of skill (for example, transferring into expanding opportunities in service industries) are likely to face a drastic reduction in income, although the time of unemployment is probably shortened. Other displaced workers may conclude that no option is feasible. They have no transferable skill, are unable to acquire new skills because of age, location, or other reasons, and are unable or unwilling to consider relocating. These will remain unemployed.

Workers, and their families, caught up in the disruption produced by technological change or other long-term factors, inevitably focus on the short-term effect on their lives. Both they and society benefit when effective assistance is provided to control the damage produced by the disruption. This must include assistance in planning, acquisition of retraining or new education, placement assistance, and help with the various personal and family problems resulting from the displacement. The long-range view shows both an increase in overall productivity and an increase in total employment, in spite of many serious short-term crises.

WORK AND MENTAL HEALTH

Yankelovich (1982) reports a recent study in which workers were asked to identify which of three concepts of work most closely reflected their view. The three concepts presented were as follows:

1. People work only because they would not otherwise have the resources to sustain themselves.
2. Work is a straight economic transaction in which people relate effort to financial return: the more money they get, the harder they work; the less money they receive, the less effort they give.
3. Work carries a moral imperative to do one's best apart from practical necessity or financial remuneration. (p. 5)

The study reports that 78 percent of the respondents selected the third response and only 15 percent and 7 percent respectively chose the first and second answer. Other studies have produced similar results. For example, Yankelovich also cites a University of Michigan survey in 1977 that found 75 percent of its sample reporting that they would continue to work even if they could live comfortably without working for the rest of their lives. These data show clearly that people generally view work as an important or essential component of their lives. Added significance must be given to this attitude when we consider that work consumes about one-third of the average adult's waking hours, probably a bigger piece of active time than any other pursuit, and its influence carries into all aspects of life.

Viewed from a broad perspective, the worker's mental health is the product of the interaction between worker and job. In this macrorelationship, one must view the worker in terms of personal values, motivations, goals, interests, and general self-concept. Similarly, one must consider the job in its totality, including the nature of the work, the setting, and the people (employer, supervisors, fellow workers) in it. Different people expect various outcomes from participation in work. As previously indicated, professional, technical, and managerial workers are more likely to seek self-satisfaction and self-fulfillment in work, while machine operators, process workers, and factory workers are more likely to give primary emphasis to income.

Different types of jobs are also able to offer differing rewards to their workers. Within certain broad limits there is some flexibility and adaptability that permits adjustment between worker and job. To the extent that sufficient "fit" is seen between worker and job, or is expected to develop in the foreseeable future, job satisfaction exists and the worker's mental health is positive. If the job permits the worker to strive for those things that are most important to him or her, whether they be self-actualization, income, security, or some other valued goal, good mental health is the product of the worker-job relationship. To the extent that the worker-job interaction is unable to accommodate those worker goals, dissatisfaction results.

Mental health is a complex and sometimes elusive concept. It is as difficult to define as it is to identify once a definition has been accepted. Kornhauser (1965) and Srebalus, Marinelli, and Messing (1982) suggest that mental health can be approximated by considering several variables. For example, one might conclude that an individual displays positive mental health if he or she tends to fall to the right of midpoint on most of the following continuums:

1. Appears tense and anxious—Generally at ease and comfortable.
2. Displays hostility toward others—Generally trustful and accepting.
3. Tends to withdraw—Usually sociable.
4. Shows depression and alienation—Displays high morale.
5. Appears goalless—Shows purposive action.
6. Expresses low self-esteem—Has high self-esteem.

In earlier sections we considered the fact that the worker brings the influence of the job into all aspects of his or her life—relationships with family and with others, social status, and so on. Of course, this involvement runs in both directions. The worker who is unhappy at home or at leisure is likely to carry that dissatisfaction and discontent to work and may express it there in outbursts toward fellow workers or supervisors, through sloppy work or low productivity, or in other ways. Our concern, however, is principally with the worker-job relationship and we will not emphasize what the worker brings to the workplace from life away from the job. These relationship types may be expressed in several ways such as the workaholic, the perfectionist, the aggressive worker, the clown, and the attention-seeker.

Overall, the worker will stay with a job that appears likely to offer a better opportunity to reach important goals, satisfy major values, or enhance self-esteem than any other job that is available or likely to be available. Even when the "fit" is less than satisfactory, the worker is likely to stay if there is no apparent better opportunity. When the work is satisfying and fulfilling, there are still often aspects of the job that produce stress, a disruptive physiological and psychological reaction to the demands of the job. This is all the more likely to occur when the worker is less certain of commitment to the job. Stress has an influence on both physiological and psychological well-being and persistent stress has been linked to allergies, cancer, heart conditions, and mental health. Considerable attention recently has been devoted to the study of stress, and seminars and workshops on stress management are widely available.

It would be difficult to identify an exhaustive list of work-related causes of stress. Nevertheless, we can list examples of such factors. It is important to keep in mind that the list is only representative and, further, that not all items will influence every worker in the same way, or even always influence a given worker in the same way. Typical sources of stress include:

Physical causes of stress at work

Continuous demand for heavy exertion *or* demand for avoidance of activity.
Prolonged and intense attention *or* unvarying monotony.
Too fast work speed *or* too slow work speed.
Demand for exact precision.
The presence of certain working conditions such as:
> Physical danger or unpredictable hazards.
> Extreme temperatures.
> Toxic conditions.
> Continuous and extreme odors, vibrations, noise.
> Poor ventilation.

Psychological causes of stress at work

Employer's work standards too demanding or too low.
Dissatisfaction with personal production rate.
Absence of job security.
Conflict with employer's ethics.
Ambiguity in employer's expectations.
Frequent change in job requirements *or* boredom caused by unchanging requirements.
Premature assignment of responsibility.
Feeling trapped in the job and unable to move.

Social causes of stress at work

Too much or too little supervision.
Uncertain relationship with supervisors.
Variable standards of supervisors.
Isolation from other workers *or* too much contact with other workers.
Personalities, attitudes, behaviors of other workers.

As many of the items above suggest, there is a middle ground that produces the optimum situation for the worker. Within that range the worker is most likely to find the work challenging, stimulating, and worthwhile. If either extreme is approached the worker may feel threatened, exhausted, or alienated. Work-related stress may result in the worker attempting to cope in unsuitable ways, such as alcoholism, addiction, aggression, or physical reactions.

For most adults, the worker-job relationship is one of continuous involvement. The worker expresses the self in numerous ways within the work-site to employer and fellow workers. The job intrudes into the off-work life of the worker. Unfortunately, this deep, persistent involvement in the mental health and life of the worker becomes most obvious when the relationship is broken. Gillett (1983) describes this wrenching experience in these words:

> The personal cost of these changes is deep and tragic. A rise in alcoholism, mental illness, heart disease, suicide, child abuse or wife-beating follows a rise in the unemployment rate. When a plant closed in Chicago, eight out of 2,000 workers committed suicide. In Wayne County, Michigan, where unemployment approaches 20 per cent, a community hotline recently reported that calls about spouse abuse have jumped over 300 per cent in a year's time. Mental health clinics report huge rises in case loads within the past two years. (p. 12)

WORK CONCOMITANT WITH LIFE

In the previous sections we have explored some of the relationships between work and the life of the individual. It is clear that work intrudes into almost every aspect of human life and its saturation is so extensive that it is difficult to identify any part of adult life that is not influenced heavily by the individual's work. Further, those few adults who have no involvement with work are often isolated and estranged from others. Many people know someone who worked a lifetime toward the goal of retirement, when it is possible to leave work forever, only to find life empty or meaningless when that goal was reached.

If work is as important to most people as the evidence overwhelmingly indicates, common sense suggests that helping individuals to develop work relationships that are meaningful and satisfying is psychologically sound, economically efficient, and socially desirable. The vast majority of adults grow up and enter an occupation that generally satisfies their needs and desires. Some could have enhanced their lives and those of their family by making better choices. Some are unable to develop choices or plans, so that they and their families live marginal lives. In both situations the individual loses, but in a larger sense all of society loses whenever lives are less effective than they could be.

As we have seen in earlier sections, the relationship between an individual and work is most complex and dynamic, often requiring adjustment or even change. The adult development specialists suggest that firm commitments to work are not completed until the person is nearly thirty years old. Many people may need help in those early years in exploring various options, making choices, and preparing for a lifetime of work. As that career develops, most people also will need help at various times in maintaining a working relationship, dealing with stress created by work or brought to work from other sources, or capitalizing on opportunities for growth or advancement. Technological or economic change and other factors may produce crises for the work relationship that require major change and realignment of career.

Because the individual and work are so closely interrelated, it is rarely possible to separate one from the other. Thus, whenever one attempts to help an individual with any aspect of career one must deal with the whole person, whether the concern is preparing for work, obtaining or keeping a job, adjusting to the demands of the work-site, or advancing in a particular field. In subsequent chapters we will examine ways that can be used to help individuals with these concerns.

REFERENCES

Banks, J. A. *Prosperity and parenthood: A study of family planning among the Victorian middle classes.* London: Routledge and Kegan Paul, 1954.

Blau, P. M., Gustad, J. W., Jessor, R., Parnes, H. S., and Wilcox, R. S. Occupational choice: A conceptual framework. *Industrial Labor Relations Review,* 1956, 9, 531–543.

Caplow, T. *The sociology of work.* Minneapolis: University of Minnesota Press, 1954.

Counts, G. S. The social status of occupations. *School Review,* 1925, 33, 16–27.

Davis, M. R. *Families in a working world.* New York: Praeger Publishers, 1982.

Deeg, M. E. and Paterson, D. G. Changes in social status of occupations. *Occupations,* 1947, 25, 205–208.

Freidson, E. Occupational autonomy and labor market shelters. In Stewart, P. L. and Cantor, M. G. (eds.), *Varieties of work.* Beverly Hills: Sage Publications, 1982.

Gillett, R. W. The reshaping of work: A challenge to the churches. *The Christian Century,* 1983, 100, 1, 10–13.

Gould, R. L. *Transformations: growth and change in adult life.* New York: Simon and Schuster, 1978.

Hakel, M. D., Hollmann, T. D., and Dunnette, M. D. Stability and change in the social status of occupations over 21 and 42 year periods. *Personnel and Guidance Journal,* 1968, 46, 762–764.

Hamilton, P. Social theory and the problematic concept of work. In Esland, G. and Salaman, G. (eds.), *The politics of work and occupations.* Toronto: University of Toronto Press, 1980.

Hodge, R. W., Siegel, P. M., and Rossi, P. H. Occupational prestige in the United States, 1925–63. *American Journal of Sociology,* 1964, 70, 286–302.

Hollingshead, A. B. *Elmtown's youth.* New York: John Wiley and Sons, 1949.

Hoyt, K. B. *Career education: Contributions to an evolving concept.* Salt Lake City: Olympus Publishing Company, 1975.

Isaacson, L. E. *Career information in counseling and teaching.* 3rd edition. Boston: Allyn and Bacon, Inc., 1977.

Kanter, R. M. *Work and family in the United States: A critical review and agenda for research and policy.* New York: Russell Sage Foundation, 1977.

Kerr, C., Dunlop, J. T., Harbison, F., and Myers, C. A. *Industrialism and industrial man.* Harmondsworth, England: Penguin Books Ltd., 1973.

Kornhauser, A. *Mental health of the industrial worker: A Detroit study.* New York: John Wiley and Sons, 1965.

Levinson, D. J., Darrow, C. N., Klein, E. B., Levinson, M. H., and McKee, B. *The seasons of a man's life.* New York: Alfred A. Knopf, 1978.

Mead, J. J. A comparison of types and amount of stress encountered by dual career, dual earner, and traditional couples. Unpublished doctoral dissertation, Purdue University, 1982.

Montagna, P. D. *Occupations and society: Toward a sociology of the labor market.* New York: John Wiley and Sons, 1977.

National Opinion Research Center. Jobs and occupations: A popular evaluation. *Opinion News,* 1947, 9, 3–13.

Oppenheimer, V. K. *Work and the family: A study in social demography.* New York: Academic Press, 1982.

Osipow, S. H. *Theories of career development.* 3rd edition. Englewood Cliffs, N.J.: Prentice-Hall, Inc., 1983.

Parsons, T. *Structure and process in modern societies.* Glencoe, Ill.: Free Press, 1960.

Rowntree, B. S. *Poverty: A study of town life.* London: Longmans, Green and Company, 1922.

Salaman, G. The sociology of work: Some themes and issues. In Esland, G. and Salaman, G. (eds.), *The politics of work and occupations.* Toronto: University of Toronto Press, 1980.

Scanzoni, J. and Fox, G. L. Sex roles, family and society: The seventies and beyond. *Journal of Marriage and the Family,* 1980, 42, 743–756.

Sears, S. A definition of career guidance terms: A National Vocational Guidance Association perspective. *Vocational Guidance Quarterly,* 1982, 31, 137–143.

Srebalus, D. J., Marinelli, R. P., and Messing, J. K. *Career development concepts and procedures.* Monterey, Calif.: Brooks/Cole Publishing Company, 1982.

Super, D. E. A theory of vocational development. *American Psychologist,* 1953, 8, 185–190.

Work in America. Report of a Special Task Force to the Secretary of Health, Education and Welfare. Cambridge, Mass.: The MIT Press, 1973.

Yankelovich, D. The work ethic is underemployed. *Psychology Today,* May 1982, 5–8.

2

A rationale for career counseling

THE NEED FOR HELPING INDIVIDUALS RELATE TO WORK

Helping individuals develop realistic and satisfying career plans has been an important human service since Frank Parsons started his work in Boston over seventy years ago. His attention was focused primarily on the disadvantaged—orphans and school dropouts; today, in contrast, there is general acceptance of the universality of the need for career counseling. In spite of this wider acknowledgment of the need for expert help in career planning and development, such assistance is sometimes difficult to obtain and less helpful than desired.

Parsons's personal experiences in the world of work undoubtedly exerted great influence on his view of the need for what at that time was called "vocational guidance." A college graduate in mathematics and engineering at age eighteen, he first accepted employment as a civil engineer for a railroad, but the company failed before he reported to work. He then worked for almost a year in a rolling mill. Next he obtained an elementary teaching position, later advancing to a high school teaching assignment. At the urging of a friend he began to "read" law, preparing for the bar examination that he successfully passed a short time later. Because of health problems, Parsons moved to New Mexico and for three years engaged in rigorous outdoor work. Following this, he returned to Boston and the practice of law; six years later he joined the faculty of a local university law school. He was an unsuccessful candidate for mayor of Boston. He subsequently moved to the midwest, becoming a professor at an agricultural and applied science college, and later became dean of the College of Liberal Arts at another institution. He returned to Boston in 1905 to organize the Breadwinner's College as part of the program of a social settlement house called Civic Service House. While in that position he organized the Vocation Bureau, and based upon his experiences there he wrote *Choosing a Vocation*. He died in 1908 and the book was published in the following year.

The introduction to that book summarizes the principles discussed by Parsons. Although we might want to change some of the words used, the ideas presented are worthy of consideration. The principles proposed by Parsons (1909) include:

1. It is better to choose a vocation than merely to "hunt a job."
2. No one should choose a vocation without careful self-analysis, thorough, honest, and under guidance.
3. The youth should have a large survey of the field of vocations, and not simply drop into the convenient or accidental position.
4. Expert advice, or the advice of men who have made a careful study of men and of vocations and of the conditions of success, must be better and safer for a young man than the absence of it.
5. *Putting it down* on paper seems to be a simple matter, but it is one of supreme importance. (p. vii)

The need of youth for assistance in career planning as recognized by Parsons has been reconfirmed by numerous research studies throughout the years. Studies by Laycock (1942) and Mooney (1942) were among the earliest extensive research projects reporting concern by youths about their educational and vocational future. Near the end of that decade, Froehlich (1948) reported that the problems brought to a free community counseling center consisted of approximately 29 percent educational topics, 60 percent vocational topics, and 11 percent personal problems. Based on an established, periodically conducted poll of high school students, Remmers and Shimberg (1949) noted that 40 to 50 percent of their group of teenagers expressed a concern for the future. Further, about 50 percent of the ninth-graders said they were already worried about how they would earn a living after high school.

Two extensive studies during the 1970s revealed no substantial change in the situation. Flanagan (1973) reported that only 13 percent of the Project TALENT sample of boys reported the same occupational choice in 1966 as they had chosen in 1960 as eleventh graders. In both 1960 and 1970, half of the eleventh grade boys indicated plans to graduate from a four-year college, although college graduation records confirmed that fewer than half of those expecting to graduate would succeed. Similarly, Prediger, Roth, and Noeth (1974) sampled eighth, ninth, and eleventh graders, both boys and girls, in thirty-three states. They found that 78 percent of the eleventh graders reported a need for more help in making career plans, with 30 percent stating a need for help with personal problems. Among the eighth graders, 73 percent wanted help with career plans and 39 percent needed help with personal problems. In the eleventh grade group, 20 percent revealed very low involvement in career planning and another 50 percent were below a desirable level of career planning.

Although these studies concentrate primarily on adolescents, one should not conclude that the need for career planning help is endemic only to youth. Research on worker alienation, decreasing worker productivity in the United States, and increasing emphasis upon midlife career change all underscore the existence of career uncertainty among a large percentage of adults.

The preceding paragraphs are not intended to suggest that every person in our society needs career counseling and that, if provided, our societal problems would melt away. Rather, an attempt has been made to suggest that we do have many individuals who express a need for such help, and that the absence of help is costly to that individual and to the rest of society as well. Ginzberg (1971) has endorsed a similar view in the following words:

> Everybody is confronted repeatedly with the need to make decisions with respect to education and work. These decisions can be facilitated if people have relevant information about the shorter and longer consequences of alternative choices.
>
> Better decision-making with respect to career development also requires the clarification of goals, the development of plans, and their implementation.
>
> People need help in learning to negotiate complex and changing institutions— the educational system, the Armed Forces, the labor market.
>
> While informal advisers such as one's peers and especially one's family help young people to define their goals and initiate them in the ways of the institutions of our society, they frequently do not have important information or objectivity. (p. 270)

Attempts have rarely been made to gauge the economic and psychological costs sustained by both individuals and society as a result of inadequate or ineffective career planning. Certainly, the figures would be mind-boggling. Human labor is a highly perishable commodity: in an economic sense, work not done today is lost forever. The differential between what a given worker produces in goods and/or services and what he or she might produce in a particular time unit if working at the most effective level is similarly an economic loss that never can be recouped. In a parallel framework, unemployment, underemployment, or misemployment carry psychological costs borne by the individual in dissatisfaction, alienation, and lack of self-esteem, and by society as it is affected by those characteristics.

It is the thesis of this book that career planning will enhance the likelihood that the individual can accomplish more of his or her life plans, find greater satisfaction in what he or she does, and attain self-actualization. This does not imply that planning will ever give the individual total control over life. The poet Robert Burns long ago recognized that the best laid plans can often go awry; similarly, each of us knows individuals whose lives are totally unplanned yet filled with bits of good fortune.

The Association for Counselor Education and Supervision (1976) has developed a position paper that speaks directly to the point we have been discussing in the foregoing pages. This document contends that all students and adults should be provided with career guidance opportunities to insure that they:

1. Understand that career development is a lifelong process based upon an interwoven and sequential series of educational, occupational, leisure, and family choices.
2. Examine their own interests, values, aptitudes, and aspirations in an effort to increase self-awareness and self-understanding.
3. Develop a personally satisfying set of work values which leads them to believe that work, in some form, can be desirable to them.
4. Recognize that the act of paid and unpaid work has dignity.
5. Understand the role of leisure in career development.
6. Understand the process of reasoned decision making and the ownership of those decisions in terms of their consequences.
7. Recognize that educational and occupational decisions are interrelated with family, work, and leisure.
8. Gather the kinds of data necessary to make well-informed career decisions.
9. Become aware of and explore a wide variety of occupational alternatives.
10. Explore possible rewards, satisfactions, lifestyles, and negative aspects associated with various occupational options.
11. Consider the probability of success and failure for various occupations.
12. Understand the important role of interpersonal and basic employability skills in occupational success.
13. Identify and use a wide variety of resources in the school and community to maximize career development potential.
14. Know and understand the entrance, transition, and decision points in education and the problems of adjustment that might occur in relation to these points.
15. Obtain chosen vocational skills and use available placement ser-

vices to gain satisfactory entrance into employment in relation to occupational aspirations and beginning competencies.

16. Know and understand the value of continuing education to upgrade and/or acquire additional occupational skills or leisure pursuits.

Many of these items are already being dealt with in some educational systems in a logical and methodical fashion in order to maximize the career development opportunities for students in those schools. On the other hand, many individuals encounter little, if any, conscious and deliberate attention to most of the items. Recently, a thrust has developed toward providing more effective assistance in dealing with these aspects. We will consider briefly the impact of career education in the next section.

CAREER EDUCATION

American education has long recognized its responsibility for assisting youth in preparing to enter vocational activities. The implementation of this responsibility has varied greatly; more often than not it has been piecemeal, erratic, and ineffective. In the early decades of this century vocational programs were added to the curriculum in many high schools. In the 1940s and 1950s many schools began to employ school counselors, a practice that rapidly accelerated with the passage of the National Defense Education Act in 1958. Concurrently, ever-increasing proportions of school-age youth were remaining in school for longer periods, so that by 1975 three-fourths of the age group were graduating from high school. Generally, the secondary schools effectively prepared those students who either pursued vocational education or college preparatory programs, but in most schools these two groups combined included less than half of the graduating class. Several factors, including high youth unemployment rates, the social malaise of public attitudes toward the Vietnam War, student protest, the search for alternate lifestyles, and an increase in public demand for accountability in the educational system exacerbated the situation and encouraged efforts toward educational reform.

Marland (1971*a*) proposed one course of action that attracted considerable attention when he stated:

all our efforts as educators must be bent on preparing students either to become properly, usefully employed immediately upon graduation from high school or to go on to further formal education. Anything else is dangerous nonsense. I propose that a universal goal of American education, starting now, be this: that every young person completing our school program at grade 12 be ready to enter higher education or to enter useful and rewarding employment.

This proposal started the development of the concept of career education, an idea that has grown and spread. No attempt was made to specify restrictively the nature and process of career education; instead, school systems and state departments of education were encouraged to interpret the concept in terms that met their needs and to create a variety of programs that reflected those local or statewide interpretations. Consequently, career education is now—and will continue to be—an evolving concept that includes very diverse programs. A few months after the above statement was made, Marland (1971*b*) explained his position in a speech with these words:

> What the term "career education" means to me is basically a point of view, a concept—a concept that says three things: first, that career education will be part of the curriculum for all students, not just some. Second, that it will continue throughout a youngster's stay in school, from the first grade through senior high and beyond, if he so elects. And third, that every student leaving school will possess the skills necessary to give him a start to making a livelihood for himself and his family, even if he leaves before completing high school.

With each state developing and following its own definition of career education, one finds considerable variation in emphasis from one definition to another. Obviously, no one can say that this one is right and that one is wrong. But although there is diversity, there is still a good deal of consensus among the various statements. Probably Hoyt (1972) has synthesized best the essence of common agreement with this definition:

> Career education is the total effort of public education and the community aimed at helping all individuals to become familiar with the values of a work-oriented society, to integrate these values into their personal value systems, and to implement these values into their lives in such a way that work becomes possible, meaningful, and satisfying to each individual. (p. 1)

This statement suggests that career education involves all school personnel—teachers, counselors, administrators, and others—and all aspects of the community—business, industry, government, labor, and individuals—in an ongoing cooperative venture that capitalizes upon opportunities in and out of school to enhance career development for all people, not just school-age youngsters. In fact, several research projects have explored successfully the viability of delivering career education services to individuals no longer in the school setting. Nevertheless, one can logically expect that the major thrust of career education will continue to be aimed toward the school-age population.

In the school setting, career education appears to be recognizing and building upon the developmental phases of life. Most programs therefore focus upon career awareness during the elementary years, providing maximum opportunity for these youngsters to gain a wide range of general information about as many jobs as possible, including what the worker does, the kinds of abilities, interests, and personality required by the job, and the satisfactions and rewards provided by the work. Learning about jobs is a lifelong process, and each of us is often discovering some occupation about which we previously were unaware, so it is not the intent of career education to concentrate this activity into early childhood. Instead, it is intended that a deliberate effort will be made during those years to widen the range of knowledge, to encourage acquiring understanding of many jobs, and to make that inquiry as productive as possible, still recognizing that it will continue in succeeding years.

The second phase of career education is introduced during the middle or junior high school years and is the major thrust until the early high school years. During this period, usually called *career exploration,* the youngsters are helped to relate occupational activities, requirements, and rewards to their own characteristics, ambitions, values, and expectations. They seek answers to such questions as the following: Would I like to do what the worker does? Could I do it successfully? Would I find the rewards satisfying? Would I like to live a life like the worker lives?

During the early high school years, many youths move into the third phase: decision making. For most, this is a gradual process, with specific refinement and focus to come later. Some career education advocates suggest that students can be helped most if attention is directed toward two broad concepts: the field or area of work as represented by the cluster concept, and the general level of work as reflected by the amount of education required. In other words, rather than trying to find "the" job, the students look toward a group of jobs that fit their interests, abilities, values, and so on and that also require generally the educational level they hope and expect to attain. Thus, a desirable goal at this stage might be "a health occupation requiring a year or two of post-high school vocational training," or "a marketing occupation at the bachelor's level," or "a construction occupation where a high school diploma is sufficient." Identification of a specific choice within this framework can be completed as the individual approaches the point where specialized preparation begins.

The next phase, career preparation, may be as brief as part of the final year of high school for the individual expecting to go to work directly, or as long as a decade for those youths contemplating professional careers. Much work remains to be completed in all levels of our educational structure before this phase can be effectively implemented. Curricular revision, when completed, will facilitate this step as well as earlier phases. Ideally, the secondary school years should prepare each youth for his or her postsecondary plans, either entrance into further education at an advanced level or entrance into work. Thus the youth whose plan is "a health occupation requiring a year or two of post-secondary vocational training" will have (1) identified the occupation and the school where the additional training can best be acquired as well as (2) completed all preparatory requirements for that training program. Further, he or she will have completed a "back-up" program enabling entrance into a related occupation at a lower level if the additional anticipated preparation becomes inaccessible. In the case of our illustration, this would mean that high school graduation also includes completion of requirements for immediate admission to an entry-level occupation related to the desired goal.

Logically, the next step after preparation for an occupation is employment. The process of job placement can occur at the end of high school (or before that point for those few individuals who elect to withdraw before graduation) or at a later point when preparation has been completed. Placement programs in educational institutions vary widely; only a few can really claim to have effective plans in operation. Certainly this activity is one that requires extensive cooperation between the educational facility and the appropriate component in the larger community.

An additional step must be incorporated into the career education process if it is to serve all individuals. Perhaps "advancement" is an appropriate label for this phase, which would provide assistance in developing paths for moving forward in the selected career. Most entry-level jobs lead to higher-level positions; often there are multiple paths leading to varied opportunities and, to some extent, the earlier phases of awareness, exploration, and decision making may need to be recycled in the specific situation facing the worker. Similarly, advancement may depend upon acquisition of additional preparation, perhaps even later return to the classroom for more formal schooling, and then back to a position of greater responsibility and opportunity, where the process may start again.

There are many obvious advantages to a comprehensive career education program. The nurturance of career planning occurs over time and in step with the psychological development of the individual. Educational experiences can be coordinated with career goals to provide realistic opportunities for awareness, exploration, tryout, revision, and so on. Exposure to a vast array of school and community resources and personnel provides an enriching experience that enhances self-understanding as well as occupational understanding, and leads to more appropriate career choices. Realistically, however, one must recognize that effective implementation of career education across the nation lies far in the future. Such implementation requires (1) retraining of all classroom teachers in the infusion process of incorporating career materials into regular classroom materials, (2) revision of the curriculum to provide more useful structure and organization, (3) revision of the daily schedule and yearly calendar to permit greater flexibility and accessibility to school offerings, (4) development of liaison contacts with community resources and personnel so that they may be incorporated into the program, and (5) modification of regulations controlling working hours of school attenders, insurance requirements for transporting students, and permitting participation in work assignments. All of these changes, and many others, require both time and money to accomplish. At best, one can hope for a gradual transition culminating eventually in a nationwide, comprehensive program.

THE PLACE FOR CAREER COUNSELING

We have considered career education in some detail because it reflects the continuing concern of professional educators and the general public for the expansion of services to assist youth in career development. As we have seen, this concern has been recognized for nearly three-quarters of a century. During that time, many innovations have been tried: some have been retained, others modified, still others abandoned. Some of the earliest efforts focused on offering classes in occupations; for example, Brewer (1942) suggests that the first known class was taught in 1908 at Westport, Connecticut. As counselors were introduced into high schools and colleges, their major, perhaps even sole, function originally was vocational guidance. Recognizing that most students also had needs and concerns that were not entirely vocationally related, counselors soon extended their activities into these other areas, thereby diluting the time available for career matters. Even if counselors had not extended their roles to deal with these other crucial topics, we probably would never have reached the point where extensive, one-to-one career counseling would have been available to all individuals.

Much effort has gone into creating activities, programs, and devices that supplement or replace counselor endeavor. As a nation highly conscious of technological modernization that is cost and energy efficient, we have become accustomed to searching for labor-saving shortcuts. We have consequently often adopted ideas that looked good in the short run but that failed to hold up over time. These often have been replaced by a later fad, similarly untried, that we will again subsequently replace or modify. Our professional behavior has also followed this pattern on occasion.

Brandt (1977) has recognized this tendency with these words:

> Today we observe a lavish display of what are termed "innovative career development programs" for the college student, involving a new world of cultish group experiences, exciting multimedia productions, sophisticated computer software, and copyrighted workbooks. This proliferation of new techniques and approaches seems to be vaguely similar to the encounter group movement of the 1960s. The only difference seems to be that the 1960s encounter group emphasized "letting it all hang out," and the new career development experiences emphasizing "getting it all together." (p. 494)

Recognizing the same developments, and perhaps also accepting them more readily, Holland (1974) has written:

> if all goes well, vocational counseling will eventually be used only for a few unusual clients and a variety of printed and audiovisual materials, workbooks,

books, and a few group activities arranged in some systematic way will dominate. (p. 26)

Probably the truth lies somewhere between the extremes of rejecting all new techniques and materials automatically and unquestioningly accepting each proposal for change that surfaces. Of course, new ideas and approaches will develop that are worthy of adoption, but not every suggestion warrants such reaction.

All persons who survive to adulthood are involved in the career development process, just as they are also involved in physical growth, personality development, and the educational process. Similarly, the career development process continues through adulthood just as physical growth and change, personality development, and the learning process also continue as lifelong aspects of the human condition. We can extend the analogy by considering the roles of the physician and the teacher. Each of us needs ongoing contact with a physician who checks to be sure we grow and mature at a reasonable rate (a developmental function), who may prescribe medicines, diet, exercise, or other treatments to eliminate a future potential problem (a preventive function), who may intercede surgically or otherwise when a serious problem does develop (a therapeutic function), and who will assist us with prosthetic devices or new living procedures when a physical problem forces major readjustments (a rehabilitative function). Similarly, the teacher provides a challenging, developmentally appropriate learning experience; anticipates and prevents potential problems by properly sequencing learning experiences and assuring skill acquisition before the skill is needed, supplying make-up sessions, individual help, or other corrective measures; and furnishes specialized procedures for learning-disabled individuals or others whose particular problems preclude progress in the usual manner. In both physical and educational development, continuous individual attention by the physician or teacher is rarely needed. However, complete lack of contact is unwise. In other words, both professionals should be involved in general monitoring of progress, accessible when possible problems might be anticipated, and definitely available when problems do occur and when change cannot be handled by the individual alone.

Correspondingly, the career counselor serves comparable functions in the career development process. One responsibility of the elementary school counselor should be to monitor the school's career awareness program to assure that each youngster is receiving a nutritious, well-balanced diet of career-related materials with which the individual is developing a sturdy, healthy body of information and attitudes toward work and its place in our society. Throughout the school years—elementary, secondary, postsecondary—the counselor should be assisting the individual to recognize approaching decision points where the student, parent, and others will be selecting among various options that have a continuing impact on the indi-

vidual's life, and helping the individual acquire the information and understanding needed to increase the likelihood of a wise and satisfying decision.
For clients in late adolescence and beyond, the career counselor should be
available for help with career choice decisions, adjustment or revision of
previously made decisions, and planning preparatory and entry programs as
needed and desired by the individual. Counselors in community agencies
such as rehabilitation programs, employment services, and adult counseling
centers should be available to assist adults who face career change either for
voluntary reasons such as a desire for midcareer change, or involuntary
reasons such as physical disability, technological obsolescence of the career,
or geographic relocation of the employer.

A recent document adopted by the Board of Directors of the National
Vocational Guidance Association (NVGA) (published in the NVGA Newsletter in June 1982) provides a definitive statement of current professional
thinking about career counseling. The document includes a definition, a
description of competency areas, and a listing of the competencies needed
by a career counselor. Because the statement relates directly to the professional preparation of those who aspire to become career counselors, it
warrants careful consideration at this point. Although the document is
lengthy, it must be viewed in its entirety. It states:

Definition: Vocational/Career Counseling consists of those activities performed or coordinated by individuals who have the professional credentials to work with and counsel other individuals or groups of
individuals about occupations, careers, life/career, career decision
making, career planning, career pathing, or other career development
related questions or conflicts.

Designated Vocational/Career Competency Areas: In order to work as a
professional engaged in Vocational/Career Counseling, the individual
must demonstrate minimum competencies in six designated areas.
These six areas are: *General Counseling, Information, Individual/
Group Assessment, Management/Administration, Implementation,*
and *Consultation.*

General Counseling—Counseling competencies considered essential
to effective vocational/career counseling.

Information—Information base and knowledge essential for professionals engaging in vocational/career counseling.

Individual/Group Assessment—Individual/Group Assessment skills
considered essential for professionals engaging in vocational/
career counseling.

Management/Administration—Management/Administration skills necessary to develop, plan, implement, and manage comprehensive career development programs.

Implementation—Knowledge and skills essential to the adoption of career development programs and strategies in a variety of settings.

Consultation—Knowledge and skills essential in relating to individuals and organizations that impact the career development process.

General counseling skills

Vocational/Career Counseling Competencies

Counseling competencies considered essential to effective vocational/career counseling.

Demonstration of

1. Knowledge of general counseling theories and techniques.
2. Skills in building a productive relationship between counselor and client.
3. Ability to use appropriate counseling techniques in effectively assisting individuals with career choice and life/career development concerns.
4. Ability to assist the client to recognize the relationship between self-understanding and effective life/career decisions.
5. Ability to assist the client in the identification of internal personal factors related to life/career decision making including personality, values, interests, aptitudes, and motives.
6. Skills in recognizing and modifying stereotypes held by clients related to career choice.
7. Ability to assist the client in the identification of contextual factors in career decision making including family, friends, educational opportunities, and finances.
8. Ability to understand and help clarify the client's decision making processes.

Information

Information base and knowledge essential for professionals engaging in vocational/career counseling.

Demonstration of

1. Knowledge of education, training, employment trends, labor market, and career resources that provide information about job tasks, functions, salaries, requirements, and future outlooks related to broad occupational fields.

2. Knowledge of basic concepts related to vocational/career counseling including career development, career pathing, and career patterns.
3. Knowledge of career development and decision making theories.
4. Knowledge of the changing roles of women and men and the linkage of work, family, and leisure.
5. Knowledge of resources and techniques designed for use with special groups.
6. Knowledge of strategies to store, retrieve, and disseminate vocational/career information.

Individual group assessment

Individual/Group Assessment skills considered essential for professionals engaging in vocational/career counseling.

Demonstration of

1. Knowledge of appraisal techniques and measures of aptitude, achievement, interest, values, and personality.
2. Knowledge of strategies used in the evaluation of job performance, individual effectiveness, and program effectiveness.
3. Ability to identify appraisal resources appropriate for specified situations and populations.
4. Ability to evaluate appraisal resources and techniques in terms of their validity, reliability, and relationships to race, sex, age, and ethnicity.
5. Ability to demonstrate the proper administration of appraisal techniques.
6. Ability to interpret appraisal data to clients and other appropriate individuals or groups of people.
7. Ability to assist clients in appraising quality of life and working environments.

Management/administration

Management/Administration skills necessary to develop, plan, implement, and manage comprehensive career development programs.

Demonstration of

1. Knowledge of program designs that can be used in the organization of career development services.
2. Knowledge of needs assessment techniques and practices.
3. Knowledge of performance objectives used in organizing career development programs, and setting goals and comprehensive career development programs.
4. Knowledge of management concepts and leadership styles us.d in relation to career development programs.

5. Ability to adjust management and administration methods to reflect identified career development program problems, and specified situational needs.
6. Ability to prepare budgets and time lines for career development programs.
7. Ability to design, compile, and report an evaluation of career development activities and programs.

Implementation

Knowledge and skills essential to the adoption of career development programs and strategies in a variety of settings.

Demonstration of

1. Knowledge of program adoption and planned change strategies.
2. Knowledge of personal and environmental barriers affecting the implementation of career development programs.
3. Ability to implement individual and group programs in career development for specified populations.
4. Ability to implement a public relations effort in behalf of career development activities and services.
5. Ability to devise and implement a comprehensive career resource center.
6. Ability to implement pilot programs in a variety of career development areas including: appraisal, decision-making, information giving, and general career counseling.

Consultation

Knowledge and skills considered essential in relating to individuals and organizations that impact the career development process.

Demonstration of

1. Knowledge of consultation strategies and consultation models.
2. Ability to provide effective career consultation to influential individuals such as parents, teachers, employers, community groups, and the general public.
3. Ability to provide career development consultation to Business and Professional groups.
4. Ability to convey program goals and achievements to key personnel in positions of authority: legislators, executives, and others.
5. Ability to provide data on the cost-effectiveness of career counseling and career development activities.

The first three competencies—general counseling skills, information, and individual/group assessment—are the competency areas addressed in this book. These three areas are concerned with the one-to-one counselor-client relationship that we will call career counseling. The remaining competencies encompass managerial and program planning tasks and consultative efforts with people other than the client.

At many points, the career counselor may have only indirect contact with the individual client. Certainly, as career education programs are incorporated into schools, many career development activities will be conducted by teachers and community resource people, with the counselor serving primarily as coordinator, organizer, and monitor. This function of the career counselor, primarily developmental and preventive, is already well developed and described in many excellent books to which the reader is referred for more detail. General references for all age levels include Healy (1982) and Herr and Cramer (1984). At the elementary and middle school level, useful books include Evans, Hoyt, and Mangum (1974), Gysbers, Miller, and Moore (1973), and Hoyt, Pinson, Laramore, and Mangum (1973). For the secondary school level, one might consult Hoyt, Evans, Mangum, Bowen, and Gale (1977), Mangum, Becker, Coombs, and Marshall (1975), Shertzer and Stone (1981), or Tolbert (1980). For postsecondary-level assistance, consider Reardon and Burck (1975).

We will focus our attention in this book on the counseling functions of the career counselor. Here we are concerned with those situations where the client, counselee, patient, or student seeks out the career counselor, requesting assistance for what purports to be a concern, difficulty, or problem in the career development process. This is most likely to occur at or near one of the previously mentioned crisis points where the individual is, or soon will be, confronted with a choice. It may also occur at any point when the individual determines that making a choice is advantageous or facilitative of further personal development, or where reassurance is desired. Although any or several of the plethora of resources such as group experiences, programmed materials, computerized systems, audiovisual materials, organized classes, workbooks, and informational files and references may be used as a substitute for the counselor, our attention will focus primarily on the activity of the career counselor as a counselor. Where application by the counselor of these other materials and techniques appears appropriate for the client we will, of course, consider their use, but our basic concern is with what the career counselor does in helping a client who seeks assistance.

REFERENCES

Association for Counselor Education and Supervision, Commission on Counselor Preparation for Career Development/Career Education. *ACES position paper.* Washington, D.C.: Association for Counselor Education and Supervision, 1976.

Brandt, J. D. Model for the delivery of career development programs by the college counseling center. *Journal of Counseling Psychology,* 1977, 24, 494–502.

Brewer, J. M. *History of vocational guidance.* New York: Harper & Bros., 1942.

Evans, R., Hoyt, K., and Mangum, G. *Career education in the middle/junior high school.* Salt Lake City: Olympus Publishing Company, 1974.

Flanagan, J. C. Some pertinent findings of Project TALENT. *Vocational Guidance Quarterly,* 1973, 22, 92–96.

Froelich, C. P. Factors related to the effectiveness of counseling. Unpublished doctoral thesis, School of Education, The George Washington University, 1948.

Ginzberg, E. *Career guidance: Who needs it, who provides it, who can improve it.* New York: McGraw-Hill Book Company, 1971.

Gysbers, N. C., Miller, W., and Moore, E. J. *Developing careers in the elementary school.* Columbus, O.: Charles E. Merrill Publishing Co., 1973.

Healy, C. C. *Career development: Counseling through the life stages.* Boston: Allyn and Bacon, Inc., 1982.

Herr, E. L. and Cramer, S. H. *Career guidance through the life span.* 2nd edition. Boston: Little, Brown and Company, 1984.

Holland, J. L. Career counseling: Then, now, and what's next? *The Counseling Psychologist,* 1974, 4, 24–26.

Hoyt, K. B., Evans, R. N., Mackin, E. F., and Mangum, G. L. *Career education: What it is and how to do it.* Salt Lake City: Olympus Publishing Company, 1972.

Hoyt, K. B., Evans, R. N., Mangum, G. L., Bowen, E., and Gale, D. *Career education in the high school.* Salt Lake City: Olympus Publishing Company, 1977.

Hoyt, K. B., Pinson, N. M., Laramore, D., and Mangum, G. L. *Career education and the elementary school teacher.* Salt Lake City: Olympus Publishing Company, 1973.

Laycock, S. R. Helping adolescents solve their problems. *The Education Digest,* November 1942, p. 32.

Mangum, G. L., Becker, J. W., Coombs, G., and Marshall, P. *Career education in the academic classroom.* Salt Lake City: Olympus Publishing Company, 1975.

Marland, S. P., Jr. Career education now. Speech delivered to the Convention of the National Association of Secondary School Principals, Houston, Texas, January 23, 1971a.

———. Marland on career education. *American Education,* 1971b, 7, 25–28.

Mooney, R. L. Surveying high school students' problems by means of a problem check list. *Educational Research Bulletin,* 1942, 21, 57–69.

National Vocational Guidance Association, Board of Directors. Vocational/career counseling competencies. *NVGA Newsletter,* June 1982, 22, 6.

Parsons, F. *Choosing a vocation.* Boston: Houghton Mifflin Company, 1909.

Prediger, D. J., Roth, J. D., and Noeth, R. J. Career development of youth: A nationwide study. *Personnel and Guidance Journal,* 1974, 53, 97–104.

Reardon, R. C. and Burck, H. D. (eds.). *Facilitating career development.* Springfield, Ill.: Charles C Thomas, Publisher, 1975.

Remmers, H. H. and Shimberg, B. *Manual for SRA youth inventory.* Chicago: Science Research Associates, 1949.

Shertzer, B. E. and Stone, S. C. *Fundamentals of guidance.* 4th edition. Boston: Houghton Mifflin Company, 1981.

Tolbert, E. L. *Counseling for career development.* 2nd edition. Boston: Houghton Mifflin Company, 1980.

3

Theoretical foundations

Work has been an essential ingredient of the human experience throughout time. In earliest days, when the most complex human organization was the family unit, differentiation of tasks probably already had been accepted as part of life. As families joined to form larger organizational units, further differentiation and specialization continued, very likely in patterns similar to those described by anthropologists as existing in present day isolated, simple cultures.

Such "job specialization" is so logical that we accept the idea almost without question. However, when we so glibly adopt that concept we must face a further set of questions: Why was A a hunter instead of a fisher, a toolmaker, a warrior, a healer, or a chieftain? Our speculation can lead us in many directions: (a) Did A have special characteristics such as strength, endurance, or agility, that suggested A might be more successful as a hunter than B, C, or D? (b) Did A's family "own the franchise" for hunting, thus limiting the competition? (c) Did A have access to the special secrets or tools of earlier hunters (his father's, perhaps)? (d) Was the tradition of "like father, like son" so strong that everyone always assumed that A would be a hunter? (e) Did the changing needs of the group suddenly require more hunters than had previously been the case? (f) Who decided that A would be a hunter—A himself, his family, the whole group, a special committee of respected elders, or did it just "happen" without an overt decision? Unfortunately, these are difficult questions to answer.

The issues we have just raised about our mythical A could be asked again and again as we contemplate the relationship between every individual who has lived since those early times and his or her work. Throughout history, career development has been subjected to powerful pressures and influences that can still be observed today. In much of today's world one still sees occupational membership determined by such factors as social status, family tradition, and societal needs. On the other hand, some opportunity for choice has also existed over the years. For example, Benjamin Franklin, in his *Autobiography*, reports an interesting event when, on his twelfth birthday (in 1718), he and his father visited the shops of several craftsmen to explore the possibilities of Benjamin's apprenticeship. The choice of printer was soon consummated.

The idea that the individual can exercise some choice in his or her career development, nevertheless, is primarily a product of this century, and mostly of very recent decades. Bandura (1974) suggests that human freedom can be defined as the availability of options and the right to exercise those options. This concept appears to be most prevalent within western democratic societies, but even there it encounters frequent challenge. However, the extension of democratic ideals to increased concern for alleviation of poverty, increased emphasis on access to opportunities for employment by minority and alienated groups, and broader attention to participatory democracy suggest the likelihood that more opportunities will become available to more individuals. Since the career counselor is basically concerned with helping each client identify appropriate and possible options and to make decisions and plans for exercising those options, the counselor is already committed to this concept of human freedom.

All professions and crafts, as well as many other occupations, require a mastery of pertinent theoretical and practical knowledge. The physician needs to know the theoretical aspects of biology, chemistry, and physics along with the practical side of anatomy, enzymology, optics, and sound conduction. The automobile mechanic must understand the theories of physics related to internal combustion, hydraulics, and electricity as well as the practical knowledge of strength of metals, heat transference, and friction reduction. To understand either a malfunctioning liver or a faulty steering mechanism one must know how these units operate normally, how they interact with other units, how the operation of the part can be influenced or changed, and how to obtain the information needed to understand the present problem. It is then possible to analyze the available data, identify possible alternatives, estimate the results likely to be produced by each option, evaluate the desirability of each result, and choose a tentative course of action.

Individuals preparing to enter the helping professions often overlook the importance of thorough grounding in both theory and knowledge. They are so concerned with building skill that they overlook the theoretical base that suggests or justifies that skill. That theoretical framework provides the basis for understanding the client, the client's problem, and possible courses of action.

Shertzer and Stone (1980) have listed four functions of theories appropriate to our discussion. First, they suggest, a theory summarizes and generalizes a body of information, permitting the user to organize material into a meaningful system. Second, a theory facilitates understanding and explanation of complex phenomena; thus the user has a basis for developing insight into complicated situations and their causes. Third, a theory serves a predictive function by providing a basis for estimating what will happen under certain conditions. Fourth, a theory stimulates further research and fact finding by assuming positions that are testable. As further research is conducted the theory is refined, extended, and completed.

The physical and biological sciences, and their related professions such as engineering and medicine, have benefited from centuries of theory-building and subsequent research. The behavioral sciences are still in their infancy in this aspect, except in areas where roots can be traced back to those early developing physical and biological sciences. This dearth of a well-developed and substantial theoretical base that is widely accepted by all professionals is a major problem in our area of concern. Several factors contribute to our lack of a solid theoretical base, including the brief period of time that career development has been studied, the impact on career patterns of vast social change occurring in the past half-century, and the lack of sophistication in basic disciplines such as psychology and sociology by career counselors and counselor educators. Although the professional literature of the past two or three decades has included much material dealing with career choice and career development, most authorities would concur with the view that our theoretical base is still sketchy and incomplete. Carkhuff, Alexik, and Anderson (1967) state that each presently existing theory of career choice has certain theoretical shortcomings.

It is very easy to assume either of two opposite positions concerning our present theoretical status. One can contend, like Warnath (1975), that our theories of career development are relevant for a continually decreasing number of individuals and that the needs of individuals are in direct conflict with the needs of our economic system, which produces the jobs people fill. He further contends that most people see no confirmation of their worth in the work they perform and that counselors should focus on helping individuals find that sense of worth in areas other than paid employment. Osipow (1983), on the other hand, states that even incomplete theory is better than none at all. He says that counselors and teachers are confronted continually with clients and students who are attempting to make choices and decisions; thus if help is to be provided, a basis for action is required. Without some theoretical base, the counselor is limited to sympathetic listening.

There is much truth in Warnath's position. Many work settings provide little opportunity for worker satisfaction, many employers have too little interest in the worker as a person rather than as a laborer, and society often emphasizes the production of goods and services rather than the recognition of human dignity. Further, there are many individuals who, for various reasons, view involvement with work in a passive, accepting way, taking whatever job comes their way and drifting with the tide. Satisfactions come primarily from extracurricular activities such as weekend camping, the bowling league, or a hobby. Career counseling has little to offer these individuals. There are many others, however, who feel a desire for self-direction, who want to make choices about what they do, how they live, who they are. Of these, some will seek or need help in making choices, building plans, acting on decisions, and for these clients the skilled career counselor can provide assistance that is honest, meaningful, and facilitative.

Even though the theories of career counseling are presently incomplete, they do offer us the best and only guidelines that we have. As Osipow states, theory precedes and accompanies empirical knowledge and orients it while it is developing. Hewer (1963) similarly suggests that many so-called theories are more truly position papers prepared for discussion and criticism by colleagues. In this chapter we will use the term *theory* loosely, referring usually to the position or point of view of the proponent and accepting the idea that the statement may be incomplete, sometimes inconsistent, often still unproven. The reader is encouraged to consider the various viewpoints from a pragmatic frame of reference that asks such questions as these: Does this help me understand human behavior? Does this provide a means for helping a client become more self-understanding and self-directing? Does this offer a better chance for estimating the future? Further, no theory is now so well developed that a counselor can afford to "buy into" or become a disciple of a single viewpoint, eschewing all others. Rather, the counselor is required to build a personal theory, accepting part of this one, a dash of that one, and possibly most of two or three others.

In this chapter the primary effort is directed toward looking at several major positions on career development, with only sufficient detail to provide the reader a base for understanding the essential ingredients of each theory. In the next chapter we will apply these theoretical positions of career development or choice to the process of career courseling, again only in enough detail to grasp the major implications for the counselor. The reader who desires more extensive coverage than our limited space permits has several options available. Books by Osipow (1983) and Pietrofessa and Splete (1975) give excellent summaries of the writings of the major theorists. Recent publications by Weinrach (1979), Herr and Cramer (1984), and Crites (1981) also give up-to-date summaries of the major writers. Whiteley and Resnikoff (1972) have edited a monograph in which several major theorists have described their viewpoint in 1970. Brown, Brooks, and associates (1984) present a 1980s evaluation and description of major theoretical positions with many of the statements prepared by the theorists.

Ultimately, the reader must turn to the statements of the theorists themselves for a detailed view of what that writer proposes.

Attempts to classify theoretical positions are often frustrating for the classifier and confusing for the reader. The clear-cut, unquestioned categorization typified by the "good guys" and "bad guys" of traditional wild-west movies is simply impossible. One finds a degree of overlap and parallelism that often confounds the categories, blurs the boundaries, and forces arbitrary actions. The classifications used here are based on convenience and "best fit." In this section we will consider the following groupings:

1. Adventitious, situational, and psychoanalytic theories.
2. Trait and factor theory.
3. Personality-based theories.
4. Developmental theories.
5. Behavioral and decision-making theories.

ADVENTITIOUS, SITUATIONAL, AND PSYCHOANALYTIC THEORIES

Economists and sociologists have sometimes been inclined to support theories of career choice that involve chance or accidental happenings in which the individual is largely subject to powerful external forces. To some extent, Warnath (1975) warns that this danger is increasing for many individuals. Often economists identify the laws of supply and demand as powerful forces in determining job opportunity and worker availability. Simply put, this concept proposes that employers will offer sufficient pay or reimbursement to attract the needed number of workers; as the pay escalates, more workers than needed are attracted. This causes the employer to reduce the pay, since there are now more workers available than needed. Reducing the pay encourages workers to search for other opportunities, results in a shortage of workers, and the cycle starts over again. Many work situations are highly sensitive to variation in economic conditions and slight changes in any direction can influence employment. At the same time, it is important to remember that many factors exist that interfere with the operation of a free market, where the supply-demand interaction occurs. Some restrictions have been developed to protect the general public, others to assist specific groups of workers, employers, or consumers. Some are the result of social custom and some come from legislative or governmental regulation.

Sociologists, such as Caplow (1954) and Miller and Form (1951), have discussed the influence of chance on career development. This is often described as "being in the right place at the right time" or as "the once in a lifetime opportunity." Movie fan magazines often exploit the story of the unknown drug store clerk or fast-food carhop who is whisked to fame by a long-searching director who wanted the perfect person to star in the movie of the decade. Similarly, but on a less spectacular scale, many of us can recall individuals whose lives have changed drastically because of accident, luck, the strange hand of fate, or other situational circumstances.

Using a broader perspective, Lipsett (1962) has identified several social factors that influence career development, including social class membership, home influences, school, community, pressure groups, and role perception. Borow mentions the influence of family and social class, and to a lesser extent the school and community, in determining the social and psychological motives upon which the individual's behavior is based. Herr and Cramer (1984) summarize a number of recent studies that have investigated the influence of social factors. They conclude that these are factors that influence every person and the extent to which any one item may serve as a constraint or as a stimulus must be determined individually.

Brill (1949) expounds an almost fatalistic view of career development, contending that occupations are simply expressions of unconscious psychic forces and, unless there is interference, the person will express sublimation in an occupational form. Thus surgeons, butchers, warriors, and hunters are simply expressing sadistic impulses, and the actor is revealing a basic exhibitionism.

TRAIT AND FACTOR THEORY

The essence of *trait and factor theory* is a joining of the concept of individual differences with the concept of job analysis. Each individual has a unique set of characteristics or *traits* that can be identified and measured by tests or other means. Each occupation also requires certain *factors* for successful performance. The counselor can identify the pattern of client traits and match this pattern against those required for successful job performance. Thus the highly verbal, aggressive, dynamic individual is a "natural" for a sales position, while the quiet, compulsive, mathematically oriented, conventional individual is encouraged to consider bookkeeping or accounting.

Several individuals contributed significantly to the trait and factor approach. In the previous chapter we considered the very early work of Parsons (1909), who suggested that a wise vocational choice required a clear understanding of self, including attitudes, abilities, interests, ambitions, resources, and limitations; also a knowledge of the requirements and conditions in various lines of work; and finally, true reasoning to discover the relation between these two sets of data. Donald G. Paterson and others in the Minnesota Employment Stabilization Research Institute concentrated on the development of tests to identify individual traits. Industrial psychologists such as Frederick Taylor and Elton Mayo focused on the characteristics of jobs and the capabilities required for successful performance. Events related to American participation in World War II greatly accelerated research and application of the trait and factor approach—within the military structure by using this system for classifying and assigning recruits and inductees to military jobs, and outside the military by using tests to identify special abilities and skills needed in essential defense jobs.

Jones, revised and updated by Stefflre and Stewart (1970), lists five assumptions basic to the trait and factor position. These include the following:

1. Vocational development is largely a cognitive process in which the individual uses reasoning to arrive at his decision.
2. Occupational choice is a single event.
3. There is a single right goal for everyone making decisions about work.
4. A single type of person works in each job.
5. There is an occupational choice available to each individual. (p. 182)

If one reads these assumptions from a strictly literal view, it is at once apparent that they can easily be negated, and if they might have been true in the '30s or '40s, they certainly don't hold true for the '80s. However, if one reads them with the insight of what we know today and accepts a loose interpretation, they are generally acceptable. For example, most of us can agree that cognition (the application of knowledge) is an essential aspect of career development, that the opportunity for occupational choice occurs *at least* once during life, that every individual has sufficient assets to be able to perform some work, and finally, that each person's characteristics can be matched with jobs that are generally compatible.

From Parsons's time until shortly after World War II, the trait and factor approach not only held dominance but, for all practical purposes, it was the only approach to what was then called vocational counseling. Since that time (the early 1950s), as we will see in the remaining pages of this chapter, it has shared the stage with other theoretical approaches. Few counselors today would advocate a pure trait and factor approach, yet in varying degrees of modification, aspects of trait and factor theory exist in about every current theory of career development.

PERSONALITY-BASED THEORIES

In this section we will consider the viewpoints proposed by two widely respected theorists, Anne Roe and John Holland. Both suggest that the appropriateness of an occupation for an individual depends upon that individual's personality, which in turn is primarily a product of earlier experience.

Roe bases her theory heavily upon the earlier writing of Maslow (1954), who proposed the concept of a hierarchy of psychological need. This idea says that lower-order needs, those necessary for maintaining life, are so strong that they take precedence over the other needs and prevent their appearance until the lower-order needs are reasonably satisfied. Maslow says each person has eight basic needs. Arranged in hierarchical order from lowest to highest they are:

1. Physiological needs.
2. Safety needs.
3. Need for belongingness and love.
4. Need for importance, respect, self-esteem, independence.
5. Need for self-actualization.
6. Need for information.
7. Need for understanding.
8. Need for beauty.

Roe's study of the personality characteristics of several groups of scientists led her to conclude that experiences occurring in early childhood are most influential in reinforcing or weakening higher-order needs and these experiences ultimately influence career development. In 1957, she presented a series of hypotheses concerning early determinants of vocational choice. These hypotheses were expanded and refined in a monograph by Roe and Siegelman (1964). Roe's position can be seen from the following quotation from the 1964 monograph:

> *Proposition 1.* Genetic inheritance sets limits to the potential development of all characteristics, but specificity of the genetic control and the extent and nature of the limitations are different for different characteristics.
> It is probable that the genetic element is more specific and stronger in what we call intellectual abilities and temperament than it is in such other variables as interests and attitudes.
> *Proposition 2.* The degrees and avenues of development of inherited characteristics are affected not only by experience unique to the individual, but also by all aspects of the general cultural background and the socio-economic position of the family.
> *Proposition 3.* The pattern of development of interests, attitudes, and other personality variables with relatively little or nonspecific genetic control is primarily determined by individual experiences through which involuntary attention becomes channeled in particular directions.
> The important word here is involuntary. The elements in any situation to which one gives automatic or effortless attention are keys to the dynamics of behavior. This proposition is clearly related to hypotheses concerning the relations between personality and perception.
> a. These directions are determined in the first place by the patterning of early satisfactions and frustrations.
> This patterning is affected by the relative strengths of various needs and the forms and relative degrees of satisfaction which they receive. The two latter aspects are environmental variables.
> b. The modes and degrees of need satisfaction determine which needs will become the strongest motivators. The nature of the motivation may be quite unconscious.

Possible variations are:
1. Needs satisfied routinely as they appear do not become unconscious motivators.
2. Needs, for which even minimum satisfaction is rarely achieved, will, if higher order (as used by Maslow, 1954), become expunged or will, if lower order, prevent the appearance of higher order needs and will become dominant and restricting motivators.
3. Needs, the satisfaction of which is delayed but eventually accomplished, will become (unconscious) motivators, depending largely upon the degree of satisfaction felt. Behavior that has received irregular reinforcement is notably difficult to extinguish (C. B. Ferster and B. F. Skinner, 1957).

   The degree of satisfaction felt will depend, among other things, upon the strengths of the basic need in the given individual, the length of time elapsing between arousal and satisfaction, and the values ascribed to the satisfaction of this need in the immediate environment.

Proposition 4. The eventual pattern of psychic energies, in terms of attention directedness, is the major determinant of interests.

Proposition 5. The intensity of these needs and of their satisfaction (perhaps particularly as they have remained unconscious) and their organization are the major determinants of the degree of motivation that reaches expression in accomplishment. (p. 5)

Roe proposed that the relationship between parent and child—the emotional climate of the home—produces these early influences that shape the individual's personality. She saw three types of emotional climate: emotional concentration on the child, avoidance of the child, or acceptance of the child. She visualized these relationships in a circular pattern with each type of climate shading into the other two types. Further, each climate type was pictured as having two subtypes which also shaded into one another and into the adjacent subcategory of the other types. These climates and subtypes are represented in the second and third inner circles of the figure proposed by Roe in the 1957 article, as shown in Figure 3–1.

Emotional concentration on the child includes subdivisions of overprotecting parents and overdemanding ones. The overprotecting parents encourage dependency in the child and restrict exploratory behavior. They are often indulgent, allow social privileges, and show affection. They limit and select the child's friendships, and protect the youngster from other children. They intrude into the child's life and expect to be told all thoughts and experiences. The overdemanding parents set very high standards for the child, and require conformity to that standard. They expect the child to be constructively busy and they select friends for the child who meet the standards they set. They dominate and direct the child's thoughts and feelings.

The avoidance climate includes both rejection and neglect. Rejecting type parents are more extreme in behavior than demanding parents. Their attitude toward the child is one of coldness, hostility, derogation, and

FIGURE 3–1   Roe's circular model. (From A. Roe and M. Siegelman, *Origin of interests*. Washington, D.C.: American Personnel and Guidance Association, 1964.)

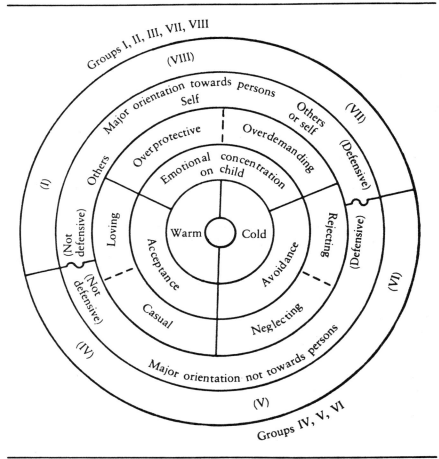

ridicule. They leave the child alone and also prevent contact with other children. They set up household rules to protect themselves from intrusions by the child into their lives. Neglecting parents, on the other hand, do not express hostility or ridicule; they simply ignore the child. They provide minimal physical care and no affection. They make no effort to avoid the child nor to establish contact or care.

The climate of acceptance can be either casual or loving. The casually accepting parents pay some attention to the child and are mildly affectionate. They accept the child as part of their general situation and are responsive to the child if not occupied with other matters. They tend to be easygoing, making few rules or exerting little effort to train the child, and usually do not enforce rules or exert training efforts. The lovingly accepting parents give the child warmth and affection. They help the child with things that are important without taking control. They usually reason with the child rather than punish. They give praise appropriately and try to help with problems. They invite the child's friends to the home, encourage independence, and allow the child to take reasonable chances in growing up.

These six types of parental behavior produce two broad types of behavior in the child. The categories of loving, overprotecting, or overdemanding attitudes produce a major orientation toward persons. The areas of casual acceptance, neglect, or rejection produce a major orientation away from persons. Both of these behaviors range from a nondefensive extreme to a defensive extreme. Occupations also are oriented toward persons or away from persons. Person-oriented areas include service, business contact, organizations, general culture, and the arts and entertainment. Non-person-oriented areas include technology, the outdoors, and science. Thus an individual whose family provided an accepting or protective environment is likely to seek an occupation working with others in service or business contact activities while the person whose parents were casual or neglectful is likely to move toward technical or outdoor occupations. Roe further suggests levels based upon responsibility or educational requirements within each of her six areas of primary focus.

Support for Roe's hypotheses has been found in subsequent research only rarely. Several problems contribute to this lack of research support. First, the emotional climate of the home, in most research to date, has been determined by recall of the research subject long after early childhood, or identified by elementary age children on the basis of very simple criteria. Second, emotional climate may be inconsistent and variable. Third, many of the propositions are somewhat vague and difficult to state in specific, researchable terms. Finally, children are subjected to many other influences even within the earliest years of childhood. This lack of research support does not justify writing off Roe's proposals. Most of us can recognize within our own childhood experience the influence of family and home and its continuing impact on our lives.

Holland, unlike Roe, spends little time considering how people became the way they are. He does suggest that earlier life history, self-perceptions, and values are among factors that have been influential. Like Roe, Holland assumes that people have developed a set of behaviors, or personality, that is characteristic, persistent, and relatively permanent. This typology is perhaps most representative of Holland's viewpoint.

Holland (1966, 1973) describes the central thrust of his theory in four basic assumptions, as follows:

1. In our culture, most persons can be categorized as one of six types: realistic, investigative, artistic, social, enterprising or conventional.
2. There are six kinds of environments: realistic, investigative, artistic, social, enterprising and conventional.

3.   People search for environments that will let them exercise their skills and abilities, express their attitudes and values, and take on agreeable problems and roles.
4.   A person's behavior is determined by an interaction between his personality and the characteristics of his environment. (1973, pp. 2–4)

Holland assumes that a person expresses personality through the choice of a vocation, and that the instruments we usually describe as interest inventories are really personality inventories. Further, each person is thought to hold stereotypical views of various occupations that have psychological and sociological relevance for the individual. Thus, Holland is saying that work is an expression of personality that reflects the basic nature of the individual as that person sees himself or herself. Let us consider briefly each of the six personality types.

Realistic persons deal with environment in an objective, concrete, and physically manipulative manner. They avoid goals and tasks that demand subjectivity, intellectual or artistic expressions, or social abilities. They are described as masculine, unsociable, emotionally stable, and materialistic. They prefer agricultural, technical, skilled trade, or engineering occupations. They like activities that involve motor skills, things, and structure, such as athletics, scouting, crafts, shop work, and the like. They avoid supervisory and leadership roles, social situations in which one would be the center of attention, and intellectual or verbal tasks that require abstract thinking. They have a single outlook, more mathematical ability than verbal, and the operation of machines, tools, and vehicles increases their sense of well-being and power.

Investigative individuals deal with environment by the use of intelligence, manipulating ideas, words, and symbols. They prefer scientific vocations, theoretical tasks, reading, collecting, algebra, foreign languages, and such creative activities as art, music, and sculpture. They avoid social situations and see themselves as unsociable, masculine, persistent, scholarly, and introverted. They achieve primarily in academic and scientific areas and usually do poorly as leaders. They have a complex outlook and score high in both verbal and mathematical aptitudes. Investigative types are more scholarly, original, independent, and self-confident, but less practical, emotionally stable, and conventional than realistic individuals.

Artistic people deal with their environment by creating art forms and products. They rely on subjective impressions and fantasies when seeking solutions to problems. They prefer musical, artistic, literary, and dramatic occupations, and activities that are creative in nature. They dislike masculine activities and roles such as auto repair and athletics. They see themselves as unsociable, feminine, submissive, introspective, sensitive, impulsive, and flexible. They are usually more original than the members of any other type and have higher verbal aptitude than mathematical.

Social types control their environment by using skills for handling and dealing with other people. They typically possess social skills and need social interactions. They prefer educational, therapeutic, and religious occupations, and such activities as church, government, community services, music, reading, and dramatics. They see themselves as sociable, nurturant, cheerful, conservative, responsible, achieving, and self-accepting. They have a positive self-image and consider themselves to be leaders, good speakers, popular, and aggressive. They tend to have high verbal but low mathematical aptitudes. They have much concern for human welfare and for helping dependent individuals.

Enterprising persons cope with their environment with choices that express adventurous, dominant, enthusiastic, and impulsive qualities. They are characterized as persuasive, verbal, extroverted, self-accepting, self-confident, aggressive, and exhibitionistic. They prefer sales, supervisory, and leadership positions, and activities that satisfy a need for dominance, verbal expression, recognition, and power. They like athletics, dramatics, public speaking, and interviewing. They dislike confining, manual, nonsocial activities. They see themselves as dominant, sociable, cheerful, adventurous, impulsive, and emotionally stable. They assert themselves by struggling for power, developing athletic abilities, acquiring possessions, and exploiting others. They differ from the conventional person by being more sociable, aggressive, dominant, original, and adventurous, and less responsible, dependent, and conservative.

Conventional people deal with the environment by choosing goals and activities that carry social approval. Their approach to problems is stereotyped, correct, and unoriginal. They create a good impression by being neat, sociable, and conservative. They prefer clerical and computational tasks, identify with business, and put a high value on economic matters. They see themselves as masculine, shrewd, dominant, controlled, rigid, and stable. They have more mathematical aptitude than verbal. They reduce stress by social conformity and by ingratiating themselves with others. They differ from social types by possessing greater self-control and being more hard-headed and less dominant and nurturant.

According to Holland, a person can be typed into one of these categories by expressed or demonstrated vocational or educational interests, by employment, or by scores obtained on such instruments as the Kuder General Interest Survey, the Strong-Campbell Interest Inventory, or the Self-Directed Search. The last instrument, developed by Holland, consists of occupational titles and activities that can be divided among the six types. The Strong-Campbell Interest Inventory scoring system includes direct translation into Holland's types.

Holland proposes that the six personality types are related to personal needs as described by Murray (1938). In other words, the various types are indicative of the needs felt by the individual. Murray was concerned not only with psychological needs but also with what he termed "environmental presses." Holland accounts for these environmental factors by identifying a set of environmental models (Assumption 2, above) that he defines as the situation or atmosphere created by the people who dominate a given environment. These environmental models reflect the personality attributes of those in control—the six types described above. Let us consider briefly each of these six environments.

The *realistic* environment involves concrete, physical tasks requiring mechanical skill, persistence, and physical movement. Only minimal interpersonal skills are needed. Typical realistic settings include a filling station, machine shop, farm, construction site, or barber shop.

The *investigative* environment requires the use of abstract and creative abilities rather than personal perceptiveness. Satisfactory performance demands imagination and intelligence; achievement usually requires a considerable time span. Problems encountered may vary in level of difficulty but they will usually be solved by the application of intellectual skills and tools. The work is with ideas and things rather than with people. Typical settings include a research laboratory, diagnostic case conference, library, working group of scientists, mathematics, and research engineering.

The *artistic* environment demands the creative and interpretive use of artistic forms. One must be able to draw on knowledge, intuition, and emotional life in solving typical problems. Information is judged against personal, subjective criteria. The work usually requires intense involvement for prolonged periods. Typical settings include a play rehearsal, concert hall, dance studio, study, library, or an art or music studio.

The *social* environment demands ability to interpret and modify human behavior and an interest in caring for and dealing with others. The work requires frequent and prolonged personal relationships. The work hazards are primarily emotional. Typical work situations include a school or college classroom, a counseling office, mental hospital, church, educational office, and recreational center.

The *enterprising* environment requires verbal skill in directing or persuading other people. The work requires directing, controlling, or planning activities of others, and an interest in others at a more superficial level than in the social environment. Typical settings include a car lot, real-estate office, political rally, and an advertising agency.

The *conventional* environment involves systematic, concrete, routine processing of verbal and mathematical information. The tasks frequently call for repetitive, short-cycle operations according to an established procedure. Minimal skill in interpersonal relations is required since the work is mostly with things and materials. Typical settings include a bank, accounting firm, post office, file room, and a business office.

Holland suggests that each model environment is sought by individuals whose personality type is similar to those controlling the environment. It is assumed that they will be comfortable and happy in a compatible environment and uneasy in one that consists of different personality types. Since it is unlikely that an individual would demonstrate a pure expression of one of the six types, one can be expected to show primary (highest score) and secondary (other high scores) types. Consistency between primary and secondary areas usually indicates stability, whereas inconsistency (opposite types) usually produces change from one category to another. Similarly, a person who demonstrates congruence between self and environment presumably can expect a more stable vocational choice, higher vocational achievement, higher academic achievement, better maintenance of personal stability, and greater satisfaction.

Holland demonstrates the concept of consistency by using a hexagonal model as shown in Figure 3–2. Each of the six types is placed at one corner of the hexagon in the sequence of closest interrelationship. Thus adjacent corners are most alike, opposite corners (R and S, I and E, A and C) are least alike, and the intermediate corners (for example, R and A, R and E) have intermediate relationships with the base corner.

Holland has developed an occupational classification system related to the model environment construct. Thus occupations have been identified that are purported to be representative of each of the major combinations of primary and secondary types. These primary and secondary types are often referred to as "Holland Codes." For example, a code of RIA means a primary area of *realistic* and secondary areas of *investigative* and *artistic*. Such a combination would be considered consistent, as reflected by close proximity on the hexagon. On the other hand, a code of RSE would be considered inconsistent because *realistic* and *social* areas are opposites.

Holland's theory has been criticized frequently in the professional literature. Major criticisms focus on the contention that a typology approach is too simplistic, that the model tends to be sexist and thus fails to recognize social changes of recent years, and that the theory doesn't deal adequately with how people develop their personality type. Nevertheless, the Holland theory has had great impact upon the field. One visible demonstration of this impact is shown by the numerous research projects stimulated by the theory.

One example of the numerous research studies relating to Holland's theory is a recent article by Warren, Winer, and Dailey (1981). The authors report a project in which sixty-five men and women, between fifty and eighty-eight years of age, were asked to complete Holland's *Vocational Preference Inventory* (VPI) and to report their first full-time job, their longest full-time job, their last job (if retired), their present job (if still employed), and hobbies. Holland one-letter codes were assigned on the basis of reported data and matched against codes obtained on the instrument. In general, those individuals assigned specific codes on the basis of their work record tended to score highest on the VPI on the appropriate scale related to that code.

FIGURE 3-2   Holland's hexagonal relationship of occupational classes. (Adapted from Holland, J. L., Whitney, D. R., Cole, N. S., and Richards, J. M., Jr. *An empirical occupational classification derived from a theory of personality and intended for practice and research.* ACT Research Report No. 29. Iowa City: The American College Testing Program, 1969.)

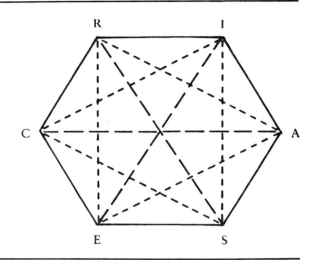

R—Realistic
I—Investigative
A—Artistic
S—Social
E—Enterprising
C—Conventional

DEVELOPMENTAL THEORIES

The theories we have considered in the previous pages should probably be labeled theories of career or vocational *choice* because they either assume or imply that the choice is an event that occurs at a specific time. Roe, to a large extent, and Holland, to a lesser degree, consider the influence of early events upon later actions, but neither seems to recognize any cumulative process. In this section we will consider three viewpoints that put basic stress upon the idea of *career development* as a process, rather than an event, extending over a very long period of time. We will consider the positions of Ginzberg and his associates (later revised by Ginzberg), of Super, and of Tiedeman.

Ginzberg, Ginsburg, Axelrad, and Herma (1951) were among the first to suggest that the developmental process was crucial to occupational choice. This team of four colleagues at Columbia University undertook a study of a group of boys and young men ages eleven to twenty-three who were attending either a university-related school or the university itself. These subjects came from upper socioeconomic backgrounds and were either college-bound or in college. A second group was added to the study including primarily the sons of white fathers employed in unskilled and semiskilled occupations. A third group included a small sample of college sophomore and senior women who were socially privileged and intelligent.

The total of the three groups was quite small and cannot be considered representative of the general population.

Drawing from the life-stages concept of Buehler (1933), they pictured the vocational choice process as covering three principal periods, which they called fantasy, tentative, and realistic periods. The *fantasy period*, they said, is an early childhood interval preceding any serious vocational consideration. The time is exemplified by arbitrary choices that lack any rational or realistic base, but that often reflect idealized choices drawn from influences within the child's environment.

The *tentative period* begins when children begin to recognize that they like or have an interest in certain activities. During this time children discover they perform some activities more ably than other activities, that they excel in some of these compared with other children, and that some activities are more highly valued than others. Finally, they begin to fit together ideas of interest, ability, and value as they give more attention to a career choice. As this correlating activity occurs they move on to the third phase of vocational choice, the realistic period.

The *realistic period* comprises three stages, including exploration, crystallization, and specification. The exploration stage covers the time in which the individual is actively involved in implementing tentative choices. Chronologically, he or she is usually at the entry job or college level and tends to evaluate vocationally related experiences in a realistic manner. As a result of the interaction of experiences and the individual's evaluation of them, he or she gradually fixes on a fairly clear vocational pattern during the crystallization stage. The specification stage is reached when a pattern has clearly focused on a particular position or occupation.

Ginzberg and his associates see the whole process from fantasy to specification covering from ten to fifteen years and consisting of a series of compromises between wishes and opportunities. The process is viewed as irreversible and consists of clearcut periods that vary considerably from person to person. The fantasy period may extend up to age ten or twelve. The realistic period is usually entered by age seventeen or eighteen, and crystallization occurs for most individuals in the period from age nineteen to twenty-one. Some individuals may appear to enter the crystallization stage and then encounter factors that upset or change what appeared to be fairly solid choices. Some individuals never progress beyond the crystallization stage. Many factors—biological, psychological, and environmental—affect the individual's progress.

The group concluded that boys from lower socioeconomic level families followed the same general pattern as did those from more favored homes. The principal difference detected between the two groups was a striking increase in passivity among the lower-income boys. They expressed interest and concern in future occupations during earlier years but were decidedly less inclined to assume an active role in bringing their hopes into actuality. The group also concluded that there were definite differences in choice patterns between men and women. They found three groups within the small sample of college women they studied. One group was career-oriented, one was marriage-oriented, and the third group hoped to combine both. Even the career-oriented women appeared to be less fixed on specific vocational goals than the boys. Ginzberg et al. concluded that the possibility of marriage and its effect on a woman's career has a heavy impact on career planning for all women.

Ginzberg (1972) restated the major points of the group's proposal in light of research that has developed in the intervening two decades. Three major components of the earlier position have been modified. These include the ideas (1) that the occupational decision-making process extends from prepuberty to the early twenties, (2) that many of the decisions have an aspect of irreversibility, and (3) that the choice process always ends in compromise.

Ginzberg now sees the decision-making process as parallel to the individual's working life. Recognition is now given to the satisfactions that the individual derives from early career choices. If these are not adequate for the individual, the likelihood of a new choice is increased. The probability of the individual's responding by making a decision to move toward other opportunities depends, in part, on the amount of flexibility—that is, freedom from family responsibilities, indebtedness, or other restrictions—and on the pressure or opportunity encountered in the present work situation.

The irreversibility factor now appears to be less influential because it is possible to delay final, firm decisions over several years and so keep one's options open for a prolonged period. Similarly, there has been an increase in what can be thought of as new opportunities for training previously considered unattainable. An example of this is acquisition of educational opportunities through military service or company programs that allow and assist the individual to pursue preparation beyond the level previously thought to be the terminal level.

Finally, Ginzberg suggests that the substitution of *optimization* for *compromise* may be more relevant to most circumstances. The word *optimization* implies a dynamic, continuing kind of adjustment and readjustment, with the worker continually attempting to coordinate changing desires with changing circumstances in a way that appears most likely to produce favorable results.

Probably no one has written as extensively about vocational development or influenced thought about the process as much as Donald Super. His earliest theoretical statements appeared shortly after those of Ginzberg, et al. and were an effort to include ideas and concepts that apparently were passed over by his Columbia colleagues. The essence of Super's theory might be described as the idea that an individual chooses an occupation that allows one to operate in a role consistent with self-concept, which in turn is an outgrowth of all one's developmental experiences. As we have done here, most authors classify Super's theory as developmental self-concept.

Super (1969), however, describes it as a theory based on differential-developmental-social-phenomenological psychology. In his 1953 *American Psychologist* article, he originally suggested ten propositions, reorganized in 1957 into a new list of eleven propositions and appearing in *Vocational Development: A Framework for Research.* These were again revised and appeared as twelve propositions in *Scientific Careers and Vocational Development Theory,* also in 1957. We will list and briefly discuss those twelve propositions, grouping them in the same combinations suggested by Super.

> *Proposition 1:* Vocational development is an ongoing, continuous, generally irreversible process.
> *Proposition 2:* Vocational development is an orderly, patterned, and predictable process.
> *Proposition 3:* Vocational development is a dynamic process. (p. 118)

Like Ginzberg and his associates, Super has drawn heavily from the life-stages concepts proposed by Buehler (1933). He identifies these life stages as growth, exploration, establishment, maintenance, and decline.

The *growth* stage consists of a period when primary emphasis is on physical and psychological development, ordinarily reaching into adolescence to perhaps fourteen or fifteen years of age. During this growth stage the individual forms attitudes and behavior mechanisms that will be important components of the self-concept for much of life. Simultaneously, experiences provide a background of knowledge of the environment generally, including the world of work, which ultimately will be used in tentative choices and in final selections.

The *exploratory* stage begins with the individual's awareness that an occupation will be an aspect of life. During the early or fantasy phase of the exploratory stage, the expressed choices are frequently unrealistic and often closely related to the play life of the individual. Examples are seen in young children's choices of such careers as cowboys, soldiers, and astronauts. These choices are nebulous and temporary and usually have little, if any, long-term significance for the individual. Some adolescents, and even adults, have not advanced beyond the fantasy phase; their understanding of self or of the world of work is not sufficiently developed to make effective choice possible. The person may be responding in terms of "if I could do anything in the world" and ignoring or refusing to accept the inevitability of compromise. In the tentative phase of the exploratory stage, the individual has narrowed choice to a few possibilities. Because of uncertainty about ability, availability of training, or access to employment opportunity, the list may contain tentative choices that will later disappear. The realistic phase of this stage, still preceding actual entrance into work, narrows the list to occupations that the individual feels are attainable and that provide the opportunities thought to be most important. This stage usually extends to the middle twenties.

The *establishment* stage, as the name implies, relates to the early encounters within the work experience. During the establishment stage, the individual, at first often by trial and error, attempts to ascertain if the vocational choices and decisions made during the exploratory stage have validity. Some of this period is simply tryout. The individual may accept a job with a definite assumption that a change in position or occupation will occur if this one does not fit. As experience and proficiency are gained, the individual becomes stabilized; that is, he or she brings aspects of this occupation into the self-concept and adjusts the position by investing self in the work. The person accepts the occupation as one offering the best chance to obtain satisfactions that are personally important. This period is thought to extend to the middle forties.

During the *maintenance* stage, the individual attempts to continue or enhance the occupational situation. Since both the occupation and the individual's self-concept have some aspects of fluidity, the maintenance stage involves a continual process of adjustment. Essentially, the person is concerned with continuing the satisfying parts of the work situation and revising or changing unpleasant and annoying aspects. Usually the maintenance period is believed to extend approximately to age sixty-five.

The *decline* stage includes the preretirement period, during which the individual's emphasis in work is focused on keeping the job and meeting the required standards of output. The worker is now more concerned with retaining the position than with enhancement. The period terminates with the individual's withdrawal from the world of work.

Super views vocational development as consisting of an interaction between the individual—in terms of behavior, attitudes, ambitions, and values—and the surrounding social factors. This dynamic interaction produces a series of compromises as the individual matches what is desired against the realities, and attempts to identify what is attainable.

> *Proposition 4:* Self-concepts begin to form prior to adolescence, become clearer in adolescence, and are translated into occupational terms in adolescence.
> *Proposition 5:* Reality factors (the reality of personal characteristics and the reality of society) play an increasingly important part in occupational choice with increasing age, from early adolescence to adulthood.
> *Proposition 6:* Identification with a parent or parent substitute is related to the development of adequate roles, their consistent and harmonious interrelationship, and their interpretation in terms of vocational plans and eventualities. (pp. 118–119)

Personality theorists have long contended that early childhood, during which most children are intensively exposed to values and interrelationships of the immediate family, has continuing influence on the individual's later life. During these years, the basic shape of self-concept is formed and its early testing occurs within the usually comfortable climate of family and elementary classroom.

As indicated above, during the preteen years most individuals increasingly see the continuing relationship between work and the adults who make up their immediate world. Since position in the world of work is important in American culture, this relationship becomes a major influence on self-concept. During the educational period, anticipated occupation or role plays a part in the development of self-concept. Each person attempts to maintain or enhance a favorable self-concept; thus the individual is attracted to activities that will permit keeping or improving the preferred self-image. As the inner drive toward this ideal self-concept pushes the individual strongly, he or she encounters restricting factors that may come from personal limitations or from the surrounding environment. These factors interfere with attaining the ideal self-concept and result in the individual's compromising to accept less than the ideal. It is developmentally logical for the person, in turn, to begin to view self in terms of some possible future relationship with work. As an individual matures, experiences provide a basis for evaluating both strengths and weaknesses and the "real world" as it is encountered. As problems are faced, persons learn to cope with these varied experiences and to find satisfying solutions.

The individual can be helped in this maturational process in two ways: (1) by assisting to develop abilities and interests, and (2) by assisting to acquire an understanding of self and strengths and weaknesses so that satisfying choices can be made. Both of these aspects emphasize the school's role and guidance program in assisting the individual to maximize development as a person. The teacher, with frequent classroom contact, can best observe latent or underdeveloped abilities and then challenge the individual to push toward higher but nonetheless attainable goals. The counselor may also discover undeveloped potential through data obtained from tests or other sources.

If the school provides adequate opportunity for youth to develop, it has built into its program frequent opportunities for reality testing. Both teacher and counselor can help each youth find more of these testing areas.

An adult role model apparently is of significant importance as the adolescent begins to take on the attributes of adulthood. This adult, who may or may not be a family member, serves as a model for many relationships, including the one with work. It appears likely that the difficulties encountered by many ghetto adolescents in adjusting to the world of work (often labeled "establishment") may be due in part to the lack of adult role models who have developed satisfactory work adjustments.

> *Proposition 7:* The direction and rate of the vertical movement of an individual from one occupational level to another are related to his intelligence, parental socio-economic level, status needs, values, interests, skill in interpersonal relationships, and the supply and demand conditions in the economy.
> *Proposition 8:* The occupational field which the individual enters is related to his interests, values, and needs, the identifications he makes with paren-

tal or substitute role models, the community resources he uses, the level
and quality of his educational background, and the occupational structure, trends, and attitudes of his community. (p. 119)

Since choice of an occupational field precedes any advancement in that
field, let us consider Proposition 8 before we discuss Proposition 7. An
individual can only choose among alternatives of which he or she is aware.
The extent of familiarity with many options is largely a product of interests
and resources, the adult role models considered important, and the local
environment in which a person is developing. If local opportunity is constricted by either economic limitations or attitudinal factors, then the impact on the individual is likely also to be narrowing. The socioeconomic
level of the adult role models makes a significant contribution, since the
early contact with the world of work is largely brought about through
parents, family, and friends. Hearing parents and their friends discuss experiences at work; observing the impact of occupational success, failure, or
frustration; and obtaining or losing chances at education, travel, or other
experience because of family circumstances greatly influence the individual's
later work history.

We can reasonably suggest that the relationship between economic
supply and demand and opportunity for vocational advancement is similar
to the relationship between genetic inheritance and later physical development. An active, expanding economy offers opportunity for vocational advancement in many areas, whereas an inactive, lethargic, or declining
economy limits opportunity and may hold many individuals in lower-level
positions longer than their ability, experience, and motivations would
otherwise suggest.

The individual's mental ability is an important contributor to academic success, which in turn will open or close many doors to and within
occupations. The ability to deal effectively with others is crucially important
in most work situations. "Being in the right place at the right time" or
"getting the breaks" is also important, since the individual must first have
an opportunity to demonstrate competency before acquiring either stability
or advancement in a job.

We often think that anyone can attain any goal, in true Horatio Alger
tradition, if only one tries hard enough. In actuality, however, factors over
which one often has no control set limits that can be surpassed or extended
only by Herculean effort, if at all.

> *Proposition 9:* Although each occupation requires a characteristic pattern of
> abilities, interests, and personality traits, the tolerances are wide enough
> to allow both some variety of individuals in each occupation and some
> diversity of occupations for each individual. (p. 119)

Many years of research have clearly established the concept of individual differences as far as abilities, interests, and personality are concerned.

The range of personal characteristics varies widely both within and among individuals. Within each person are traits or abilities so pronounced that often they are used to caricature the individual. At the same time, there are other areas in which the person is relatively weak or inept.

The range of abilities, personality characteristics, and other traits is so wide that every person has the requisites for success in many occupations. Research in the field of rehabilitation has demonstrated that even the severely handicapped individual has a choice of many occupations in which that individual can perform satisfactorily. For the person without serious physical or emotional impairment, the gamut of possibilities is wide indeed.

Few occupations require special abilities, skills, or traits in excessive quantity. Just as most athletic activities involve only certain muscles or muscle groups, so too most jobs require only a few specific characteristics. A person, then, can perform successfully in any occupation for which he or she has the qualifying characteristics. The lack of a certain skill, or its presence in minute quantities, excludes a person from an occupation only if the occupation requires that skill in larger quantities.

For each ability or trait required in the performance of a particular occupation one might expect to find a modal quantity that best fits the nature of the work. On either side of this amount is a band or range of this characteristic that still will meet satisfactorily the demands of the work. To illustrate, picture an extremely simple task that requires, hypothetically, only a single characteristic. In studying this task we might ascertain the quantity of this trait that would best meet the requirements of the job. We would expect that a person could perform satisfactorily even though he or she possesses somewhat less or more of the trait, as long as it surpasses the minimum requirement. Obviously, the range for different traits will vary in each occupation, and the range in a given trait will vary among occupations.

To illustrate this point further, let us imagine three different workers with variable amounts of three different characteristics. Worker A has a high amount of the first trait, an average amount of the second trait, and a low amount of the third trait. Worker B has a low amount of the first trait, an average amount of the second trait, and a high amount of the third one; Worker C has an average amount of all three traits. Let us further assume that the minimums held by Workers A and C exceed the minimum threshold required to perform a job that demands only these three characteristics, and that their maximums are not so great as to impede their performance. Each worker, although different from the other two, can therefore perform the job successfully.

Since the patterns of characteristics required in various occupations rarely will be unique, one can expect to find considerable overlap from one job to another. Thus there will be some occupations in which a particular distribution of assets can result in satisfactory performance, just as there will be some patterns of ability that can result in satisfactory performance in a given occupation.

Proposition 10: Work satisfactions depend upon the extent to which the individual can find adequate outlets in his job for his abilities, interests, values, and personality traits.

Proposition 11: The degree of satisfaction the individual attains from his work is related to the degree to which he has been able to implement his self-concept in his work. (pp. 119–120)

The individual who finds pleasure and satisfaction in work does so because the position held permits use of characteristics and values in a way that is important. In other words, the experiences encountered in work are compatible with the mental image held of self—they give sufficient opportunity to be the kind of person he or she pictures self to be.

If the work performed does not provide the possibility to be the type of person pictured, discontent develops. This dissatisfaction will usually cause the person to look for a work situation where the possibility to play the role sought seems brighter.

The relationship of the work situation to the individual's role must be thought of in the broad sense. The professions and higher managerial positions probably provide the greatest opportunities, as viewed by most, for the intrinsic satisfactions that come from work itself. Many individuals gain great satisfaction from work that to some appears boring and monotonous. Other workers find satisfaction in jobs that they, too, may consider routine and unchallenging but that provide them the chance to be the kind of persons they want to be, to do the things they want to do, and to think of themselves as they wish.

Proposition 12: Work and occupation provide a focus for personality organization for most men and many women, although for some persons this focus is peripheral, incidental, or even nonexistent, and other foci such as social activities and the home are central. (p. 120)

Recent changes in the relationship of women to the world of work and the now generally accepted view of considering homemaking as an occupation make necessary some revision in this proposition if it is to have relevance today. Essentially, the major point here is that for many people, regardless of the nature of the job they fill, the work they do is an expression of their personality. For other individuals, both men and women, the work in which they engage is simply a means to an end and they seek opportunities for self-expression in places other than their work.

The extensive writing that Super and his colleagues have placed in the professional literature is research based. Much of Super's research has been longitudinal in nature and focused on a group of ninth grade boys who were first studied in 1951. This group was followed regularly in the Career Pattern Study for nearly a quarter century. In addition to these studies, many writers have built hypotheses on Super's theory, many of which are reviewed by Osipow (1983).

Super (1980) has recently summarized much of his previous thinking and writing in a brief article describing a life-career rainbow that encapsulates his view of the interrelationship between each person and career throughout the life span. He sees most individuals involved at various times of life, and in variable degrees of intensity, in the roles of child, student, leisurite, citizen, worker, spouse, homemaker, parent, and pensioner. The usual theaters in which these roles are played include the home, the community, the school, and the workplace. Super incorporated all roles into his definition of career and uses "occupational career" to refer to those work-related experiences that we will equate with career. As the importance of various roles increases or decreases, the lifestyle changes, and decision points are encountered that have further impact on the total life cycle of the individual. The choices made at these various decision points are the result of the interaction of several personal and situational determinants including genetic endowment as modified by life experiences, and all the geographic, social, cultural, and economic conditions that the person has experienced.

The proposal of a theoretical position by one professional influences another to react, question, modify, and counterpropose. In such manner are the writings of Tiedeman (1961), O'Hara and Tiedeman (1959), and Tiedeman and O'Hara (1963) related to the work of Super and also to Ginzberg and his associates. Tiedeman and O'Hara have drawn certain concepts from both sources and then proceeded to modify or develop further the earlier proposal.

Tiedeman and O'Hara suggest that career development is a process of organizing an identification with work through the interaction of the individual's personality with society. They consider personality development as a process in which the person is involved in both differentiation and integration. *Differentiation* focuses on the ways in which one uniquely expresses individuality—in other words, how one shows self as different from all other individuals. *Integration* refers to the ways in which one adjusts self to others so that one is an acceptable part of society.

Tiedeman and O'Hara suggest that one key aspect of their proposal is an emphasis on the relationship between personality and career as it is developed in the process of making career choices. Like Super, they see career development as spanning most of the individual's lifetime. The vocational aspects of a person's life, if they are not to dominate and control all of his or her actions, must be fitted into a larger life pattern. Tiedeman and O'Hara use the term *ego identity* to refer to the personal meanings, values, and relationships upon which the individual builds broader integration with society. The ego identity is formed through the interaction of three factors: the individual's biological constitution, psychological make-up, and the society or subculture in which he or she exists.

Tiedeman sees decision as crucial to vocational development. The decisions made by the individual regarding school, work, daily activities, and similar facets of total life will form and structure vocational development. Each decision includes two periods or aspects; each of these periods has substages, as indicated in the following outline:

I. The period of anticipation

A.   Exploration
B.   Crystallization
C.   Choice
D.   Specification

II. The period of implementation and adjustment

A.   Induction
B.   Transition
C.   Maintenance

During the exploration stage, the person considers a number of alternatives or possible goals. Within the range of the alternatives is the context of choice. He or she attempts to consider self in relation to the possible choices that are seen and enters the stage of crystallization as the choices become clearer, better understood, and evaluated. As a person chooses a particular goal, this goal influences his or her behavioral system. The greater the certainty with which the choice is made, the greater the impact on behavior. The final stage of the anticipatory period occurs after the choice has been made and before the individual moves to implement the choice. During this specification stage, he or she elaborates and perfects the image anticipated as a result of this choice.

The period of implementation begins as the person moves to act on the choice made. At this stage of induction, the individual is involved in fitting goal and field into the broader framework of the group and of society. As he or she gains confidence, the interaction between person and group expands, and he or she undertakes an effort to incorporate group goals into personal goal and field. If successful, a modification and an accommodation of group and individual goals is the result. The person then enters the maintenance stage, in which he or she tries to continue this satisfying equilibrium.

Tiedeman and O'Hara see the movement from one stage to another as a reversible process, so that the person may move in either direction at any given moment. Both advance and retreat occur in the decision-making process. Advancement usually predominates, so the person moves ultimately from indecision to choice to action.

Vocational development is thus seen as the summation of a complex series of decisions made by the individual over a considerable span of time, with each previous decision having an impact on later choices. Not all decisions occur longitudinally or sequentially. Thus, at any given moment the person may be at several different stages of choice on related aspects of life. The crystallization and resulting action on one of these aspects has an impact on all of the other aspects that are in process as well as on subsequent decisions. In the same way, the experiences the person encounters as a result of a decision will affect other decisions. The implied role of the counselor is to be a catalyst in freeing the person to make decisions and act on them in relation to choices already made and those still possible.

BEHAVIORAL AND DECISION-MAKING THEORIES

The viewpoints that we will consider in this section are related to the developmental position in many ways. Both groups, for example, recognize the impact of physical inheritance, family, school, and the developmental years. There is, at the same time, significantly different accentuation on the learning process, goal orientation, and factors influencing choice. We will consider the positions of John Krumboltz, as representative of the behavioralists, and H. B. Gelatt and Martin Katz as decision-making theorists.

Krumboltz (1976) has recently proposed a social learning theory of career decision making. He identifies four kinds of factors that influence career decision making; these include the following:

1. *Genetic endowment and special abilities.* Krumboltz recognizes that certain inherited characteristics can be restrictive influences on the individual, as Tiedeman similarly identifies biological constitution. Some illustrative examples are race, sex, and physical appearance. There are also some other factors where inheritance, at least in part, may set limits: these include various special abilities such as intelligence, musical and artistic ability, and physical coordination.

2. *Environmental conditions and events.* This factor includes those influences that may lie outside the control of anyone but which bear upon the individual through the environment in which the individual exists. Some influences may be man-made in the broadest sense, others may be due to natural forces. These human or natural elements may cause events to occur that also bear upon the individual in the educational and career decision process. Examples of influences of this type include existence of job and training opportunities, social policies and procedures for selecting trainees or workers, rate of return for various occupations, labor and union laws and regulations, physical events such as earthquakes and floods, existence of natural resources, technological developments, changes in social organization, family training experiences and resources, educational systems, and neighborhood and community influences.

3. *Learning experiences.* All previous learning experiences influence the individual's educational and career decision making. Recognizing the extreme complexity of the learning process, Krumboltz identifies only two types of learning as illustrative examples. These include instrumental learning experiences and associative learning experiences. He describes *instrumental learning experiences* as those situations where the individual acts on the environment to produce certain consequences. *Associative learning experiences* are described as situations where the individual learns by reacting to external stimuli, by observing real or fictitious models, or by pairing two events in time or location.

4. *Task-approach skills.* The skills that the individual applies to each new task or problem are called *task approach skills.* Examples of these include performance standards and values, work habits, and such perceptual and cognitive processes as attending, selecting, symbolic rehearsing, coding, and so on. The application of these skills affects the outcome of each task or problem and in turn is modified by the results.

Krumboltz sees the individual as constantly encountering learning experiences, each of which is followed by rewards or punishments that in turn produce the uniqueness of the individual. This continuous interaction with learning experiences produces three types of consequences which Krumboltz labels as self-observation generalizations, task approach skills, and actions. A *self-observation generalization* is an overt or covert self-statement that evaluates one's own actual or vicarious performance in relation to learned standards. The generalization may or may not be accurate, just as one's self-concept may or may not coincide with the concept others have of an individual. *Task approach skills* are thought to be efforts by the person to project into the future self-observation generalizations in order to make predictions about future events. They include work habits, mental sets, perceptual and thought processes, performance standards and values, and the like. *Actions* are the implementations of behavior such as applying for a job or changing a major field of study. The behavior produces certain consequences that affect behavior in the future.

In summary, we see an individual, born into the world with certain genetic characteristics such as race, sex, physique, and special abilities or handicaps who, as time passes, encounters environmental, economic, social, and cultural events and conditions. The individual learns from these encounters, building self-observations and task approach skills that are applied to new events and encounters. The successes and failures that accrue in these encounters influence the individual in choosing courses of action in subsequent learning experiences, increasing the likelihood of making choices like previous ones that led to success and avoiding choices like those that led to failure. The process is complicated by aspects of instability, since the individual changes as a result of the continuous series of learning experiences, and the situation also changes because environmental, cultural, and social conditions are dynamic.

Several authors have proposed models of vocational decision making. These are reviewed and compared in an excellent article by D. A. Jepsen and J. S. Dilley (1974). We will consider briefly only two of these positions, one suggested by H. B. Gelatt and one by Martin Katz.

Gelatt (1962) and Clarke, Gelatt, and Levine (1965) draw upon the earlier work of Bross (1953) and Cronbach and Gleser (1957) to develop a theoretical model for vocational decision making. Emphasis is given to a developmental approach rather than a single event by stating that decision making is a series of decisions in which each one influences subsequent decisions as well as some previously made decisions. Since decisions may relate to events of the immediate future, the intermediate future, or the distant future, all of those relating to the last two groups are subject to influence by decisions made before those events come to pass. Gelatt sees the major function of guidance and counseling services as that of turning potentialities into realities, and this, he thinks, can best be accomplished by building decision-making skills.

As Bross (1953) had suggested, Gelatt sees the individual processing information to produce a course of action or decision. The process involves a *predictive system* (a system to assess the possible alternative actions, the possible outcomes, and the probabilities), a *value system* (a means of weighing the desirability of different outcomes), and a *decision criterion* (a way to integrate and select an appropriate action). The three steps are seen as occurring in cyclical fashion to produce a decision that may be to collect further data; or to an outcome that changes the situation, the strategy, or the objective; or an outcome that achieves the purpose. Using this system leads the individual to consider wider ranges of alternatives and possible outcomes and to weigh the desirability of those possibilities not previously contemplated. The decision is a good decision when the decider is willing to accept responsibility for the consequences.

Clarke, Gelatt, and Levine (1965) describe four types of information to be processed by the decider. These include the following:

1.   *Information: Alternative actions.* This includes information about those courses of action that are available to the individual.
2.   *Information: Possible outcomes.* This carries the above alternatives to considerations of their results or consequences.
3.   *Information: Probabilities linking actions to outcomes.* Since each alternative course of action can likely lead to several distinct outcomes, one must estimate the probability of each action producing each possible outcome. Some will be certain but most will involve risk taking and uncertainty. Complicating the situation further is the existence of

branching points within the various alternative courses of action that in turn may carry differing probabilities.

4.   *Information: Preferences for the various outcomes.* The decider must be able to determine the desirability of each outcome. Outcomes may be instrumental in that they in turn make other, subsequent outcomes possible, or they may be intrinsic and be satisfying in their own right.

This approach suggests that the individual is better able to direct self-development toward desired outcomes if he or she can understand the possible sequences of experiences that lie ahead. This understanding includes the nature of the courses of action, the major branching points, the factors that bear upon the directions at the branching points, and the associated probabilities.

Katz (1963, 1966, 1969, 1973) proposes a model that has special significance because it has since served as the basis for the *System for Interactive Guidance and Information,* a computerized system considered by many to be one of the most sophisticated in present use. The unique aspect of Katz's viewpoint is the preeminence given to values, a matter to be dealt with before considering alternatives, information, and probabilities.

Katz also accepts a developmental position that emphasizes that one is continually involved in one decision after another, with each decision influencing both subsequent and previously made decisions. Using self-concept as a major basis in career development, Katz contends that an individual's value system is the main aspect of that self-concept and thus the major force in decision making. While Gelatt et al. listed information about preferences for various outcomes as the last type of information processed in decision making, Katz contends it must be the first to be considered, followed by an information system and a prediction system.

Early consideration of alternatives or probability of outcomes is largely wasted effort, Katz maintains, since the significance of each will vary from person to person. The individual should first come to some understanding of his or her values. This requires consideration of influences that have been exerted by family, church, peers, socioeconomic status, and similar factors to produce the existing pattern of values, and also comparison of the individual's pattern to the patterns of others. Helping the person to identify and define these values, work through these perceptions rationally, and apply them to making a choice becomes the primary aspect of career decision making.

Although the boundaries and characteristics of values are still largely unexplored, there are starting points that permit progress. Katz points out that even simple systems of arbitrary lists such as money-income, power-authority, stability-security, adventure-excitement-change, provide satisfactory bases for further consideration. In any given decision, Katz believes, the number of pertinent values is usually small, involving perhaps four to six factors. Each of these factors can be divided into convenient segments—for example, desired annual income can easily be put in terms of range of income.

Values differ in significance not only from person to person, but also within the individual. Thus the person must be aware of the different weights he or she ascribes to the values considered pertinent. Katz proposes that some overall total weight be used, for example one hundred points, and each value can then be assigned a proportionate share of this total weight to reflect the significance carried by that value.

After the individual clearly understands his or her value system, it is appropriate to view the options or alternatives as part of the information system. At this point, the person is concerned with identifying the "strength of return" offered by each option or alternative. In other words, to what extent does this option offer a payoff most compatible with the values espoused? Often "hard" information about such payoffs is unavailable, and only "soft" estimates can be used. The individual often will need help in assessing the quality of the information.

Finally, the prediction system is used by applying regression equations or expectancy tables to determine the likelihood of success in each option. This probability of entry or success can be combined with the value return to produce a combination of what Katz labels *expected value* for each option. Major difficulties in applying this system relate to unavailability of hard data for both identifying "strength of return" and "likelihood of success." Limited but significant progress has been made in both areas, although it tends to remain patchy and incomplete. For example, many colleges and universities have developed "likelihood of success" data for various programs based upon SAT scores, high school rank, grade in a relevant early course, or similar data.

AN ECLECTIC SUMMARY

The various positions or theories we have considered approach the topic of career choice from several different frames of reference; some are based on specific personality theories, others almost totally ignore personality formation, some are concerned with human development throughout the lifetime, and others focus on a specific period. There are, of course, many other fundamental differences among them.

Since the positions have been developed from differing bases, there is considerable risk in attempting to mix them together. Nevertheless, there are some generalizations on which several writers appear to agree. The reader is already aware of several common threads that tie many of the positions together.

The following tentative generalizations are proposed as reflecting a synthesis of ideas drawn from many of the theorists considered in this chapter. Each reader is encouraged similarly to develop a personal synthesis of career development theory. This author suggests the following:

1. The career development process is an ongoing, lifelong aspect of human existence.
2. Since the process is essentially developmental in nature, it is generally predictable but also can be modified by changing circumstances, even to the point of being reversible as the individual attempts to optimize the benefits and satisfactions derived from the worker-job relationship.
3. Individuals have differing patterns of abilities, interests, and personality as a result of the interaction of genetic inheritance and environmental factors. These characteristics are influenced by parental attitudes and behaviors, the impact of other role models, and the experiences that make up the life of the individual.
4. Occupations also have differing patterns of characteristics required or expected of successful workers. In most situations, some accommodation of variation is possible using a "band concept" identifying the tolerable limits for most successful participants.
5. The extent to which a person develops and applies his or her unique pattern of individual characteristics depends on attitudes, motivations, and values. These patterns can be approached from either the basis of psychological need or the development of self-concept. They impinge on the individual's perception of reality (now) and possible reality (future) and probably determine the extent to which the individual responds to existing opportunity.
6. The individual learns about jobs and their relationship to the individual specifically and to society generally from many sources, including the family, peer groups, community, school, media, and the planned and unplanned experiences of everyday life. The attitudes toward and knowledge of work developed in the growth, exploration, and crystallization periods of childhood and adolescence will have lasting influence on the worker-job relationship of the adult years.
7. The optimization that the individual seeks in the worker-job relationship is the product of the interaction between the individual (including abilities, interests, personality, values, and so on) and the realities of his or her situation (including economic conditions, opportunity, and chance factors of either positive or negative value). The ability and desire of the individual to capitalize on these interactions influence the level of optimization.
8. The degree of satisfaction experienced by the worker (either the extent to which the individual's self-concept is implemented or psychological needs are met) is largely determined by the extent

to which the potential for optimization is apparent to the individual and is viewed as agreeable and acceptable.

REFERENCES

Bandura, A. Behavior theory and the models of man. *American Psychologist,* 1974, 29, 859–869.

Borow, H. (ed.). *Man in a world at work.* Boston: Houghton Mifflin Company, 1964.

Brill, A. A. *Basic principles of psychoanalysis.* New York: Doubleday and Company, Inc., 1949.

Bross, I. D. *Design for decision.* New York: Macmillan Co., 1953.

Brown, D., Brooks, L., and associates. *Career choice and development.* San Francisco: Jossey-Bass Publishers, 1984.

Buehler, C. *Der menschliche lebenslauf als psychologisches problem.* Leipzig: Hirzel, 1933.

Caplow, T. *The sociology of work.* Minneapolis: University of Minnesota Press, 1954.

Carkhuff, R. R., Alexik, M., and Anderson, S. Do we have a theory of vocational choice? *Personnel and Guidance Journal,* 1967, 46, 335–345.

Clarke, R., Gelatt, H. B., and Levine, L. A decision-making paradigm for local guidance research. *Personnel and Guidance Journal,* 1965, 44, 40–51.

Crites, J. O. *Career counseling: Models, methods, and materials.* New York: McGraw-Hill Book Company, 1981.

Cronbach, L. and Gleser, G. C. *Psychological tests and personnel decisions.* Urbana, Ill.: University of Illinois Press, 1957.

Gelatt, H. B. Decision-making: A conceptual frame of reference for counseling. *Journal of Counseling Psychology,* 1962, 9, 240–245.

Ginzberg, E. Toward a theory of occupational choice: A restatement. *Vocational Guidance Quarterly,* 1972, 20, 169–176.

Ginzberg, E., Ginsburg, S. W., Axelrad, S., and Herma, J. L. *Occupational choice: An approach to a general theory.* New York: Columbia University Press, 1951.

Herr, E. L. and Cramer, S. H. *Career guidance and counseling through the life span.* 2nd edition. Boston: Little, Brown and Company, 1984.

Hewer, V. H. What do theories of vocational choice mean to a counselor? *Journal of Counseling Psychology,* 1963, 10, 118–125.

Holland, J. L. *The psychology of vocational choice.* Waltham, Mass.: Blaisdell Publishing Company, 1966.

————. *Making vocational choices: A theory of careers.* Englewood Cliffs, N.J.: Prentice-Hall, Inc., 1973.

Jepsen, D. A., and Dilley, J. S. Vocational decision-making models: A review and comparative analysis. *Review of Educational Research,* 1974, 44, 331–344.

Jones, A. *Principles of guidance.* 6th edition, revised and updated by B. Stefflre and N. R. Stewart. New York: McGraw-Hill Book Company, 1970.

Katz, M. *Decisions and values: A rationale for secondary school guidance.* New York: College Entrance Examination Board, 1963.

————. A model of guidance for career decision-making. *Vocational Guidance Quarterly,* 1966, 15, 2–10.

———. Theoretical formulations of guidance. *Review of Educational Research,* 1969, 39, 127–140.

———. The name and nature of vocational guidance. In Borow, H. (ed.), *Career guidance for a new age.* Boston: Houghton Mifflin Company, 1973.

Krumboltz, J. D., with Mitchell, A. M., and Jones, G. B. A social learning theory of career selection. *The Counseling Psychologist,* 1976, 6, 1, 71–81.

Lipsett, L. Social factors in vocational development. *Personnel and Guidance Journal,* 1962, 40, 432–437.

Maslow, A. H. *Motivation and personality.* New York: Harper & Row, Publishers, 1954.

Miller, D. C. and Form, W. H. *Industrial sociology.* New York: Harper & Row, Publishers, 1951.

Murray, H. A. *Explorations in personality.* New York: Oxford Press, 1938.

O'Hara, R. P. and Tiedeman, D. V. Vocational self-concept in adolescence. *Journal of Counseling Psychology,* 1959, 6, 292–301.

Osipow, S. H. *Theories of career development.* 3rd edition. Englewood Cliffs, N.J.: Prentice-Hall, Inc., 1983.

Parsons, F. *Choosing a vocation.* Boston: Houghton Mifflin Company, 1909.

Pietrofessa, J. J. and Splete, H. *Career development: Theory and research.* New York: Grune and Stratton, 1975.

Roe, A. Early determinants of vocational choice. *Journal of Counseling Psychology,* 1957, 4, 212–217.

Roe, A. and Siegelman, M. *The origin of interests.* APGA Inquiry Studies No. 1. Washington, D.C.: American Personnel and Guidance Association, 1964.

Shertzer, B. E. and Stone, S. C. *Fundamentals of counseling.* 3rd edition. Boston: Houghton Mifflin Company, 1980.

Super, D. E. A theory of vocational development. *American Psychologist,* 1953, 8, 185–190.

———. The natural history of a study of lives and of vocations. *Perspectives on Education,* 1969, 2, 13–22.

———. A life-span, life-space approach to career development. *Journal of Vocational Behavior,* 1980, 16, 282–298.

Super, D. E. and Bachrach, P. B. *Scientific careers and vocational development theory.* New York: Teachers College, Columbia University, 1957.

Super, D. E., Crites, J. O., Hummel, R. C., Moser, H. P., Overstreet, P. L., and Warnath, C. F. *Vocational development: A framework for research.* New York: Teachers College, Columbia University, 1957.

Tiedeman, D. V. Decision and vocational development: A paradigm and its implications. *Personnel and Guidance Journal,* 1961, 40, 15–20.

Tiedeman, D. V. and O'Hara, R. P. *Career development: Choice and adjustment.* New York: College Entrance Examination Board, 1963.

Warnath, C. F. Vocational theories: Direction to nowhere. *Personnel and Guidance Journal,* 1975, 53, 422–428.

Warren, G. D., Winer, J. L. and Dailey, K. C. Extending Holland's theory to the later years. *Journal of Vocational Behavior,* 1981, 18, 104–114.

Weinrach, S. G. (ed.). *Career counseling.* New York: McGraw-Hill Book Company, 1979.

Whiteley, J. M. and Resnikoff, A. (eds.). *Perspectives on vocational development.* Washington, D.C.: American Personnel and Guidance Association, 1972.

4

The application of
theory to career
counseling

As a consequence of viewing the individual and the environment and the interaction between the two from different perspectives, the theoretical positions considered in the previous chapter suggest differing approaches to the process we call career counseling. In this chapter we will consider some of the effects, both facilitative and restrictive, that the various theoretical positions imply or impose on the process. Our concern will be to identify major influential factors without attempting to spell out or identify the many lesser nuances of each theoretical position. We will look primarily at how the counselor functions, what resources the counselor uses, and what outcomes are expected by the counselor within each major theoretical framework.

SITUATIONAL THEORIES

Few, if any, counselors view economic and sociological theories of career development as sufficiently comprehensive to warrant consideration as the foundation for their personal theory because, according to these views, the client and the counselor are placed in a position of essential helplessness. At the same time, there are few counselors who would totally disregard the factors included in these theoretical positions.

Economic theories place major emphasis upon the influence of the marketplace and the interaction of supply and demand factors. These are elements that operate on a massive scale, ponderously and incessantly, with a force that overwhelms the individual. In such circumstances the counselor's role would have to focus primarily upon helping the client read the signs that are most predictive of marketplace activity and then devise ways by which the client could best position himself or herself to capitalize upon that activity as it occurs. In many ways the counselor would function like an economic adviser or an investment counselor attempting to determine long-range market forecasts. While the career counselor's client is concerned with investing time and effort rather than capital and facilities, the approach would be much the same.

Since the major focus would fall on economic matters, our hypothetical counselor would be skillful in observing and predicting economic change and in applying those measurements and formulae used to estimate business and employment trends. Attention would be paid to bank deposits, interest rates, wholesale inventories, construction starts, business mergers, changes in imports and exports, and stock market indices. Counselors would read with regularity *Business Week, Monthly Labor Review, Fortune,* the *Wall Street Journal,* and other periodicals and news reports that focus on present and anticipated business conditions.

If counselors were to operate predominantly on an economic base, the major outcome expected would be for clients to be favorably positioned to maximize benefits as market conditions change: to be prepared to enter fields where the supply of workers falls short of demand; to be situated so that they have vacated fields before oversupply of workers forces incomes and other perquisites downward; or to be entrenched in their positions so firmly that they are relatively immune to the downward income cycle.

Sociological theories put major emphasis on social and cultural factors and tend to view the individual as the product of the interactions of those factors. Lipsett (1962), for example, stresses the influence of social class membership, home influences, school, community, pressure groups, and role perception as influential factors in career development. Caplow (1954) and Miller and Form (1951) have considered the influence of "being in the right place at the right time" or a "chance" factor in career development. More recently, Krumboltz (1976) has argued persuasively that instead of "chance" these should be labeled as "unanticipated events."

If counselors used the sociological approach *exclusively* they would be confronted with helping clients to accept with some degree of resignation whatever fate is about to hand them. The possibility that careful planning, effective development of aptitudes and abilities, motivation, and industrious application separately and collectively could have an impact on career development would be largely disregarded because "what will be will be." Counselor function might be viewed as primarily predictive since the items listed by Lipsett, for example, are identifiable and mostly quantifiable. The counselor would be likely to use interview procedures, tests, and survey instruments that identify the client's status with regard to the various social factors previously listed. Since the role of the counselor is clouded in a circumscribed situation such as the one we are dealing with, it is difficult to specify expected outcomes.

Most counselors would insist that sociological factors are an important aspect in career development and must be considered in dealing with a client who wishes to make career plans. Many theoretical positions, including those of the psychological need theorists, the developmentalists, and the behavioralists, include sociological factors as a part of the total picture. Our concern at this point is based on making these factors the only consideration. (Since the psychoanalytic theory advocated by Brill and others considers the counselor unnecessary, there is no way to consider the functions of the counselor in this framework.)

In summary, one can say that the situational theories contribute to understanding the relationship between individual and job in the career development process. Certainly economic events, sociological factors, personality characteristics, even chance, influence the choices that are made by individuals and the events that occur as the individual pursues that choice. Nevertheless, each of these positions leaves unconsidered too many factors that appear to bear on career development.

TRAIT AND FACTOR THEORY

In simplest terms, the trait and factor approach is based on the idea that the individual differences of people can be measured and then matched against the various differing requirements of occupations. As described in the previous chapter, the matching concept is often traced to the early writing of Parsons, and the measurement concepts date back to the Minnesota group of Paterson, Darley, Williamson, and others. During the heyday of trait and factor counseling and continuing from that period, occupational requirements have often been identified by measuring the characteristics possessed by workers in the specific occupation. The implicit assumption is that whatever characteristics are commonly held by the workers are required for successful performance of the work. One illustration of this approach is the *General Aptitude Test Battery* which provides "occupational" norms and "occupational aptitude patterns" based on the scores obtained by those workers ranking in the upper two-thirds of workers tested. This application of test data to predict possible success in the occupation has sometimes resulted in the trait and factor approach being labeled as an actuarial system.

Williamson (1939, 1950) suggested that individuals seeking counseling for vocational planning can be sorted into four categories. He labeled these as (1) no choice, (2) uncertain choice, (3) unwise choice, and (4) discrepancy between interests and aptitudes. He saw the vocational counseling process as one in which the client is diagnosed as belonging to one of these categories, and once diagnosis is made, a plan of action is developed to resolve the difficulty. He viewed the counselor as completing six steps in this career counseling process. These six steps include the following:

1. *Analysis*—gathering information about the client, primarily from interview procedures but supplemented by data from tests and other sources, including information about aptitudes, interests, motives, physical health, emotional balance, family background, knowledge, educational progress, and other factors.
2. *Synthesis*—organizing the data to gain an understanding of the counselee, searching for a pattern of consistency in the data, and seeking the unique or individual characteristics of the client.
3. *Diagnosis*—reviewing case data to arrive at the counselor's statement of the client's problem, using a clinical method involving both verifiable data and "clinical hunches" matched against available information in order to make a critical appraisal and to get behind the raw data to factors causing the problem.
4. *Prognosis*—predicting the future development of the problem according to the counselor's evaluation of the data. When predictions can be made validly about future behavior, Williamson suggests that this step is often combined with diagnosis. This step includes identifying alternative courses of action or alternative adjustments that can be made by the client.
5. *Counseling*—helping the client marshal and organize personal and other resources to assist in achieving the optimum adjustment either now or in the future. The counselor presents evidence for or against the student's educational or vocational choice or other matters of concern, indicates favorable and unfavorable data and the weight of each, and explains why he or she advises a specific course of action.
6. *Follow-up*—helping the client further, usually at a later time, with either new problems or recurrences of the same problem, or checking to determine the effectiveness of counseling.

In these six steps, as viewed by Williamson and other early trait and factor counselors, the counselor assumed a role similar to that of the physician in determining a patient's problem, prescribing treatment to correct the problem, and later checking to ascertain success of the treatment. This active leadership of the counselor produced the label of "directive" counseling by the "nondirectivists" who resisted that role.

The trait and factor counselor uses a wide array of resources and typically applies many of them with each client. In the analysis stage, the counselor acquires information about the client from interviews, school records, and other sources of subjective data. In addition, testing, often extensive, is used to collect objective data. The counselor's integrative skills are of primary importance in the stages of synthesis, diagnosis, and prognosis. The counselor organizes and evaluates information about the individual and uses "occupational" or career information to support or refute client plans or to help the client develop or accept a plan. In the counseling stage, the client is actively involved in discussing and planning a course of action. Williamson sees the counselor as involved in establishing rapport, cultivating self-understanding, advising or planning a program of action, and sometimes carrying out a plan or referring the client to another individual for additional assistance. If needed, Williamson could also see the counselor forcing conformity, changing the environment, selecting a needed environment, teaching needed skills, or attempting to change attitudes. To accomplish these results, the counselor might be persuasive, explanatory, or direct.

The outcome expected by the trait and factor counselor is the resolution of the client's present problem. Obviously the final step of follow-up suggests that further readjustment or refinement of the developed plan might later be necessary. It is also assumed, as Thompson (1954) points out, that solving this specific problem assists the individual in being better able to solve future problems because problem solution is expected to lead to effective self-management.

PERSONALITY-BASED THEORIES

In the previous chapter we considered two "theories" identified as personality-based theory: those of Anne Roe and of John Holland. Roe relates her theory quite explicitly to the hierarchy of needs proposed earlier by Maslow. On the other hand, Holland only infers a need factor by stating that career choice is basically an expression of personality. Because there is considerable difference between the two theories, as discussed in the earlier chapter, we will consider them separately here.

Osipow (1983) has pointed out that Roe's theoretical statement includes no recommendation relevant to counseling. We are therefore unable to identify specifically how Roe visualizes her theory being applied by a counselor. Many other theories incorporate the importance of psychological needs and also recognize the impact of early childhood experiences as described by Roe. Further, her two-dimensional system for classifying occupations is widely used by both counselors and teachers in helping individuals understand the world of work. As Osipow suggests, we can draw inferences from Roe's theory that would suggest the type of counselor behavior appropriate to the theory.

One would logically infer from Roe's emphasis upon Maslow's need structure that the counselor would give major attention to identifying and helping the client understand personal needs. The career counselor, further, would certainly try to assist the client in relating these needs to occupations by identifying those where the opportunity to satisfy existing needs would be greatest. Osipow (1983) also proposes that occasionally, where unusual factors have thwarted or distorted the development of an appropriate pattern of psychological needs, the client may need psychotherapy to help understand, clarify, and perhaps restructure a pattern of needs more appropriate to adult life. Such intensive therapy might well be beyond the career counselor's professional skill or interest and a referral to resolve this deficiency before resuming career counseling may be necessary. We will consider in the next chapter, in more detail, the importance of determining if such contravening factors warrant consideration and treatment before proceeding with career counseling.

One would expect the counselor using Roe's theory to use interview procedures and perhaps appropriate psychological testing to identify the client's needs pattern. Once the point is reached where both counselor and client have a relatively clear understanding of the "needs" and "presses" that bear upon the client, two options are faced. One of these options is to proceed to a consideration of occupations appropriate to that set of needs. Roe's occupational classification system provides a structure for implementing this action since it is already geared to such a construct. This system permits the client to identify typical occupations representative of the appropriate needs pattern at various levels related to responsibility and educational demands. These can then be studied or investigated through the use of suitable materials and techniques.

The second option facing counselor and client is a determination of whether the existing needs pattern offers the potential for a satisfying and fulfilling life for the client. If the answer is an affirmative one, counselor and client would proceed as we have discussed above. If the answer is negative, the counselor—or an appropriate referral—would have to undertake the process of helping the client restructure the needs pattern. Since most needs theorists view these aspects as long-lived and relatively permanent, undertaking change might require extensive as well as intensive therapy. One might hypothesize that such counseling would involve a process such as Bordin's psychodynamic approach or Rogers' client-centered approach. Hypothetically, upon successful completion of that process, the counselor and client would consider appropriate occupations in light of the modified or rebuilt needs.

Expected outcomes, in either case, would be anticipated to be the involvement of the client in work that is personally satisfying. Roe's classification system groups occupations in very broad clusters related to need patterns developing from early childhood. Those broad groupings have since been sustained by research of other theorists (Holland, 1973; Hanson, 1974). Further, her theory recognizes differences in ability, family influences, access to resources, and so on. The classification grid proposed by Roe is used by counselors with varied theoretical positions to assist clients in building a framework for understanding the world of work.

The essence of Holland's theory is his six personality types and the six environments in which they are found. Because of this fundamental emphasis on personality characteristics, his theory is usually classified, like Roe's theory, as being based on psychological need theory. As previously indicated, he gives little consideration to the biological or psychological antecedents that produce the personality characteristics of the client. Holland (1974) refers to himself as an adherent of a modified trait and factor view. Further, as stated in Chapter 3, Holland views one-to-one vocational or career counseling as a last resort to be used by those few individuals who remain confused, uncertain, or undecided after other types of career development assistance have been provided.

Responding to an article in which Crites (1976) describes a series of seven counseling interviews with "Karen," Holland (1976) describes succinctly how he would have dealt with this client. The following quotations summarize Holland's hypothetical handling of the case:

> I might have seen Karen for about 5 to 15 minutes. I would have started with "What do you have in mind?" When she talked about whether it should be social work or teaching, I would have mumbled to myself: "There is not much difference between an SIA or SAE. . . ." I then would have asked, or she might have asked to take the Self-Directed Search (SDS). . . . I would have loaned her a copy of the Occupational Outlook Handbook and told her to come back when she was ready.

> . . . If Karen came back to see me for a second interview (I lose some), I would have asked "How did the SDS go?" "What did you get out of the Occupational Outlook Handbook?" Or, she might have taken the initiative because the SDS supported social work more than teacher, or because she now saw more alternatives. Our discussion would have focused on the alternatives—questions she might have, where to get more information about training? What's it like to be a social worker? What led to the current alternatives, how she justified each alternative, and so on.

> In the second interview, I would have relied on the SDS to learn whether or not she was a well-differentiated person and therefore a good decision-maker. . . . I would have reinforced the need to continue exploring those vocational alternatives that were appealing via reading and work experiences, and I would have told her that it was not necessary for people to always know what they are going to do. . . .

> . . . My fictitious work with Karen might have increased the options she considered, clarified why some made more sense than others, given her more

understanding of herself in vocational terms, and a structure she might use to relate to the vocational world. . . .

In general, the exploratory view consists in focusing on the exploration of vocational alternatives with the subordination of the concerns of diagnosis, personal adjustment, examining one's values, or similar counseling concerns. (p. 14)

Elsewhere, Holland (1973) suggests that the counselor might use the Vocational Preference Inventory (VPI), the SDS, or the Holland scales for the Strong Vocational Interest Blank to assess client characteristics. Presumably the Holland scales on the Strong-Campbell Interest Inventory, published since Holland's 1973 statement, would also be viewed as acceptable. It would be difficult to use other interest inventories since they have not been keyed to Holland's typology. He further suggests that data acquired from interviews, tests, reports or other sources could also be incorporated into the typology structure. Similarly, to facilitate client use, career information could be coded and filed in a system based on the Holland codes. Finally, Holland suggests that further exposure of clients or students to career information via class projects, speakers, audiovisual materials, visits, and other methods can be checked against the Holland code structure to assure a balanced and comprehensive program.

Holland (1973) states that maladaptive vocational development probably arises from one of five causes, including:

1.   Insufficient experience to acquire well-defined interests, competencies, or perceptions of self.
2.   Insufficient experience to learn about the work environments.
3.   Ambiguous or conflicting experience about interests, competencies, or personal characteristics.
4.   Ambiguous or conflicting information about work environments.
5.   Lack of self-information or confidence needed to translate personal characteristics into occupational opportunities. (pp. 89–90)

Holland suggests that counselors who encounter clients unable to resolve their own vocational decisions may find it helpful to involve the client in reviewing and discussing these five maladaptive conditions with the purpose of identifying the cause of their own indecision. The counselor can also use any decision about the appropriateness of one of the five conditions to determine the type of treatment the client should receive. For example, Holland suggests that a person with a well-defined profile (Holland code) probably needs only access to information to make an adequate career choice while an individual with a confused profile may need extensive counseling or psychotherapy in order to develop a better self understanding.

The anticipated outcome with Holland's approach would be satisfactory vocational adjustment of the client, based on a clear understanding of self and self-profile to enable the individual to make career choices appropriate to that profile.

DEVELOPMENTAL THEORIES

The developmentalists view career choice as a process extending over a considerable period of time and thus the counselor may have differing inputs according to the stage in which the client is operating at the time he or she encounters the counselor. Since the developmental theorists hold many viewpoints in common, it will be less confusing for the reader if we consider them jointly rather than individually. Actually, the Ginzberg group gave no particular attention to the role or place of counselors in the career development process. Osipow (1983) states this clearly by saying:

> It seems that the theory is too vague to suggest techniques for counselors beyond a general notion that experiences should be arranged for young people that will facilitate their progress through whatever stage they happen to be in. If the theory has any accuracy and validity, it can be used to highlight developmental tasks and bring them to the attention of counselors, teachers, and parents. (p. 203)

Super, on the other hand, has written much about developmental career counseling and his approach will dominate our consideration of this theoretical position. The reader will find an excellent description of Super's approach to career counseling in the review prepared by Crites (1974, 1981).

Developmental career counseling as described by Super combines the developmental process (life stages) with a modified trait and factor approach that Super (1954) refers to as an *actuarial method*. Incorporating the life-stages concept recognizes that career counseling needs and processes will vary depending on the developmental status of the client. Thus, a youngster in the early high school years is likely to have quite different career concerns than the individual at age twenty-five. Further, both of these may be ahead of, approximately even with, or behind their respective peer groups in planning and implementing career development plans. This aspect of comparison with appropriate peer groups has led to the development of the concept of career maturity (Super, 1955, 1974; Crites, 1973).

Career counseling typically starts with the determination of the client's career maturity, since this status indicates not only where the client is developmentally and what his or her counseling needs are, but also suggests what counselor activities are appropriate. The immature client is helped to develop skills in understanding and exploring self and occupations before consideration is given to choosing and trying-out (Super and Overstreet, 1960). On the other hand, the mature client is more likely to be ready to deal with information about self and the environment in a choice-making process. The young and immature individual is assisted in many ways, often in a noncounseling relationship, to acquire the information and skills appropriate at that stage of career development. When the individual approaches the decision-making stage and has developed appropriate levels of career maturity, career counseling proceeds.

Super (1957*a*) sees the counselor using a spiraling or cyclical rotation of directive and nondirective interviewing. In the first interview, the counselor is essentially nondirective, permitting and encouraging the client to describe and explore the problem, view of self, and the realities of his or her psychological world. In many ways this encounter parallels the traditional intake interview, and the process continues until counselor and client feel that the problem has been adequately identified and defined by the client.

At this point, the counselor shifts to a directive approach in which topics for subsequent counseling sessions are identified and priorities are established. The identification of needed additional data related either to the individual or to his or her world and ways in which those data may be acquired are also considered. When data can best be obtained by testing, the client is included in the consideration of this approach and in the decision to use such instruments. Tests are used selectively to obtain specific information when it is needed, rather than as a broad, general test battery applied in "shotgun" fashion. A schedule and other operational details may be considered, along with the goals and limitations of the counseling process.

After completing this phase the counselor resumes a nondirective role to permit the client opportunity to react to the proposed plan, its implications and demands. This change of pace allows the client to clarify feelings and attitudes, accept responsibility for the mutually developed plan for counseling, and increase self-acceptance and insight.

Subsequent sessions in which the counselor assists the client to acquire and understand test results, career information, or other factual material, are conducted in a directive manner. Since counselor and client are dealing with data often involving format and terminology unfamiliar to the client, the counselor may assume a quasi-teaching role. The objective of these sessions is to assist the client to obtain additional needed information and assimilate that knowledge in a way that the client can use in the decision-making process.

The broadening of perspective through acquisition of additional data requires the reexamination of attitudes and feelings. Consequently, the counselor reverts to a nondirective role. The client is assisted in understanding and clarifying his or her attitudes and feelings as viewed against this broader view of self and the world in which he or she exists. This nondirective approach is continued by the counselor as the client works through feelings and attitudes and moves forward in the decision-making process.

Shifting between directive and nondirective procedures need not be confusing for either client or counselor. Essentially, Super is separating approaches to fit the content of the counseling sessions. When the major content is factual, such as developing procedural plans, considering test data, or discussing career information, the counselor assumes a directive approach. When the content is primarily attitudinal, such as exploring self-concept and previous experiences, identifying the client's willingness to proceed with counseling as proposed by the counselor, discussing the client's feeling toward test data, tryout experiences, and other reality testing, the counselor assumes a nondirective stance. In the first role the counselor uses interpretation, explanation, and summarization. In the second role the counselor responds with reflection, restatement, and clarification.

The developmental counselor draws on a wide range of resources. These include interview procedures, tests, and a variety of career materials and experiences. As indicated earlier, the choice and application of appropriate resources relate to the developmental stage of the client and the goals and outcomes that are compatible with the client's career maturity.

Although somewhat oversimplified, the primary purpose of applying these procedures is to assist the client in an appraisal process that includes evaluation of the presenting problem, the client, and predictive estimates of future career adjustment. Unlike the trait and factor adherents, Super sees both client and counselor cooperatively involved in the appraisal process. Thus the client is given access to new information about self, occupations, and the broader environment but is still required to deal with feelings and incorporate them into overall career development.

The developmental counselor has access to the entire array of test instruments as a means of helping the client to learn more about self. Super's early book (1949), later revised with Crites (1962), is still considered one of the definitive statements on using tests. Super (1950) suggests that tests be used to obtain information that appears to be crucial for the client in understanding either self or the larger environment. Instead of selecting and administering a lengthy general battery of tests to all clients, Super proposes that tests be selected to provide specific data and used when client and counselor agree those data are needed. The counselor must have a thorough mastery of available tests to assure consideration of the instrument that best fits the client's needs as perceived by counselor and client together.

The developmental counselor also helps the client use information about jobs and the world of work or larger environment in which those jobs exist. These materials, too, range across the gamut of available information forms, from printed materials to direct contact materials such as shadowing (spending a day with a worker, watching what is done) and tryout experiences. The primary reason for using career information is to assist the client in personal appraisal and in prognostic appraisal—helping to identify present or potential strengths and weaknesses and estimating the degree to which those characteristics can predict later success or satisfaction.

Crites (1974, 1981) emphasizes that the most useful type of career information for the developmental counselor is that which provides a "career pattern" approach, and further, that this type of information is least available. Some materials of this type are becoming available from the results of Project TALENT (for example, Flanagan et al., 1973) and data now being released from Super's own twenty-year Career Pattern Study (for example, Jordaan and Heyde, 1979). These data do show more clearly than any other available information the developmental paths through which the subjects passed from early high school years until their mid-thirties. Caution in the use of such data is still crucial since the influence and forces encountered by adolescents two decades ago are not identical to those encountered today. Neither the internal forces of values, motivations, and goals nor the external forces of opportunity, social mores, and economic and political conditions are factors that remain static over long periods of time.

The developmental counselor expects that career counseling will result in the client acquiring a clearer understanding of self that results in appropriate decisions in the present, compatible with client self-concept. Further, the counselor expects the client to be able to adjust or modify present decisions to fit changing circumstances encountered in the future.

BEHAVIORAL AND DECISION-MAKING THEORIES

Krumboltz proposed his social learning theory of career selection in 1975, and it was first published in 1976 in *Counseling Psychologist*. This statement was reprinted in Whiteley and Resnikoff (eds.) (1978). Essentially the same statement appeared in Mitchell, Jones, and Krumboltz (eds.) (1979). Two brief responses by Holland (1976) and Roe (1976) have appeared. A reply by Krumboltz (1976) does provide a sketchy view of some aspects of the theory's application to counseling.

This theoretical statement appears to be a logical extension and, to some extent, a summarization of earlier writing by Krumboltz and colleagues (1966; Krumboltz and Thoresen, 1969; Krumboltz and Baker, 1973). Thus it seems reasonable to assume that those earlier statements of a behavioralist approach fit reasonably well into the more recent statement. The reader will find an excellent summary of Krumboltz' earlier statements contrasted with a more theoretical behavioral approach in the previously cited review by Crites (1974).

Behavioral theory is built largely on the psychology of learning; in fact, Krumboltz' label of "social learning" merely emphasizes this. One can then expect that the counselor may often be involved in a teaching relationship with the client. That teaching may be either direct—for example, transmission of knowledge—or indirect—for example, unknowingly serving as a role model, in using or developing learning situations to build understanding and attitudes and thereby produce behavior.

Krumboltz and Thoresen (1969) state that the counselor must first be concerned with what they call problem identification. They identify seven types of problem that clients may present in counseling. Of these, three are directly related to career counseling and the remaining four are more involved in personal and social areas, touching career problems only tangentially. The three career counseling problems include: (1) the absence of a goal, or indecision, (2) expressed feeling of concern about high aspirations, or unrealism, and (3) a conflict between equally appropriate alternatives, or multipotentiality. The goals of counseling are established pragmatically in terms of the identified presenting problem, usually expressed as the elimination of the problem.

Krumboltz and Baker (1973) identify a series of eight steps in the career counseling process. In many ways the list is comparable to the previously described phases of trait and factor or developmental counseling. These eight steps include the following:

1. Defining the problem and the client's goals.
2. Agreeing mutually to achieve counseling goals.
3. Generating alternative problem solutions.
4. Collecting information about the alternatives.
5. Examining the consequences of the alternatives.
6. Revaluing goals, alternatives, and consequences.
7. Making the decision or tentatively selecting an alternative contingent upon new developments and new opportunities.
8. Generalizing the decision-making process to new problems.

Krumboltz (1976) suggests that the impact of the social learning theory on the way counselors operate will include the teaching of decision making as a skill, revising the criteria of success in vocational counseling, and a more systematic development of occupational preferences and skills. As we saw in the previous chapter, this emphasis on decision making is supported by other behavioralists such as Gelatt, Katz, and Hilton. Krumboltz contends that teaching decision-making skills will assist the client later when changing conditions inevitably require modification of previously made decisions. The client, having learned a generalizable approach to such situations, should now be able to make satisfactory decisions independently. Secondly, he suggests that the crucial criterion for measuring successful vocational counseling should not be the degree of certainty the client has about the present decision, but instead, the extent to which appropriate decision-making procedures were used in making the decision. Finally, he advocates that counselors must spend more time helping clients explore career possibilities so that they acquire accurate occupational concepts, including considering positive and negative aspects of the alternatives.

One can see from the eight steps in counseling proposed by Krumboltz and Baker that the interview plays a major part in behavioral counseling. Except for portions of the third and fifth steps, which focus on occupational exploration of various types, almost the entire process consists of counselor-client interaction. Interviews are likely to serve a variety of functions, including information collecting, attitude and feeling exploration, and reinforcement, and may range from teaching relationships to nondirective counseling sessions. Krumboltz and Thoresen (1969) include many specific examples of the counselor's application of interview procedures.

Since tests are rarely mentioned by Krumboltz, Thoresen, Gelatt, or others, one must conclude that little use is made of these instruments in behavioral career counseling. Crites (1974, 1981) suggests that this disregard for tests may be related to the behavioralists' focus on the interaction between the individual and the environment, whereas tests usually provide data that indicate interpersonal differences.

On the other hand, career information materials are extensively used by behavioral counselors. Emphasis is usually focused on reality-oriented types of material such as shadowing, simulated work exercises, on-the-job tryout, and work experience programs. For example, the Job Kits developed by Krumboltz and his colleagues are widely recognized as excellent examples of the use of simulation in career information. Krumboltz (1976) anticipates increased emphasis on assisting adolescents to learn more about jobs, develop both breadth and depth in that knowledge, and acquire more job related skills, if his social learning theory is adopted widely.

The counseling outcome expected by behavioral counselors is usually directly related to the client's presenting problem. Pragmatically stated, the outcome sought is the elimination of that problem. From a more theoretical position, Krumboltz (1966) has identified three goals or expected outcomes. These include (1) changing maladaptive behavior, (2) learning the decision-making process, and (3) preventing problems.

ECLECTIC APPROACHES

By now it should be clear to the reader that each of the previously described viewpoints has certain advantages for the counselor who is an adherent of that particular approach. Similarly, each has limitations and disadvantages that impede or restrict the effectiveness of the counselor who holds counseling activities within the boundaries established by that theoretical approach. Other authors have also attempted to combine aspects of several approaches into a broader, more flexible system. A notable example of such an effort is the comprehensive approach suggested by Crites (1976, 1981).

Career development theory, in spite of the efforts of many writers, remains both incomplete and fragmented. This situation is at least partly due to the need for more time in which research can be completed to provide a basis for revision and clarification of existing viewpoints. In the meantime, as Osipow (1973) points out, counselors each day encounter clients and must help them with assorted needs and problems. It is proposed therefore that these variable needs of clients can be met most effectively by drawing selectively from existing theoretical approaches and using those techniques and resources that appear to offer the greatest likelihood of rendering substantial assistance to each client within a logical and appropriate framework.

This pragmatic approach will sometimes result in choosing or suggesting procedures that appear inconsistent with one or more of the theoretical positions previously considered. It should nevertheless be consistent with the basic criterion of what will best help the client at this point. It is also likely that the action is consistent with other theories we have considered. In other words, theoretical consistency may be less important than effective client growth.

Our approach will involve role changes for the counselor. On occasion the counselor may be the directive expert suggested by the trait and factor theorists. At other times, he or she may be a reflective counselor or a teacher in the developmental model. In addition to these roles and many others, the counselor will most often assume a collaborative role as described by Crites (1976, 1981). At one time, it was felt that the counselor must maintain a consistent role to prevent confusion on the part of the client. Such a view may have merit for counseling seriously disturbed clients, but it does not appear valid in dealing with most clients who seek career counseling.

Similarly, a wide range of resources is available to the counselor and these can be used selectively to assist the client. The interview skill of the counselor constitutes the most important resource since this provides the basis for the counselor-client relationship that is foundational for all that takes place in career counseling. Client problems and concerns may arise from self-oriented or internal aspects of the client or they may arise from external or environmentally oriented factors. Sometimes these problems require information or evaluation best obtained by tests or other data-gathering, data-assessing techniques. In some situations, there may be a need for skill development or enhancement, and a different set of techniques may be more useful. In still other circumstances, the need may focus on evaluating and understanding external data that may be important in decision making, such as what a job really is like, how one prepares for it, the rewards and satisfactions that accompany it. Frequently, clients who request career counseling may reveal self-oriented or externally oriented problems of sufficient magnitude to impede or prevent effective career counseling. The counselor then must give priority to these impediments before proceeding to the client's stated reasons for contacting the counselor.

Like counselors with narrower theoretical frames of reference, eclectic counselors seek effective resolution of the client's problem as the expected outcome of counseling. With some clients this may be a relatively simple process of identifying and removing whatever prevented an appropriate decision. In other cases, the process may be straightforward but time-consuming. With other clients, intervening aspects must be resolved before proceeding to the presenting problem. Nevertheless, the counselor's *raison d'etre* is assisting the client with the problem he or she brings to the counselor.

In the following chapters we will consider how the eclectic counselor meets this responsibility.

REFERENCES

Caplow, T. *The sociology of work*. Minneapolis: University of Minnesota Press, 1954.

Crites, J. O. *Theory and research handbook for the Career Maturity Inventory*. Monterey, Cal.: CTB/McGraw-Hill Book Company, 1973.

————. Career counseling: A review of major approaches. *Counseling Psychologist*, 1974, 4, 3, 12–17.

————. Career counseling: A comprehensive approach. *The Counseling Psychologist*, 1976, 6, 3, 2–12.

————. *Career counseling: Models, methods, and materials*. New York: McGraw-Hill Book Company, 1981.

Flanagan, J. C., Tiedeman, D. V., Willis, M. B., and McLaughlin, D. H. *The career data book: Results from Project TALENT's five-year follow-up study*. Palo Alto, Cal.: American Institutes for Research, 1973.

Hanson, G. *ACT research report 67: Assessing the career interests of college youth*. Iowa City, Iowa: American College Testing Program, 1974.

Holland, J. L. *Making vocational choices: A theory of careers*. Englewood Cliffs, N.J.: Prentice-Hall, Inc., 1973.

————. Career counseling: Then, now, and what's next. *The Counseling Psychologist*, 1974, 4, 3, 24–26.

————. A new synthesis for an old method and a new analysis of some old phenomena. *The Counseling Psychologist*, 1976, 6, 3, 12–15.

Jordaan, J. P. and Heyde, M. B. *Vocational maturity during the high school years*. New York: Teachers College Press, 1979.

Krumboltz, J. D. (ed.). *Revolution in counseling: Implications of behavioral science*. Boston: Houghton Mifflin Company, 1966.

————. This Chevrolet can't float or fly. *The Counseling Psychologist*, 1976, 6, 3, 17–19.

Krumboltz, J. D. and Baker, R. D. Behavioral counseling for vocational decision. In H. Borow (ed.), *Career guidance for a new age*. Boston: Houghton Mifflin Company, 1973.

Krumboltz, J. D., with Mitchell, A. M., and Jones, G. B. A social learning theory of career selection. *The Counseling Psychologist*, 1976, 6, 1, 71–81.

Krumboltz, J. D., Mitchell, A. M., and Jones, G. B. A social learning theory of career selection. In J. M. Whiteley and P. Resnikoff (eds.), *Career counseling*. Monterey, Cal.: Brooks/Cole Publishing Company, 1978.

Krumboltz, J. D. and Thoresen, C. E. (eds.). *Behavioral counseling: Cases and techniques*. New York: Holt, Rinehart and Winston, 1969.

Lipsett, L. Social factors in vocational development. *Personnel and Guidance Journal*, 1962, 40, 432–437.

Miller, D. C. and Form, W. H. *Industrial sociology*. New York: Harper & Row, Publishers, 1951.

Mitchell, A. M., Jones, G. B., and Krumboltz, J. D. (eds.). *Social learning theory and career decision making.* Cranston, R.I.: The Carroll Press, 1979.

Osipow, S. H. *Theories of career development.* 3rd edition. Englewood Cliffs, N.J.: Prentice-Hall, Inc., 1983.

Roe, A. Reactions to Krumboltz and Crites. *The Counseling Psychologist,* 1976, 6, 3, 16–17.

Super, D. E. *Appraising vocational fitness.* New York: Harper & Row, Publishers, 1949.

———. Testing and using test results in counseling. *Occupations,* 1950, 29, 95–97.

———. Career patterns as a basis for vocational counseling. *Journal of Counseling Psychology,* 1954, 1, 1, 12–20.

———. The dimensions and measurement of vocational maturity. *Teachers College Record,* 1955, 57, 151–163.

———. The preliminary appraisal in vocational counseling. *Personnel and Guidance Journal,* 1957a, 36, 154–161.

———. *The psychology of careers.* New York: Harper & Row, Publishers, 1957b.

———. *Measuring vocational maturity for counseling and evaluation.* Washington, D.C.: National Vocational Guidance Association, 1974.

Super, D. E. and Crites, J. O. *Appraising vocational fitness.* Rev. ed. New York: Harper & Row, Publishers, 1962.

Super, D. E. and Overstreet, P. L. *The vocational maturity of ninth grade boys.* New York: Teachers College Bureau of Publications, 1960.

Thompson, A. S. A rationale for vocational guidance. *Personnel and Guidance Journal,* 1954, 32, 533–535.

Williamson, E. G. The clinical method of guidance. *Review of Educational Research,* 1939, 9, 214–217.

———. *Counseling adolescents.* New York: McGraw-Hill Book Company, 1950.

5

Getting started—the initial interview(s)

Idealistically, one could expect that the development of effective career education programs in American schools might eliminate the need for career counseling entirely. After all, one might reason, if we provide continual opportunity to learn about oneself, to understand society's work-oriented values, and to have extensive contact with the world of work, it should be a simple matter for every individual to make a satisfying and fulfilling career choice. Realistically, one might just as reasonably conclude that providing an effective program of hygiene and health education through schools and the communication media will eliminate the need for medical care. Both programs, career education and health education, would be of great benefit to many individuals, but each is insufficient to cope with the myriad problems, concerns, and needs encountered by some members of society. Just as there are varying tolerance levels for physical pain, allergic reactions to different substances, irregular developmental processes, deficiencies, diseases, and other physical anomalies, so too are there many factors that prevent, impede, or disrupt career development.

Many, perhaps even most, individuals will deal effectively with career problems and decisions, just as many people cope successfully with matters of health. There are times in the lives of most individuals, however, when they wish to consult a physician. The reasons as viewed by the individual at the time are of sufficient consequence to justify the action. From the professional viewpoint of the physician, some of those reasons or symptoms may soon be established as insignificant and meaningless and others may require immediate, even massive, treatment to restore the well-being of the individual. Further, many individuals misread, ignore, or suppress physical danger signals until the physician can no longer help. Therefore, it is common practice for many physicians to tell their patients that if the patient has a problem, or thinks he or she has a problem, to let the physician help in determining its severity.

This behavior of the physician perhaps provides a role model for the counselor. Although everyone is a potential client for career counseling, most people, most of the time, do very well on their own. Sometimes, however, for varying reasons and with differing levels of validity, some individuals will wish to consult the counselor. At this point, the counselor knows neither the nature of the problem nor its severity, but knows only that this person comes because of a desire to see and talk to a counselor. On this basis, preconditions and assumptions are unnecessary. The client may be unnecessarily distressed about a very minor matter or, on the other hand, in desperate need for extensive and intensive therapy with a highly skilled specialist. It seems reasonable for the counselor to be involved at this point in exploring the nature and gravity of those concerns so that appropriate subsequent action or referral is chosen. Thus the counselor deals with the client, recognizing that the client's self-diagnosis may be precisely accurate, totally erroneous, or somewhere between the two extremes.

Career counseling, like counseling in general, requires the counselor to identify properly and respond appropriately to feelings, thoughts, attitudes, and behaviors expressed by the client and to assist the client in developing desired and appropriate behaviors that reflect the increased understanding and insight resulting from counseling. Further, it requires the counselor to be competent in assisting the client in acquiring, processing, and applying information and skills required in effective decision making and subsequent implementation of plans. While many clients may focus on personal or social aspects of life, the majority of clients served by most counseling centers indicate primary concern about matters that are career-oriented, and a large portion of the other cases may well involve career elements.

In this chapter we will consider the first contact between client and counselor. Occasionally, but not often, the activities usually completed in the first interview may extend over two or three sessions rather than the customary first interview. Similarly, and also rarely, the activities completed by client and counselor may include more than those we propose as first interview business. Discrepancies from the usual pattern are of less significance than a pace that is comfortable for both client and counselor and compatible with the needs of the client. We will consider the typical first interview to extend from the initial face-to-face contact through the development of tentative plans or goals for further counseling and/or supporting action and the arrangement of specific next steps for the client.

GOALS OF THE FIRST INTERVIEW

The specific content, format, and sequence of the first interview may vary considerably from client to client. Nevertheless, the counselor usually has certain fairly clear-cut objectives for the period or periods we are calling the first interview. Several authors concur on the basic purposes of this session.

Cottle and Downie (1960) open their discussion of the initial interview with the following paragraph:

> The initial interview has at least four primary purposes. One of these is to establish a good working relationship between the counselor and the client which will last throughout counseling. Another is to validate and expand the data about the client collected prior to the interview. Still a third is to observe the client directly and to collect information which will show client feelings about values, interests, attitudes, and goals. In addition this first interview is used to establish the structure within which counseling will take place. (p. 59)

Tyler (1969) includes similar purposes in her statement, as follows:

> We have been thinking about three objectives the counselor has in mind for the initial interview: (a) getting a sound counseling relationship started, (b) opening up the psychological realms of feeling and attitude within the person, and (c) clarifying the structure of the helping process. The order in which these have been stated corresponds to their importance. (p. 63)

Hansen, Stevic, and Warner (1977) have drawn directly from Tyler's position when they identify the three purposes of the initial interview as follows:

1. To lay the foundation for the counseling relationship.
2. To begin opening all the psychological realities in the client's situation.
3. To structure the situation for the client. (p. 311)

Stewart et al. (1978), describing a "systems" approach to counseling, summarize their view of initiating the counseling process, in part, with the following:

> Successful counseling practice is based upon the concurrent development of two types of understanding. On the one hand, counselors attempt to create a relationship of trust and understanding with each client. Concurrently, they develop a comprehensive model or "picture" of client concerns.
>
> At some time during the initial interview, counselors describe the process commonly used in counseling as one vehicle for establishing a sound relationship with the client. Elements of the process identified are the purpose of counseling, the respective responsibilities of both the client and counselor,

the focus or convergence of attention upon one concern at a time, and the limits within which counseling is conducted. This shared understanding of the counseling process provides a sound foundation for the development of mutual trust that is so essential in counseling.

Along with developing a comfortable working relationship with clients, counselors are concerned, during the early phases of counseling, with helping clients to "tell their story". (p. 113)

Finally, Hackney and Cormier (1979) describe their view of this activity in these words:

Based on what has been said about the client who is entering counseling, it follows that you would have some fairly clear responsibilities. These responsibilities are above and beyond creating a favorable climate for counseling, even beyond being a good and caring listener. It is your role to hear the unmet needs as clients describe their problems, and to help them hear those needs as well. It is then necessary to help clients translate these needs into wants in order that the working mode can be translated from a passive to an active one. You must listen for those solutions the client has tried that have become part of the problem, and help the client see this. Next it is your role to help clients formulate goals that will help meet the needs from these goals, plans of action may be constructed, implemented, and evaluated. (p. 107)

Essentially, there are three major purposes for the initial interview. These include: (a) establishing a relationship so that counseling can continue, (b) developing the client's psychological realities so that the goals of counseling can be conceptualized, and (c) agreeing on the structure and plan for further counseling and related activities. As Tyler has suggested, the first of these is absolutely essential, for without this foundation further activity will not occur. The sequence of the remaining steps may vary in specific situations; however, it is logical to assume that ordinarily some exploration of the client's concerns and needs would certainly precede any development of plans to deal with those needs.

One should keep in mind that we are not necessarily proposing that the first interview will break into three sequential sections that correspond to these three purposes. One can usually expect that client statements, questions, concerns, and needs may easily lead appropriately to some jumping about from topic to topic. More often than not, attention will be given to establishing a relationship throughout the first interview(s) and the other two purposes alternately provide the vehicle by which this is accomplished. Starting at a rather superficial level, one would expect more depth and detail to develop later as client trust in the relationship expands.

BEGINNING THE SESSION

Counselors need to reflect regularly on the difference between counselor and client as the first contact approaches. All of the cards have been stacked in the counselor's favor: the counselor knows that he or she is kind, gentle, concerned, and eager to help; is familiar with the office and setting in which one meets with clients; has a fairly good idea of what will happen in the interviews; and expects to be able to do whatever the situation calls for—after all, the rules and procedures were established by the counselor. The client, on the other hand, believes he or she has a problem or concern that can be resolved best by seeking help from someone else. Beyond that, the client has little information of substance about the counselor or the counseling relationship. Except for the trifling information that is obtained "through the grapevine," sketchy comments by other clients, modest efforts to advertise counseling services, or an occasional well-informed referrer, the client knows little about the counselor or the counseling relationship—a situation that inevitably must increase client anxiety and uncertainty.

Some school and college counselors are successful in minimizing client uncertainty by establishing personal contact before the need for counseling arises, usually in situations where the pool of potential clients is limited or perhaps individually assigned. Further, some clients, as a result of an earlier positive experience with a counselor, arrive without the overlay of anxiety described above. In addition, some counselors and some counseling centers have been so effective in informing potential clients of the nature of available services that the clients arrive almost "preconditioned" and ready to go to work on their problem. However, this is not true for most clients.

Thus, as we face the question of how to begin our first session, the only sensible global answer is the one on which the military has long relied: "It depends on the situation and the terrain." Our assumption will be that both client and counselor are starting essentially from scratch. Prior personal contact, familiarity with setting and services, or similar pluses may shorten the first interview somewhat but are not likely to change the basic structure and purposes.

Establishing rapport

The common social courtesies that accompany any first encounter with another individual apply to the first counseling interview. The immediate preliminary matters, mundane but essential, include a warm greeting and self-introduction, indication of where the client may put any books, wraps, or similar paraphernalia, and an indication of where the client might sit.

Providing the client with comfortable privacy; demonstrating interest, concern, and regard for the client, as well as knowledgeable competency; and establishing an atmosphere of ease and a sense of rapport are essential ingredients of the opening minutes of the initial interview. To some extent, the personality of the counselor will determine precisely how he or she accomplishes each of these. This first contact between counselor and client is of extreme importance. During this brief period the client decides whether this counselor can be trusted, if he or she is likely to be of assistance and if the counselor can build a relationship worthy of the client's time.

Beginning counselors often ask about what should be done once introductions are completed. The counselor's immediate concern is to help the client feel accepted and comfortable, so actions must be taken to promote that feeling in the client. This will sometimes suggest that a few moments of "small talk" may be appropriate. One might hypothesize that counselor-oriented topics are least desirable, neutral topics are only slightly more satisfactory, client-oriented topics are much more useful, and, if they can be identified readily, topics of mutual interest are most advantageous. Since the counselor has only a very few moments to read the clues, it will often be necessary to settle for a client-oriented topic, for which suggestions are always more abundant. A move of this type is most appropriate if the client displays signs of hesitancy or nervousness and seems to need a little time to settle in and feel comfortable.

Once the client is seated, some counselors pause briefly, thus allowing the client to open the interview if he or she is ready to talk. While this allows the client maximum freedom to begin discussing any desired topic, it also can produce some discomfort if the client is uncertain or hesitant. A counselor who uses this technique should be ready to pick up, perhaps using some opening lead like one of those listed below, if the client fails to respond to the silent invitation.

If the client appears to be relatively at ease or is obviously problem-oriented, preliminary chit-chat is not only unnecessary but probably impedes the development of the client's feeling of acceptance. The counselor's gambit in this circumstance is to provide an easy, nonthreatening opening that allows the client to start wherever he or she wishes. Typical counselor statements might be:

> "Would you like to tell me why you asked for a counseling appointment?"
>
> *never* "How can I help you?"
>
> * "What brings you to the counseling center?"
>
> "Tell me what you'd like to discuss."
>
> * "What would you like to talk about this period/today/now?"
>
> "Where would you like to start?"

Counselors must learn to recognize and read the signs that are present during those first moments in order to select an approach that helps the client feel at ease as soon as possible. This requires adjusting the opening to fit the counselor's estimate of client attitude, mental status, concern, and self-control almost instantly. Obviously, a set approach for all clients is likely to be inappropriate most of the time.

There are real advantages in an opening that permits the client maximum flexibility. First, the client is reassured about any doubts or concerns relative to seeking counseling because it can be seen at once that some control of the situation has been retained. The client can start at the level and in the area where he or she wishes and where he or she feels most comfortable. Further, the counselor makes no assumption prematurely, thus reducing the possibility of a false start.

The client who is momentarily more concerned about procedural matters will ask questions in that area first. Counselor answers should be sufficient to reduce the concern or anxiety and they should be focused only on this interview. If preliminary consideration of structure seems necessary, it would ordinarily include a statement by the counselor of his or her view of counseling, the confidentiality of the relationship, the limits imposed on counseling, and a request for client permission to tape or otherwise record the session if the counselor uses such devices. At this point in the session the concern with structure is only to meet the questions of the client or to establish necessary procedures such as taping. More discussion of structure will occur later when more is known about the client's concerns. The important point is that the counselor should communicate, by both language and behavior, that he or she is primarily concerned with substance—the client and the client's problem—and less concerned about form—the structure of the interview. Too much attention to structure early in the first interview may suggest to the client that the reverse is true. Often the receptionist (or whoever schedules the appointment) can easily indicate the amount of time assigned to the interview so that this question is already answered.

Client openings

When the client opens with some statement that is problem-oriented, he or she should be encouraged to talk further. One must recognize and accept that most clients will be conservative and cautious in their opening remarks. After all, there has not yet been sufficient time to build very much confidence and trust. It is much easier for the counselor, in familiar circumstances and knowledgeable about procedures, to accept the client than vice versa. So, at best, the client's statement is likely to be somewhat vague and superficial, but it is enough for a starting point. The counselor can respond appropriately to encourage the client to express feelings about the topic presented with a variety of techniques such as reflection of feelings, restatement, and request for clarification, using language suitable to the client. Focusing upon client feeling, accepting the client warmly and nonjudgmentally, and encouraging the client to select and direct early discussion helps to establish the rapport that permits the client to proceed. Gradually, as the relationship is established, the client can move freely to a broader consideration of the problem at a more significant level.

Tyler (1969) has stated that building this relationship can be assisted by finding out what the client wants, takes pride in, and is really concerned about. This suggests that establishing a counseling relationship and opening the psychological realities in the client's world are so closely related that they meld. In other words, what we as counselors are trying to accomplish is to help the client feel sufficiently at ease to invite us into his or her world so that we may see "reality" from the perspective of his or her viewpoint. This is most likely to occur in the easy, comfortable conditions described above.

Client opening statements may provide considerable insight into the client's concern, be largely innocuous, or even serve as an intentional or unintentional smokescreen. The counselor accepts whatever is said in a manner that helps the client expand and elaborate on that starting point. The counselor becomes able to evaluate the opening remarks only after the interview has continued for a time. We will discuss this in more detail in the next section of this chapter. Classifying client presenting statements is difficult because each client is unique and comes to us with a unique set of previous experiences. For our purposes here and in the next section, we will consider three broad categories of such opening remarks. A few examples of each type are included in the following list:

Type 1 presenting statement (uncertain, indefinite)

1. I saw a notice $\begin{pmatrix} \text{on the bulletin board} \\ \text{in the newspaper} \end{pmatrix}$ about counseling.
2. Someone said I could take a test here.
3. My $\begin{pmatrix} \text{principal} \\ \text{teacher} \\ \text{friend} \end{pmatrix}$ sent me for counseling
4. My spouse and I have split up.

Type 2 presenting statement (suggests other problem may be present)

1. My major doesn't seem right for me.
2. I like _____ but I'm not doing well in it.
3. I don't like the $\begin{pmatrix} \text{school} \\ \text{major} \\ \text{job} \end{pmatrix}$ I'm in.
4. There seems to be no job in my field.
5. I think I'm ready to make a change.
6. Every time they fire me they tell me to get some counseling.
7. I don't want to work, but it looks like I'll have to.
8. My job requires more $\begin{pmatrix} \text{time} \\ \text{effort} \\ \text{travel} \\ \text{etc.} \end{pmatrix}$ than I want to give.

Type 3 presenting statement (probably career counseling)

1. I want to be sure I'm going into the right field.

2. I can't decide on a $\begin{pmatrix}\text{college}\\\text{major}\\\text{job}\end{pmatrix}$.

3. The only jobs I know are _____ and _____, but I $\begin{pmatrix}\text{don't want either}\\\text{like both}\end{pmatrix}$ of them.

4. I want a job that involves $\begin{pmatrix}\text{interest}\\\text{activity}\\\text{value}\\\text{opportunity}\end{pmatrix}$, what is there?

5. I don't want to be in the same rut as my $\begin{pmatrix}\text{parents}\\\text{sibling}\\\text{friend}\end{pmatrix}$.

6. My children are now in school so I'd like to do something outside the home.

AS THE SESSION CONTINUES

The first purpose or objective—that of establishing a relationship so that counseling can continue—is ongoing and extends not only through the first interview but actually continues throughout all of the sessions. As the relationship develops, the counselor devotes less time and attention to this purpose, but it is safe to say that the point is never reached where this goal can be disregarded. Thus, even though little further discussion is devoted to this topic, keep in mind that, along with whatever other activities are concerned as the interview(s) continue, the counselor is constantly striving to maintain and enhance that relationship of trust and confidence.

With a viable relationship developing, the counselor can focus attention on the other primary purposes of the initial interview: to open up the client's psychological realities and agree on the structure and plan for further action. Often, some aspects of both of these already may have entered the picture. Any questions by the client or statements by the counselor regarding structure of the first interview touch to some extent on future plans. Similarly, as suggested above, the counselor really establishes a working relationship only as he or she begins to see and understand the client's world. Thus, to a lesser degree, the second and third purposes are also ongoing in nature. In other words, enough of a relationship should be established to encourage the client to give a glimpse of that personal world so that: enough structure can be provided to help the client open the door further; the relationship can deepen; and a plan can be proposed that aids the client in reaching his or her goals in counseling. If the relationship is progressing effectively, one can expect client statements to be spiraling in nature, providing both additional breadth and depth to earlier statements. A photographic analogy is bringing a fuzzy picture into sharper focus.

Answering ethical questions

At some point, the client will have provided enough information to permit the counselor to answer two questions: "Can I help this client?" and "How can I help this client?" While the counselor may choose to discuss both questions at some point where attention is being given to structure and future sessions, they must be considered and answered as early as possible. Unless the first question has a positive answer, the second question can only be answered with an appropriate referral. In some settings—for example, high schools—the counselor may have prior access to client information from cumulative school records or from statements of referral sources, such as teachers or parents, to answer the basic question before contact with the client. Ordinarily, that is not the case when the client is self-referred.

In considering whether the counselor can help the client, the major, but not exclusive, question is the professional competence of the counselor relative to his or her best estimate of the client's problem. If, for example, it appears that the client's need is for intensive psychotherapy at a level beyond the counselor's skill, the only ethically proper behavior for the counselor is to refer the client to a person or agency competent to provide that service.

Even when the counselor concludes that the client's need lies within the counselor's range of competency, there are several secondary factors that may lead the counselor to conclude that he or she cannot continue with the client. Examples of this type of question for the counselor are "Do I have the time in my schedule for this client?" "Do I have access to the facilities, materials, or equipment that will be needed to help this client?" "Does this client show sufficient interest and motivation to expect he or she will carry through the counseling process?"

A third factor must also be considered before the counselor can answer affirmatively that he or she can help the client. This factor relates to personal characteristics of the counselor and the interpersonal relationship with the client. Stewart et al. (1978) suggest that the counselor must ask "Do I have any personal inadequacies that would make it impossible to work effectively with this client?" Tyler (1969) expresses concern for the situation where the counselor feels a dislike for the client. She states that it is not unusual for a counselor to feel negatively toward a client at the beginning of the interview because of the client's mannerisms, language, attitudes, personal appearance, or similar reason; but if this feeling persists to the end of the first interview, the counselor should terminate involvement in the case.

Classifying clients and problems

Consideration of the two questions by the career counselor requires him or her to reach some tentative decisions about the client. Trait and factor theorists would refer to this decision as *diagnosis,* and developmentalists would likely use the term *appraisal.* Essentially, we are concerned with developing the best possible estimate of what is the problem, concern, need, care, worry, or difficulty on which the client is presently focusing. Obviously, the counselor's identification of this factor underlies the answer to our two questions, since attention to professional competence, case load, facilities, and the like, and any determination of future actions can only be considered in terms of the client's problem.

The counselor often feels some pressure to reach the point where these decisions can be made, and a sense of proper timing is essential. If the counselor decides too soon, the danger of error is greatly enhanced. On the other hand, delaying the decision results in inefficiency, loss of client time, perhaps even the development in the client of a feeling that the counselor is unsure or incompetent. Again, there is no easy answer to this dilemma. In some cases things fit together so neatly and so rapidly that the counselor feels completely confident to decide within a very few minutes. In other cases, a second or third session may still leave enough fuzziness, loose ends, incongruities, and uncertainties that the counselor feels the need for extreme caution. Recognizing that one may always be wrong and that later information may require revision of plans, the counselor should face this basic issue just as soon as sufficient data are on hand to make a reasonably good judgment. In most cases this will likely occur considerably before the closing moments of the first interview.

There are at least three factors that will help the counselor to identify a career counseling case. The first, and most obvious, of these clues is the client's presenting statement. If the client's opening remarks involve either direct or indirect reference to educational program, occupational choice or adjustment, or any aspect of career, one must consider the likelihood that the client is a career counseling case. Examples of typical opening remarks of this kind are listed as Type 2 and Type 3 Presenting Statements in the previous section of this chapter. Vague and indefinite opening statements, such as those listed as Type 1, simply require further information and clarification before any decision can be made. Remember that clients will sometimes invent some reasons for seeing the counselor, in order to determine if they can trust him or her sufficiently to discuss some other matter that they consider more personal, sensitive, or difficult to talk about. The counselor is not justified in discarding the client's presenting statement prematurely, because this subterfuge is sometimes used. If we are to be honest, forthright, and accepting with clients we must proceed with what they tell us. There is sufficient time to revise plans if or when the client tells us he or she is more concerned about something else.

Secondly, the counselor should listen carefully to what the client is saying in at least two senses. The words and statements used by the client are important. Equally important, or more so, are the feelings, needs, pressures, and uncertainties that those words reflect. If there is conflict between statements and feelings, primary attention should be given to the feelings expressed by the client. Helping the client to elaborate on these feelings may well lead to a better understanding of the words and language being used by the client and thus increase the congruence between words and feelings.

The third clue is probably the most important and certainly is the most comprehensive. It consists of the counselor's overall evaluation of what the client has said so far, plus an evaluation of nonverbal factors observed since the interview started. The counselor uses all available data relative to client characteristics including physical status, behavior, functioning level, cultural and educational background, learning style and ability, stress patterns, and self-descriptive statements. In those settings where prior data such as school records or preinterview information forms are routinely used, the material from these sources is also filtered into the evaluation.

If all three clues suggest a career counseling case, the counselor has reached the point where he or she can begin to consider the second question of how the client can be helped. On the other hand, as long as the counselor believes there is conflict or incongruity among these three factors, the client should be encouraged to continue discussing the concerns and feelings that led to the request for counseling.

Until the counselor is quite certain that the client is presenting a career counseling case, he or she proceeds as any counselor would. The counselor actions described up to this point closely parallel the procedures discussed in most books on counseling techniques. This is exactly as it should be, since no planning can occur until the counselor has a clear picture of the client's concerns.

Having reached the decision that he or she is working with a career counseling case, the counselor ordinarily next considers what type of career counseling case is being presented. This step is necessary before plans can be developed for counselor-client action in resolving the difficulty. One must assume that such action is related to the nature of the client's problem, and this inevitably requires some type of classification system. Even though recognizing that each client presents a unique problem arising from the interaction between a unique individual and a personal environment, rather clear-cut clusterings of these unique problems still can be seen. Thus, a classification, or diagnostic, system is used to suggest a basic procedure that is constantly adjusted to fit the uniqueness of the individual client.

Several classification systems were described in Chapter 4 as we considered how various theorists would deal with a career counseling client. It may be helpful to review briefly some of those typologies to provide a basis for the plan to be proposed here.

Williamson (1939, 1950), as a trait and factor advocate, proposed that career counseling clients can be divided into four groups. These were labeled as follows:

1.   No choice.
2.   Uncertain choice.

3. Unwise choice.
4. Discrepancy between interests and aptitudes.

Holland (1973) stated that maladaptive vocational development usually is produced by one of five causes. These five causes include the following:

1. Insufficient experience to acquire well-defined interests, competencies, or perceptions of self.
2. Insufficient experience to learn about the work environment.
3. Ambiguous or conflicting experience about interests, competencies, or personal characteristics.
4. Ambiguous or conflicting experience about work environments.
5. Lack of self-information or confidence needed to translate personal characteristics into occupational opportunities. (pp. 89–90)

Krumboltz and Thoresen (1969) have proposed seven types of problems that clients bring to counseling. Of these, only three are specifically related to career problems. These include the following:

1. The absence of a goal, or indecision.
2. Expressed feeling of concern about high aspirations, or unrealism.
3. A conflict between equally appropriate alternatives, or multi-potentiality.

Crites (1969, 1976) has proposed a system that is somewhat more complicated, but at the same time provides definite advantages of comprehensiveness. He suggests that three kinds of diagnosis are necessary if one is to understand the client. These three types of diagnosis include the following:

1. *Differential diagnosis* is the effort made by the counselor to identify *what* the client's problem is. Essentially, this system attempts to eliminate subjective judgment and to depend upon identifying discrepancies between career choice and client aptitudes and interests. The categories used include the following:
    A. Problems of adjustment—adjusted/maladjusted.
    B. Problems of indecision—multipotential/undecided/uninterested.
    C. Problems of unrealism—unrealistic/unfulfilled/coerced.
2. *Dynamic diagnosis* is the attempt by the counselor to determine *why* the client has this problem. Crites is concerned with learning how the client has dealt with other problems encountered previously. For example, is the client whom Williamson might label "uncertain choice" and Krumboltz as "multipotentiality"

unable to choose because he or she is facing simple indecision, or is this a more serious situation of pervasive indecisiveness? Exploring this area requires some examination of developmental and behavioral data.

3. _Decisional diagnosis_, according to Crites, is necessary because both differential and dynamic diagnosis are primarily concerned with the content of career choice but neither provides information about how the client makes decisions. Crites suggests that scores on the *Career Maturity Inventory* would provide information useful in evaluating the client's decisional skills.

Each of these taxonomies has certain advantages. One can also see a high degree of similarity among the various systems. Most are relatively simple, easily applied and understood. However, as Crites (1969) has emphasized, persistent problems exist with such classification methods, including unreliability, lack of mutual exclusiveness, and lack of exhaustiveness. He attempted to surmount these shortcomings by developing the system described above.

Each taxonomy, including that of Crites, assumes that career counseling can proceed immediately with all clients, without regard to personal or environmental factors that might impede or prevent successful counseling and subsequent follow-through. A more realistic approach recognizes that clients who come for career counseling bring with them all aspects of their lives. Some clients may be ready to enter the career counseling process, while others may need to resolve difficulties that would interfere with the process. Analogous situations can be found in many other aspects of life— for example, a student who wants to study a specific course may first need to complete prerequisite courses, or a person desiring to travel to a foreign country must first obtain a passport, perhaps a visa and required inoculations, sometimes special clothing, language skills, and other equipment.

The system that we will use suffers from some of the same disadvantages as other arrangements. On the other hand, it has the specific advantage of resolving the problem we have just been considering. It is relatively simple, provides a basis for client and counselor action, and avoids labels that can cause problems. Further, it is a system that is also appropriate to use with clients who are not career counseling cases.

Tyler (1969) has proposed a plan that seems to fit the needs of career counselors. She suggests that the counselor, on the basis of the evaluation of the client and the client's situation, can estimate the likelihood of the client having the "possibilities" to make and carry through decisions that are satisfying to the client and to society. If those possibilities appear strong enough to indicate a positive response, counselor and client can focus on *choice*. Typical clues for this classification include a fairly accurate client self-appraisal with no indication of actual or potential obstacles of serious magnitude, and client statements that suggest that career development has reached an appropriate level. On the other hand, if the client's statements suggest problems that limit or prevent choice, the counselor and client must focus on *change*. Clues that suggest a "change" classification include any indication that client assets and expressed goals do not mesh, or that physical, psychological, or environmental obstacles exist and are of sufficient magnitude to block or impede effective planning and execution of career goals. Tyler suggests a temporary third category of *doubtful* for those cases where the counselor lacks sufficient information to classify the client and his or her problem.

At the next level, depending on the initial counseling objective, both *choice* and *change* categories can be divided into two subcategories. *Choice* cases can be separated into those where client need is either for a comprehensive survey of possibilities or for a decision or commitment. Classification into one of these groups depends partly on the career maturity that Crites emphasizes and partly on other factors such as timing or proximity to completion of formal education. The individual who expresses great uncertainty about a career choice (Williamson's "no choice" or Krumboltz's "indecision") would fit into the first group. Someone who has progressed in career development to the stage of focusing on two or three possibilities but is having trouble selecting a specific goal (Williamson's "uncertain choice" or Krumboltz's "multipotentiality") would represent the second group. Similarly, *change* cases are those who need either the removal of an obstacle that is blocking progress in a promising direction, or the development of one or more new possibilities not now being considered.

Figure 5–1 is a modification of one proposed by Tyler and is intended to clarify the classification system described above.

Tyler's classification system takes into account the present status of the client, his or her apparent potentialities, and the possibility of existing problems or obstacles that might prevent or impede making appropriate career choices. It provides a "holding" category for those occasional clients whose confusion, uncertainty, reluctance to be self-revealing, or other characteristics prevent an early and confident decision about type of case. Finally, the proposed system also provides for counselor-client goal-directed action based on client need.

Developing structure

Having ascertained that the client's problem falls within the counselor's competence, and having also made a tentative classification of the client problem, including the initial objectives of counseling, the counselor is now in a position to discuss structure. Frequently, some reference or explanation of ground rules may have already occurred. For example, many counseling centers have a brief prepared statement, often included in the brochure describing services, assuring confidentiality, emphasizing the voluntary nature of the relationship, and identifying ethical responsibility. In other situa-

FIGURE 5–1   Tyler's classification system for counseling. (Adapted from Tyler, L. E. *The work of the counselor.* 3rd edition. New York: Appleton-Century-Crofts, 1969, p. 70)

| Counselor's judgment of the client and his situation leads to classification | Initial counseling objective to meet client's expressed or inferred need |

| **DOUBTFUL CASES** Client's present possibilities cannot be evaluated without greater understanding of him or her | ▶ | Search for structure to replace confusion |

| **CHANGE CASES** Client's present possibilities are inadequate or unpromising for future development | ▶ | Remove obstacles blocking possible avenues of choice |
| | ▶ | Create new possibilities |

| **CHOICE CASES** Client's present possibilities are adequate for future development | ▶ | Make a comprehensive survey of possibilities |
| | ▶ | Decision or commitment |

tions these items may have been included in the opening moments of the first session. If the counselor tapes sessions, some of these topics will have been included with the request for client permission.

Beyond these preliminary "rules of the game," some of which may have already been discussed with the client, lie other aspects of structure that warrant special consideration. These topics can be discussed most effectively if they are presented in relation to the client's problem. It is for this reason that it seems most appropriate to delay this topic until sufficient data about the client are available to permit casting the discussion in those terms. When these topics are considered at the very beginning of the first session, they must be discussed in very general terms. When consideration is delayed until later in the first interview, it becomes possible to approach matters from a viewpoint that emphasizes the client's needs.

Stewart et al. (1978) suggest that discussion of structure covers four topics including *purpose, responsibilities, focus* and *limits* of the counseling process. Shertzer and Stone (1974) state that structure consists of the way the counselor defines the nature, limits, roles, and goals within the counseling relationship. The extent to which each of these topics is discussed depends on client concern, degree of familiarity with the counseling process, and whether the topic has already been dealt with as the interview has progressed. Some authors suggest that counselors have an ethical responsibility to establish structure formally, others disagree. The recent increase in professional malpractice court cases suggests quite clearly that counselors must assure themselves that their clients clearly understand these aspects of structure.

The purpose or nature of counseling is much more clearly understood by the counselor than by the client. This situation sometimes causes the counselor to overlook the fact that this may well be the first encounter this client has ever had with a counselor. It is entirely possible that the client may have brought serious misconceptions that could lead to future complications and difficulties. The counselor should explain that counseling attempts to help the client to identify, understand, and cope with concerns or problems that the client has found vexing.

The counselor should also explore with the client the roles or responsibilities that each accepts in the counseling relationship. Clients often transfer to the counseling relationship their previous experience with physicians who may have prescribed medication or treatment for a particular problem, and expect the counselor to do the work while they passively accept whatever is prescribed. The counselor can use the time in establishing structure to emphasize clearly the active role of each participant in the counseling relationship and the necessity of the client assuming responsibility for completing assigned tasks and ultimately making and executing decisions.

Each counselor works under certain limits, some of which may be self-imposed and others that are created by the setting or institution in which the counselor functions. The kinds of limits to be discussed with the client would usually include any restriction on type of problem dealt with, the extent to which voluntary participation remains within client control, the confidentiality of the relationship, and the access to information by others. The counselor should also mention any constraints on length of interview time, frequency of appointments, available hours, and so forth.

Developing plans for counseling

Discussion of focus or goal leads logically to a detailed development of a plan of action for a specific client with a specific problem. For this reason, it is advantageous for consideration of planning to be taken up after other aspects of structure have been satisfied. If the topic of focus or counseling goals arises early in the first interview, the counselor can describe general procedures and point out that specific plans can only be made after more is known about the client and his or her problem. Before that specific plan is developed with the client, he or she has a right to know the various possibilities or approaches that the counselor considers appropriate. This general discussion of counseling focus can serve as a natural bridge to the development of a tentative course of action or plan that is specific for this client.

Having already made a tentative classification of the problem troubling the client, the counselor is ready to discuss those client needs that seem to be most pressing. If counselor and client agree on the nature of the problem, they next begin to establish counseling goals and appropriate action to alleviate that problem. Clients often may present several problems that stand independently or may be interwoven into a very complicated tangle. In either case, counseling is more likely to succeed by clearly agreeing upon one specific concern, among the many, to be dealt with first. This may even necessitate establishing some priority among the array of problems so that first things do remain first. The classification system provides for an initial course of action that can be used as the basis for describing the plan of action being proposed by the counselor. One advantage of such a system is that it relates the counselor's plan directly to client need.

Although the plan will quite likely be modified somewhat as counseling progresses, it should be spelled out as completely as possible at this time. The client has a right to know, as clearly as possible, how much time (in terms of both interviews and independent assignments) he or she is tentatively committing and what kinds of activities, other than interviews, are likely to be involved. Client concurrence on goals and proposed activities is an absolute necessity, since the reluctant client is soon a nonclient. Once counselor and client agree on the goals to be pursued and on a general plan, they should develop a tentative time schedule. This includes the counselor's best estimate of the number of interviews likely to be scheduled, their length, the usual interval between sessions, and the amount of time likely to be needed for other activities such as testing, participation in group sessions, or completion of assigned exercises such as collecting information from experts in various occupations, simulation, computer exercises, or tryout work experiences.

Understanding the client's world

As previously indicated, the counselor may reach a decision to discuss structure and counseling plans either relatively early or near the close of the first interview or, occasionally, only after a second or third session with the client. This negotiation should transpire as soon as the counselor feels that he or she has an adequate understanding of the client's major concern. When this occurs early in the first interview, the counselor may have developed only a very sketchy picture of the client's world. On the other hand, when negotiation is delayed, the counselor may have acquired as much information as needed at this point. Further, in some counseling settings the client is required to provide fairly comprehensive personal data by completing a questionnaire or form used by the counseling center prior to the first interview.

The counselor who feels that there are significant gaps in his or her insight into the client's psychological realities may wish to turn to further discussion of these areas. Only those topics that relate to the counseling plan deserve time for elaboration, and the relevance to counseling must be obvious to the client. Counselors disagree on how much information is needed to help the client. Some take the position that the counselor should limit himself or herself to that information proffered by the client. The result may be that information of great significance to the counseling process may lie hidden for a long time. Others contend that a fairly complete case history is necessary to assure counselor accountability and effective use of counseling time. The result may be extensive exploration into relatively unimportant topics and an increasing passivity on the part of the client. A middle ground seems most advantageous for both counselor and client. It appears reasonable to expect sufficient information to permit a good understanding of the client's present world or psychological realities and enough background to answer some of the "why" questions Crites (1969) suggests as dynamic diagnosis.

Topics that are frequently discussed with most career counseling clients include the following:

Self

1. *Client's view of self*—How does the client generally view his or her self and his or her world? What factors contribute to a generally positive or negative view? Which of these does he or she feel are within his or her control? If there are problems or negative factors, are they real or attitudinal? Does the client appear to take charge of his or her life, accepting both responsibility and accountability for present status and likely future status?

2. *Client characteristics*—What are the client's abilities, achievements, aptitudes, attitudes, interests, values? How well developed are each of these? How aware is the client of his or her strengths or weaknesses in each of these? Are these characteristics stable or variable? Is there evidence that the client is motivated?

3. *Client's view of the future*—Is the client positive and optimistic or apprehensive and uncertain? Has he or she reached the level of career maturity that is normal for his or her developmental peer group? What are his or her dreams and goals for the future? Are they fantasy or realistic, improbable or highly accurate?

4. *Health and physical status*—Does the client have either positive or negative physical characteristics that must be considered in developing career plans?

Family and background

5.   *Family*—Who are they? What kind of people are they? What has been their influence, past and present, on the client? How strong are the ties, loyalties, and desires of client to please family members? Which, if any, have been or are role models for the client? What are the attitudes of family toward the client? What are their desires, ambitions, hopes for the client? What are the client's attitudes toward the family?

6.   *Educational background*—What is the client's attitude toward past and present educational experiences? What has been the general quality of previous education? Has the client encountered educational experiences that have been either limiting and handicapping or challenging and growth-producing? Within the client's educational experience are there, or have there been, individuals or experiences that are either extremely positive or negative in influence? Do client abilities, attitudes, and experience support the possibility of further education if unfolding plans suggest this?

External factors

7.   *Work experience*—What kinds of work (both paid or unpaid) has the client experienced? What attitudes exist toward work as a result of these experiences? Is the client evaluating his or her attitudes and experiences realistically? Has the contact with work (either vicarious or participatory) contributed to or impeded client career maturity? What factors, if any, from previous work contact have relevance for future career development?

8.   *Significant individuals*—Who are the significant individuals in the client's past and present who influence career planning? What was/is their impact? Does the client assess their influence fairly accurately? Positively or negatively? Does their presence or influence sustain and enhance or denigrate and restrict the client's view of self?

9.   *Significant experiences*—What events have been influential in the client's life? How have they influenced his or her life? What previous decisions has the client confronted, successfully or unsuccessfully? How were successful decisions made? Why did the others fail? How has the client coped with difficulties, disappointments, problems?

Some or many of these questions may be irrelevant for a particular client. In other cases, even more detail about some of the general topics may be highly desirable. In still other cases, topics not included above may have considerable importance in both classifying the client and his or her prob-

FIGURE 5–2 Estimate of client attributes for career counseling.

1. View of self	negative	. . . . .	positive
2. Self-direction	passive	. . . . .	take-charge
3. Age range	low teens	. . . . .	over 50
4. General ability	very low	. . . . .	very high
5. Special abilities	few apparent	. . . . .	many
6. Self-awareness	very limited	. . . . .	insightful
7. Career development	retarded	. . . . .	well-developed
8. Motivation	lacking	. . . . .	very high
9. General health	serious problems	. . . . .	appears healthy
10. Interpersonal skills	lacking	. . . . .	well-developed
11. Family attitudes	hindering	. . . . .	supportive
12. Extent of education	limited	. . . . .	post-BA or BS
13. Quality of education	poor	. . . . .	excellent
14. Attitude toward education	negative	. . . . .	positive
15. Extent of work experience	very limited	. . . . .	extensive
16. Level of work experience	unskilled	. . . . .	highly skilled
17. Attitude toward work	negative	. . . . .	very positive
18. Attitude toward planning	indifferent	. . . . .	eager
19. Cooperativeness	resistant	. . . . .	helpful
20. Obvious problems	serious	. . . . .	none apparent
21. Other significant factors			

lem and understanding the psychological realities that surround the client. The list above is not intended as a checklist, but rather is to show the breadth of client information that can relate significantly to the career development and career choice process that is often called career counseling.

Client attributes can easily be organized in checklist fashion, and sometimes that approach is helpful for the beginning counselor. At least it provides some reassurance to counselor and client that most client aspects pertinent to career counseling have been reviewed and are being considered in the counseling process. Figure 5–2 is a sample of how such a checklist might be organized.

A somewhat comparable approach to identifying important aspects of the client's world has been reported by O'Neil and Bush (1978), O'Neil, Meeker, and Borgers (1978), and O'Neil et al. (1980a, 1980b). They propose that six broad factors influence the career decision-making process. They have asked career decision clients, in three reported research studies, to rate the degree of influence that the components of these factors exerted upon career decisions. The six factors and the component subcategories parallel quite closely the topics listed above. In these studies, sampling a total of more than 2600 individuals, they report the rank order of effect for the six factors to be listed below. The subcategories are listed under each factor to demonstrate the general nature of each factor.

1. *Individual factors*

   A. Self-expectancies
   B. Abilities
   C. Interests
   D. Attitudes
   E. Achievement needs

2. *Familial factors*

   A. Early childhood experiences
   B. Mother's role model
   C. Father's role model

3. *Socioeconomic factors*

   A. Social class
   B. Race
   C. Sex discrimination
   D. Supply and demand of jobs

4–5. *Psychosocial emotional factors*

   A. Fear of failure
   B. Fear of success
   C. Lack of confidence
   D. Lack of assertiveness
   E. Role conflict

6. *Situational factors*

   A. Chance
   B. Course of least resistance

BEFORE THE INTERVIEW ENDS

During this first interview (occasionally more than one may be required to reach this point), the counselor has been concerned with three main purposes: establishing a relationship so that counseling can continue, developing the client's psychological realities so that the goals of counseling can be conceptualized, and agreeing on the structure and plan for further counseling and related activities. The first of these purposes permeates all the counseling sessions, but probably the time and attention given to this goal diminish as rapport and trust develop. Thus, the remaining two goals really set the perimeters of the first interview. Once these two goals are satisfactorily attained, the counselor should turn attention to closing the interview. At least two matters need to be dealt with before that point is reached. These include summarizing the session's activities and arranging for immediate next steps.

Either counselor or client can summarize the main points of the session. There are definite advantages to either method. Usually, the primary reasons for summarizing are to be sure the counselor is understanding the client and his or her concerns and that the client understands and accepts the plan for resolving the problem.

When the counselor does the summary, one major advantage is expediency. Having the advantage of seeing many clients, the counselor can usually identify more rapidly and express more succinctly the major topics that have been discussed. If the time allotted for the interview is running short, the counselor can probably cover more territory in less time and still include the major topics mentioned by the client. A second advantage of counselor summarization is client reassurance. It can be most encouraging to the client to hear the counselor restating those items the client presented earlier—he or she realizes the counselor *really* heard and *really* understands.

There also are disadvantages to counselor summarization. Many counselors feel that the major responsibility for progress rests on the client. Thus any counselor action that involves leadership or responsibility may diminish client responsibility. This is probably less the case in career counseling, since the counselor must exert leadership at many points in the process. A more serious disadvantage can be the possibility that the counselor has missed some feelings and nuances that are important to the client and to the counseling process. As the counselor summarizes, the client may not catch the fact that these items have been missed or misunderstood by the counselor. Sometimes the client lacks the self-assurance needed to tell the counselor that something important has been ignored.

An advantage of client summarization is that the counselor has the opportunity to recheck his or her conclusions about client attitudes, client view of the major concern, and client understanding of the various points discussed. In other words, after the story has been pieced together during the interview, the counselor can now hear the client saying what he or she believes are the major elements of their earlier discussion. This also permits the client to benefit from his or her own synopsis of the session.

The major disadvantages may be client uncertainty about the amount of detail to include, perhaps a tendency to repeat factual matter rather than feelings and attitudes, and sometimes the belief that the counselor hasn't really heard him or her.

Another option does exist, and often may be most advantageous for both parties. This alternative has both involved in the summarization. Probably this mutual activity eliminates most of the disadvantages previously enumerated as well as retaining most of the advantages.

The counselor will ordinarily develop an approach to the summarization phase that fits his or her personality and counseling technique. Often it will be something like the following:

Our time today is very nearly gone, but before we stop let's spend a little time summarizing what has happened in this session. Why don't you share the things that are most significant in your thinking, and then I'll try to add any others that have occurred to me as we've spent this time together.

Before the client leaves, he or she should clearly understand what the next steps will be, and what actions he or she is responsible to complete. Those items depend on the plans discussed earlier in the interview. If they were not dealt with specifically at that point, they must now be handled in detail. Usually, a general plan has been outlined at the time of the earlier discussion, so that now it is only necessary to be sure that the client agrees on the next step, and knows what he or she is to do, and how. For example, if there has been agreement that the client will complete a test before the next interview, he or she should know where and when this is to be accomplished as well as why the step is being taken. If some type of homework assignment is to be completed, the client should understand exactly what is to be done and why. Often, an appointment card showing the time and place for the next session with the counselor can also include any special information about such assignment for the client. A written note of what is to be done, and when and where, increases the likelihood of the client understanding and complying with the plan.

Focusing attention on the next steps in the final moments of the first interview helps the client see that a plan is under way to deal with the concern that brought him or her to counseling in the first place. This results in an optimistic tone, making it easier for the client to continue. It also provides for a closure or termination of the session that permits the session to end smoothly and gracefully.

REFERENCES

Cottle, W. C. and Downie, N. M. *Procedures and preparation for counseling.* Englewood Cliffs, N.J.: Prentice-Hall, Inc., 1960.

Crites, J. O. *Vocational psychology.* New York: McGraw-Hill Book Company, 1969.

———. Career counseling: A comprehensive approach. *The Counseling Psychologist,* 1976, 6, 3, 2–12.

Hackney, H. L. and Cormier, L. S. *Counseling strategies and objectives.* 2nd edition. Englewood Cliffs, N.J.: Prentice-Hall, Inc., 1979.

Hansen, J. C., Stevic, R. R., and Warner, R. W., Jr. *Counseling theory and process.* 2nd edition. Boston: Allyn and Bacon, Inc., 1977.

Holland, J. L. *Making vocational choices: A theory of careers.* Englewood Cliffs, N.J.: Prentice-Hall, Inc., 1973.

Krumboltz, J. D. and Thoresen, C. E. (eds.). *Behavioral counseling: Cases and techniques.* New York: Holt, Rinehart and Winston, 1969.

O'Neil, J. M. and Bush, B. Psychosocial factors affecting career development of adult women. In D. P. Garner (ed.), *The career educator.* Vol. 3. Dubuque, Iowa: Kendall-Hunt, 1978.

O'Neil, J. M., Meeker, C. H., and Borgers, S. B. A developmental, preventive, and consultative model to reduce sexism in the career planning of women. *JSAS Catalog of Selected Documents in Psychology*, 1978, 8, 39 (MS. no. 1684).

O'Neil, J. M., Ohlde, C., Barke, C., Prosser Gelwich, B., and Garfield, N. Research on a workshop to reduce the effects of sexism and sex-role socialization on women's career planning. *Journal of Counseling Psychology*, 1980a, 27, 355–363.

O'Neil, J. M., Ohlde, C., Tollefson, N., Barke, C., and Piggott, T. Factors, correlates, and problem areas affecting career decision making of a cross-sectional sample of students. *Journal of Counseling Psychology*, 1980b, 27, 571–580.

Shertzer, B. E. and Stone, S. C. *Fundamentals of Counseling.* Boston: Houghton-Mifflin Company, 1974.

Stewart, N. R., Winborn, B. B., Burks, H. M., Jr., Johnson, R. R., and Engelkes, J. R. *Systematic counseling.* Englewood Cliffs, N.J.: Prentice-Hall, Inc., 1978.

Tyler, L. E. *The work of the counselor.* 3rd edition. New York: Appleton-Century-Crofts, 1969.

Williamson, E. G. The clinical method of guidance. *Review of Educational Research*, 1939, 9, 214–217.

———. *Counseling adolescents.* New York: McGraw-Hill Book Company, 1950.

6

Helping clients deal with change

Change occurs in the life of everyone. It is persistent, ongoing, and unending. Much of it is accepted with scarcely a thought, or at most a brief pause of recognition that things are different, and then we resume the onward flow of our lives. Sometimes we resist change and seek ways to return to the former status quo because we like things the way they were. Thus we may find change an irritant, a disruptive force that we fight against as we attempt to resume an earlier pattern. Sometimes change becomes a major compelling force that is threatening or even incapacitating until it is managed.

The difficulty we encounter in dealing with change is not necessarily a product of the size of the change required. Each of us, at different times and in varying circumstances, has confronted a very major change that we handled effectively, wisely, and with resulting satisfaction, and at another time we faced a relatively trivial change that caused us worry, confusion, despair, and dissatisfaction. Regardless of size or intensity, if the situation confronting the individual prevents that person from moving forward with his or her life or opening new opportunities, attention must be directed to resolving that problem and enabling change to occur before devoting major attention to career counseling. Sometimes the early steps of career counseling can proceed as the client is helped to resolve restricting problems, but until the client has faced the difficulty and developed a plan for handling it, he or she cannot assess accurately how to deal with problems of choice and career development. The situation that is restricting or blocking the individual must be seen as also likely to restrict or block that individual's efforts to make plans or implement those plans. Thus, ordinarily, restricting problems must be resolved before proceeding with career counseling.

As indicated in the previous chapter, Tyler (1969) states:

> the most basic evaluation the counselor must make if he is to be of assistance to the client is whether the person's present possibilities are adequate enough so that a course of action he might now choose is likely to lead to a kind of development that will be rewarding to himself and to society. If so, the counseling emphasis can be on the kinds of thinking and activity that will lead to good choices. If not, the counseling emphasis will be on changes in the person's behavior or situation designed to *open up* one or more promising possibilities for constructive development so that good choices can then be made. (p. 68)

Clients with quite disparate concerns can be classified properly as *change cases*. For example, a client may be fully aware that certain behaviors, attitudes, or lack of skill interfere with interpersonal relationships and/or pursuit of tentative or definite career plans, but be unable to instigate coping or resolving actions to produce change. On the other hand, another client may see only vaguely that problems exist that complicate his or her life and frustrate his or her plans; this client is unable to define those problems, much less contemplate action leading to change. Further, another client may be able to focus clearly on a personal or interpersonal problem but be unaware of its intrusion on career planning and development. The essence of the change category is that those clients reveal the existence of obstacles that impede or prevent their choosing or progressing satisfactorily toward a career goal. Common logic would suggest attention to either removing the obstacle or creating new possibilities as replacements for the blocked objectives before proceeding to *choice* activities.

Counseling change clients can be described as developmental, personal, or therapeutic. Similarly, acquiring new skills or information may be thought to be "learning activity," and developing new behaviors or attitudes may be called "therapy." Regardless of label, the goal is the same, as Stefflre (1972) has said:

> a free, informed, responsible person conscious of himself—his strengths and weaknesses, his sickness and health—and capable of viewing the world unblinking and unafraid; capable, too, of making decisions for himself in harmony with his unique nature and at least minimal societal requirements. (p. 302)

The counselor must help the client accept the necessity of dealing with those restricting conditions that limit the possibility of making and implementing effective career choices. Sometimes clients may view this proposal as unnecessary delay or a superfluous side trip. Such client resistance is often likely to occur when the client, having delayed contact with the counselor, is now faced with some imminent deadline such as declaring a major, choosing a program, or registering for next term. Obviously, the most persuasive rationale is the reality of the situation: that the perceived conditions are in fact limiting or restrictive to the point that client options are reduced or even foreclosed. Again, to help the client understand the reason for not immediately addressing the career choice problem, one can easily draw upon medical care analogies, where correction of one physical condition is often necessary before another problem can be treated. Further, discussion of a tentative time schedule, as described in the previous chapter, may help the client to see that the career concern will be handled at an appropriate and not far distant time. It is important for the client to understand that what is being proposed is a logical and necessary sequencing of activities and not a "bait-and-switch" technique that allows the counselor to move in a direction differing from the client's original concern.

Agreement by the client that factors do exist that impede or limit career choice or implementation provides the basis for proceeding with change counseling. Because the problem or problems are already evident, counselor and client can move expeditiously toward resolution. Often this will involve identifying the dimensions and severity of the problem, setting a reasonable goal, determining strategies, agreeing on intermediate objectives, planning steps required to reach the first objective, executing those steps, evaluating progress, revising steps for the first objective or planning those necessary to the second objective, and so forth until the difficulty is reduced to the agreed level.

Selecting counseling strategies appropriate for a change client depends on the counselor's skill, theoretical framework, and understanding of the client. These aspects of counseling have been thoroughly discussed in a number of references to which the counselor can turn, including Hackney and Cormier (1979), Hansen, Stevic, and Warner (1977), Shertzer and Stone (1980), and Stewart et al. (1978). These and other comparable references provide more detailed discussion of suitable counseling procedures than can properly be included here. Therefore, we will review only briefly various techniques that can be employed by the counselor to help change clients realize their goal.

Problems with sufficient severity to impede or interfere with effective choices are seldom simple. Often there may be a network of interrelated difficulties with varying levels of severity, so that treating a superficial action may only result in its being replaced by other unsatisfactory behavior. For example, helping a client to overcome eating binges may require looking for and dealing with factors that cause the client to participate in that type of behavior. The symptomatic behavior and the underlying attitude may require different treatment with different techniques or strategies.

The problems or obstacles that block or impede change clients arise from two basic sources. The first area is internal to the client and can be thought to consist of *self-oriented factors*. The second group of problems arises from the conditions or environment that surround the client and can be labeled as *externally oriented factors*. Client problems may also arise from an interaction between components of these two areas.

SELF-ORIENTED FACTORS

Obstacles or problems arising from within the client often reflect the need for information, behavioral change, attitudinal change, or skill acquisition. Problems often have roots in more than one of these areas. The counselor and client can determine whether multiple facets should be dealt with sequentially or concurrently.

Need for information

Ignorance is the cause of many problems. Sometimes the client doesn't know, and sometimes the client doesn't know that he or she doesn't know. There is a difference between not knowing and not knowing where to find answers, and even, occasionally, not knowing how to use answers. The counselor may very well be involved in all three aspects: are there answers, where are they, and how can they be applied?

Lack of self-oriented information probably consists of inadequate self-understanding and is relative to standards that appear reasonable or typical for the client's peer group. Certainly, a ninth-grade student would usually be expected to possess less self-understanding than a thirty-year-old adult. The client may lack information about either physical or psychological characteristics, including what is typical, or even what the usual limits of normality encompass. For example, an individual whose visual or auditory acuity was marginally normal during the developmental years may be unaware of a gradual deterioration that some time later has produced a serious deficit. Another illustration might be the individual who doesn't know how to deal effectively in interpersonal relationships because circumstances prevented learning this at an appropriate developmental stage or because the role models at that time were inadequate or conflicting. Teachers may have tried to encourage one type of response while parental influence pushed in another direction. The personal advice and medical advice columns in many newspapers and popular magazines amply demonstrate the frequency with which teenagers and adults lack basic information about typical physical and psychological functioning of the human organism.

Serious deficits of information may become apparent to the observant counselor almost at once. Others will appear as counseling proceeds. In cases where the counselor is convinced that lack of information is producing an impediment to choice, specific counselor effort may have to be aimed at evaluating this factor.

Once client and counselor perceive that lack of information is an obstacle that requires attention, several avenues for action are available. The simplest of these is to help the client gain access to the information through whatever medium is appropriate for the situation, including appropriate reading material ranging from pamphlets to books, audiovisual materials such as films, film strips, audio- and videotapes, referral to experts or significant others, and the use of simulation.

The scope and quality of knowledge in many areas—for example, personal hygiene, health, sex education, and personality characteristics— can be ascertained by existing tests or questionnaires. Often the instrument may serve as the indicator of specific knowledge needed by the client as well as identifying related misconceptions and misinterpretations.

Some people, once exposed to new knowledge, easily incorporate the information into their frame of reference by relating it to other previously acquired concepts and modifying subsequent behavior. Others may hold the information, or parts of it, in an encapsulated form, unable to relate it to previous data or apply it to their own behavior. Thus, information that cannot be used is no more useful than no information at all. The counselor can help the client incorporate and accept the new information in several ways. One way is to apply frequently used facilitating techniques such as acceptance, clarification, reassurance, and encouragement in the usual counseling relationship.

Both Hackney and Cormier (1979) and Stewart et al. (1978) discuss the use of social modeling as an appropriate strategy for this situation. Hackney and Cormier describe *live, symbolic,* and *covert* modeling in which, respectively, the counselor may serve as the live model, films or tapes are used to provide symbolic models, or the client imagines a model applying the new information. Hosford (1966) and Krumboltz and Thoresen (1964) report research that supports the use of symbolic models for effective learning and applying new information.

Role play and simulation are additional techniques by which the client can learn to apply knowledge to behavior. Role play between client and counselor, or between client and other clients in a group setting, permits the individual to act out a situation where the use of that knowledge is required. Learning and using can be enhanced by repetition, reversing roles, varying the situation, or by role playing misuse or lack of information. Simulation, usually somewhat more formal and involved than role playing, permits the client to apply the knowledge in a structured but still artificial situation.

Both role playing and simulation have many advantages. They permit a client to imagine and act out immediately a situation he or she expects to meet sometime in the future. They both allow learning to be demonstrated, revised if needed, and tried again without risk. Learning can be applied in increments that match client needs, and the situations can be controlled to maximize the effectiveness of the learning.

Programmed learning activities can be used to assist clients to evaluate their knowledge as well as to acquire new knowledge and process it for later use. The materials may be as simple as very brief exercises requiring only a few minutes to complete or as complex as extensive workbooks requiring several sessions to finish. A wide array of high-quality self-instructional material focusing on various aspects of personal development is now available from several educational publishers and similar sources. Learning from self-instructional packets is usually more effective when the learner is highly motivated and able to accept responsibility. Unless the counselor is particularly knowledgeable in the subject, he or she may need to consult media specialists or subject matter experts to ascertain the source of relevant and usable materials. If the client is not referred to such a subject specialist who will supervise the learning experience, the counselor must schedule time with the client to discuss materials and concepts learned in order to ascertain that the learning has occurred and the client can apply the knowledge effectively.

Participation in an appropriate group may help a client to assess information and acquire and apply needed information. Such group involvement should have direct relevance to the client's needs. When the counselor works in educational or community settings, where the clientele often have many common characteristics, arranging a group with similar needs is a relatively easy task. The group experience may provide encouragement, reassurance, insight, and motivation for the client along with such side products as increased social skills, enhanced self-confidence, and independence.

Helping clients acquire and process information so that they can apply it appropriately to improve their lives emphasizes the teaching aspects of counseling. Like a highly skilled teacher, the counselor must clearly identify the client's needs and determine how the client can learn the needed information most effectively. The materials and techniques selected are chosen because they appear to facilitate best that effort.

Need for behavioral or attitudinal change

Counselors frequently encounter clients who describe personal behavior that they view as undesirable or disadvantageous, and almost in the same breath rationalize its perpetuation by some statement like "but that's the way I am!" The implication, of course, is that an individual's behavior is unchangeable, and when it is inappropriate one can only lament the heavy hand of fate. Although almost everyone knows the story of George Bernard Shaw's character of Eliza Doolittle, made famous in *My Fair Lady*, we are rarely able to apply the lesson to ourselves. There also are many individuals who would like to behave in certain ways (for example, to initiate comfortably conversations with strangers) but find themselves unable to perform these desired activities. Most psychologists agree that behavior is learned, and therefore it can be unlearned, changed, or relearned. Similarly, attitudes that are often more elusive than overt behavior are also learned and can be unlearned or changed. The steps involved in helping clients change behavior are similar to those in changing attitudes.

The counselor can use the counseling relationship to help the client gain understanding of his or her behavior. Carkhuff (1971) suggests steps that can be taken by the counselor to assist in self-exploration. Hansen, Stevic, and Warner (1977) also describe the process of helping the client in self-exploration move gradually to deeper exploration that will lead to insight, self-understanding, and the initiation of action. Although behavior can be changed without developing client understanding and insight, change is more likely to contribute to client well-being and self-actualization if it is consciously understood by the client.

When the client reaches the point in the counseling process where the need for new behaviors or the changing or elimination of old ones is recognized, there are several techniques that the counselor can use to facilitate the change. Basically, the process of instigating new behaviors requires the development of a reward system that reinforces and emphasizes the desired action. Changing or modifying existing behavior involves helping the client to view the modification as desirable and to build a self-disciplining or -rewarding system that accomplishes the change. Extinguishing behaviors involves helping the client to view the present behavior as undesirable and controllable and to develop a method (often a reward system) for eliminating the action.

Krumboltz and Thoresen (1969) have discussed various techniques for changing behavior and have included numerous examples of effective application.

The strategies of social modeling, role play, and simulation discussed in the previous section are all applicable to behavioral change, particularly in helping a client acquire new behavior. Further attention will be given to this topic in the next section.

The most frequently used technique for modifying behavior is some variation of the reinforcement principle. This principle suggests that the strength of a response (behavior) depends upon its result. If the result is favorable, pleasant, or good (as viewed by the person) the behavior is likely to be repeated—in other words, it is reinforced. If the action does not result in an "acceptable" reward it is less likely to occur in the future. Although this appears simple and straightforward, presumably producing "good" behavior and eliminating "bad" behavior, it does not always work that way. Sometimes the individual gains satisfaction from behavior that others might view as unsatisfactory because the reward system was inappropriate or distorted. Sometimes the learning situation is too limited or restricted to allow appropriate experiences to occur. Occasionally old behaviors that are recognized as unsatisfactory are retained because it seems so hard to learn new replacements. The counselor using this technique deliberately attempts to strengthen those behaviors that are agreed by client and counselor to be favorable or positive and to weaken those that they have agreed are unsatisfactory or counterproductive.

The use of reinforcement strategies is often called *behavior modification*. Considerable research has demonstrated its usefulness in replacing ineffective behavior with more appropriate action (Premack, 1965; Ullman and Krasner, 1965; Cohen, 1968; Kanfer and Phillips, 1970). Elementary teachers have often used token systems to accelerate learning activities, combined with complimenting and praising positive behavior while ignoring inappropriate or attention-seeking activity. Distributing small rewards to students helps them to keep working at long and difficult tasks.

Changing behavior is a complex task that can be accomplished only incrementally over considerable time. Reinforcement strategies can be used successfully to accomplish these devised changes. The process requires that counselor and client agree specifically on the response to be reinforced (including the appropriate circumstances and the minimum amount of response required), select suitable reinforcing rewards, and establish a means of monitoring the behavior and dispensing the reward at the proper time. Some behavior can be assessed in terms of frequency (the number of cigarettes smoked per day) or in units of time (lengthening the time spent studying assignments) or in completing a complex series of items (researching, writing, and turning in a major course paper on time).

Effective remarks (reinforcers) must fit the specific client; some rewards are useful with one client but not with another. Social reinforcement—verbal or nonverbal signs of approval, praise, attention, or recognition by others—is effective with many people. This can be as simple as an appropriately timed smile or congratulatory slap on the back or as formal as the granting of a certificate or diploma. Verbal feedback on the progress being made is effective when the task can be divided into relatively small units. Those individuals who do not respond to social reinforcement may react positively to tangible rewards (the token system). The reward can be toys, candy, money, or tokens that can be exchanged for various rewards, or any concrete item identified by the client as valuable. Another type of reinforcer is access to some desired activity. Numberless little boys have been kept at their piano lessons by the promise that "as soon as you play the last piece perfectly, you may go outdoors and play ball."

Dispensing the reward at the appropriate time can be done by the counselor, the client, or by some other individual. The counselor has probably been reinforcing behavior throughout the counseling process, so there are many situations in which he or she is the logical person to provide reinforcement. The client, if he or she is willing and able to accept the responsibility, can dispense the reward. The advantage to this approach is that the client is required to accept and develop responsibility for his or her actions. Parents, teachers, friends, spouses, or significant others can also observe behavior and reinforce appropriate actions.

Eliminating undesirable behavior involves a process quite similar to that used to modify or change behavior. Stopping smoking is an example of extinguishing behavior. It may be approached in a "cold turkey," substitution, delaying, or self-disciplinary manner. The counselor's task is to help the client view the behavior as undesirable and to help select and implement an appropriate strategy for eliminating the behavior.

The principle involved is similar to that of reinforcement. If behavior occurs because the individual views the result as rewarding, then that behavior can be eliminated either by removing the reward or by making the reward undesirable. Sometimes the reward obtained by the individual for inappropriate behavior is positively reinforced, for example, the attention-seeking behavior of a child who obtains the desired attention. Sometimes the behavior is negatively reinforced or used to remove some threat, as when an individual isolates himself or herself from others because of fear of rejection.

The "cold turkey" approach to extinguishing behavior is difficult but effective when the client can be motivated sufficiently to apply the self-discipline required. Social reinforcement often is used to help the client through those periods when urge or pressure for participation in the undesired behavior is strongest. Alcoholics Anonymous has used this approach in overcoming alcoholic dependence, and it is also a common treatment for substance abuse.

<u>Substitution</u> is probably the most frequently used <u>method for eliminating undesired</u> behavior. This is the modification process described above, in which a new behavior is substituted for an old behavior. Many former smokers have tried this system by reaching for candy or gum when they felt the desire for a cigarette. This example demonstrates the need for careful selection of an appropriate substitute behavior, since many previous smokers who switched to candy soon found that they then needed a weight-reduction program.

The *delaying system* for eliminating behavior requires the individual to stretch out the time between behavioral incidents. For example, if a smoker has been consuming a pack of cigarettes a day, he or she can be helped to reduce that to ten cigarettes a day by waiting longer between smokes, and then to five and then to two and then to none at all. Similarly, the student who can only study for ten minutes at a time can be helped to build that to twenty and to forty minutes and then an hour, and so on to the agreed goal.

Undesirable behavior can also be eliminated by <u>helping the client to develop self-management techniques</u>. This strategy places the responsibility for eliminating the behavior on the client and helps the client assume responsibility for self. Hackney and Cormier (1979) discuss ways in which the client can be taught to engage in self-monitoring, self-reward, and self-contracting as methods for changing or extinguishing behavior.

Irrational thoughts, attitudes, fears, and worries can be dealt with using the same kinds of strategies used to develop, modify, or extinguish behavior. Assistance in overcoming fears or troublesome attitudes is sometimes provided by using *systematic desensitization* as described by Wolpe (1958). In this technique the counselor first teaches the client methods of deep muscle relaxation, then helps the clients to arrange the aspects of the fear or anxiety in a hierarchy from least to most frightening. Finally, the counselor helps the client to maintain a state of deep relaxation while confronting or considering the least disturbing aspect on the hierarchical list. If this can be done by the client, he or she is then encouraged to face the next-weakest aspect on the list. When the client can deal with this idea and maintain the state of relaxation, client and counselor progress to the next step on the list and continue this system until all aspects of the fear can be encountered.

Cognitive restructuring and *thought-stopping* are procedures suggested by Hackney and Cormier (1979) to assist clients in replacing illogical thoughts or anxieties with positive or self-enhancing views. Clients are taught how to identify negative attitudes, how to interrupt them, and then how to switch to coping thoughts.

Need for skill acquisition

Social graces, how to study, managing a checking account, driving a car, preparing an IRS 1040, or dealing kindly and effectively with others can all be mastered by "how-to-do-it" procedures. Where needed skills are relatively simple and easily learned, the counselor may assume a teaching role and directly assist the client in developing competency. Because skill acquisition is essentially the process of learning new behavior, the techniques discussed in the two previous sections are applicable to this client need. A common sequence for teaching skills is to use social modeling followed by role playing and rehearsal, then trying new skills first in simulated situations and next in controlled-reality settings. Another technique involves the use of exercises or similar programmed materials that are designed to develop the specific skills. Some of these are designed to maximize self-learning. Often these materials can be incorporated in the role playing, simulation, and other tryout experiences to assure that the client has developed proficiency at the agreed-upon level.

We are not concerned here with acquisition of vocational skills used in learning or performing occupational tasks; that will come in a later chapter. We are focusing here on acquiring needed skills that either will permit the client to overcome obstacles that prevent developing and implementing effective career choices, or will help the client build new approaches to planning and fulfilling career plans. These skills can range from overcoming educational deficiencies, such as penmanship, reading ability, or numerical skills, to personal hygiene and care, to interpersonal actions such as manners, accepting supervision or direction, and dealing effectively with others.

Learning complex skills requires an instructor who possesses teaching skill as well as proficiency in the skill, and a considerable period of time for mastery by the recipient. Consequently, attempting to meet client needs of this type within the counseling relationship may be impractical, inefficient, and a misuse of counseling time. The counselor will need to know or be able to find referral resources to which the client can be sent to learn complex skills.

Local educational institutions, mental health centers, other agencies, and counselors familiar with local resources can be helpful in identifying possible references. Because the counselor must respect and protect the client's well-being, referrals can be made only with care. Ascertaining that the reference meets ethical and quality standards and is appropriate for this specific client is a necessary prelude to actual referral.

In this section we have considered techniques that counselors can apply to assist clients in resolving obstacles or problems that arise within the client. Many difficulties arise from other sources to impede or prevent the client from making effective career choices. These will be discussed in the next part of this chapter.

EXTERNALLY ORIENTED FACTORS

Individuals often are inclined to say, "I'm my own worst enemy." They usually mean that many of the problems they face have been internally caused by inappropriate behaviors or attitudes, lack of self-understanding, or lack of skill. Very few, however, would agree that all their problems are self-caused. Those problems that originate outside the individual can be thought to be environmentally or externally related. In this usage the term "environment" is broadly applied to include not only the physical environment that surrounds the individual, but also the other people encountered by the individual and the social and psychological climate created by the interaction of those others with each other, the individual, and with the physical environment. These will be considered under the headings of need for social and environmental information, need for career-related information, and need for situational or social change.

Need for social and environmental information

A frequently quoted saying states "Ignorance of the law is no excuse." But it certainly can be a means of producing great troubles for some individuals. Similarly, unfamiliarity with local custom, cultural attitudes, social and behavioral expectations, or accepted practices and procedures can lead to frustration and failure in interpersonal relations and in career development. Clashes between the individual and society or some subsection of society may result from that person's lack of information, and the product of that encounter can be devastating.

The social and environmental information ordinarily needed by an individual is acquired in the developmental years from a variety of sources. Much of the knowledge is provided by the formal educational structure that transmits information within the regular classroom and via the various contacts between the individual and teachers, peer groups, and others. Some information is acquired from extracurricular experiences such as clubs, athletics, school trips, lectures, and the like. Non-school-related activities, including church groups, civic, fraternal, and social clubs, also provide part of the information acquired by the individual. Further, much knowledge comes from significant others, including parents, family, close friends, or additional people with whom the person has regular or important contact.

Learning deficits can occur for many reasons, including various failures in the system or in the individual. One frequently cited illustration of this problem is the absence of male role models for boys who grow up in homes where the father is missing. Another example can be seen among children who have difficulty relating to a work-oriented society when they have had no close contact with employed adults. Geographic mobility has also produced many problems that fit this category because many customs, attitudes, and practices are local or regional in nature; thus a youngster who grew up in a small rural community may encounter great difficulty in coping with life in the city.

The counselor, using traditional counseling techniques such as restatement, reflection, or interpretation, can help the client understand why and how his or her behavior, attitudes, or understandings differ from those held by peer group members. Such counseling reassures the client and helps engender confidence in the individuality apparent in the differences. However, this resolves only part of the difficulty faced by most clients since it does not do anything to narrow that gap between the person and his or her peers. While the gap can never be eliminated, if we accept the idea that the individual is the product of the interaction of self, total environment, and the experiences encountered, much can be done to help the person acquire more comprehensive social and environmental information. Because behavior is usually evaluated in terms of local or regional standards, the individual who desires to "fit in" must overcome those learning deficits that produce the "different" behavior.

The public media provide one useful source of social and environmental information. These include newspapers, periodicals, books, radio, television, and so on. The client whose problem is identifying acceptable or customary modes of dress, for example, might be helped by viewing and discussing illustrations and advertisements in newspapers and magazines or appropriate television programs, or some of the instructional films, filmstrips, or slides available in most educational institutions. The individual who has difficulty with local dialect or speech patterns might use radio or television programs or educational tapes or records to increase understanding. All of these resources provide examples of symbolic social modeling. In addition to those resources normally available in everyday life, such as the local daily newspaper and local radio and television programs, there are vast resources available in public and institutional libraries and media centers.

Some information is unlikely to be in print or public media vehicles because of the currency of the information, its tendency to fluctuate rapidly, or other unique characteristics. Identifying people who have the needed information may be appropriate. Although consultation with lawyers and physicians is common practice, their counterparts in other fields are often overlooked. Very often the kind of information needed is a fairly common variety, for which there are many available consultants—peers, fellow club members, neighbors, fellow workers, for example.

Various agencies, public or private, fee or free, local, regional, or centralized may be appropriate sources for certain types of information. The person who needs a license for some type of activity, wishes to apply for citizenship, wants to determine eligibility for certain benefits because of parental veteran status, or has some similar problem may often be unaware of whom to contact to initiate action. Large communities may very often have an agency directory available. In other communities the information about local agencies is relatively difficult to obtain and use. If the counselor is not familiar with the appropriate agency to deal with the client's problem, he or she must be familiar with sources of information that will lead to identifying the agency.

The client may also, in some circumstances, be the logical collector of needed information. He or she may be able to apply basic principles of observation, listening, interviewing, or resource searching to collect the information. Occasionally the counselor may be the logical or appropriate collector of data. The client may need some help in identifying what to ask or look for, how to ask, whom to ask, and where.

Need for career-related information

Career education specialists have often labeled the first phase of career development as the *awareness stage*. This is the period in which the individual develops insight and understanding of self, and a broad comprehension of the general structure of the world of work, including its various components and how the system works. Awareness of the world of work is recognized as an essential foundation for later career development stages such as exploration and decision making. The awareness phase is an ongoing, lifelong process, but developmentally it is largely concentrated in the preadolescent or early adolescent years. Individuals usually have an adequate basis for exploratory and preliminary decision making by the time they reach high school.

Counselors may often encounter clients seeking assistance in the career choice process whose awareness of work is so limited or distorted that it effectively blocks progress. Holland (1973) lists insufficient experience to learn about the work environment as one of five causes of maladaptive vocational development. Crites (1973) would describe such an individual as immature in career development. There is probably little advantage in attempting to determine the cause of the condition. There are, on the other hand, many steps the counselor can take to help the client overcome the condition. Providing assistance first necessitates determining the extent and type of help needed by the client. Some examples of the types of problems include inadequate or erroneous understanding of any of the following:

1. How jobs relate to one another to form broad families or job clusters.
2. How different jobs require different kinds of worker characteristics.
3. The impact of job on the worker in lifestyle, income, status and opportunities.
4. General relationships between levels of educational attainment and responsibility and status in work.
5. The various educational and experience paths leading to different fields of work.
6. The role and function of the various agencies and institutions available to help the individual successfully operate the system.

The scope of missing information can range from little or no understanding of one or more of these general topics to quite narrow, but significant, deficiencies. An example of this more restricted type of problem is the lack of understanding of such matters as the admission requirements in a highly competitive field, health standards for food preparation occupations, length of formal training for highly skilled jobs, or public expectations of job holders in a specific occupation.

With all clients there is the possibility of resolving the problem in an individual or group setting. Group approaches include formally structured classes available in educational settings, and informal groups or workshops of variable length created by the counselor, a community agency, or an educational institution to help those with such problems. Individual help may come from the counselor or appropriate referral to someone else. Some states now provide for the preparation and certification of career information technicians or specialists who can be particularly useful in resolving problems of this type.

The resources available for assisting clients are numerous. They include printed materials that range from brief brochures to full-length books, and may encompass fictional presentations as well as purely factual statements. Audiovisual materials, including films, filmstrips, slides, audiotapes, combinations of visual and aural matter, videotapes, and similar products are available for purchase from commercial services, or for rental or free use at many media centers. Programmed materials ranging from single page exercises to lengthy workbooks focus on many difficulties in this category. Computerized programs applicable to problems of this type are increasing. There are also simulation programs that are useful in helping clients acquire needed information. These various information systems will be discussed in more detail in a later chapter. Extensive descriptions also can be found in Isaacson (1977) and in Norris et al. (1979).

Clients are encountered occasionally who have well-developed and appropriate career plans and usable skills but are unable to obtain or hold a position because they cannot operate the system effectively. They may be lacking in interview skills, in interpersonal relations, or in understanding such basic job-holding characteristics as punctuality, regularity of attendance, acceptance of supervision, and cooperation with fellow workers. Counseling or job information materials or exercises may be sufficient to reduce or overcome the handicap.

Need for situational or social change

Many clients face problems arising from their personal situation that impede or block effective career planning. These can be as varied as unsuitable housing conditions, transportation problems, indebtedness, money management difficulties, or paucity of opportunity. Problems frequently arise from relationships with significant others, such as restrictive attitudes of parents, spouse, or others, need for child care services, coordinating time schedules with those of others, interpersonal conflicts regarding ambitions, desired lifestyle, philosophy, and so on.

Throughout this chapter our focus has not been on whether problems exist, but whether they impinge on the client with sufficient severity that they limit the possibility of successful choice counseling. This emphasis is particularly true of situational factors because such problems exist, to some extent, in almost every person's life. Client awareness of the restrictive impact of the problem may vary from a vague awareness to an intense and painful recognition of the precise dimensions of it.

Here, as in earlier sections of this chapter, the counselor's goal is to help clients realize that they can take charge of their lives and to help develop effective ways of dealing with problems so that they do take charge. Thus, counseling with these clients usually has two distinct phases or emphases, sometimes pursued sequentially and sometimes concurrently. The first of these involves counseling in a traditional or classical sense, aimed at helping the client develop insight and understanding of self, situation, and problems. The counselor provides a support system in which the client feels secure enough to look introspectively at his or her world, sort out relationships, build some understanding, and develop attitudes of self-confidence and self-direction. In the second aspect the counselor helps the client develop problem-solving or decision-making skills that are applicable specifically to the present problem or concern and applicable generally to future situations.

Both aspects of counseling are essential for the change client. If the counselor focuses exclusively on the first phase, the client may develop complete insight and understanding, even to an exquisitely painful level, but may be immobilized in resolving the problem. If the counselor provides only "how-to-do-it" skills, the immediate symptom may be removed, but the underlying difficulty of lack of self-awareness will soon emerge in another part of the client's life. Either aspect of counseling, by itself, tends to leave the client in a dependent state. By helping the client who faces situational or social problems develop self-understanding *and* decision-making skills, the counselor serves the basic goal of counseling: to help the client be his or her own person and to be able to strive for the goals he or she has established.

The introductory section of this chapter listed several references to which the reader can turn for detailed discussion of counseling techniques and strategies appropriate for the first phase of counseling the client with situational/social problems. Discussion of strategies for building decision-making skills is also available in several references, for example, Krumboltz and Thoresen (1976), Shertzer and Stone (1976), and Stewart et al. (1978). We will summarize briefly the major steps in the decision-making process. Although the number of steps proposed by various writers varies somewhat, the differences are primarily due to the extent to which some steps are combined or identified separately.

Decision making for the client with situational/social problems involves the following steps:

1. *Identify the problem.* If counselor and client have started logically with the first phase of developing an awareness of self and of the situation, this first step will have been accomplished and agreement can be consummated easily on the problem to be given immediate attention. It is crucial that the client be able to verbalize the problem and to "own" it—that is, recognize and accept that the problem is his or hers and that he or she must deal with it.

2. *Clarify relevant values and goals.* Problems usually become problems because they interfere with establishing or attaining goals. Sometimes, however, this interference is not clearly perceived. The client can only understand and evaluate the problem as he or she contrasts the situation with those personal values and goals that are relevant. The comparison of problem to

values and goals is similar to the old psychological example of the Grecian urn to illustrate perception. The client's problem becomes the urn and is seen clearly only as it contrasts with the background of values and goals. The importance of identifying client values and goals becomes obvious in the next two steps.

3. *Develop alternatives.* The client is helped to develop a list of possible solutions to the problem. Some counselors encourage clients to engage in a free-wheeling brainstorming exercise listing every solution that comes to mind regardless of rationality or appropriateness. Usually clients, having recently discussed values and goals, use those factors as a monitoring system and are more inclined to propose suggestions that are reasonable and possible. Clients who have struggled with a specific problem over a considerable period may have developed a circular approach that limits their view of possible solutions. They may need assistance in seeing new approaches to the situation.

4. *Evaluate alternatives.* Once client and counselor agree that most possible solutions have been identified they must turn their attention to evaluating each proposal. Consideration must be given to the degree of compatibility with those previously listed values and goals. Conflicting options will probably be discarded at this point. The remaining items must be weighed in terms of what each would demand in effort, time, money, and similar factors. The possibility of success or failure of each must be estimated along with side effects and residual factors.

5. *Rank order the alternatives.* Once each possible solution has been identified and evaluated, the next step is to find the one that is best. Unlike fairy-tale solutions, reality usually provides no easy answer, and several solutions will incorporate both positive and negative aspects. The client must be helped to identify which positives are most important to him or her and to determine if the accompanying negatives are acceptable. Often the first alternative involves a compromise of these factors.

6. *Plan action for the first alternative.* One cannot assume that identifying the best course of action automatically leads to its implementation. Many counselors have often heard clients say, "I know what I should do, I just can't do it!" Thinking through the action, identifying the various steps, considering the matters of when, where, and how, helps the client to prepare to carry out something that is obviously viewed as risky. Many of the techniques discussed earlier in the section on changing behavior and attitude are appropriately used in this step.

7. *Implement action.* Once the best alternative is chosen and a plan of action developed, execution of the plan should logically occur. Sometimes it is possible for a client to arrange a tryout before full commitment is required. When this can be done, the

client has additional data available for determining outcomes. Implementation of the action should start when the probabilities of success fall within the range of risk that the client is willing to accept.

8. *Evaluate outcomes.* Very soon after implementation begins, some data are available to indicate if the plan is progressing as expected. If this feedback is favorable, the client continues executing the plan as originally established. If small adjustments appear to be called for, those adaptations can be made at appropriate times.

9. *Correct plan or commit to action.* If major flaws appear as the plan is implemented, drastic changes may be required. When the client can identify the cause of the difficulty, he or she may be able to develop compensatory action. If the plan of action is clearly a failure, the client may need to return to step 5 and review another option. If, on the other hand, the plan is working as expected, the client is now in a position to commit himself or herself completely to its execution.

10. *Identify fall-back alternatives.* This step is necessary only when the problem is a major one and the plan of action is long and complex. Many situational/social problems are of that nature, and others involve aspects of fluidity caused by changing conditions and other factors. Where such instability is a potential influence before the plan is completed, the client may need to consider several possible "what if's." Anticipation of possible changes and consideration of appropriate adaptations provide the client with some reassurance, as well as helping him or her to meet unanticipated changes with a greater likelihood of success.

During this second phase of counseling the client with situational/ social problems, the counselor is often involved in a teaching role in which the client is not only finding a solution to the specific problem that brought him or her to the counselor, but also is learning how to deal with all problems. One major purpose of counseling is to help the client reach this point where he or she can face problems and identify and implement satisfactory solutions as a self-directing individual.

Our attention in this chapter has focused on helping clients change aspects of their lives so that they can participate successfully in the choice process—the focus of the remainder of this book. Early consideration of change must occur if a counselor finds that the client faces obstacles that impede or prevent making a choice or implementing that choice. Unless problems of this magnitude are made manageable and the client has controlled or limited their influence, they may make the choice process a frustrating experience that results in a wishful dream. This is not to say that every problem, regardless of size and impact, must first be expunged; but those that can be seen to interfere with satisfactory progress must be resolved before effective choices can be made.

In this chapter we have considered how the counselor can help clients to gain control of difficulties that either impede or block their opportunities for making and implementing effective career choices. We have considered two broad types of problems that restrict clients: those that are self-oriented and come from within the client, and those that are externally oriented and arise from social or environmental factors that exist in the life of the client. Once the client has developed sufficient self-managing skills so that restrictive problems appear to be under reasonable control, consideration can be given to the career choice process.

REFERENCES

Carkhuff, R. R. Helping and human relations: A brief guide for training lay helpers. *Journal of Research and Development in Education*, 1971, 4, 17–27.

Cohen, H. L. Educational therapy: The design of learning environments. In J. N. Shlien (ed.), *Research in Psychotherapy*. Washington, D.C.: American Psychological Association, 1968.

Crites, J. O. *Theory and research handbook for the Career Maturity Inventory*. Monterey, Cal.: CTB/McGraw-Hill Book Company, 1973.

Hackney, H. and Cormier, L. S. *Counseling strategies and objectives*. 2nd edition. Englewood Cliffs, N.J.: Prentice-Hall, Inc., 1979.

Hansen, J. C., Stevic, R. R., and Warner, R. W., Jr. *Counseling theory and process*. 2nd edition. Boston: Allyn and Bacon, Inc., 1977.

Holland, J. L. *Making vocational choices: A theory of careers*. Englewood Cliffs, N.J.: Prentice-Hall, Inc., 1973.

Hosford, R. E. Determining effective models for counseling clients of varying competencies. Unpublished doctoral dissertation, Stanford University, 1966.

Isaacson, L. E. *Career information in counseling and teaching*. 3rd edition. Boston: Allyn and Bacon, Inc., 1977.

Kanfer, F. H. and Phillips, J. S. *Learning foundations of behavior therapy*. New York: John Wiley and Sons, 1970.

Krumboltz, J. D. and Thoresen, C. E. The effect of behavioral counseling in group and individual settings on information-seeking behavior. *Journal of Counseling Psychology*, 1964, 11, 324–333.

Krumboltz, J. D. and Thoresen, C. E. (eds.). *Behavioral counseling: Cases and techniques*. New York: Holt, Rinehart and Winston, 1969.

———. *Counseling methods*. New York: Holt, Rinehart and Winston, 1976.

Norris, W., Hatch, R. N., Engelkes, J. R., and Winborn, B. B. *The career information service*. 4th edition. Chicago: Rand McNally and Company, 1979.

Premack, D. Reinforcement theory. In David Levine (ed.), *Nebraska symposium on motivation*. Lincoln, Neb.: University of Nebraska Press, 1965.

Shertzer, B. E. and Stone, S. C. *Fundamentals of guidance*. 3rd edition. Boston: Houghton Mifflin Company, 1976.

———. *Fundamentals of counseling*. 3rd edition. Boston: Houghton Mifflin Company, 1980.

Stefflre, B. A summing up. In B. Stefflre and W. H. Grant (eds.), *Theories of counseling*. 2nd edition. New York: McGraw-Hill Book Company, 1972.

Stewart, N. R., Winborn, B. B., Johnson, R. G., Burks, H. M., Jr., and Engelkes, J. R. *Systematic counseling*. Englewood Cliffs, N.J.: Prentice-Hall, Inc., 1978.

Tyler, L. E. *The work of the counselor*. 3rd edition. New York: Appleton-Century-Crofts, 1969.

Ullman, L. P. and Krasner, L. *Case studies in behavior modification*. New York: Holt, Rinehart and Winston, 1965.

Wolpe, J. *Psychotherapy by reciprocal inhibition*. Stanford, Cal.: Stanford University Press, 1958.

7

Sizing up self

Janis and Mann (1977) suggest that the decision-making process starts when the individual receives or becomes aware of an authentic warning of impending danger. Following a similar vein, Remer and O'Neill (1980) have stated that the first step in the career-choice process is the recognition by the individual that he or she faces a problem (must make a choice) and, further, is responsible for resolving the problem.

The model of emergency decision making proposed by Janis and Mann (1977, p. 55) shows the individual who has just realized the existence of impending danger, first asking himself or herself if the risk is great if no action is taken. The decision maker who concludes there is little risk in no action moves to a stage of unconflicted inertia and dismisses the consideration of further action. Physicists would explain this phenomenon by referring to the accepted law of physics stating that a body at rest tends to remain at rest. Psychologists would refer to the tendency of individuals to maintain the status quo. High school and college teachers and counselors immediately would recognize many students who appear to be approaching crisis points but whose behavior is clearly that of unconflicted inertia. According to the model, only the individual who answers the question "Is the risk great if no action is taken?" with a yes or a maybe continues the search for the best coping action.

The client's coming to the counselor is *de facto* evidence that the person has reached the first step and has decided that further action is necessary. Some clients are also implying by that action that they accept responsibility for resolving the problem, and they are ready to get on with the process. Others, however, may be seeking someone who will take charge and solve the problem for them. As the counselor and client discuss the structure of the counseling relationship (described earlier in Chapter 5), the counselor will be able to clarify that the client must accept responsibility. Clients who are unwilling or unable to assume a responsible role will usually discontinue counseling and, according to the model, assume a condition of defensive avoidance typified by wishful thinking, rationalization, and procrastination.

Having acknowledged the need to make a decision, and having assumed some responsibility for taking action, the client is ready to begin. When counselor and client agree that prevailing circumstances and behavior suggest that change counseling (see Chapter 6) is not presently required, they can undertake the choice-counseling process. This process first requires self-knowledge on the part of the client. To be useful in the choice process, self-knowledge must be not only comprehensive but also sufficiently integrated so that the client sees and understands the "why" of his or her behavior. Crites (1976, 1981) also discusses these two aspects of client behavior by applying the label of *differential diagnosis* to the question "What is the client's career decision problem?" and the label of *dynamic diagnosis* to the question of "Why does the client have this problem?" It is important to recognize that our concern with the nature and development of the client's problem is not for diagnostic labeling but instead is to help the client progress through the decision-making process. Decision making starts with the recognition of risk and uncertainty. The client can determine whether that danger requires some defensive retreat or offers the challenge of new opportunity only when he or she knows self sufficiently well to be aware of the resources that can be applied to the situation.

One can argue effectively that the individual who understands self sufficiently to be able to match personal characteristics, values, and potentials, with the uncertainty or challenge being confronted and who is able to develop a plan of action that is cognitively and affectively acceptable is not in need of counseling, and likely will not seek it. Conversely, the individual who lacks that self-understanding or who is unable to develop an acceptable plan is in need of counseling.

IDENTIFYING GAPS

Information about the client begins to surface almost as soon as the client enters the counselor's office. The observant counselor recognizes many clues that provide insight into the client, even when the client is discussing other topics. The initial interview is usually highly productive of verbal and non-verbal information about the client and the client's world. In fact, the data volunteered about self during that first interview usually shape the format for the later discussion of self.

We considered in Chapter 5 the problem of how much information about the client is needed to help him or her. We proposed there that a reasonable rule of thumb is to have sufficient information to provide both counselor and client a good understanding of the client in his or her present world as well as enough background to answer some of the "why" questions. How much information is enough depends on many factors. It seems obvious that the client who comes for help in resolving a commitment problem consisting of choosing among two or three apparently appropriate choices has more self-understanding than the client who hasn't started the process at all. More time must be spent with the second client in exploring self and helping organize the data in useful forms. For the purpose of this chapter, we will assume that our client is of the second type and essentially is starting from scratch.

Who the client is today is the product of the interaction of the client, including biological inheritance, with the physical and social environments that have surrounded him or her in the past. This interaction of *who* and *what* produces the *why* of today's behavior. The who, what, and why of human behavior are thoroughly mixed together, and clients will sometimes experience difficulty in sorting them out. Fortunately, the career counselor is usually not too concerned about sorting each item into its exact pile. Instead, counseling's aim is to help the client clarify self-perception and how it evolved—including both the what and why. Of particular importance to client and counselor are those "whats" and "whys" that bear upon the different aspects of the career-choice process.

Chapter 5 included an array of questions related to several general topics that usually are relevant to self-understanding in the choice process. The topics presented in that list include the following:

1. Client's view of self.
2. Client characteristics, including ability, achievement, aptitude, interests, motivations, values.
3. Client's view of future, including aspirations, dreams, goals, hopes.
4. Health and physical status.
5. Family.
6. Educational experience.
7. Work experience.
8. Significant individuals in the client's life.
9. Significant experiences.

The relationship of each topic to career planning is readily apparent, although the special importance of any one subject will vary considerably from one client to another. For example, with younger clients of high school or immediate postsecondary age, family and educational experience usually will be of considerable importance and work experience often will be insignificant. On the other hand, if the client is more mature—a displaced homemaker, for example—one might expect self-concept, significant experiences, and significant others to be relatively important while educational experiences of a decade or more ago, and family, especially parents and siblings, to be somewhat less important as influential factors.

The personal characteristics are almost always of significance because they often identify the outer limits or maximum goals that the individual might attain under ideal circumstances. The individual's view of self and attitude toward the future can provide essential indicators of how much effort the client will exert to move toward those maximum goals. Thus highly competitive occupations, the professions for example, may be appropriate goals if compatible client characteristics are supplemented by a high level of motivation, strong competitive drive, willingness to accept delayed gratification, recognition of the years of work and study that must be invested to attain the goal, access to the resources needed to pursue the goal, and similar relevant factors. Another client with comparable personal characteristics may prefer goals that require less competition, can be attained in less time, or can be reached with less formal education.

Later in the decision-making process, as alternative choices are evaluated, the counselor will be responsible for assisting the client to relate knowledge of self to requirements of various occupations. At this time the counselor's attention is focused on helping the client answer global questions such as the following: Who am I? What am I really like? How am I similar to and different from others? What are the characteristics and experiences that have produced my uniqueness? What commitments am I prepared to make to attain career goals? What goals and aspirations that are unrelated to career are important to me, and how important are they?

Questions like these cannot be answered with broad generalizations. Instead they are answered in little pieces, a bit at a time. In some ways, the process is analogous to working a jigsaw puzzle—at first there are several distinctly separate aspects that can be seen, but as additional pieces are put in place the several parts are tied together into a total design or pattern. The counselor's task at this stage is to help the client find the pieces and fit them with others that have already been put together so that a clearer idea of the "big picture" is possible.

As is true with the puzzle, gaps and unidentified pieces may later prove to be significant parts of that total picture. Similarly, there may be gaps in the self-understanding of the client. Because the picture we are dealing with is more abstract and nebulous than a jigsaw puzzle, these gaps are harder to recognize, evaluate, and manage. Thus, in addition to helping the client find and put together the available pieces, the counselor is also responsible for helping the client become aware of gaps or missing pieces that leave the present picture incomplete.

Frequently, clients can report quite easily and assess accurately those aspects that are relatively objective in nature—family background, educational experiences, health, work, significant others, and important experiences. They often find more difficulty in self-reporting those matters that might be described as subjective—personal characteristics, self-concept, and view of the future. Not only are these matters more central to the individual's private world, they also are more difficult to evaluate, compare, and define. The sensitive and competent counselor can help the client explore these areas in ways that enhance both client self-esteem and self-understanding.

Counselors can help clients in the self-appraisal process by helping them evaluate known information not previously considered from this viewpoint. For example, some clients request an interest inventory to provide information about interests or an aptitude test to assess their abilities when discussion of their reaction to work and/or educational experiences, leisure activities, successes and failures, and other significant parts of their daily lives will provide a wealth of personally oriented information. Look beyond the client, or use other techniques, when the client is unable to assess self accurately or lacks confidence in that self-appraisal, but such devices may be unnecessary if the client has sufficient self-understanding. Clients often need encouragement to recognize that they already know far more about themselves than anyone else can possibly know. They may need some help in organizing that information and sometimes in evaluating it, but client self-knowledge is a rich vein that deserves careful mining before rushing off to other sources.

As gaps in client self-understanding are identified, the counselor has two responsibilities. The first of these is to help the client determine if the gap is an area that is important to resolve in light of the decision that the client is presently confronting. If the answer is clearly a no, further attention to this area, beyond ascertaining that the client is cognizant of his or her hazy knowledge, is unnecessary. The second responsibility arises when the answer to the question about relevance is either a yes or a maybe. The counselor is obliged to propose to the client methods by which accurate and sufficient data can be acquired expeditiously to satisfy present needs. Many counselors turn to tests almost automatically when clients need further information about themselves. There often are other techniques that will supply the information more easily and rapidly, and with more client understanding and acceptance. In making recommendations, the counselor is answering the question "How can we obtain efficiently accurate and trustworthy information in a form that is most meaningful?"

FILLING IN GAPS: NONTEST TECHNIQUES

Because clients are usually not in the habit of asking themselves where they can acquire additional information about themselves, they frequently overlook rich reservoirs of data that can be used to expand self-understanding. Occasionally, individuals are simply unaware of possible sources; at other times, they may not have known that feedback was possible or how to obtain it, or even how to evaluate and use information when it was provided. One obvious supplementary source of information is observation of the client by the counselor. It is plain that the counselor has been watching the client since he or she first arrived at the counselor's office. The client's general appearance, including attire, size and body build, posture, care given to hands, face, and hair, smiling or serious countenance, and similar physical characteristics tell much about him or her. As soon as the client begins to speak, he or she reveals through language usage, diction, grammar, accent, slang, and other vocal properties much more than the meaning conveyed by the spoken words. Further, the use of gestures, mannerisms, tics, eye contact, what the client does with hands, how he or she sits, apparent poise or lack of self-control, and other nonverbal behaviors will also tell a great deal about the client. From these observed data the counselor can form tentative hypotheses about the client, or confirm or question self-descriptive statements made by the client.

Not to be overlooked are the observations made by others whose impressions are available to counselor or client. For example, where both are involved in an educational institution, there are numerous others, such as teachers, who will have had extensive contact with the client in noncounseling circumstances, and whose report may add significant supplementary data. In other settings, there are often individuals whose scrutiny of the client extends over a far longer period than that of the counselor, for example, friends, relatives, spouse, or employer. When data from such outside observers appear useful to the counseling process, the counselor and client should develop a plan for acquiring that information. Many times in schools, employment situations, or social agencies an anecdotal record system may already be in place and accessible to an "inside" counselor. A counselor unaffiliated with the organization may need only a signed consent form to obtain access to client records.

The academic record or school cumulative file is a rich source for insight into clients who are still in school or who have only recently completed their educational activities. Information about the types of courses undertaken and completed, grades earned, attendance records, and participation in nonclass activities can confirm or refresh client recollections and may often provide insight into broad patterns of behavior that the client only sees in piecemeal fashion. Obviously, the school record is of diminishing importance as the client is farther removed from that experience. Clients who are several years away from school may have employment records that will include similar data that are of greater usefulness.

In addition to observation and the academic work records that are available for practically every client, there often are other sources of client information that can be used to develop a more complete picture of that individual. Many of these are described in detail in other references, such as Shertzer and Stone (1976). Some of these other sources include questionnaires, sociometric information, rating scales, case studies, and autobiographical devices such as logs and diaries.

USING APPRAISAL INSTRUMENTS

Career development theorists have almost universally endorsed the use of tests in the career counseling process. Even those theorists who adhere most closely to a client-centered approach emphasizing counseling outcome as reorganization of self and counselor role as nonjudgmental reflection, have seen a place for tests in career counseling. Patterson (1964) and Grummon (1972), for example, suggest that tests can be used because they supply information that is needed and wanted by the client.

Perhaps this almost wholesale acceptance of testing in career counseling has led to some of the abuses and misuses of tests that have occurred in recent years. For example, career counseling has sometimes been described as "three sessions and a cloud of dust," in which occur a brief intake interview, routine assignment of a lengthy battery of tests, a test interpretation session, and a brief final session relating test data to occupational characteristics, after which the client departs in a cloud of dust. Equally dismaying is the frequent "group career counseling" that transpires in many college dormitories, consisting of the administration of an interest inventory such as the *Strong-Campbell Interest Inventory* followed by a brief, usually inadequate, group explanation of the test profiles. Similarly, college counselors find it commonplace for clients to say "I want to take that test that tells me what I should do." It is often difficult to convince clients that tests are not crystal balls, magic wands, fortune cookies, or shortcuts to the future, nor should they be used in that way.

Cottle and Downie (1960) long ago emphasized that two reasons for using tests are to save time and to obtain information that cannot be secured in any other way. These two reasons are related but different. As indicated above, the counselor's task is to help the client develop sufficient self-understanding to be able to apply that knowledge in the career decision-making process. Gaps in self-understanding may occur in areas that can be labeled personal characteristics, including such items as interests, aptitudes, abilities, personality traits, values, and other areas.

Data relevant to these factors are often available from a variety of sources. For example, if the client is able to evaluate his or her interests adequately through expressed or demonstrated interests, it may be unnecessary to inventory them. Further, a college sophomore may find that his or her previous college academic record sufficiently answers questions about scholastic ability so that testing of that trait is superfluous. On the other hand, the college sophomore with an indifferent academic record who believes he or she can compete effectively with classmates can collect information from an ability test in far less time than the semester or two of tryout that otherwise would be required.

Clients often encounter difficulty in trying to estimate relative strengths of characteristics like interests, aptitudes, and abilities. Although they often can identify readily what they like most and least, they are at a loss to estimate the strength of this characteristic compared with other individuals. Thus, they cannot ascertain if this interest is unique or relatively so, or simply something that is liked by almost everyone.

There will be times, then, when data available from other sources may be sought via tests because tests will save time. In other situations, tests may sometimes take longer to provide information, but once obtained it includes data not available from other sources. Before suggesting that the client take tests, the counselor must ascertain that one or the other of these reasons is operative.

There is general agreement that counselors use tests for four different purposes (Cronbach, 1970; Hansen, Stevic, and Warner, 1977; Herr and Cramer, 1984). These purposes are usually identified as prediction, diagnosis, monitoring, and evaluation. Of the four purposes, the first two are of most importance to the counselor and are most frequently applied.

Tests may be used for predictive purposes when the client's question is "Can I succeed at that type of activity?" The kinds of tests used for this purpose are usually labeled *aptitude* or *ability tests,* although achievement test results are also frequently used for predictive purposes. College entrance examinations such as the *Scholastic Aptitude Test* or the *American College Test* are required when one applies for admission to college because the college believes that the scores can help predict the likelihood of success in programs offered by the college.

Using test results alone for prediction is a discouraging and unsatisfying process because a limited sample of behavior (the test results) is used to predict a complex, global result (such as college success). Clients, and counselors too, sometimes overlook the fact that the selected criterion (college success, often defined as grade point index) has great variability from student to student. Aside from the student input of effort, ability, and motivation are many uncontrollable factors such as what courses were chosen, who taught the courses, what grading system was used, what competition existed within the class, and other factors. Even if it were possible to control completely the variability on the criterion side, difficulty would still be encountered because tests have not yet reached the stage of precision where perfect prediction is possible. Measurement experts would explain that such predictions are based on a regression equation that assumes a perfect relationship between the predictor and the criterion. For example, if basketball skill were perfectly correlated with height, we could be certain that we had the best team by securing the tallest players. When the correlation is less than perfect, as it always is with tests, predictive accuracy declines and we must fall back on the standard error of estimate, a statistical device that provides a range within which a given forecast is likely to occur. In terms of the basketball players, while height is an important factor, other elements such as speed, stamina, dexterity, jumping and shooting skill, and knowledge of the game will moderate and diminish the influence of height as a predictor of success.

Prediction for an individual client is also difficult because most test data are based on group results in an actuarial sense. In other words, it can be estimated fairly accurately that a high proportion of students with SAT scores above a certain point will succeed in a given college program, but almost never that all students with such scores will succeed. The dilemma then faced is whether the client is one of that large group or one of the smaller portion.

The limitations of tests sometimes lead counselors to conclude that they should simply rely on their hunches or clinical judgment. The evidence, however, suggests that in spite of the limitations, predictions based on actuarial data seem to be stronger and more reliable than those based on clinical judgment alone. Meehl's (1954) study is still considered a classic in this area. Predictive accuracy is usually increased when data from multiple predictors are combined, so counselors should seek confirming and supplementary data to combine with test scores when they attempt to make predictions.

Tests may be used for diagnostic purposes when the client asks such questions as "What am I like? Where am I strongest or weakest? With what groups am I similar?" Questions like these are so global that a simple answer is impossible. Fortunately, the client is usually asking something much more restricted than the words imply. For example, the first question usually refers to such smaller domains as any one of the following: "How do my interests compare to those of my peers? Can I handle math/language/science/etc. sufficiently well that I can safely choose this major? It always seemed like high school was pretty easy; did I learn as much as students who attended really tough schools? Do I have the interests and abilities to be a _____? If not, what fields should I consider? I think I'm less domineering and assertive than a lot of people, but I think I understand how others feel better than most. How can I be sure I'm right?" The counselor may suggest interest inventories, aptitude or ability tests, or personality inventories to obtain the information the client is seeking in these more specific areas.

At one time counselors frequently prescribed an extensive battery of tests in order to collect a massive amount of data to answer client questions such as "What am I like?" This approach is unrealistic in several ways. It assumes that only test data can be trusted, that information is not available from any other source, that tests will collect the information faster or more accurately than other techniques, that the client has unlimited time and willingness to spend hours taking tests, and that if enough tests are assigned something of value will be learned by the client. Unfortunately, there probably also were occasional counselors who were uncertain about what to do next or who felt the client expected to take a test and suggested some tests to fill that time and expectation. Long ago, Super (1950) discussed the "precision" use of testing as contrasted with a "saturation" system. He described *precision testing* as the process of getting necessary facts as the client needs them and is able to use them. This corresponds to the approach we have been discussing of assisting the client to identify the specific kinds of information needed and then helping to find that information as efficiently as possible. If it is agreed that testing is to be that method, then the counselor must be able to suggest the test or tests that will provide that information most accurately and understandably.

Diagnosis sometimes involves the use of tests to answer a different set of questions, such as "What's wrong? Why am I encountering this problem? Why can't I do _____ or _____?" The counselor's concern is to identify the nature and extent of the problem or special needs and, as appropriate, the causes of the situation. The purpose is to provide a base for planning remedial or rehabilitative action where that is possible, or to help the client adjust to or compensate for the situation if it cannot be changed.

Tests may be used for monitoring purposes when the client asks such questions as "Am I keeping on target? Am I where I should be in this program? How am I doing?" Questions of this nature are most likely to be asked of teachers, instructors, or supervisors, but they do come to counselors as well. Mainly, they focus on developmental processes or on skill acquisition. Achievement tests are the most typical kinds of tests used for monitoring purposes. A comparison to a different area is the daily or weekly "weigh-in" to monitor progress in a weight-reduction program.

Tests may be used for evaluative purposes when the client or counselor asks "How did I do?" The client's concern is usually directed toward the level of skill acquired or some similar goal and the testing time is at the end of the program or course or allotted time period. Counselors similarly may use tests, checklists, questionnaires, or rating scales to determine the extent to which counseling goals were accomplished.

Counselor education programs universally require counselors-in-preparation to include courses in measurement and testing. The proper place to discuss in detail the theoretical and statistical basis of tests, as well as their development, use, and interpretation, is in such measurement classes. Our purpose here is to consider briefly examples of the kinds of tests frequently used by counselors to help clients acquire more self-understanding. There are several widely accepted references to which the career counselor can turn for a more detailed discussion of tests used in career counseling than we can include here. Extensively used among this group are texts by Cronbach (1970), Goldman (1971), Anastasi (1976), and Shertzer and Linden (1979). Recent publications such as *A Counselor's Guide to Vocational Guidance Instruments* by National Vocational Guidance Association (Kapes and Mastie, eds., 1982) and *Using Assessment Results in Career Counseling* by Zunker (1982) are valuable handbooks for information about specific tests.

In addition to these textbooks, there are at least three other valuable sources of information about specific tests with which the counselor should be thoroughly familiar. These include the Buros *Mental Measurement Yearbooks,* test manuals, and current journal articles and reviews.

The *Mental Measurement Yearbooks,* edited by Oscar Buros, represent a herculean task of organizing and presenting usable information about tests. They include information on several hundred tests, including original reviews for most of them and excerpts of previously published reviews for many others. In addition they provide an up-to-date bibliography of published references for most of the listed tests. Also included is such demographic information as name of publisher, date of publication, forms used, age level, price at the time the yearbook was compiled, and similar useful data. Few test experts would challenge the assertion that the *Yearbooks* are the most useful available resource on tests.

Standards established by the American Psychological Association and other groups that represent frequent users of tests have led to remarkable improvement in information available in test manuals. Much more detailed technical and interpretive data are now provided to users than previously was the case. Many test publishers now have divided the materials furnished to test purchasers into a manual that includes instructions for administration and interpretation and another manual, often labeled as a technical manual, that includes necessary statistical data such as evidence of reliability, validity, and other information useful for evaluating the instrument.

Finally, counselors should be alert to the publication in professional journals of both critical reviews and reports of research related to frequently used tests. Research reports in particular may have significant impact on what we know about specific tests. Such reports appear in almost any professional journal relevant to the field of counseling. Experience reveals, however, that information of this type appears regularly in *Educational and Psychological Measurement, Journal of Consulting Psychology, Journal of Counseling Psychology, Journal of Vocational Behavior,* and *Measurement and Evaluation in Guidance.*

If tests are to be used with a client, he or she must be included in the planning for that usage and must be a willing participant. The client must agree that tests can probably provide some additional needed information or confirm information about which he or she is presently somewhat uncertain, and must also agree to make a reasonable and conscientious effort in the testing process. Unless the client trusts the counselor, the results will be questionable and of doubtful value. Similarly, the counselor must be able to suggest appropriate instruments that are most likely to provide helpful, usable information. When the tests have been agreed on, the counselor must be certain that tests are properly administered, scored, and reported. Finally, the counselor must be able to explain the results in a meaningful manner so that the client can expand self-understanding.

In the following pages we will look briefly at examples of the types of tests used frequently in career counseling. These are tests that are appropriate for general settings where clients may vary considerably on a number of factors. No attempt has been made to make the list comprehensive or to include tests that are used most frequently for specialized clientele. Readers should turn to the test manuals for detailed specific information about each instrument and to the appropriate Buros *Yearbook* for critical evaluations by test specialists. The tests are arranged according to type—career maturity, interest inventories, ability and aptitude tests, and personality, temperament, and values instruments. Within each section, tests are arranged alphabetically.

Career maturity measures

Career development inventory

Authors: Donald E. Super, Albert S. Thompson, Richard H. Lindeman, Jean P. Jordaan, and Roger A. Myers.

Date of publication: School Form, 1979; College and University Form, 1981.

Publisher: Consulting Psychologists Press, Inc., 577 College Avenue, Palo Alto, CA 94306.

Description: The purpose of the *Career Development Inventory* (CDI) is to measure the readiness of individuals to make choices about educational and vocational issues. It is a self-administering, machine-scorable instrument that purports to measure attitudes, knowledge, and skills used in making career choices.

Parts: Both forms of the CDI include five scales grouped in two parts as follows:

Part I	Career Planning (CP)	20 items
	Career Exploration (CE)	20 items
	Decision Making (DM)	20 items
	World-of-Work Information (WW)	20 items
Part II	Knowledge of Preferred Occupational Group	40 items

Within Part I, additional scores are obtained by combining scale scores as follows:

Career Development—Attitudes = CP + CE
Career Development—Knowledge and Skills = DM + WW
Career Orientation Total = CP + CE + DM + WW

The CP section asks the individual how much planning he or she has done in several areas of career preparation and how much knowledge he or she has about the work being considered. The CE section asks whether the client would consult certain sources in making career plans and the extent to which those sources have already been consulted. The DM section asks the person to identify the best action for given situations. The WW section asks questions about the person's knowledge and view of the world of work. Part II first asks the individual to choose an occupational group from twenty given sets and then to answer questions about that group concerning characteristics of jobs in that group, special ability requirements, interests compatible with the group, and the degree to which jobs in the group might satisfy certain values.

Time factor: The CDI is untimed. Both sections usually can be completed in about one hour.

Norm groups: The School Form has percentile norms by gender and grade level based on approximately 5000 students from ten different schools. The College and University norms are based on approximately 4000 college students.

Scoring system: The CDI must be machine scored by the publisher.

Appropriate groups: The instrument is intended to be used with high school or college level individuals.

Major advantages: The major advantages of the CDI include the following:

1. Information obtained by the CDI is useful in identifying the kinds of career development help needed by the individual or, in group administrations, by the group.
2. The time required is brief enough to fit easily into counseling and testing programs.
3. The scales have been carefully developed and reliability data suggest that most scales can be used with confidence.
4. The scoring service includes options of additional summary data when group or school materials are submitted simultaneously.

Major disadvantages: The major disadvantages of the CDI include the following:

1. The necessity of machine scoring by the publisher delays access to the results.
2. The keying of some items appears difficult to rationalize.

3.   Many items are transparent and therefore easily faked. Caution must be used to prevent any apparent advantage to such action.

Summary: The CDI was in the developmental stage for many years while the authors attempted to refine and improve the instrument. The result has been a brief inventory that appears to offer much hope for the counselor and the curriculum development director. It includes areas that are generally thought important and the user's manual includes many data that document the fact that this test does appear to tap those areas appropriately.

Career maturity inventory

Author: John O. Crites.

Date of publication: 1978. Formerly named *Vocational Development Inventory.*

Publisher: CTB/McGraw-Hill, Del Monte Research Park, Monterey, CA 93940.

Description: The *Career Maturity Inventory* (CMI) purports to measure attitudes and abilities of an individual that are believed to be important to the career decision-making process. The test is based on the assumption that career choice is a process extending over several years and includes several related but different attitudes and skills. The *Attitude Scale* includes fifty or seventy-five true-false items and the *Competence Test* has five parts with twenty items in each section. The CMI is based on a well-developed theoretical foundation and is supported by extensive research.

Parts: The CMI has two parts. The *Attitude Scale* purports to measure five variables that are included in how the individual looks at the career choice process. These five variables include:

1.   Decisiveness in career decision making.
2.   Involvement in career decision making.
3.   Independence in career decision making.
4.   Orientation to career decision making.
5.   Compromise in career decision making.

There are two forms of the *Attitude Scale.* The Screening Form is a fifty-item test that yields a single score. The Counseling Form includes seventy-five items and provides a score for each of the five variables.

The second part of the CMI is the *Competence Test.* This part purports to measure five cognitive variables involved in choosing an occupation, including the following:

1. Self-appraisal.
2. Occupational information.
3. Goal selection.
4. Planning.
5. Problem solving.

Time factor: Both parts of the CMI are untimed tests. The *Attitude Scale* can be administered in approximately thirty minutes for the Screening Form and forty minutes for the Counseling Form. The *Competence Test* requires approximately two hours, with a suggested working time of about twenty minutes for each section. Total time for the entire test is about two and one-half hours. Only a minute or two is needed for hand scoring.

Norm groups: Norm tables that translate raw scores to standard scores and percentiles are available for each grade level from grade six through grade twelve. Although the manual suggests that the CMI can be used with college students, norms are not provided beyond grade twelve. Local norms can be developed for a specific school where the number of students tested is sufficiently large to justify such action.

Scoring system: On all parts of the CMI the raw score is based on the number of correct responses. The Screening Form of the *Attitude Scale* produces a single score. The Counseling Form of the *Attitude Scale* provides five subscores. The *Competence Test* produces five subscores.

Appropriate groups: Because the CMI has a sixth-grade reading difficulty level, it is inappropriate for use with younger children and should be used only with those individuals in grade six and beyond who read at least at sixth grade level. The manual states that the CMI can be used appropriately with students between grade six and college senior level. Students at the sixth grade level or below are unlikely to have progressed far enough in the career development process to make testing a useful exercise.

Major advantages: The major advantages of the CMI include the following:

1. The CMI attempts to measure those aspects of career development that are generally considered by counselors to be significant aspects of that process.
2. The *Theory and Research Handbook* provides a careful explanation of the CMI's theoretical base.
3. Areas of ongoing research to be reported in later editions of the *Handbook* are identified.

Major disadvantages: Reviewers in the Buros *Eighth Mental Measurements Yearbook* have identified several major disadvantages of the CMI, including the following:

1. The test is built on the assumption that the number of correctly answered items will increase across grade levels; although this

happens, the amount of change per grade is very modest—about one and one-half items per grade on the *Attitude Scale.*

2. Most of the items on the *Attitude Scale* (forty-three of fifty on the Screening Form, sixty of seventy-five on the Counseling Form) are keyed "false."

3. Several sections of the *Competence Test*, while theoretically sound, have serious structural problems. For example, the first section on self-appraisal asks the person to evaluate hypothetical others, supposing that if one can see others clearly, self-understanding can be assumed. Further, the response pattern for each item is set—one response is "don't know," one is "dependence on others," one involves overinterpretation of the data, one involves underinterpretation, and one (the correct response) is just right. The shrewd test-taker can probably select the correct response by reading only the response items. Other sections are similarly structured in response pattern.

4. The intercorrelations among the various parts of the *Competence Test* across grades are quite high (range of all coefficients of correlation .45 to .71, range of the means across parts .55 to .68), suggesting that cognitive ability may be a major aspect in the test. This may mean that the sections have limited diagnostic value.

5. The *Competence Test* clearly is still in the developmental stage, and probably cannot yet accomplish all the tasks that it may be able to do when further research has been completed. If used with individuals, it must be interpreted cautiously.

Summary: The CMI has a substantial theoretical base and has been used more widely than any of its presently available counterparts. It attempts to measure an area of development that counselors recognize as extremely important in many career counseling cases. Items were retained for inclusion in the *Attitude Scale* that a majority of twelfth graders answered in the same way; thus "career maturity" is operationally defined in a way that may make some counselors quite uncomfortable. Content validity is claimed on the basis that 80 percent of expert judges agreed with the majority of twelfth graders on 75 percent of the items. Counselors who choose to use the CMI with individual clients may find the normative data of little value. If used, the test may be most helpful as a device to assist the client gain awareness of the aspects of career development, leaving the instrument unscored.

Interest inventories

Jackson vocational interest survey

Author: Douglas N. Jackson.

Date of publication: 1977.

Publisher: Research Psychologist Press, Inc., P.O. Box 984, Port Huron, MI 48060.

Description: The *Jackson Vocational Interest Survey* (JVIS) includes 289 pairs of statements that describe occupational activities. Individuals are asked to choose the item in each pair that either represents their preferred choice or is more characteristic of them. Items generally describe familiar activities in relatively simple terms. The test includes thirty-four scales consisting of seventeen items each, arranged in a format that permits easy hand scoring. Reading is at the seventh grade level.

Scales: The JVIS provides scores on thirty-four scales grouped in eleven families of vocational interests. Eight scales (three groups) represent work styles and twenty-five scales (nine groups) are named for work roles. One group includes scales for both work roles and work styles. Scales marked with an asterisk in the list below are work style scales and unmarked items are work role scales. The scales are as follows:

A. The Arts
   1. Creative Arts
   2. Performing Arts
B. Science and Mathematics
   3. Mathematics
   4. Physical Science
   5. Engineering
   6. Life Science
   7. Social Science
C. Practical, Outdoor Activities
   8. Adventure
   9. Nature–Agriculture
   10. Skilled Trades
D. Service Activities
   11. Personal Service
   12. Family Activity
E. Medicine and Health
   13. Medical Service
F. Interpersonal and Job-related Work Styles
   14. Dominant Leadership*
   15. Job Security*

    16. Stamina*
    17. Accountability*
G. Teaching and Social Welfare Activities
    18. Teaching
    19. Social Service
    20. Elementary Education
H. Business, Administrative, and Related Activities
    21. Finance
    22. Business
    23. Office Work
    24. Sales
    25. Supervision
I. Legal, Professional, Persuasive Work Roles
    26. Human Relations Management
    27. Law
    28. Professional Advising
J. Literary, Academic
    29. Author Journalism
    30. Academic Achievement*
    31. Technical Writing
K. Work Styles Related to Job Activities
    32. Independence*
    33. Planfulness*
    34. Interpersonal Confidence*

Time factor: Most individuals can complete the JVIS in forty to sixty minutes. Hand-scoring the answer sheet requires approximately five minutes, and the profile can be completed in about the same amount of time.

Norm groups: The norms are based on three large groups including the following: (1) A group of 658 male and 815 female college students drawn randomly from sixteen United States and Canadian colleges and universities; (2) a group of 1057 male and 850 female grade twelve students, mostly from Pennsylvania high schools, who had been admitted to Pennsylvania State University; (3) a representative group of 2157 male and 2273 female students from grades nine through thirteen in twenty-eight representative high schools in the province of Ontario, Canada. The profile sheet provides comparison with the combined group of males and females as well as comparison with both gender groups separately.

Scoring system: The format of the hand-scoring answer sheet permits easy and rapid scoring without the use of scoring stencils. The scores are obtained by counting certain designated choices in vertical columns and other designated choices in horizontal rows. The seventeen columns and seventeen rows provide the raw scores for the thirty-four scales. There is also a computer-scored form available with scoring service provided by the publisher. The profile for the computer-scored form includes additional comparative data not available on the hand scoring form.

Appropriate groups: The JVIS appears to be appropriate for use with high school or college age individuals or with older individuals.

Major advantages: Some of the major advantages of the JVIS include the following:

1. The hand-scoring system permits counselor and client to have results immediately available.
2. The JVIS is relatively easy to administer, complete, score, and profile, with minimal possibility for producing errors, although error can occur.
3. Comparison can be made to a combined group of males and females, or to either gender separately.
4. The manual includes descriptive statements for each scale.
5. The results provide information on both roles and styles.
6. Work-role scales are generally representative of groups or clusters of occupations.
7. The profile shows areas in which the person has low scores, generally interpreted as dislike or low interest.
8. The manual is well-organized and contains a large amount of valuable information for the counselor, including profiles for occupational groups, extensive counselor aids for interpreting profiles, detailed statistical data on the development and nature of the JVIS, and an extensive summary of completed research using the JVIS.

Major disadvantages: Some of the more obvious disadvantages of the JVIS include the following:

1. The JVIS is a relatively new instrument; hence follow-up studies, further research, and counselor reports based on extensive usage are still unavailable.
2. Some individuals find the forced-choice format difficult and/or boring.
3. JVIS results show inventoried interests *in* areas of activity, not interests *like* certain occupational groups.
4. Some comparative data useful to counselor and client are available only from the computer scored form.

Summary: Because the JVIS is quite new, it must be applied cautiously until more data concerning its usefulness are available. The excellent manual and careful development suggest that it will prove to be a highly valuable instrument. Probably, it will be of greatest help with clients who are in intermediate ranges of career development—that is, they have identified very broad global areas of interest and now desire to make more specific choices. It may also be helpful in counseling the late-entry client with limited prior work experience, such as the displaced homemaker or retired military person, or the physically disabled worker who is now seeking a new possibility. The work-style scales appear to be useful in helping clients understand the temperament aspects of career fields.

Kuder occupational interest survey—DD

Author: G. Frederic Kuder

Date of publication: The manual states that the *Kuder Occupational Interest Survey* (KOIS) was first published in 1966. It is an outgrowth of the *Kuder Preference Record—Occupational* (Form D) and is closely related to Forms B and C. It was revised in 1979.

Publisher: Science Research Associates, 155 North Wacker Drive, Chicago, IL 60606.

Description: Like the other Kuder tests, Form DD consists of brief descriptions of activities presented in triads. In each of the one hundred triads, the person is asked to indicate the most liked item and the least liked item. Unlike the earlier *Kuder Preference Record—Vocational* (Forms B and C) with norms based on boys and girls in high school, Form D introduced a new concept in scoring based on occupational groups. Form DD continues and extends this scoring system and now includes college major groups as well as occupational groups. The test can only be scored by computer.

Scales: The individual's responses are compared with 119 occupational groups including forty scales for women and seventy-nine scales for men, of which twenty are common to both. There are also comparisons with forty-eight college major groups including twenty-nine male groups and nineteen female groups, of which twelve are common to both.

Occupational scales

Accountant, Public	M	F	Automobile Mechanic	M	
Architect	M	F	Automobile Salesperson	M	
Audiologist/Speech			Bank Clerk		F
Pathologist	M	F	Banker	M	F

Occupational scales

Occupation	M	F
Beautician		F
Bookkeeper	M	F
Bookstore Manager	M	F
Bricklayer	M	
Building Contractor	M	
Buyer	M	
Carpenter	M	
Chemist	M	
Clothier (retail)	M	
Computer Programmer	M	F
Counselor (high school)	M	F
County Agricultural Agent	M	
Dean of Women		F
Dental Assistant		F
Dentist	M	F
Department Store Salesperson		F
Dietician (administration)		F
Dietician (public school)		F
Electrician	M	
Elementary School Teacher	M	
Engineer		F
Engineer, Civil	M	
Engineer, Electrical	M	
Engineer, Heating, Air Conditioning	M	
Engineer, Industrial	M	
Engineer, Mechanical	M	
Engineer, Mining/Metal	M	
Farmer	M	
Film/TV Producer or Director	M	F
Florist	M	F
Forester	M	
Home Demonstration Agent		F
Home Economics Teacher (College)		F
Insurance Agent	M	F
Interior Decorator	M	F
Journalist	M	F
Lawyer	M	F
Librarian	M	F

Occupation	M	F
Machinist	M	
Mathematician	M	
Math Teacher (high school)	M	F
Meteorologist	M	
Minister	M	
Nurse	M	F
Nutritionist		F
Occupational Therapist		F
Office Clerk		F
Optometrist	M	
Osteopath	M	
Painter, House	M	
Pediatrician	M	
Personnel Manager	M	
Pharmaceutics Salesperson	M	
Pharmacist	M	
Photographer	M	
Physical Therapist	M	F
Physician	M	F
Plant Nursery Worker	M	
Plumber	M	
Plumbing Contractor	M	
Podiatrist	M	
Police Officer	M	
Postal Clerk	M	
Primary School Teacher		F
Printer	M	
Psychiatrist	M	
Psychologist		F
Psychologist, Clinical	M	F
Psychologist, Counseling	M	
Psychologist, Industrial	M	
Psychology Professor	M	
Radio Station Manager	M	
Real Estate Agent	M	
Religious Education Director		F
Science Teacher (high school)	M	F
School Superintendent	M	
Secretary		F
Social Caseworker	M	F

Occupational scales

Social Worker, Group	M	F	Television Repairer	M	
Social Worker, Medical		F	Travel Agent	M	
Social Worker, Psychiatric	M	F	Truck Driver	M	
Social Worker, School		F	Veterinarian	M	F
Statistician	M		Welder	M	
Stenographer		F	X-ray Technician	M	F
Supervisor, Industrial	M		YMCA Secretary	M	

College major scales

Agriculture	M		Foreign Language	M	F
Air Force Cadet	M		Forestry	M	
Animal Husbandry	M		Health Professional		F
Architecture	M		History	M	F
Art and Art Education	M	F	Home Economics		
Biological Sciences	M	F	Education		F
Business Accounting and			Law—Graduate School	M	
Finance	M		Mathematics	M	F
Business and Marketing	M		Military Cadet	M	
Business Education and			Music and Music		
Communication		F	Education	M	F
Business Management	M		Nursing		F
Drama		F	Physical Education	M	F
Economics	M		Physical Science	M	
Elementary Education	M	F	Political Science	M	F
Engineering, Chemical	M		Pre-Med/Pharmacy/Dental	M	
Engineering, Civil	M		Psychology	M	F
Engineering, Electrical	M		Social Science, General		F
Engineering, Mechanical	M		Sociology	M	F
English	M	F	Teaching Catholic Sister		F

In addition to these scales, the KOIS provides scores on a Verification Scale and on eight experimental scales.

Time factor: Most people can complete the inventory in about thirty minutes.

Norm groups: Each scale of the inventory provides a direct comparison to individuals in the named group. Occupational criterion groups, obtained in various ways, included only subjects between twenty-five and sixty-five years of age who had been in the occupation at least three years and who met standards of job satisfaction. College major groups were obtained by inventorying 12,000 seniors at 119 colleges and universities who were in their final month and expressed satisfaction with their major.

Scoring system: Form DD can be scored only by computer.

Appropriate groups: The inventory is appropriate for use with upper-high-school- and college-age students and with adults.

Major advantages: The major advantages include the following:

1. The KOIS makes direct comparison with occupational and college major groups rather than using a general reference group as the basis for contrast.
2. The sixth grade reading level and specific instructions make administration relatively easy.
3. The profile lists scores in rank order and indicates by an asterisk all scores that appear to be equivalent to the highest score for each sex group.
4. Other sex comparisons are easy since all scores for each gender appear in rank order on the profile.
5. A verification score gives some evidence of the subject's sincerity and reliability.
6. The range of occupations on the profile is broader than for most other interest inventories.
7. The manual is carefully developed, attractive, and useful.

Major disadvantages: The major disadvantages include:

1. Because the inventory is relatively new, far fewer data on validity, predictive value, reliability, and the like are available compared with older, better-established inventories.
2. A disadvantage shared by all interest inventories is that they do not necessarily produce comparable results for norm groups that carry identical labels. Although this predicament can be explained by the fact that different items were asked of different representatives of the criterion group, it is still disconcerting to client and counselor alike.
3. Since computer scoring is necessary, there is considerable delay between administration time and access to profile results.

Summary: The KOIS offers the counselor an opportunity to use an interest inventory with broadly diverse occupational criterion groups. This is often important when clients express little interest in the competitive professional fields. The KOIS appears to be useful with high school seniors, college freshmen, or out-of-school adults who desire some comparison with college major or occupational criterion groups.

Kuder general interest survey—form E

Author: G. Frederic Kuder.

Date of publication: First published in 1963, Form E is a revision and downward extension of earlier Forms B and C. Form C, including the same ten scales presently used in Form E, was first published in 1948 and is still available. The manual was revised in 1975.

Publisher: Science Research Associates, 155 North Wacker Drive, Chicago, IL 60606.

Description: The *Kuder General Interest Survey—Form E* consists of 168 triads, each consisting of three brief descriptions of activities. The student is asked to identify the one item he or she most likes and the one item he or she most dislikes in each triad. On the hand-scoring version, the individual records his or her response by punching the appropriate circle with a pin. Vocabulary is at the sixth grade level.

Scales: The individual's preferences for activities in ten job family groups are obtained. These include the following:

1. Outdoor
2. Mechanical
3. Scientific
4. Computational
5. Persuasive
6. Artistic
7. Literary
8. Musical
9. Social Service
10. Clerical

There is also a Verification Scale that gives some indication of whether the subject has indicated responses sincerely and correctly.

Time factor: Most students complete the test in forty-five to sixty minutes. Hand scoring requires approximately five minutes.

Norm group: Scores can be compared with boys or girls in grades six through eight or in grades nine through twelve on the ten scales.

Scoring system: The hand-scoring version is easily scored by following the specific information printed in the answer pad. The individual starts at the indicated arrow for each scale and follows the chain of circles, counting each circle in which a hole has been punched, and records the number in the box at the end of each chain. These totals are transferred to the appropriate grade level profile sheet where the same-sex norm chart is used to graph the profile.

Appropriate groups: Kuder E is intended primarily for use with students in grades six through eight or in grades nine through twelve. Because scores are reported that show the level of preference in such broad areas as mechanical, persuasive, and social service, *Kuder E* may be useful with some adults who have not yet developed sharply differentiated interests, for example, displaced homemakers without prior employment, released criminal offenders, and released military personnel.

Major advantages: The *Kuder E* has the following major advantages:

1. The test is easy to administer and score. Most students can complete the test with little difficulty and also can score and profile their own results.

2. A group explanation of results and meaning of scores is often sufficient for most students.

3. The scores identify only broad areas of interest.

4. *Kuder E* scores are particularly helpful with those individuals who are beginning to explore career interests, since the scores identify areas in which the individual can focus reading and other exploratory activities.

5. *Career Guidance and the Kuder Interest Inventories* includes lists of occupations related to each of the ten scales, with each occupation keyed to the more commonly used career information reference systems and to the *Occupational Outlook Handbook* and the *Dictionary of Occupational Titles*, useful for encouraging exploration.

Major disadvantages: The major disadvantages of the *Kuder General Interest Survey* include the following:

1. Some individuals find the forced choice and triad format unpleasant. Some test experts raise serious questions about using forced-choice, ipsative (providing intra-individual comparison) type scores with a normative interpretive profile.

2. Although the publisher's catalog, the manual, and the profile sheets suggest that it can be used with students in grades six through eight, the manual points out that there are questions about using the *Survey* with average sixth grade students. It further suggests that it be used only with those sixth graders that the counselor feels are mature enough to answer the test sincerely and correctly. Probably that warning applies to some seventh and eighth graders as well if there is any indication of immaturity, low reading level, or short attention span.

3. The span of usefulness is relatively narrow, extending from somewhere in junior high school to someplace in high school, depending on how rapidly the individual begins to develop differential career plans and interests.

4. Even though the test is widely used and highly respected, only limited reliability and validity data are made available in the manual and no information is provided on the test's predictive usefulness.

Summary: The *Kuder General Interest Survey—Form E* appears to be a helpful instrument to use with those individuals who are only beginning to explore career possibilities and need self-information about interests only in very broad terms. It is best used with young people in grades eight through ten to motivate exploration of self and occupations.

Ohio vocational interest survey II

Authors: Ayres G. D'Costa, David W. Winefordner, John G. Odgers, and Paul B. Koons, Jr. developed the first edition of *Ohio Vocational Interest Survey* (OVIS).

Date of publication: First published in 1970. OVIS II appeared in 1981.

Publisher: The Psychological Corporation, 757 Third Avenue, New York, NY 10017.

Description: The OVIS II Student Booklet includes 253 items to be answered on a separate answer sheet. The *Career Planning Questionnaire* collects background information and allows a school or other agency to add as many as 18 additional locally pertinent questions if machine-scorable answer sheets are used. The items are brief descriptors of work activity. The individual responds on a five-point scale ranging from "Like very much" to "Dislike very much," without regard to the amount of education or training required. The items are related to twenty-three OVIS II interest scales, with eleven items assigned to each scale. The twenty-three scales are based on the Cubistic classification system related, in turn, to the data, people, things component of the *Dictionary of Occupational Titles*.

Scales: OVIS II provides scores for twenty-three scales including the following:

1. Manual Work (L-L-L)
2. Basic Services (L-L-L)
3. Machine Operation (L-L-A)
4. Quality Control (A-L-L)
5. Clerical (A-L-L)
6. Health Services (A-L-L)
7. Crafts and Precise Operations (A-L-H)
8. Skilled Personal Services (A-L-H)
9. Sports and Recreation (A-A-L)
10. Customer Services (A-A-L)
11. Regulations Enforcement (H-L-L)
12. Communications (H-L-L)
13. Numerical (H-L-L)
14. Visual Arts (H-L-H)
15. Agriculture and Life Sciences (H-L-H)
16. Engineering and Physical Sciences (H-L-H)
17. Music (H-A-L)
18. Performing Arts (H-A-L)
19. Marketing (H-A-L)
20. Legal Services (H-H-L)
21. Management (H-H-L)
22. Education and Social Work (H-H-L)
23. Medical Services (H-H-L)

The parenthetical three letter codes listed above with the scale titles indicate the scale location in the Cubistic system where L = low involvement, A = average involvement, and H = high involvement with data, people, and things respectively.

Time factor: Usually sixty to ninety minutes are needed to complete the OVIS II. If additional questions are added to the *Questionnaire,* more time is needed. Slow readers or young students will generally require longer time. Two separate sittings are recommended for eighth- and ninth-grade students.

Norm groups: Schools using the OVIS for groups of students have access to three norm groups. National norms are based on a national sample of approximately 23,000 males and 23,000 females in grades 8–12 drawn from schools in ten widely scattered states representing ten regions of the country. Schools may choose local norms based on the scores obtained by students in the local group if the group taking the test is sufficiently large (at least one hundred of each sex). Finally, schools may choose a combination of national and local norms. National norms are based on separate sex groups by grade level.

Scoring system: Scoring may be done either by hand or machine, and scoring services are available from the publisher. *Scale scores* (raw scores) represent the sum of the student's responses to the items on each of the twenty-three scales, with a weight of five for "Like very much" and a weight of one assigned to "Dislike very much." Scale scores are translated to percentile ranks. The *scale clarity index* provides a measure of consistency of client response.

Appropriate groups: The OVIS II is intended for use with students in grades eight through fourteen. Reading difficulty and the time factor for completion probably make its usefulness at a lower level quite limited. Most individuals beyond grade fourteen will have passed the point where the kind of data provided in OVIS scores could be helpful.

Major advantages: The OVIS II has the following advantages:

1. Based on the Cubistic classification system (the worker traits and worker functions section of the *Dictionary of Occupational Titles*) OVIS II permits maximum use of the *Dictionary of Occupational Titles* and the *Occupational Outlook Handbook*.

2. The Cubistic system helps individuals to relate their characteristics to the data-people-things structure of occupations.

3. Data provided by OVIS II scores form a useful base for curriculum development in career education by the local school system.

Major disadvantages: Principal limitations include the following:

1. The test is difficult for younger students or those with limited ability and attention span. The five-point evaluation of each item, unfamiliarity with some items, the relatively long time period cause problems for some students.

2. If the test is sent to a scoring service, there is considerable delay between administration and availability of scores. Counselors will often find this delay disadvantageous.

Summary: The OVIS II is probably most useful with groups such as school classes. It provides a practical approach to relating individual characteristics to occupational requirements and should be helpful in stimulating career exploration in schools or similar settings with high-school-age youth. Its value for individual counseling is probably most likely to arise from its prior use in a group setting.

Author: John L. Holland

Date of publication: 1977. The *Self-Directed Search* (SDS) was originally published in 1970 as an outgrowth of the *Vocational Preference Inventory,* first published in 1953. Between 1970 and 1977 several minor revisions occurred.

Publisher: Consulting Psychologists Press, Inc., 577 College Avenue, Palo Alto, CA 94306

Description: The Assessment Booklet of the SDS includes sixty-six activities arranged in six groups of eleven, sixty-six competencies similarly arranged, eighty-four occupations arranged in six groups of fourteen, a section in which the individual estimates his or her traits, an explanation of how to score the SDS, an explanation of what the summary code means and how to use the *Occupations Finder,* and finally a list of steps the individual can undertake to clarify career interests and plans. The individual responds to activities by indicating those liked and disliked, to competencies by identifying those done well and never or poorly, and to occupations by indicating those that are appealing or uninteresting. The *Occupations Finder* includes a list of 500 of the most common occupations in the United States arranged according to Holland three-letter codes and including the *Dictionary of Occupational Titles* code number and an indication of the general educational level demanded by each listed occupation. Reading level is considered to be at the seventh to eighth grade level.

Form E of the SDS was developed for individuals with limited reading skill. It consists of 203 items (compared with 228 items on the regular form) using only fourth grade level words. The scoring system has been simplified and produces two-letter codes. The *Jobs Finder* is used with this form and includes 456 jobs grouped according to the two-letter codes. There is also a special version of the SDS available for individuals who are visually disabled.

Scales: The SDS provides the person with a three-letter code that reflects his or her choices in terms of Holland's occupational typology. The first letter represents the individual's highest score, and secondary and tertiary areas constitute the remaining letters in the three-letter code. The six areas are as follows:

R—Realistic
I—Investigative
A—Artistic
S—Social
E—Enterprising
C—Conventional

Time factor: Most people can mark and score the SDS in forty to fifty minutes. Compliance with the "Next Steps" section would extend that time, depending on the degree to which each person applies the suggestions.

Norm groups: Norms in the usual sense are not provided. The use of the SDS requires an acceptance of Holland's occupational typology and its basic assumptions.

Scoring system: The scoring system is incorporated in the format of the SDS. The person counts the number of "Like" or "Yes" responses for each section, tallies these on one page, and sums up the various columns.

Appropriate groups: The manual states, "The SDS is clearly suitable for persons age 15 and older . . ."

Major advantages: The major advantages of the SDS include:

1. Most people can self-direct the completion of the instrument, controlling time and input.
2. Directions for completion are simple, straightforward, and easy to follow.
3. Reading level is low enough to cause few people problems. Form E is available for limited readers.
4. The SDS can be applied to group and individual use.
5. It provides all the help some people need.
6. The comprehensive and detailed manual includes an excellent chapter on interpretation and a counselor self-test to check counselor familiarity and understanding of the SDS.

Major disadvantages: The major disadvantages include:

1. Some individuals will have difficulty in following the instructions, and errors can occur in the scoring process that result in erroneous conclusions.
2. The two- and three-letter code system confuses some individuals, resulting in misinterpretations.
3. Many items appear to sustain sex-role stereotypes because access to many of the listed competencies has often been available in the past to single-sex groups.
4. Approximately 14 percent of those taking the SDS will have a summary code for which no occupation is listed in the *Occupations Finder* or the *Job Finder*.

Summary: The very wide usage of the SDS suggests that many counselors believe the instrument is helpful for their clients. Although the instructions are clear and the individual can move from section to section at his or her own pace, the SDS is probably not as "self-directing" as the name implies. It is likely to be most useful with clients who are relatively sure of themselves and their plans, but who are seeking a little reassurance. Because access to many of the activities and competencies has been gender-restricted in the past, the SDS must be used with extreme caution, especially with female clients.

Strong-Campbell interest inventory

Authors: E. K. Strong, Jr. Revisions in the 1960s and 1970s were completed under the direction of David P. Campbell. The 1981 revision is primarily the work of Jo-Ida C. Hansen.

Date of publication: The men's form of the *Strong Vocational Interest Blank* (SVIB) was first published in 1927. The women's form was published in 1933. Each form underwent several revisions until 1974, when a major change occurred. At that time the two forms were merged into a single booklet requiring a single answer sheet and using a single profile form. The General Occupational Themes (based on Holland's theory) were introduced and a new, enlarged manual was produced. The 1981 revision added several new Occupational Scales and replaced some old ones, revised the profile form and the manual, but left the inventory unchanged.

Publisher: Stanford University Press, Stanford, CA 94305.

Description: The *Strong-Campbell Interest Inventory* (SCII) and its antecedent, the SVIB, are unquestionably the best-known of the interest inventories. The SCII contains 325 items, mostly drawn from earlier forms. The items consist of occupations, school subjects, activities, amusements, types of people, preference between two activities, and personal characteristics. In the first five sections (281 items) the individual responds by indicating feelings about each item by marking *L* if he or she likes or would like it, *I* if he or she is indifferent to the activity, and *D* if he or she dislikes the item. In the penultimate section the person expresses a preference between two optional activities, and in the final section he or she indicates if a statement is like him or her by marking a yes or a no. The later revisions (1974 and 1981) attempt to eliminate sexist terminology as well as culture-bound items, dated items, and extremely popular or unpopular items.

Scales: The SCII provides scores for three types of scales and a fourth set of data that is helpful in interpreting the results. The three types of scores include:

6 General Occupational Themes
23 Basic Interest Scales
162 Occupational Scales

The six General Occupational Themes are related directly to Holland's six occupational types. The twenty-three Basic Interest Scales assess the strength and consistency of specific interest areas, for example, mechanical, artistic, social service, or sales. The Occupational Scales measure the degree of similarity between the individual's responses and those made by men and women in the various occupations. Most of the 162 Occupational Scales have keys for both men and women, although they will not always appear under the same General Theme. The specific titles included under each of the three types of scales are listed below. The reader must be aware that the Basic Interest Scales and the Occupational Scales both relate to the General Occupational Themes, but they do not relate directly to each other.

General occupational themes	*Basic interest scales*	*Occupational scales*	
R—Realistic	Agriculture	Air Force Officer	f/m
	Nature	Army Officer	f/m
	Adventure	Navy Officer	m/f
	Military Activities	Police Officer	f/m
	Mechanical Activities	Vocational Agriculture Teacher	m
		Farmer	f/m
		Forester	m
		Skilled Crafts	m
		Radiology Technician (x-ray)	f/m
		Forester	f
		Engineer	f/m
		Veterinarian	m
		Licensed Practical Nurse	f
		Occupational Therapist	f/m
I—Investigative	Science	Veterinarian	f
	Mathematics	Chemist	f/m
	Medical Science	Physicist	f/m
	Medical Service	Geologist	f/m
		Medical Technician	f/m
		Dental Hygienist	f
		Dentist	f/m
		Optometrist	f/m
		Physical Therapist	f/m

General occupational themes	*Basic interest scales*	*Occupational scales*	
		Physician	f/m
		Registered Nurse	m
		Math-Science Teacher	m/f
		Systems Analyst	f/m
		Computer Programmer	f/m
		Chiropractor	f/m
		Pharmacist	m/f
		Biologist	f/m
		Geographer	f/m
		Mathematician	f/m
		College Professor	f/m
		Sociologist	f/m
		Psychologist	f/m
A—Artistic	Music/Drama	Architect	f/m
	Art	Lawyer	f/m
	Writing	Public Relations Director	f/m
		Advertising Executive	f/m
		Interior Decorator	f/m
		Musician	f/m
		Commercial Artist	f/m
		Fine Artist	f/m
		Art Teacher	f/m
		Photographer	f/m
		Librarian	f/m
		Foreign Language Teacher	f/m
		Reporter	f/m
		English Teacher	f/m
S—Social	Teaching	Speech Pathologist	f/m
	Social Service	Social Worker	f/m
	Athletics	Minister	f/m
	Domestic Arts	Registered Nurse	f
	Religious	Licensed Practical Nurse	m
	Activities	Special Education Teacher	f/m
		Elementary Teacher	f/m
		Physical Education Teacher	f/m
		Recreational Leader	f/m
		YWCA Director	f
		YMCA Director	m
		School Administrator	f/m
		Guidance Counselor	m/f
		Social Science Teacher	f/m

General occupational themes	Basic interest scales	Occupational scales	
E—Enterprising	Public Speaking	Flight Attendant	f/m
	Law/Politics	Beautician	m/f
	Merchandising	Department Store	
	Sales	Manager	f/m
	Business	Realtor	f/m
	Management	Life Insurance Agent	f/m
		Elected Public Official	f/m
		Public Administrator	f
		Investment Fund Manager	m
		Marketing Executive	f/m
		Personnel Director	f/m
		Chamber of Commerce	
		Executive	m
		Restaurant Manager	m/f
		Chamber of Commerce	
		Executive	f
		Buyer	f/m
		Purchasing Agent	f/m
		Agribusiness Manager	m
		Home Economics Teacher	f
		Nursing Home	
		Administrator	m/f
		Dietitian	f/m
C—Conventional	Office Practices	Executive Housekeeper	f/m
		Business Education	
		Teacher	f/m
		Banker	f/m
		Credit Manager	f/m
		IRS Agent	f/m
		Public Administrator	m
		Accountant	f/m
		Secretary	f
		Dental Assistant	f

The nonoccupational scales include two special scales and a set of administrative indexes. The special scales include an *Academic Comfort* scale that discriminates between students who do well in academic settings and those who do not. Advanced degree holders earn higher scores on the average than those who have less academic experience. College freshmen score lower than college graduates. The second special scale is an *Introversion-Extroversion* scale that measures introversion with item content related to working with people in various settings.

The administrative indexes include a record of total responses indicating whether the person has answered all items, infrequent responses indicating the tendency for the person to choose unpopular items, and the like preferences (LP), indifferent preferences (IP), and dislike preferences (DP) for each of the seven sections. The LP, IP, and DP percentiles are useful in evaluating the significance of high and low scores on the various scales since a considerable deviation from the usually balanced division of approximately 33/33/33 will be reflected in all of these sets.

Time factor: The average adult can complete the SCII in approximately thirty minutes.

Norm groups: The General Theme Scales were developed by identifying 20 test items that represent each of the six themes as described by Holland. The responses to these items by 300 males and 300 females served as the basis for standardizing the scores. Although the printed standard score for each person is based on the total group of 600, the interpretive statement is based on the same-sex group of 300. The Basic Interest Scales are statistically developed scales consisting of items that cluster together. For the most part, these scales were developed on the separate gender forms of the earlier SVIB and have now been merged for the SCII with relatively minor change. They are most useful in interpreting the Occupational Scales. They, too, were standardized against the general reference group of 300 men and 300 women. The Occupational Scales are scales that have been empirically developed by contrasting the responses of a sample of individuals in a specific occupational group with the responses made by the individuals in the general reference group, and then identifying those items that distinguish the special group from the general reference group. Sampling is an important factor in establishing the validity of the scale. It is also important to remember that the contrast between people in general and the special group provides the basis for the scale. This contrast eliminates the influence of universally popular items and increases the discriminatory power of the scale. Those differentiating items were then assigned weights and the scales were normed by establishing standard scores on the original occupational sample. The Academic Comfort scale is normed on a sample of individuals holding a doctorate degree. Present scores correlate very closely with older SVIB scores that were based on college graduates. The Introversion-Extroversion scale has been continued from the earlier SVIB forms. It was originally developed by comparing the SVIB responses of college students identified as introverts or extroverts on the *Minnesota Multiphasic Personality Inventory.*

Scoring system: SCII answer sheets can be scored only by authorized computer scoring centers. Because of the complex system of weights used on each of the scales, hand scoring would be extremely tedious and difficult. Inasmuch as the assigned weights for each item on each scale are not made public, it is impossible to develop hand-scoring keys, even if one wished to do so. The computer scoring centers use approved profile forms for reporting scores on which the standard scores are reported and an asterisk is used to plot the score for same-sex norms on a continuum based on standard scores ranging from very low or very dissimilar to very high or very similar.

Appropriate groups: As the manual states, the SCII should be used in the larger context of career planning (Campbell, 1978). Although it is widely used within this general framework, it is of limited value to many people who may be involved in career planning. It is rarely useful with individuals who have not yet reached the last year or two of high school, who have average or less interest in postsecondary education, who are still immature in their career planning, or who appear to be passive, apathetic, or personally confused. The SCII is likely to be useful for those individuals who are considering occupations usually involving college preparation, appear to have some understanding of their career potentials, and are able to identify their likes and dislikes. Like all other tests, the SCII should be used only with those individuals for whom the counselor has clear evidence that the test is appropriate and likely to provide information that the individual wants and needs.

Major advantages: The major advantages of the SCII include the following:

1.   The SCII is considered a paragon in the psychometric field. Its stature has grown over its half-century of use.
2.   The manual, with its vast statistical base, has long been recognized as excellent.
3.   Data from the profile form are provided at three levels: broad and general on the General Theme Scales, cluster or group on the Basic Interest Scales, and occupationally specific on the Occupational Scales.
4.   Follow-up data from earlier forms provide powerful evidence of test validity.
5.   Most people can complete the form in a short time and with little difficulty or confusion.

Major disadvantages: The major disadvantages of the SCII include the following:

1.   Centralized scoring requires an inevitable delay, usually of a week or more, before results are available.
2.   Individual response style affects the scores. The individual with few like responses may be highly certain of his or her preferences and have a very specific, firmly established career orientation, or on the other hand may be very passive, dependent, and uncertain.
3.   Inconsistencies that are confusing to clients can appear between basic interest scores and occupational scales.

4.   The present SCII is based on data from occupational samples collected at an earlier time; hence scores for young women whose education has included less emphasis on traditional sex-role stereotypes may be unfairly compared to scores of more traditional women.

Summary: The SCII is an interest inventory with impeccable credentials. When used appropriately by a properly trained, skilled counselor it can provide a great deal of extremely valuable and helpful information for a client. When used inappropriately it is not only uninformative, but likely to be misleading and even dangerous. The care, skill, and precision with which a Rolls Royce or a Mercedes-Benz is built does not assure that it will be properly driven or maintained.

Ability and aptitude tests

Differential aptitude tests

Authors: George K. Bennett, Harold G. Seashore, and Alexander G. Wesman

Date of publication: Forms S and T were published in 1974; Forms V and W became available in 1982. The first edition appeared in 1947 and newer forms have been published periodically since that time.

Publisher: The Psychological Corporation, 757 Third Avenue, New York, NY 10017

Description: The *Differential Aptitude Tests* (DAT) are an integrated battery of aptitude tests intended for use with junior and senior high school students. Each of the eight tests produces a score indicating the individual's strength or weakness in that particular ability; in addition, two scores are combined to produce a ninth score that provides an index of scholastic ability. The types of item vary across the different tests. Most of the tests are essentially power tests, allowing the taker ample time, thus reducing the pressure of a speed test; hence, completing the battery requires approximately three hours. DAT scores appear to be effective predictors of future course grades. They include measures of general and special abilities.

Parts: The eight tests that comprise the DAT include:

1.   *Verbal Reasoning* measures the ability to understand and use concepts based on words. It is an analogy type test in which the subject must choose among five pairs of words the one pair that will best fill the first and last positions in a given four-word analogy. Working time is thirty minutes.

2. *Numerical Ability* measures skill in quantitative reasoning and the use of basic mathematical competencies. Items are mostly of the computational type, minimizing reading skill but requiring appropriate application of quantitative concepts. Working time is thirty minutes.

3. *Abstract Reasoning* measures the subject's reasoning ability without depending on language skill. The items consist of series of figures that differ in a particular way; the examinee must discern the principle that is operating and apply that principle by identifying the figure that would occur next in the sequence. Working time is twenty-five minutes.

4. *Clerical Speed and Accuracy* is a measure of the speed of response in a simple perceptual task. The person must identify a marked combination of letters or numbers in the test booklet, mentally retain this combination while searching for it on the answer sheet, and finally indicate the appropriate space on the answer sheet. Speed of perception and response are the primary factors. Working time is six minutes (two sections of three minutes each).

5. *Mechanical Reasoning* measures the ability to understand and solve relatively simple problems involving physical laws. Each item consists of a mechanical problem presented in a simple pictorial manner and a question about the problem. Working time is thirty minutes.

6. *Space Relations* measures the ability of a person to perceive a two-dimensional pattern and to visualize its appearance if it were formed in three dimensions. Items consist of a given pattern and several possible options of how that object would appear if viewed in three-dimensional space. Working time is twenty-five minutes.

7. *Spelling* measures the ability to recognize whether a word is correctly spelled. Working time is ten minutes.

8. *Language Usage* measures ability to recognize proper sentence structure, punctuation, and similar rules of formal written communication. Items consist of sentences with marked portions within which the examinee determines if an error exists. Working time is twenty-five minutes.

9. A ninth score is produced by adding the Verbal Reasoning and the Numerical Ability scores to produce the Scholastic Ability score. The sum of these two correlates highly with other measures of mental ability and is a good predictor of academic success in school or college.

Time factor: The working time required for each of the tests is listed in the section above. Total working time is 181 minutes. Several options are available for dividing the test into different length testing periods when testing must be done within a structured schedule. Two periods of approximately two hours each are sufficient to complete the entire battery. If hand-scoring forms are used, an entire battery can be scored in about ten minutes.

Norm groups: Percentile norms and stanine norms are available by sex for each grade level eight through twelve. Norms were developed on a nationwide sample of students. Because differing kinds of machine-scored answer sheets affect the scores on the Clerical Speed and Accuracy Test, norm tables are provided for that test according to the answer sheet used in testing. Except at the extremes, percentiles are provided only in five point increments.

Scoring system: Separate answer sheets are required for each form of the test. Five different machine-scorable answer sheets are available to permit access to a variety of machine-scoring services. The publishers also provide three levels of scoring service, ranging from a roster of individuals and their scores plus sheets of press-on labels that permit easy recording of scores on student record forms, to individual profiles of scores with a computer printout of career planning information. Hand-scoring keys are also available and easily used when the number of tests to be scored is small.

Appropriate groups: The DAT is intended for use with individuals in grades eight through twelve and appropriate norms are provided for these groups. The tests can be used with adults when the information sought can be properly interpreted using school level norms.

Major advantages: The *Differential Aptitude Tests* have the following advantages:

1. The long history of widespread usage clearly indicates acceptance by a national clientele of schools and counselors who appear to consider the DAT as the best of its kind.
2. Special norms are available for parochial school systems.
3. The manual is generally considered excellent.
4. The profile sheets used with students are clear, well-written, and easily understood. The take-home material is also appropriate, helpful, and easily understood.
5. The additional career planning service, available separately with machine scoring service from the publisher, is useful for most students in a school setting to motivate future planning.

Major disadvantages: The major disadvantages for the DAT include the following:

1. The DAT appears to predict success in future academic work quite well, but there is little evidence that it can predict occupational success or failure.
2. Most of the tests show relatively high intercorrelations with the

other tests. Two-thirds of the reported average intercorrelations are above .50. This suggests that the tests are primarily measuring general intelligence.

3. Translating the raw scores to percentiles in increments of five points probably causes some loss of precision.

4. The tests appear to be unnecessarily male-oriented. One critic has pointed out that the only illustration involving a female in the Mechanical Reasoning test (the only section with pictorial representation) shows her in a wheelchair. Some items in the Language Usage section also appear to be sexist. These problems are reported to be resolved in Forms V and W.

Summary: The DAT is extremely useful in helping high school age clients answer questions about how well they might be able to compete in further academic settings. There is, unfortunately, little evidence to show that the DAT can make differential predictions of success among various future academic programs; it can help answer the question "Should I go to college?" but it doesn't provide much help in answering "What should I study in college?"

Flanagan aptitude classification test

Author: John C. Flanagan

Date of publication: First published in 1953, revised in 1958 and 1960.

Publisher: Science Research Associates, Inc., 155 North Wacker Drive, Chicago, IL 60606.

Description: The *Flanagan Aptitude Classification Test* (FACT) consists of sixteen tests developed to test various job elements and intended to be used in varying combinations as those elements reflect the totality of job demands. The tests are all paper-and-pencil tests with varying time limits.

Parts: The FACT includes the following tests:

1. *Inspection* tests the individual's form perception ability by asking the test-taker to identify the one object among a group of five that is unlike the model. (twelve minutes)

2. *Coding* requires the individual to assign the proper code, obtained from a brief list that is supposed to be memorized, to a variety of items such as sales districts and colors of paint. (thirty minutes)

3. *Memory* requires the individual to continue the coding process of Test 2 without access to the lists of codes provided in the previous test. (five minutes)

4. *Precision* intends to measure the ability to do precise work in small areas by asking the person to draw lines between concentric circles and squares with limited space between the borders. (fifteen minutes)
5. *Assembly* tests spatial judgment by asking the person to identify the finished shape when several solid parts are assembled. (eighteen minutes)
6. *Scales* measures the ability to obtain accurate information from graphs. (twenty-eight minutes)
7. *Coordination* requires the person to perform a series of tracing tasks. (eight minutes)
8. *Judgment and Comprehension* is a measure of reading comprehension, asking the person a series of questions about a paragraph of information. (thirty-five to forty minutes, no time limit)
9. *Arithmetic* measures speed and accuracy with basic mathematical fundamentals. (twenty minutes)
10. *Patterns* requires the subject to reproduce geometrical designs on a grid, sometimes changing the position of the figure. (twenty-eight minutes)
11. *Components* asks the person to visualize forms that are concealed in a variety of complex drawings. (twenty-four minutes)
12. *Tables* measures the student's ability to obtain accurate information from various tables. (fifteen minutes)
13. *Mechanics* is a measure of mechanical comprehension in which the person responds to questions about various mechanical devices. (twenty-five minutes)
14. *Expression* is a language usage test to measure correctness and effectiveness of expression as shown in a series of sentences. (twenty-five to thirty-five minutes, no time limit)
15. *Reasoning* measures arithmetic reasoning by asking the student to solve story problems. (thirty minutes)
16. *Ingenuity* requires the individual to solve a problem situation described in brief statements. (thirty minutes)

Time factor: The time required for each test, including administration, sample exercises, and working time, is estimated above. The total time for all sixteen tests amounts to nearly seven hours.

Norm groups: Percentiles and stanines are provided for ninth-, tenth-, eleventh-, and twelfth-grade students. Described as national norms typical of students throughout the country, the normative data have been criticized for coming preponderantly from two school systems.

Scoring system: Each test booklet is self-scoring. As the subject marks answers on the booklet, a carbon paper backing transmits the choice to a preprinted scoring stencil, so it is only necessary to open the sealed edge and count the correct responses.

Appropriate groups: The FACT is intended for use with high school students and adults. It would appear to be most useful when clients are asking questions about their ability to perform the types of tasks that are measured by the various tests. Because the norms do not provide for direct comparison to workers in the specific occupation being considered, care must be used in making predictive statements.

Major advantages: The major advantages of the FACT include:

1. The basic assumption of measuring identified job elements and combining tests of those basic elements to estimate possible success appears to be logical.
2. Students usually find each test interesting and challenging.
3. The test accessories—Student Booklet, Counselor's Booklet, and the Technical Report—are thorough, well-organized, and informative.

Major disadvantages: The more important disadvantages of the FACT include the following:

1. The absence of usable occupational norms seriously restricts the usefulness of the test. Even the school norms provided appear to lack the representativeness that is desirable.
2. Because the difficulty level on several tests is relatively flat rather than spiral, there is often very little difference between the various grade-level norms.
3. Because the tests are based on job elements, the FACT appears to be of limited value for use with students who are considering occupations that require college preparation. Nevertheless, there is some evidence that good students tend to score high on most tests and poor students score low.
4. Administration of the tests is very complex and difficult because of variations in time periods for sample exercises and work sessions, and because of frequent change of instructions for the different tests.
5. The total battery requires eight to nine hours of time. Even in that very long period, some of the tests have relatively brief work periods where the combination of speed and difficulty can prove to be very frustrating to slower students.

Summary: The FACT appears to be a test with great possibilities—logical theoretical base, carefully crafted parts, high face validity—but seriously restricted by inadequate normative data. It is easy to accept the job element approach but disappointing to be unable to make useful comparisons with occupational groups. Even so, clients and counselors can use combinations of FACT tests to obtain some limited information about the client. With presently available norms there is probably little justification for using the entire battery for any client.

The *Flanagan Industrial Tests* include eighteen brief tests drawn from the FACT. Several of the tests relate to entry-level work and are suitable for testing applicants for such positions.

Author: Developed by the United States Employment Service

Date of publication: 1947. Test booklets, answer sheets, aptitude patterns, and norms have been revised at various times since original publication.

Publisher: Test booklets and manuals are published by the Government Printing Office. Performance sections of the test are manufactured by K & W Products Company, Warwick Products Company, and Specialty Case Manufacturing Company. The test, released for use by State Employment Services, is available to nonprofit institutions for counseling purposes. Orders for tests and all accessories must be cleared through a State Employment Service office.

Description: The *General Aptitude Test Battery* (GATB) consists of twelve parts, including eight paper-and-pencil sections and four dexterity tests requiring special equipment. Screening exercises are available to identify those individuals who are deficient in reading skill, and consequently should be tested with nonreading adaptations of the test. The paper-and-pencil sections are available in an expendable booklet version and in a separate answer sheet edition. Relatively brief time limits impose speed factors upon the examinee. Scores are translated into Occupational Aptitude Patterns that permit comparison with individuals in various occupations.

Parts: The twelve tests in the GATB include the following:

1. *Name Comparison* is a test of clerical speed and accuracy. Subjects are asked to identify pairs of names and discriminate between identical and different sets.
2. *Computation* is a test of arithmetical ability consisting of items that require performance of basic mathematical functions.
3. *Three Dimensional Space* measures the ability to visualize how a two-dimensional pattern would appear in three-dimensional space.
4. *Vocabulary* measures the ability to identify pairs of synonyms or antonyms in a given set of words.
5. *Tool Matching* is a test of form perception in which the subject is asked to compare representations of common tools and in each set to find the two representations that carry the same shading.

6. *Arithmetic Reasoning* tests the ability to solve story problems.

7. *Form Matching* is another test of form perception. In this test the individual is presented two sets of irregular, two-dimensional figures; in one set the figures are located differently and sometimes turned to different positions. The task is to identify the identical pairs.

8. *Mark Making* is a test of motor coordination that is measured by determining the number of sets of marks (two vertical marks and one horizontal mark) that the individual can put in a sequence of small squares within a very limited time.

9. *Place* measures manual dexterity by requiring the individual to move pegs bimanually from one board to another as rapidly as possible.

10. *Turn* also measures manual dexterity by asking the individual, using only the favored hand, to pick up the same pegs used in the *Place* test singly, turn them over, and return them to the same space on the board in very limited time periods.

11. *Assemble Test* measures finger dexterity by requiring the subject to use the favored hand to pick up a small metal pin from the upper section of the board while removing a small washer from a rod on the board with the other hand, insert the pin in the washer, and then, using the favored hand only, insert the assembled unit in the lower portion of the board.

12. *Disassemble Test* is a further test of finger dexterity. It requires the person to reverse the procedure followed in the *Assemble Test*. With the favored hand the person picks up an assembled unit from the lower portion of the board, separates the pin and washer, and while placing the pin in an appropriate hole in the upper portion of the board with the favored hand returns the washer to the rod with the other hand.

The twelve tests provide scores for nine aptitudes. Some aptitude scores consist of the sum of more than one test and some tests contribute to more than one aptitude. The aptitudes and tests contributing to that score are as follows:

G—Intelligence: Tests 3, 4, and 6.
V—Verbal: Test 4.
N—Numerical: Tests 2 and 6.
S—Spatial: Test 3.
P—Form perception: Tests 5 and 7.
Q—Clerical perception: Test 1.
K—Motor coordination: Test 8.
F—Finger dexterity: Tests 11 and 12.
M—Manual dexterity: Tests 9 and 10.

Time factor: Time limits for all of the tests are comparatively brief, introducing a speed factor that has occupational relevancy. The time allowed varies from a minute to six minutes. Even though several practice exercises are provided on the performance tests and careful instructions on the others, the total time required to complete the entire test runs only a little over two hours. Hand-scoring time for the paper-and-pencil tests requires not more than five minutes.

Norm groups: Recently developed norms now permit comparison with successful workers in a wide range of occupations. This comparison is accomplished by means of Occupational Aptitude Patterns that include the scores on the two, three, or four most important aptitudes for each of the occupations. Multiple cut-off scores have been established for each OAP by identifying the score on each aptitude above which two-thirds of successful workers between eighteen and fifty-four years of age would place. This upper two-thirds range is then divided into standard scores and percentiles.

Scoring system: Scoring is simple and straightforward. An overlay stencil is used to identify the number correct for each of the paper-and-pencil tests. The performance tests are scored by counting the number of units attempted in the timed exercise. Scores are recorded on a standard test record card.

Appropriate groups: The GATB is intended for use with individuals age sixteen or older. Special forms are available for those who have limited reading ability.

Major advantages: The major advantages of the GATB include:

1. Test experts generally agree that the GATB is the most thoroughly researched of all multiple aptitude tests.
2. GATB testing is available at all State Employment offices, so clients can be tested even when the counselor has neither GATB training or materials.
3. Direct comparisons are made to aptitude patterns representative of individuals in specific occupations.
4. Total testing time is relatively brief (a little over two hours) and results are immediately available.

Major disadvantages: The major disadvantages include:

1. The lack of computerized data restricts comparisons to those that easily can be made by the counselor; consequently, much valuable information remains unused.
2. The test probably measures current ability in the various test areas rather than ability to learn the skills.
3. The test is over thirty-five years old. Much change has occurred in the world of work, with tremendous expansion in the service and clerical areas. The skills required in many new jobs may not be adequately tested by the GATB.
4. The test's capacity for differential prediction may be restricted

by its emphasis on speed and its disregard for other factors besides ability.

Summary: The GATB does what very few other tests do: it permits comparison of client characteristics with those of actual workers in specific jobs. Thus, it can help clients answer such questions as "Can I compete with typical workers in that occupation?" or "In what occupations can I perform better than most workers?" It was developed to assist State Employment Service counselors in placement activities and in its present format it serves that function adequately. Many other counselors deal with clients earlier than the placement stage, and they would find more extensive computerized reports very helpful. GATB scores coupled with scores on the new Employment Service Interest Inventory will provide a very useful base for assisting clients to explore occupational possibilities in the *Guide to Occupational Exploration,* the *Occupational Outlook Handbook,* and the *Dictionary of Occupational Titles.* High school counselors can refer seniors not planning to pursue further education to employment service testing.

Otis-Lennon mental ability test

Authors: Arthur S. Otis and Roger T. Lennon

Date of publication: The current forms of this test were first published in 1967. The present test is a revision and modernization of widely used earlier tests, including some that are still in use such as the *Otis Quick-Scoring Mental Ability Test* and the *Otis Self-Administering Test of Mental Ability.* These, in turn, trace their lineage to the very beginning of group tests of mental ability in the United States.

Publisher: The Psychological Corporation, 757 Third Avenue, New York, NY 10017.

Description: The Otis-Lennon Mental Ability Test (OLMAT) has six levels, ranging from Primary I for kindergarten through to the Advanced level for grade 10 and above. For our purposes, we will be concerned only with the Intermediate and Advanced Levels, since these tests cover grades seven and upward. Two parallel forms exist at each level. The earliest form of the test was developed before theories of mental ability had been clearly formulated. More recent versions follow the Spearman g approach (Spearman, 1927). The test measures the so-called verbal-educational aspects of g by using items that sample verbal ability, numerical ability, abstract reasoning, and so on, and produces a single score. Both levels consist of eighty items arranged in a spiral omnibus format.

Parts: The OLMAT consists of a single part.

Time factor: The working time on the test is forty minutes, so total time including administration is usually not more than fifty minutes. Hand scoring either a booklet or answer sheet requires only a minute or two.

Norm groups: Raw scores can be translated to deviation IQ based on chronological age, with data provided to nearest quarter year. Deviation IQs can then be translated to percentile ranks and stanines based on age. Raw scores can also be translated directly to percentiles and stanines based on grade level, divided into half-year units.

Scoring system: The raw score is a sum of the right answers.

Appropriate groups: The OLMAT is appropriate for school-age individuals and adults for whom school-age norms are meaningful. This test is not appropriate for an individual whose educational, social, economic, and cultural background would clearly affect his or her results. Individuals whose age or grade places them in the lower range of one level and who might be expected to encounter difficulty with that level test can be given the next lower level test. Similarly, high-achieving individuals in the upper range of one level can be tested with the next higher level test.

Major advantages: The major advantages of the OLMAT include:

1. The test's long history attests to the recognition of its careful construction and norming. Those standards have been continued with the current forms.

2. Scores are available in deviation IQs, percentiles, or stanines, permitting comparisons that are most meaningful and useful.

3. The test is relatively brief, easily scored, and provides a good prediction of scholastic success.

Major disadvantages: It is difficult to criticize a test that has survived and prospered as long as the OLMAT and its antecedents. Some users will feel that grouping what appear to be different types of ability (verbal, numerical, spatial, and so forth) into a single score may conceal information that client and counselor would find helpful. Others will suggest that the relatively brief time limit may put undue emphasis on speed, although required time is comparable to other similar tests.

Summary: The OLMAT is a useful test when one wants an estimate of scholastic ability reflected in a single score and available in a minimum time. It is probably most useful for teachers, curriculum planners, and other school personnel who need information about the level and range of general ability in groups of students. Counselors sometimes encounter clients who have been away from the academic environment for several years and who now are considering a course in a vocational or trade school or similar setting, where the challenges of study and classroom appear frightening. They are likely to raise questions about their academic abilities and the chances for success. The OLMAT may provide sufficient information to answer questions of this kind.

Personality, temperament, and values instruments

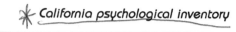 California psychological inventory

Author: Harrison G. Gough

Date of publication: The *California Psychological Inventory* (CPI) was originally published in 1957. It was revised in 1964, 1969, and 1975.

Publisher: Consulting Psychologists Press, Inc., 577 College Avenue, Palo Alto, CA 94306

Description: The CPI consists of 480 mostly self-descriptive items that the subject identifies as true or false. This test was developed in an effort "to use descriptive concepts which possess broad personal and social relevance" and "of devising brief, accurate, and dependable subscales for the identification and measurement of the variables." The 480 items yield eighteen standard scores grouped in four broad categories. Each scale is intended to forecast what a person will say or do in certain circumstances or to reflect how others familiar with the individual might describe him or her.

Scales: The eighteen scales of the CPI are divided into the four classes indicated below by Roman numerals:

I. Measures of poise, ascendancy, self-assurance, and interpersonal adequacy

   1. *Do—Dominance* measures factors of leadership ability, dominance, persistence, and social initiative. A high score suggests the person is aggressive, confident, outgoing, organized, and self-reliant. A low score describes a person who appears retiring, inhibited, indifferent, nonverbal, and lacking confidence.

   2. *Cs—Capacity for status* provides an index of the person's capacity to achieve or deal with status. A high score connotes an active, ambitious, forceful, insightful, resourceful, ascendant individual. A low score indicates an apathetic, shy, conventional, stereotyped, restricted person.

   3. *Sy—Sociability* identifies persons with outgoing, sociable, participative temperament. A high score implies a confident, enterprising, ingenious, outgoing, competitive

individual. A low score manifests awkwardness, conventionality, submissiveness, passivity, and suggestibility to reactions of others.

4. *Sp—Social presence* measures poise, spontaneity, and self-confidence in personal and social interaction. A high score demonstrates a clever, enthusiastic, imaginative, spontaneous, vigorous person. A low score denotes a deliberate, moderate, patient, self-restrained, indecisive, and unoriginal client.

5. *Sa—Self-acceptance* assesses sense of personal worth, self-acceptance, capacity for independent thinking. A high score reflects an intelligent, outspoken, cool, versatile, witty, self-confident person. A low score suggests a methodical, conservative, dependable, quiet, self-abasing, passive individual.

6. *Wb—Sense of well-being* identifies those who minimize worries, and are free of self-doubts and disillusionment. A high score indicates an ambitious, alert, versatile, and productive individual. A low score implies an unambitious, leisurely, cautious, conventional, apologetic, constricted person.

II. Measures of socialization, maturity, and responsibility

7. *Re—Responsibility* identifies people who are conscientious, responsible, and dependable in disposition and temperament. High scores denote individuals who are responsible, thorough, progressive, capable, independent, and dependable. Low scores reflect awkwardness, changeability, immaturity, moodiness, bias, and impulsiveness.

8. *So—Socialization* measures the degree of social maturity, probity, and rectitude attained by the person. High scores demonstrate honesty, industry, sincerity, modesty, and responsibility. Low scores manifest defensiveness, resentment, rebelliousness, undependability, deceitfulness, and ostentation.

9. *Sc—Self-control* indicates the degree of self-regulation and self-control possessed by the individual. High scores connote calmness, patience, practicality, self-approval, thoughtfulness, thoroughness, and conscientiousness. Low scores describe individuals who are impulsive, shrewd, excitable, irritable, uninhibited, and aggressive.

10. *To—Tolerance* identifies persons with permissive, accepting, nonjudgmental social beliefs and attitudes. High scores suggest enterprising, informal, quick, tolerant, clear-thinking, resourceful, broadly interested individuals. Low scores describe persons who are inhibited, aloof, wary,

judgmental, disbelieving, and distrustful in personal and social outlook.

11. *Gi—Good impression* identifies persons capable of creating a favorable impression and who are concerned about how others react to them. High scores indicate a cooperative, enterprising, outgoing, warm, helpful, diligent individual. Low scores connote an inhibited, shrewd, wary, resentful, distant, self-centered person.

12. *Cm—Communality* indicates the extent to which an individual's reactions and responses conform to the common pattern established for the CPI. High scores imply that the person is moderate, tactful, reliable, sincere, patient, steady, conscientious, and shows good judgment. Low scores manifest impatience, changeability, complexity, nervousness, restlessness, confusion, guile, forgetfulness, and inner conflict.

III. Measures of achievement potential and intellectual efficiency

13. *Ac—Achievement via conformance* identifies interest and motivation that facilitate achievement in situations requiring conformance. High scores denote a capable, cooperative, organized, responsible, stable, persistent, industrious person. Low scores demonstrate a coarse, stubborn, awkward, insecure, easily disorganized individual.

14. *Ai—Achievement via independence* identifies the interest and motivation that facilitate achievement in situations of autonomy and independence. High scores reflect maturity, forcefulness, dominance, foresightedness, independence, and self-reliance. Low scores reflect an inhibited, anxious, cautious, dissatisfied, submissive person.

15. *Ie—Intellectual efficiency* indicates the degree of personal and intellectual efficiency that the individual has developed. High scores describe the person who is efficient, clear-thinking, intelligent, progressive, thorough, alert, and well-informed. Low scores suggest confusion, caution, defensiveness, shallowness, lack of ambition, conventionality, and a lack of self-direction.

IV. Measures of intellectual and interest modes

16. *Py—Psychological mindedness* measures the extent to which the person is interested in and responds to the inner needs, motives, and experiences of others. High scores indicate an outgoing, spontaneous, quick, resourceful, changeable, fluent individual. Low scores imply an apathetic, serious, unassuming, deliberate, conforming person.

17. *Fx—Flexibility* measures the amount of flexibility and adaptability in a person's thinking and social behavior.

High scores denote a person who is insightful, informal, adventurous, humorous, rebellious, idealistic, assertive, sarcastic, and concerned with personal pleasure. Low scores reflect a person who is deliberate, worrying, industrious, guarded, methodical, rigid, formal, and deferential.

18. *Fe—Femininity* assesses the masculinity and femininity of interests. High scores describe individuals who are appreciative, patient, helpful, gentle, moderate, sincere, respectful, conscientious and sympathetic. Low scores imply a person who is hard-headed, ambitious, masculine, active, robust, opportunistic, blunt, and impatient.

Time factor: The manual states that testing time is usually about forty-five minutes to one hour. Because individual scoring stencils are used for each scale, hand scoring requires about ten minutes.

Norm groups: The profile chart for each sex is based on a large composite group including 6,200 males and 7,150 females. The group includes diversification by age, socioeconomic group, and geographic area, but is not purported to be a true random sample. Means and standard deviations for each scale obtained on nineteen male and eleven female occupational and educational groups are included in the manual. These groups provide some basis for comparison when the regular norm sample may be inappropriate or when one of the special groups is particularly pertinent.

Scoring system: The answer sheet is ordinarily scored by hand, using an overlay stencil for each scale. The score obtained for each scale is recorded in the indicated box at the bottom of the answer sheet. From this it is easily transferred to the appropriate side of the profile chart. Computer-scoring service is available but should probably only be used when large numbers of answer sheets must be scored.

Appropriate groups: The CPI appears to be appropriate for use with apparently normal individuals who are of high-school age or older.

Major advantages: The major advantages of the CPI include the following:

1. The test is very widely used, especially for counseling in academic settings.
2. A variety of forms is available for special needs. For example, a short form (Personal Values Abstract) requires about fifteen minutes to measure three scales. Translations of the test in four European languages are also available.
3. There is some research evidence supporting the appropriate use of the CPI across other cultures.
4. The manual is well-developed, with extensive information on validity, means, and standard deviations for many groups and a good explanatory section on interpretations.

5. The test includes three scales that are particularly useful in detecting faking or distortion.

Major disadvantages: The major disadvantages include:

1. Although most scales on the CPI have been empirically developed, there appears to be extensive overlap among many of the scales, and factor analysis suggests that only a few unique traits are actually being measured.
2. Research shows applicability across cultures but there is limited evidence supporting the use of the CPI with the ethnic minorities within this country.
3. Many of the data in the present manual, such as validity information, are the same as that appearing in the original manual over twenty years ago.
4. Although the test purports to measure "self-concept" traits and personality characteristics, interpretation of the test is difficult and probably requires more counselor skill than most paper-and-pencil personality inventories.

Summary: The CPI's very wide use suggests that many counselors find this a helpful and dependable personality inventory. It has been applied in a great many research studies (references in Buros' *Eighth Mental Measurement Yearbook* now approach 1400) and the results are available to test users. Cross-cultural validation confirms its value with a wide array of individuals in many diverse settings. The CPI is probably most appropriate for college clients.

Edwards personal preference schedule

Author: Allen L. Edwards

Date of publication: The *Edwards Personal Preference Schedule* (EPPS) was originally published in 1953. The manual was revised in 1959.

Publisher: The Psychological Corporation, 757 Third Avenue, New York, NY 10017

Description: The EPPS consists of 225 pairs of self-descriptive items that are presented in a forced-choice format, with the subject selecting the item that is more descriptive of self. Items in each pair are alleged to be matched for social desirability. The test uses as a theoretical base Murray's manifest need system; thus fifteen needs are presumably measured. Fifteen pairs of items are repeated as a measure of consistency.

Parts: The EPPS measures fifteen variables (or the degree to which the person feels the identified need) that are described in the manual as follows:

1. *ach Achievement:* To do one's best, to be successful, to accomplish tasks requiring skill and effort, to be a recognized authority, etc.

2. *def Deference:* To get suggestions from others, to find out what others think, to follow instructions and do what is expected, to praise others, to tell others that they have done a good job, etc.

3. *ord Order:* To have written work neat and organized, to make plans before starting on a difficult task, to have things organized, to keep things neat and orderly, etc.

4. *exh Exhibition:* To say witty and clever things, to tell amusing jokes and stories, to talk about personal adventures and experiences, to have others notice and comment on one's appearance, etc.

5. *aut Autonomy:* To be able to come and go as desired, to say what one thinks about things, to be independent of others in making decisions, to feel free to do what one wants, to do things that are unconventional, etc.

6. *aff Affiliation:* To be loyal to friends, to participate in friendly groups, to do things for friends, to form new friendships, to make as many friends as possible, etc.

7. *int Intraception:* To analyze one's motives and feelings, to observe others, to understand how others feel about problems, to put one's self in another's place, to judge people by why they do things rather than by what they do, etc.

8. *suc Succorance:* To have others provide help when in trouble, to seek encouragement from others, to have others be kindly, to have others be sympathetic and understanding about personal problems, etc.

9. *dom Dominance:* To argue for one's point of view, to be a leader in groups to which one belongs, to be regarded by others as a leader, to be elected or appointed chairman of committees, to make group decisions, etc.

10. *aba Abasement:* To feel guilty when one does something wrong, to accept blame when things do not go right, to feel that personal pain and misery suffered does more good than harm, to feel the need for punishment for wrong doing, etc.

11. *nur Nurturance:* To help friends when they are in trouble, to assist others less fortunate, to treat others with kindness and sympathy, to forgive others, to do small favors for others, etc.

12. *chg Change:* To do new and different things, to travel, to meet new people, to experience novelty and change in daily routine, to

experiment and try new things, to eat in new and different places, etc.

13. *end Endurance:* To keep at a job until it is finished, to complete any job undertaken, to work hard at a task, to keep at a puzzle or problem until it is solved, to work at a single job before taking on others, etc.

14. *het Heterosexuality:* To go out with members of the opposite sex, to engage in social activities with the opposite sex, to be in love with someone of the opposite sex, etc.

15. *agg Aggression:* To attack contrary points of view, to tell others what one thinks about them, to criticize others publicly, to make fun of others, to tell others off when disagreeing with them, etc.

Time factor: Most people can complete the EPPS in about forty-five minutes. Scoring and profiling can be completed in about five minutes.

Norm groups: The manual provides percentiles for college men based on a sample of 760, and college women based on 749 at various universities and colleges. A general adult sample of 4031 males and 4932 females obtained from a consumer purchase panel was used to establish percentiles for general adult men and women.

Scoring system: The EPPS is easily scored in two steps. First an overlay stencil is used to identify and mark the items that are repeated to provide the consistency score. Next, excluding the repeated pairs, the number of first-item selections (*a*s) are determined in each row of the answer sheet and recorded, and the number of second-item selections (*b*s) are determined in each column and appropriately recorded. These two tallies (first-row *a*s plus first-column *b*s, second-row *a*s plus second-column *b*s, etc.) are summed to produce the raw score for each trait. The consistency score is obtained by examining the two pairs identified by the template in each column and checking the box at the bottom of the column if the pairs are answered identically. The consistency score is the sum of the checkmarks. The profile chart appears on the reverse side of the answer sheet. Raw scores are easily transferred to the profile side, percentile equivalents are obtained from the appropriate table in the manual, and the percentile scores can be plotted on the chart.

Appropriate groups: The EPPS is suggested as appropriate for individuals of college age and older.

Major advantages: The major advantages of the EPPS include the following:

1. The test is based on a recognized personality theory.
2. Controlling social desirability for each pair of items reduces one major cause of falsification.
3. The test was originally developed for use with college students and appears to have adequate norms for this purpose.

4.   Including a consistency score provides additional information that is helpful in interpreting the other scores.
5.   The test is widely used for research purposes. The *Eighth Mental Measurement Yearbook* records 1640 references.
6.   The scores are ipsative because of the forced-choice format, and thus differences within the individual are revealed for use in counseling.

Major disadvantages: The major disadvantages of the EPPS include:

1.   The forced-choice format introduces problems in establishing validity that remain unanswered.
2.   The social desirability of the items was determined in a different format, so one cannot be certain that social desirability is really equated in forced-choice pairings.
3.   The scales appear to be interdependent and fakable.
4.   There is still little evidence that the scales predict socially important variables; thus, its use in counseling is restricted.
5.   Caution must be used in applying percentile ranks to ipsative scores. Many psychometrists consider this an inappropriate step.

Summary: The obvious advantages of a theoretically based personality inventory with controlled social desirability is largely cancelled by questions of validity, whether social desirability is really controlled, and the use of normative scores with ipsative responses. While the literature clearly underscores the wide use of the EPPS in research activities, its use in counseling is still questioned. It appears to be most useful in counseling if scores are kept as raw scores and used to help the client explore his or her areas of high and low response. It appears reasonable to expect such discussion to lead to clarification of insight and self-understanding. Thus questions can be explored such as "What kind of behaviors do I most often or least often choose?" and "How do I consistently picture myself?"

Guilford-Zimmerman temperament survey

Authors: J. P. Guilford, J. S. Guilford, and W. S. Zimmerman

Date of publication: First published in the present form in 1949 as a consolidation of earlier inventories (*Guilford-Martin Inventory of Factors (GAMIN), Guilford-Martin Personnel Inventory,* and *Inventory of Factors STDCR* that appeared as early as 1943.

Publisher: Sheridan Psychological Services, Inc., P.O. Box 6101, Orange, CA 92667

Description: The GZTS consists of 300 items measuring ten personality factors identified earlier by factor analysis. Individuals respond with a yes, question marks, or no to items that describe behavioral characteristics, attitudes, feelings, or emotional reactions. Items usually are stated in the form of "You do," "You are," "You would like," "You usually," and so on.

Parts: The *Guilford-Zimmerman Temperament Survey* (GZTS) provides scores for ten traits that are labeled with a word descriptive of the positive end of a continuum (M-F trait is scored according to the sex of the subject). The word representing the negative end of the continuum is given in parentheses in the following descriptions.

1. *G—General activity (Inactivity).* High scores suggest a rapid pace of activities, high energy and vitality, a tendency to remain active, a preference for speed, and enthusiasm. A low score implies the opposite type of characteristic: preference for a slower pace, tendency to tire easily, low output, and need for plenty of rest.

2. *R—Restraint (Impulsiveness).* A high score suggests a tendency toward being serious-minded, deliberate, persistent, and controlled. A low score describes a carefree, impulsive individual who prefers a lot of excitement.

3. *A—Ascendance (Submissiveness).* High scores imply self-defense, leadership, preference for persuasive activities and being conspicuous. Low scores suggest submissiveness, tendency to follow, reluctance to speak, and avoidance of conspicuousness.

4. *S—Sociability (Shyness).* High scores indicate a preference for many friends, an active conversationalist, and liking for social activities and social contacts. Low scores suggest a preference for a small circle of friends, minimal social activities and contacts, shyness, and avoidance of the limelight.

5. *E—Emotional stability (Emotional instability).* A high score describes an evenness of moods, cheerfulness, being self-composed, and feeling in good health. A low score indicates fluctuation of mood, pessimism, daydreaming, feeling in poor health, and loneliness.

6. *O—Objectivity (Subjectivity).* A high score implies not being sensitive or hurt by criticism. A low score denotes unusual sensitivity, self-centeredness, and suspiciousness.

7. *F—Friendliness (Hostility).* A high score reflects tolerance of hostile action, acceptance of domination, and respect for others. A low score indicates belligerence, resentment, desire to dominate, resistance to domination, and contempt for others.

8. *T—Thoughtfulness (Unreflectiveness).* A high score demonstrates reflectiveness, observation of the behavior of others, an

interest in thinking, a philosophical inclination, and mental poise. A low score manifests an interest in overt activity, mental disconcertedness, and unawareness of the behavior of others.

9. P—*Personal relations (Criticalness).* A high score connotes a tolerance for people, belief in social institutions, absence of suspicion and self-pity. A low score suggests a tendency to find fault, to be critical and suspicious of others and social institutions, and to engage in self-pity.

10. M—*Masculinity (Femininity).* This trait is scored with M the positive end for males and F the positive end for females. A high M score suggests an interest in masculine activities, being difficult to disgust, hard-boiled, resistant to fear, inhibited in emotional expression. A high F score indicates an interest in feminine activities, being easily disgusted, sympathetic, having romantic interests, and ability to express emotions.

Time factor: The test is untimed. Most individuals can complete it within forty-five minutes.

Norm groups: The profile chart provides norms based on "a fairly large sample of individuals mostly at the college level." The profile chart includes separate norms for males and females on the Ascendance, Masculinity, and Femininity scales. The manual provides means and standard deviations for males and females in high school and college groups for each trait. Additional normative data are included in an extensive, supplementary handbook.

Scoring system: Each of the ten traits is represented by thirty items arranged so that five traits are placed on each side of the answer sheet. Items are scored right if the response tends toward the positive end and wrong if it tends in the negative direction. The score is the number of right responses for each trait. The answer sheet is easily scored with two overlay stencils, and scoring and profiling requires only two or three minutes.

Appropriate groups: The GZTS is useful with adults in the general population and with college and high school students. One must bear in mind that the profile chart norms are basically derived from college students. There are additional norms in the *Handbook* for a number of special groups including such diverse bodies as drinking drivers, military personnel, various student specialties, managers, teachers, musicians, police officers, and others.

Major advantages: The principal advantages of the GZTS include the following:

1. The various traits carry titles in nonpsychological terms that are generally better understood and more acceptable to clients.

2. Test items are easily understood and do not include questions that might be considered offensive or prying.

3. The test is easily scored, requiring only two stencils, one for the front and one for the back of the answer sheet.

4. Because the test was constructed on a factor analytic basis, inter-correlations between the scales are generally low and one can be assured that the tested traits are relatively independent.

5. The factor analytic construction permits some indication of the presence of bias in test responses since it is very unlikely that all, or almost all, scores would be either elevated or depressed unless bias were operating.

6. The manual includes excellent statements describing the meaning of high and low scores for each scale.

Major disadvantages: The major disadvantages of the GZTS include:

1. The profile chart is based on a population that consisted mostly of college students. The manual includes means and standard deviations for male and female high school students and college students, showing some differences between the educational levels; thus, noncollege clients will face some distortion on the profile chart.

2. Like most personality inventories, correct interpretation is difficult and the counselor must use great care to maximize rapport with the client before administering the instrument as well as during interpretation of results.

Summary: The GZTS is a good personality inventory that can be used with so-called "normals" to help them gain insight into personal characteristics. Its use of nontechnical labels increases its value for answering client questions such as "Does my pattern of personality traits fit the requirements in that occupational field? Which of my traits appear to be the ones that I could capitalize on in choosing an occupational field? What kinds of positions best match my temperament traits?" It is not an appropriate instrument for diagnosing personality deviance and should not be used when the counselor suspects the presence of disabling personality problems.

Work values inventory

Author: Donald E. Super

Date of publication: 1968–1970

Publisher: Houghton Mifflin Company, One Beacon Street, Boston, MA 02107

Description: The *Work Values Inventory* (WVI) consists of forty-five self-reporting items to which the subject responds on a five-point Likert-type scale indicating the importance of the concept to him or her. The WVI measures fifteen values related to work. Values are described as related to interests but differ by being the qualities sought rather than the activities or objects that embody them. Therefore, values are more fundamental to this inventory than to others.

Parts: The WVI measures fifteen values that are named and briefly described in the manual as follows:

1. *Altruism.* Present in "work which enables one to contribute to the welfare of others."
2. *Esthetic.* Inherent in "work which permits one to make beautiful things and to contribute beauty to the world."
3. *Creativity.* Associated with "work which permits one to invent new things, design new products, or develop new ideas."
4. *Intellectual Stimulation.* Seen in "work which provides opportunity for independent thinking and for learning how and why things work."
5. *Achievement.* Connected with "work which gives one a feeling of accomplishment in doing a job well."
6. *Independence.* Related to "work which permits one to work in his own way, as fast or as slowly as he wishes."
7. *Prestige.* Linked with "work which gives one standing in the eyes of others and evokes respect."
8. *Management.* Associated with "work which permits one to plan and lay out work for others to do."
9. *Economic Returns.* Connected with "work which pays well and enables one to have the things he wants."
10. *Security.* Present in "work which provides one with the certainty of having a job even in hard times."
11. *Surroundings.* Inherent in "work which is carried out under pleasant conditions—not too hot or too cold, noisy, dirty, etc."
12. *Supervisory Relations.* Seen in "work which is carried out under a supervisor who is fair and with whom one can get along."
13. *Associates.* Characterized by "work which brings one into contact with fellow workers whom he likes."
14. *Way of Life.* Linked with "work that permits one to live the kind of life he chooses and to be the type of person he wishes to be."
15. *Variety.* Related to "work that provides an opportunity to do different types of jobs."

Time factor: Most people can complete the WVI within fifteen minutes. Hand scoring can be completed in two to three minutes.

Norm groups: Percentile norms are provided by sex for each grade level for grades seven through twelve. The norms are based on fairly large groups, the smallest one being 672 twelfth-grade boys. In addition, means and standard deviations for each value are provided for an array of occupational groups.

Scoring system: Although the test booklets are designed for machine scoring, hand scoring is very easy as one need only ascertain the sum of weights for three items for each of the fifteen values. These weights range from a minimum sum of three to a maximum of fifteen for each value. These can be translated to percentiles by using the appropriate chart in the manual.

Appropriate groups: The manual states that the WVI may be used with junior high school students and anyone older who has completed at least an elementary education. Vocabulary is at the seventh-grade level.

Major advantages: The principal advantages of the WVI include the following:

1. The WVI does appear to measure characteristics that differ from interests—perhaps, as the manual suggests, traits that are more basic.

2. There is some evidence that work values tend to remain fairly constant so that twelfth-grade norms may be appropriate for adults.

3. Even though there is obvious overlap and intercorrelation, factor analysis shows at least four dimensions being measured by the WVI.

4. The vocabulary is relatively easy, yet the instrument is applicable to a wide age range.

5. Reliability appears to be adequate for three-item tests and there appears to be some evidence of concurrent validity.

Major disadvantages: Limitations of the WVI include:

1. The manual provides no information about predictive validity so there is, as yet, no way to judge if the results are useful.

2. The reliability information is based on a small group of tenth-grade students. Data based on a larger and more diverse group would be reassuring.

3. Some of the data included in the manual have been based on earlier versions of the WVI. It is not clear that all data are totally relevant to the present form.

4. The items are very transparent and are easily faked; therefore, the counselor must be certain that rapport and trust have been established.

Summary: The WVI easily and quickly provides information about a client that is not conveniently available from other instruments or sources. It can help the client develop self-understanding that explains other behavior such as interests, work preferences, and goals, which will contribute to better career planning. Probably, the instrument is just as useful when only raw scores are considered and when attention is given only to those areas where high and low scores have been reported.

Selecting tests

The tests that we have examined are representative of those used by counselors who assist typical clients in the career choice process. Few counselors would find sufficient depth in this brief list to provide feedback for all questions raised by clients in that process. Every counselor will find additional tests useful, and will expand his or her repertoire according to the work setting and type of clientele served.

Counselors employed in secondary school settings will usually be involved in the testing program that the school system regularly uses to assess all students periodically. Because the school system is concerned with identifying student needs in order to plan curricular experiences, or monitoring student progress in order to evaluate teaching and learning activities, school testing programs often are heavily loaded with ability and achievement tests. The information provided by these tests is helpful in expanding student self-understanding and often may be a more accurate assessment of student ability and potential than the grades recorded on the student's transcript. The existence of such information, usually obtained every two or three years, will frequently make unnecessary any additional testing of ability or achievement.

Individuals with special learning problems or other nontypical needs require assessment by different types of tests. A broad array of instruments for use with these students already exists. Again, detailed testing information may already be a part of the school record. When adequate test data are not available, the counselor must exercise considerable caution and care in selecting tests to use with clients who have special problems. Often it will be advisable to consult with the special education teacher, the school psychologist, or other personnel who are involved in the educational program for special students.

The personality tests that we have examined are of limited value in diagnosing special problems or personality disorders. Instead, those included have been developed for use with individuals who can best be described as normal. If the counselor begins to develop data suggesting that the client has problems that exceed the usual boundaries of normalcy, a referral to a competent therapist is appropriate.

Further consideration to testing problems with clients whose characteristics place them in groups that appear to differ from the usual will be given in a later chapter. Here we have been primarily concerned with the client who fits the usually broad and generally undefined adjective of "normal."

Interpreting test data

If the counselor has included testing in the career counseling process, this has been done to obtain information that will assist the client in answering questions about self, and thus to develop a more complete and accurate self-understanding. Reporting test results to the client should be accomplished in a way that keeps the attention of both counselor and client focused on that goal. It may be advantageous to review together those questions or uncertainties, identified earlier, that led to the use of tests to obtain supplementary information.

The counselor ordinarily adopts a teaching role as attention is turned to consideration of test results. He or she assumes that client familiarity with the psychometric world is limited and consequently may include misconceptions, perhaps unrealistic expectations or concerns. The immediate, short-term goal probably is to help the client understand enough about tests and the testing process so that his or her comprehension of the results will be accurate and useful. Test results, by themselves, are meaningless to most clients and may induce unnecessary concern or invalid assumptions; on the other hand, the client usually does not need to know everything the counselor has learned about tests in his or her professional career.

Most clients are likely to be unfamiliar with terms such as *percentile, stanine, standard score,* or *norm group.* "Percentile" is especially susceptible to misunderstanding, probably because so many spelling and arithmetic lessons in elementary school were graded on the basis of percentage of correct answers. Even general terms such as *reliability, scholastic ability,* and *temperament* take on special meaning when used in a psychometric frame of reference. If any technical terms are to be used to explain test results, clients must first understand what those terms mean in the context in which they are being applied. Ordinarily, professional jargon is unnecessary because one important counselor skill is the ability to communicate effectively with a client by using the client's language and terminology.

Additional communication problems may arise if the counselor uses profile charts or graphs to illustrate test results. These also must be reviewed for terminology that can be misleading or misunderstood. Further, unspoken implications can confuse the client, for example, if a bar graph based on a meaningless zero-point is used rather than a bar graph based on the midpoint of the appropriate norm group. Some of the personality instruments use titles for test scales that may be psychologically loaded for some clients—for example, dominance, masculinity, exhibition, and other words. Others use initials or abbreviations that sometimes arouse needless curiosity or concern. Nevertheless, profile charts are generally helpful since they assist the client in visualizing the information that is being transmitted verbally.

As test results are explained, the counselor can help the client internalize and understand their meaning if the data can be related to what is already known about the client. Items that are particularly useful are comments that the client has made about self in earlier sessions or on personal data forms, or observations made by the counselor. The objective is to provide the client with information that relates to the bigger picture and helps the client see that picture more clearly and use that additional insight in resolving the present problem. Client comments, degree of animation, body language, facial expression, and similar signs will reveal the extent to which the client is accepting and comprehending the information. Providing frequent opportunities for the client to react and talk will also help the assimilation process. Asking the client to summarize occasionally allows feedback that demonstrates the extent to which the client can organize and use the data in his or her framework.

Discussing test information may lead to the identification of some data that may appear to require further validation or substantiation. This is more likely to be necessary if the questioned results seem to be crucial to the decision facing the client. Sometimes areas for additional investigation arise because of unexpected test results—a flat profile on an interest inventory, for example, may raise questions as to whether these scores truly reflect the client and, if so, why? This result may suggest exploring areas of personality and self-concept. It may imply that an inappropriate interest inventory was administered, or even that this one was incorrectly marked or scored. It may also suggest to the client something that he or she wants to explore further. Questions then may arise about how the results can be confirmed or validated. Several possibilities may be readily apparent, such as reading appropriate materials, retesting with a different instrument, various exercises or workbook programs, discussion with other individuals such as friends or instructors, tryout explorations, or other activities.

The counselor may move back and forth from counseling role to teaching role and back to counselor role again as test results are considered. This movement is easily accomplished, rarely confusing to the client, and need not be philosophically distressing to the counselor. Although some counselors feel that they can only maintain a counseling role, such rigidity may result in disservice to a client whose need to know information may momentarily require a teacher-learner relationship. The confident and able counselor has sufficient flexibility to make these short-term role changes without damage to the basic counseling relationship and without building an undesirable and unnecessary dependence.

In this chapter we have considered the importance of information about self in the decision-making process. We have also explored ways by which clients and counselors can identify areas where information is needed. We looked at a variety of ways by which clients might obtain a more complete picture of self, including the discussion of a representative group of assessment instruments frequently used by counselors. Finally, we have considered briefly some of the problems encountered in discussing test results with clients.

REFERENCES

Anastasi, A. *Psychological testing.* 4th edition. New York: Macmillan Co., 1976.
Buros, O. K. (ed.). *The eighth mental measurement yearbook.* Highland Park, N.J.: Gryphon Press, 1978.

Campbell, D. P. *Manual for the SVIB-SCII Strong-Campbell Interest Inventory.* 2nd edition. Stanford, Cal.: Stanford University Press, 1978.

Cottle, W. C. and Downie, N. M. *Procedures and preparation for counseling.* Englewood Cliffs, N.J.: Prentice-Hall, Inc., 1960, p. 164.

Crites, J. O. Career counseling: A comprehensive approach. *The Counseling Psychologist,* 1976, *6,* 3, 2–12, p. 4.

———. *Career counseling: Models, methods, and materials.* New York: McGraw-Hill Book Company, 1981, pp. 174ff.

Cronbach, L. J. *Essentials of psychological testing.* 3rd edition. New York: Harper & Row, Publishers, 1970.

Goldman, L. *Using tests in counseling.* Revised edition. New York: Appleton-Century-Crofts, 1971.

Grummon, D. L. Client-centered theory. In B. Stefflre and W. H. Grant (eds.), *Theories of counseling.* 2nd edition. New York: McGraw-Hill Book Company, 1972, pp. 73–135.

Hansen, J. C., Stevic, R. R. and Warner, R. W., Jr. *Counseling theory and process.* 2nd edition. Boston: Allyn and Bacon, Inc., 1977.

Herr, E. L. and Cramer, S. H. *Career guidance through the life span.* 2nd edition. Boston: Little, Brown and Company, 1984.

Janis, I. L. and Mann, L. *Decision making.* New York: Free Press, 1977.

Kapes, J. T. and Mastie, M. M. (eds.). *A counselor's guide to vocational guidance instruments.* Falls Church, Vir.: National Vocational Guidance Association, 1982.

Meehl, P. E. *Clinical versus statistical prediction.* Minneapolis: University of Minnesota Press, 1954.

Patterson, C. H. Counseling: Self-clarification and the helping relationship. In H. Borow (ed.), *Man in a world at work.* Boston: Houghton Mifflin Company, 1964, pp. 434–459.

Remer, P. and O'Neill, C. Clients as change agents: What color could my parachute be? *Personnel and Guidance Journal,* 1980, 58, 425–429.

Shertzer, B. E. and Linden, J. D. *Fundamentals of individual appraisal.* Boston: Houghton Mifflin Company, 1979.

Shertzer, B. E. and Stone, S. C. *Fundamentals of guidance.* 3rd edition. Boston: Houghton Mifflin Company, 1976, pp. 245–277.

Spearman, C. *The abilities of man.* New York: Macmillan Co., 1927.

Super, D. E. Testing and using test results in counseling. *Occupations,* 1950, 29, 95–97.

Super, D. E. and Crites, J. O. *Appraising vocational fitness.* Rev. ed. New York: Harper & Row, Publishers, 1962.

Zunker, V. G. *Using assessment results in career counseling.* Monterey, Cal.: Brooks/Cole Publishing Company, 1982.

8

The world of work

Counseling requires the counselor to identify properly and respond appropriately to feelings, thoughts, attitudes, and behaviors expressed by the client, and to assist the client in developing desired and suitable behavior that reflects the increased understanding and insight resulting from counseling. When we focus on career counseling, the counselor is also required to be competent in assisting the client to acquire, process, and apply information and skills needed in effective career decision making and subsequent implementation of career plans. Specifically, "information" includes relevant data about the world of work and all its aspects.

The counselor who expects the client to suggest all the occupations he or she might want to consider is somewhat analogous to the physician who treats patients only on the basis of patient self-diagnosis, or the lawyer who specifies that clients are expected to develop their own legal defense. Such an approach drastically reduces the value of professional assistance, in some cases even removing the need for consulting the specialist. The career counselor who is to be most useful to the client not only must assist in the self-appraisal process, as discussed in the previous chapter, but also must aid the client in understanding the world of work in sufficient detail that counselor and client can develop an expanded list of occupational alternatives. Later, the counselor will help in acquiring and evaluating information about those opportunities in sufficient detail and relevance to the client so that the list can be narrowed ultimately to the best choice and a small number of fall-back possibilities.

The counselor's competency in the career area is at least two-fold. First, the counselor must have a fairly thorough general understanding of the world of work, including the occupations of which it consists; how these differ from one another as well as how they are related; how they can be grouped in families or clusters; what they require of workers; what rewards they offer; and so forth. Second, the counselor must know sources of information and appropriate techniques that can help the client develop a significant list of suitable occupations and subsequently identify the best options in that array. In this chapter, we will survey the general structure of the world of work, its anticipated changes, and some of the available types and sources of information. Chapter 9 will include a discussion of how clients can be helped to expand alternatives and narrow options.

The counselor who desires more depth than can be included in this brief chapter has several usable resources. The most prolific source of current, reliable data about the world of work is the United States Department of Labor. Several of its subordinate agencies are specifically charged with the tasks of collecting and disseminating facts about jobs, employment, wages, hours, and other work-related material. Particularly helpful for counselors are such publications as *Monthly Labor Review, Occupational Outlook Quarterly, Dictionary of Occupational Titles, Guide for Occupational Exploration,* and the *Occupational Outlook Handbook.* Discussions of the use of these and similar materials can be found in Fredrikson (1982), Hoppock (1976), Isaacson (1977), and Norris et al. (1979).

STRUCTURE OF THE WORLD OF WORK

The world of work is a dynamic, constantly changing system. Some of the changes that influence occupational opportunity occur in the short run and their impact soon disappears. Other factors, however, exert pressure over a long period, producing an influence that lasts for decades. One example of this enduring type of change can be seen in population changes such as reduction in the birth rate. Such a factor not only influences the number of workers available in the future, but also modifies the demand for products and services in terms of both type and quantity. Population factors that deserve attention include changes in size, changes in the age structure, and geographic distribution within the country.

The population of the United States increased rapidly in the "baby boom" years following World War II. For example, between 1945 and 1960 the average annual increase was about 1.7 percent. During the 1960s this figure declined, and through the decade of the 1970s held fairly constant at about .8 percent. Bureau of the Census estimates anticipate little change in this figure during the 1980s, perhaps increasing only to .9 percent annual increase.

The high birth rate of 1945–1960, followed by the much lower rate beginning in the 1960s, has a heavy impact on the present nature of the labor force. The most striking feature is the sharp decline in the number of individuals aged sixteen to twenty-four—the age group that includes most of the entrants into the labor force. Other factors, more difficult to quantify, can influence the available number of workers. While the number of individuals of a given age can be identified accurately long before they reach working age, it is harder to estimate the impact of such factors as fertility rates (changes in this factor not only influence future population size, but also affect women's participation in the labor force), changes in attitude toward women's involvement in work outside the home (if recent increases in participation by women ages twenty-five to twenty-nine were projected ahead, their participation in the work force would exceed that of similarly aged men before 1990), economic opportunity, still-existent remnants of discrimination based on race, sex or age, and such imponderables as inflation rates, desire for extended schooling, increased or decreased adequacy of retirement programs, and so on.

Because of uncertainties such as these, Bureau of Labor Statistics projections are often developed with three possible paths or scenarios. One of these is usually based on a conservative approach, assuming that the combination of factors will produce a low-growth factor. A second approach takes an optimistic outlook, suggesting that the interaction of factors will produce a high-growth pattern; the third, middle-of-the-road approach assumes a moderate or intermediate growth pattern. Another way to view these three paths is to view the first two as setting the minimum and maximum limits, with the third pattern suggesting the most likely figures if all other things are equal. Table 8–1 shows the projected civilian labor force for 1995 using the three growth rate predictions. These data are from *Monthly Labor Review, Nov. 1983*, prepared by the Bureau of Labor Statistics.

All three of the projected patterns shown in Table 8–1 use certain common assumptions. These include further rises in the labor force participation by teenagers, continued increase in participation by women, and further declines in participation by older workers. Table 8–2 shows the civilian labor force broken down according to sex, age, and race as actually distributed in 1970, 1980, and 1982 and as projected for 1990 and 1995. The intermediate growth pattern assumes that participation by men will decrease slightly, dropping from 76.6 percent in 1982 to 76.1 percent in 1995. Further, teenage men will increase their participation during that period from 56.7 percent to 62.9 percent. Women's involvement in the labor force is predicted to continue rapidly for a time, then slow gradually

TABLE 8—1   Projections of the civilian labor force in 1995, by alternative demographic scenarios

Labor group	Labor force (in thousands)			Participation rate		
	High scenario	Middle scenario	Low scenario	High scenario	Middle scenario	Low scenario
Total, age 16 and over	140,973	131,387	125,058	72.7	67.8	64.5
Men	73,005	69,970	67,541	79.4	76.1	73.5
16 to 24	11,321	10,573	10,013	79.8	74.5	70.6
25 to 54	52,545	51,358	50,130	95.5	93.4	91.2
55 and over	9,139	8,039	7,398	40.1	35.3	32.5
Women	67,968	61,417	57,517	66.7	60.3	56.5
16 to 24	11,155	10,557	9,792	75.7	71.6	66.4
25 to 54	49,525	44,852	41,964	86.9	78.7	73.6
55 and over	7,288	6,008	5,761	24.2	19.9	19.1
White	119,560	112,393	107,170	72.5	68.1	65.0
Men	62,451	60,757	58,839	79.2	77.0	74.6
16 to 24	9,463	9,271	8,755	80.8	79.1	74.7
25 to 54	44,815	44,232	43,406	95.7	94.5	92.7
55 and over	8,173	7,254	6,678	40.2	35.6	32.8
Women	57,109	51,636	48,331	66.4	60.0	56.2
16 to 24	9,330	9,025	8,316	77.9	75.4	69.5
25 to 54	41,384	37,433	35,097	87.0	78.7	73.8
55 and over	6,395	5,178	4,918	24.1	19.5	18.6
Black and other	21,413	18,994	17,889	74.8	65.1	61.9
Men	10,554	9,213	8,709	80.0	70.2	66.7
16 to 24	1,858	1,302	1,253	75.9	52.7	50.9
25 to 54	7,730	7,126	6,725	94.6	87.1	82.3
55 and over	966	785	722	40.3	32.8	29.9
Women	10,859	9,781	9,182	68.7	61.2	58.0
16 to 24	1,825	1,532	1,471	65.7	55.4	53.2
25 to 54	8,141	7,419	6,863	86.8	78.7	72.9
55 and over	893	830	847	24.5	22.9	23.1
Black	16,517	14,833	13,984	72.5	65.6	61.7
Men	8,125	7,297	6,775	79.4	70.7	66.4
16 to 24	1,432	1,055	984	73.9	54.3	50.4
25 to 54	5,974	5,549	5,246	93.4	87.1	82.2
55 and over	719	583	549	38.2	31.0	29.1
Women	8,392	7,646	7,217	67.0	61.7	57.8
16 to 24	1,407	1,180	1,148	63.8	53.8	51.8
25 to 54	6,311	5,805	5,413	85.7	78.1	73.2
55 and over	674	661	650	23.6	22.3	22.7

Source: Fullerton, H. N., Jr. and Tschetter, J. The 1995 labor force: a second look. *Monthly Labor Review*, 1983, *106*, 11, p. 8.

TABLE 8–2 Civilian labor force, by sex, age, and race, 1970–82, and middle growth projection to 1995

	Labor force (in thousands)					Participation rate				
Labor group	1970	1980	1982	1990	1995	1970	1980	1982	1990	1995
Total, age 16 and over	82,771	106,940	110,204	124,951	131,387	60.4	63.8	64.0	66.9	67.8
Men	51,228	61,453	62,450	67,701	69,970	79.7	77.4	76.6	76.5	76.1
16 to 24	9,725	13,606	13,074	11,274	10,573	69.4	74.4	72.6	74.7	74.5
16 to 19	4,008	4,999	4,470	4,123	4,043	56.1	60.5	56.7	62.3	62.9
20 to 24	5,717	8,607	8,604	7,151	6,530	83.3	85.9	84.9	84.4	84.1
25 to 54	32,213	38,712	40,357	48,180	51,358	95.8	94.2	94.0	93.8	93.4
25 to 34	11,327	16,971	17,793	19,569	18,105	96.4	95.2	94.7	93.7	93.1
35 to 44	10,469	11,836	12,781	17,469	19,446	96.9	95.5	95.3	95.6	95.3
45 to 54	10,417	9,905	9,784	11,142	13,807	94.3	91.2	91.2	91.3	91.1
55 and over	9,291	9,135	9,019	8,247	8,039	55.7	45.6	43.8	37.4	35.3
55 to 64	7,126	7,242	7,174	6,419	6,311	83.0	72.1	70.2	65.5	64.5
65 and over	2,165	1,893	1,845	1,828	1,728	26.8	19.0	17.8	14.9	13.3
Women	31,543	45,487	47,755	57,250	61,417	43.3	51.5	52.6	58.3	60.3
16 to 24	8,121	11,696	11,533	10,813	10,557	51.3	61.9	62.0	69.1	71.6
16 to 19	3,241	4,381	4,056	3,778	3,761	44.0	52.9	51.4	56.8	58.2
20 to 24	4,880	7,315	7,477	7,035	6,796	57.7	68.9	69.8	78.1	82.0
25 to 54	18,208	27,888	30,149	40,496	44,852	50.1	64.0	66.3	75.6	78.7
25 to 34	5,708	12,257	13,393	16,804	16,300	45.0	65.5	68.0	78.1	81.7
35 to 44	5,968	8,627	9,651	14,974	17,427	51.1	65.5	68.0	78.6	82.8
45 to 54	6,532	7,004	7,105	8,718	11,125	54.4	59.9	61.6	67.1	69.5
55 and over	5,213	5,904	6,073	5,941	6,008	25.3	22.8	22.7	20.5	19.9
55 to 64	4,157	4,742	4,888	4,612	4,671	43.0	41.3	41.8	41.5	42.5
65 and over	1,056	1,161	1,185	1,329	1,337	9.7	8.1	7.9	7.4	7.0

(continued)

TABLE 8–2 continued

Labor group	Labor force (in thousands)					Participation rate				
	1970	1980	1982	1990	1995	1970	1980	1982	1990	1995
White	73,556	93,600	96,143	107,734	112,393	60.2	64.1	64.3	67.3	68.1
Men	46,035	54,473	55,133	59,201	60,757	80.0	78.2	77.4	77.4	77.0
16 to 24	8,540	11,902	11,371	9,854	9,271	70.2	76.7	74.9	78.5	79.1
25 to 54	29,000	34,224	35,565	41,864	44,232	96.3	95.0	94.9	94.8	94.5
55 and over	8,494	8,345	8,197	7,483	7,254	55.8	46.1	44.2	37.8	35.6
Women	27,521	39,127	41,010	48,533	51,636	42.6	51.2	52.4	58.1	60.0
16 to 24	7,141	10,179	10,013	9,285	9,025	52.1	64.4	64.7	72.5	75.4
25 to 54	15,690	23,723	25,619	34,081	37,433	48.9	63.4	66.1	75.6	78.7
55 and over	4,690	5,226	5,378	5,167	5,178	24.9	22.4	22.4	20.1	19.5
Black and other	9,218	13,340	14,062	17,217	18,994	61.8	61.7	61.6	64.8	65.7
Men	5,194	6,980	7,317	8,500	9,213	76.5	71.5	71.0	71.0	70.6
16 to 24	1,185	1,702	1,702	1,420	1,302	64.5	61.6	60.0	55.9	52.7
25 to 54	3,212	4,488	4,792	6,316	7,126	91.9	88.6	88.0	87.6	87.2
55 and over	796	790	822	764	785	54.7	40.8	40.5	34.3	32.6
Women	4,024	6,359	6,745	8,717	9,781	49.5	53.6	53.9	59.7	61.7
16 to 24	982	1,516	1,520	1,528	1,532	46.3	49.3	48.8	53.7	55.3
25 to 54	2,517	4,164	4,529	6,415	7,419	59.2	67.0	67.9	75.8	78.7
55 and over	524	678	695	774	830	30.0	26.4	25.5	23.5	22.8

Source: Fullerton, H. N., Jr. and Tschetter, J. The 1995 labor force: a second look. Monthly Labor Review, 1983, 106, 11, p. 5.

to a moderate rate of increase, showing 52.6 percent participation in 1982, 58.3 percent in 1990, and 60.3 percent by 1995. Participation of older workers would continue to decline in the labor force but at a slower pace than shown over the 1970–1982 period. The rate of working men over fifty-five is expected to drop from 43.8 percent in 1982 to 35.3 percent in 1995, and that of women over 55 to drop from 22.7 percent to 19.9 percent in that same period. Recent changes in mandatory retirement practices may change these figures somewhat. Finally, it is expected that overall participation by whites will grow faster than participation by blacks and others.

The high-growth pattern accords greater weight to a continuing rapid increase in participation in the labor force by women; a halt in the downward trend for men; a reversal in participation rates by black men that would lead to convergence with rates for white men by the year 2000; and no decrease in participation by workers age sixty-five or over. The low-growth pattern assumes that the decrease of participation of adult men will continue; fertility rates will rise, causing a slowdown of participation rates of women; participation of older workers will continue to decrease; and the participation rate of teenagers will slow.

The decline in rates of workers ages sixteen to twenty-four and the increase of workers ages twenty-five to fifty-four, caused by the baby boom of the 1950s and the declining birth rates in the 1960s and after, is shown in Figure 8–1. These data are from the *Occupational Outlook Handbook, 1980–81* and support the information included in Table 8–2.

FIGURE 8–1 Through the 1980s, the number of workers in the prime working ages will grow dramatically. (*Source:* Bureau of Labor Statistics.)

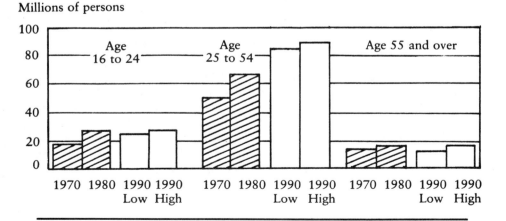

Millions of persons

Industrial sectors

Another way to view the world of work is to consider the various industrial sectors that collectively constitute it. Economists and others think of the world of work in terms of two broad categories: goods-producing and service-producing activities. These two areas in turn are divided into nine industrial sectors. *Goods-producing sectors* include agriculture, mining and petroleum, construction, and manufacturing. *Service-producing sectors* include government; wholesale and retail trade; services; transportation, communication, and public utilities; and finance, insurance, and real estate. The nine sectors are subdivided into industries where even finer subdivisions can be made. For example, the agricultural sector is thought to consist of dairy and poultry products, meat animals and livestock, cotton, food and feed grains, and other agricultural products. The trade sector is divided into two parts, wholesale and retail. Within each of these industries can be found the myriad sets of tasks that are called *occupations*. Table 8–3 reports employment figures for these various sectors for 1959, 1969, 1979, and 1982, and shows estimates of these figures for 1990, and 1995. The largest fields—manufacturing, wholesale and retail trade, and services—are expected to increase by four, six, and nine million workers respectively from 1982 to 1995. Except for agriculture, which is expected to decline, the other industrial sectors are anticipated to show modest growth.

More rapid growth and decline can be seen in different occupational groups within the various industries. Comparisons can be made in two different ways, sometimes producing what appear to be contradictory data. Table 8–4 lists the occupations that are expected to show the largest job growth between 1982 and 1995 in actual numbers of new jobs created. Because many of the occupations on the list already involve very large numbers of workers, the percentage change, in many cases, appears to be quite modest. Tables 8–5 and 8–6 list those occupations expected to show the fastest rate of growth and decline in percentage figures. If the number of workers in the occupational group is quite small it can double and still be relatively small when compared with occupations with very large numbers of workers.

In the next few pages we will briefly consider each of the major industrial sectors as they are listed in Table 8–3. A widely used system for grouping industries is called the Standard Industrial Classification System (SICS) (U.S. Office of Management and Budget, 1972). This system has ten major divisions that in turn are divided into eighty-four classifications that include specific industries. The ten major industrial sectors, slightly rearranged and regrouped in Table 8–3, include the following:

A   Agriculture, forestry, and fishing
B   Mining
C   Construction

TABLE 8–3 Actual and projected employment by major sectors, 1959–95

| | | | | | Employment (in thousands) | | | | | |
| | | | | | 1990 | | | 1995 | | |
Sector	1959	1969	1979	1982	Low	Moderate	High	Low	Moderate	High
Total	67,705	82,401	102,211	102,315	116,943	118,315	119,399	125,251	127,563	130,299
Farm	5,491	3,495	2,861	2,815	2,630	2,652	2,672	2,500	2,550	2,595
Nonfarm	62,214	78,906	99,350	99,500	114,313	115,663	116,727	122,751	125,013	127,704
Government	8,083	12,195	15,947	15,803	16,830	16,750	17,060	17,180	17,230	17,760
Federal	2,233	2,758	2,773	2,739	3,202	2,989	3,096	3,163	2,960	3,139
State and local	5,850	9,437	13,174	13,064	13,628	13,761	13,964	14,017	14,270	14,621
Private	54,131	66,711	83,403	83,697	97,483	98,913	99,667	105,571	107,783	109,944
Mining	612	501	704	742	775	781	760	842	864	844
Construction	3,825	4,386	5,903	5,491	7,020	6,963	7,052	7,798	7,925	8,004
Manufacturing	16,985	20,469	21,406	19,234	21,686	22,236	22,635	22,963	23,491	24,132
Durable	9,560	12,081	12,989	11,326	13,218	13,550	13,871	14,266	14,496	14,965
Nondurable	7,425	8,388	8,417	7,908	8,468	8,686	8,764	8,696	8,995	9,167
Transportation and public utilities	4,304	4,718	5,534	5,543	6,152	6,202	6,287	6,488	6,637	6,746
Trade	13,245	16,704	22,352	22,536	25,885	26,355	26,649	27,764	28,545	28,859
Finance, insurance, and real estate	2,923	3,864	5,523	5,899	7,021	7,113	6,667	7,607	7,685	7,788
Services	9,663	13,747	20,258	22,617	27,501	27,863	28,225	30,814	31,290	32,203
Private households	2,574	2,322	1,723	1,635	1,443	1,400	1,392	1,295	1,346	1,368

(continued)

TABLE 8–3 continued

Sector	1959	1969	1979	1982	1990 Low	1990 Moderate	1990 High	1995 Low	1995 Moderate	1995 High
					Percent distribution					
Total	100.0	100.0	100.0	100.0	100.0	100.0	100.0	100.0	100.0	100.0
Farm	8.1	4.2	2.8	2.8	2.2	2.2	2.2	2.0	2.0	2.0
Nonfarm	91.9	95.8	97.2	97.2	97.8	97.8	97.8	98.0	98.0	98.0
Government	11.9	14.8	15.6	15.4	14.4	14.2	14.3	13.7	13.5	13.6
Federal	3.3	3.3	2.7	2.7	2.7	2.5	2.6	2.5	2.3	2.4
State and local	8.6	11.5	12.9	12.8	11.7	11.6	11.7	11.2	11.2	11.2
Private	80.0	81.0	81.6	81.8	83.4	83.6	83.5	84.3	84.5	84.4
Mining	.9	.6	.7	.7	.7	.7	.6	.7	.7	.6
Construction	5.6	5.3	5.8	5.4	6.0	5.9	5.9	6.2	6.2	6.1
Manufacturing	25.1	24.8	20.9	18.8	18.5	18.8	19.0	18.3	18.4	18.5
Durable	14.1	14.7	12.7	11.1	11.3	11.5	11.6	11.4	11.4	11.5
Nondurable	11.0	10.2	8.2	7.7	7.2	7.3	7.3	6.9	7.1	7.0
Transportation and public utilities	6.4	5.7	5.4	5.4	5.3	5.2	5.3	5.2	5.2	5.2
Trade	19.6	20.3	21.9	22.0	22.1	22.3	22.3	22.2	22.4	22.1
Finance, insurance, and real estate	4.3	4.7	5.4	5.8	6.0	6.0	5.6	6.1	6.0	6.0
Services	14.3	16.7	19.8	22.1	23.5	23.5	23.6	24.6	24.5	24.7
Private households	3.8	2.8	1.7	1.6	1.2	1.2	1.2	1.0	1.1	1.0

Average annual rate of change

	1959–69	1969–79	1979–82	1982–90			1990–95			1982–95		
				Low	Moderate	High	Low	Moderate	High	Low	Moderate	High
Total	2.0	2.2	.0	1.7	1.8	1.9	1.4	1.5	1.8	1.6	1.7	1.9
Farm	-4.4	-2.0	-.5	-.8	-.7	-.6	-1.0	-.8	-.6	-.9	-.8	-.6
Nonfarm	2.4	2.3	.1	1.7	1.9	2.0	1.4	1.6	1.8	1.6	1.8	1.9
Government	4.2	2.7	-.3	.8	.7	1.0	.4	.6	.8	.6	.7	.9
Federal	2.1	.1	-.4	2.0	1.1	1.5	-.2	-.2	.3	1.1	.6	1.1
State and local	4.9	3.4	-.3	.5	.7	.8	.6	.7	.9	.5	.7	.9
Private	2.1	2.3	.1	1.9	2.1	2.2	1.6	1.7	2.0	1.8	2.0	2.1
Mining	-2.0	3.5	1.8	.6	.7	.3	1.7	2.0	2.1	1.0	1.2	1.0
Construction	1.4	3.0	-2.4	3.1	3.0	3.2	2.1	2.6	2.6	2.7	2.9	2.9
Manufacturing	1.9	.4	-3.5	1.5	1.8	2.1	1.2	1.1	1.3	1.4	1.5	1.8
Durable	2.4	.7	-4.5	1.9	2.3	2.6	1.5	1.4	1.5	1.8	1.9	2.2
Nondurable	1.2	.0	-2.1	.9	1.2	1.3	.5	.7	.9	.7	1.0	1.1
Transportation and public utilities	.9	1.6	.1	1.3	1.4	1.6	1.1	1.4	1.4	1.2	1.4	1.5
Trade	2.3	3.0	.3	1.7	2.0	2.1	1.4	1.6	1.6	1.6	1.8	1.9
Finance, insurance, and real estate	2.8	3.6	2.2	2.2	2.4	1.5	1.6	1.6	3.2	2.0	2.1	2.2
Services	3.6	4.0	3.7	2.5	2.6	2.8	2.3	2.3	2.7	2.4	2.5	2.8
Private households	-1.0	-2.9	-1.7	-1.6	-1.9	-2.0	-2.1	-.8	-.3	-1.8	-1.5	-1.4

Source: Personick, V. A. The job outlook through 1995: Industry output and employment projections. *Monthly Labor Review,* 1983, *106,* 11, p. 26.
Note: Data include wage and salary workers, the self-employed, and unpaid family workers.

TABLE 8–4   Forty occupations with largest job growth, 1982–95

Occupation	Change in total employment (in thousands)	Percent of total job growth	Percent change
Building custodians	779	3.0	27.5
Cashiers	744	2.9	47.4
Secretaries	719	2.8	29.5
General clerks, office	696	2.7	29.6
Salesclerks	685	2.7	23.5
Nurses, registered	642	2.5	48.9
Waiters and waitresses	562	2.2	33.8
Teachers, kindergarten and elementary	511	2.0	37.4
Truckdrivers	425	1.7	26.5
Nursing aides and orderlies	423	1.7	34.8
Sales representatives, technical	386	1.5	29.3
Accountants and auditors	344	1.3	40.2
Automotive mechanics	324	1.3	38.3
Supervisors of blue-collar workers	319	1.2	26.6
Kitchen helpers	305	1.2	35.9
Guards and doorkeepers	300	1.2	47.3
Food preparation and service workers, fast food restaurants	297	1.2	36.7
Managers, store	292	1.1	30.1
Carpenters	247	1.0	28.6
Electrical and electronic technicians	222	.9	60.7
Licensed practical nurses	220	.9	37.1
Computer systems analysts	217	.8	85.3
Electrical engineers	209	.8	65.3
Computer programmers	205	.8	76.9
Maintenance repairers, general utility	193	.8	27.8
Helpers, trades	190	.7	31.2
Receptionists	189	.7	48.8
Electricians	173	.7	31.8
Physicians	163	.7	34.0
Clerical supervisors	162	.6	34.6
Computer operators	160	.6	75.8
Sales representatives, nontechnical	160	.6	27.4
Lawyers	159	.6	34.3
Stock clerks, stockroom and warehouse	156	.6	18.8
Typists	155	.6	15.7
Delivery and route workers	153	.6	19.2
Bookkeepers, hand	152	.6	15.9

TABLE 8–4 continued

Occupation	Change in total employment (in thousands)	Percent of total job growth	Percent change
Cooks, restaurants	149	.6	42.3
Bank tellers	142	.6	30.0
Cooks, short order, specialty and fast food	141	.6	32.2

Source: Silvestri, G. T., Lukarsiewicz, J. M. and Einstein, M. E. Occupational employment projections through 1995. *Monthly Labor Review*, 1983, *106*, 11, p. 45.
Note: Includes only detailed occupations with 1982 employment of 25,000 or more. Data for 1995 are based on moderate-trend projections.

TABLE 8–5   Twenty fastest growing occupations, 1982–95

Occupation	Percent growth in employment
Computer service technicians	96.8
Legal assistants	94.3
Computer systems analysts	85.3
Computer programmers	76.9
Computer operators	75.8
Office machine repairers	71.7
Physical therapy assistants	67.8
Electrical engineers	65.3
Civil engineering technicians	63.9
Peripheral EDP equipment operators	63.5
Insurance clerks, medical	62.2
Electrical and electronic technicians	60.7
Occupational therapists	59.8
Surveyor helpers	58.6
Credit clerks, banking and insurance	54.1
Physical therapists	53.6
Employment interviewers	52.5
Mechanical engineers	52.1
Mechanical engineering technicians	51.6
Compression and injection mold machine operators, plastics	50.3

Source: Silvestri, G. T., Lukarsiewicz, J. M. and Einstein, M. E. Occupational employment projections through 1995. *Monthly Labor Review*, 1983, *106*, 11, p. 46.
Note: Includes only detailed occupations with 1982 employment of 25,000 or more. Data for 1995 are based on moderate-trend projections.

TABLE 8—6   Twenty most rapidly declining occupations,
1982–95

Occupation	*Percent decline in employment*
Railroad conductors	−32.0
Shoemaking machine operatives	−30.2
Aircraft structure assemblers	−21.0
Central telephone office operators	−20.0
Taxi drivers	−18.9
Postal clerks	−17.9
Private household workers	−16.9
Farm laborers	−15.9
College and university faculty	−15.0
Roustabouts	−14.4
Postmasters and mail superintendents	−13.8
Rotary drill operator helpers	−11.6
Graduate assistants	−11.2
Data entry operators	−10.6
Railroad brake operators	−9.8
Fallers and buckers	−8.7
Stenographers	−7.4
Farm owners and tenants	−7.3
Typesetters and compositors	−7.3
Butchers and meatcutters	−6.3

Source: Silvestri, G. T., Lukarsiewicz, J. M. and Einstein, M. E. Occupational employment projections through 1995. *Monthly Labor Review*, 1983, *106*, 11, p. 46.
Note: Includes only detailed occupations with 1982 employment of 25,000 or more. Data for 1995 are based on moderate-trend projections.

D   Manufacturing
E   Transportation, communications, and electric, gas, and sanitary services
F   Wholesale trade
G   Retail trade
H   Finance, insurance, and real estate
I   Services
J   Public administration

Government service provided jobs for about 15.8 million civilian workers in 1982. Of these, approximately one worker in six worked for the Federal Government and the rest were employed by state and local units, including counties, cities, townships, school districts, and similar divisions.

Approximately two million other persons are members of the Armed Forces. Many military jobs are identical to civilian jobs; others are unique to the military. Nevertheless, members of the Armed Forces are considered to be outside the public and private domains of the civilian economy. Thus when one refers to the government sector, this does not include the Army, Navy, Marine Corps, Air Force, or Coast Guard.

Because of the special character of governmental activities, the distribution of workers differs considerably from that of the so-called private domain. For example, two-thirds of government workers are white-collar workers while less than half of the private domain workers fit this category. Thirty-five percent of government workers are professional or technical, compared with only 11 percent of private industry workers. Only 14 percent of government workers are blue-collar workers, but 37 percent of workers in private industry are classified as blue collar.

As mentioned above, agricultural employment is expected to continue its decline through the 1980s, although probably at a slowed pace. Large increases in productivity in agriculture have permitted fewer workers to produce more food and fiber than in previous years. For example, output per hour of all workers in the farm sector increased almost five percent per year between 1959 and 1977 while nonfarm workers increased productivity at a two or three percent rate before 1973 and at a one percent rate since 1973. These rapid gains started to slow in the early 1980s and the decrease in agricultural jobs began to moderate.

The mining and petroleum sector produces much of the raw material and energy sources used by industry and private consumers. Within the energy areas are coal mining and the finding and extraction of crude petroleum and natural gas. These industries account for approximately 75 percent of the workers in this sector. Other industries in this sector include iron mining, copper mining, mining of other metals such as gold, stone and clay mining and quarrying, and chemical and fertilizer mineral mining. The total sector employed 742,000 workers in 1982. Even with the growth expected to be produced by increased efforts to become more energy self-sufficient, this sector will probably continue to include only about one percent of the labor force.

The construction sector includes the building of new homes, nonresidential buildings, public utilities, highways, all other new construction, and maintenance and repair construction. Over five million workers were employed in this sector in 1982. About 80 percent were blue-collar workers, with more than half of the total group being craft workers such as carpenters, electricians, painters, and plumbers. About half of the workers in this sector are employed by special trade contractors who often subcontract to perform specific parts of a larger construction job. About one-third work for general building contractors. The remaining one-fifth are involved in heavy construction projects such as dams, bridges, and roads.

Manufacturing is one of the largest industrial sectors, employing almost one-fourth of all workers. The sector's size also reflects its diversity. It consists of two broad areas, durable goods and nondurable goods. The first of these includes fifty-nine industries and about three-fifths of the workers, and the second encompasses thirty-six industries. Some of these industries, motor vehicle and apparel, for example, are each larger than the entire mining and petroleum sector. In spite of the tremendous range of products created by the manufacturing sector, ten industries employ approximately 75% of all manufacturing workers. These ten industries include the following:

Durable goods	*Nondurable goods*
Machinery, except electrical	Food products
Electric and electronic equipment	Clothing and other textile products
Transportation equipment	Printing and publishing
Fabricated metal products	Chemicals
Iron, steel, and other primary metals	Textile mill products

As is true of the other sectors, manufacturing has its own unique composition of workers. Nearly two-thirds are blue-collar workers, and of these the largest group consists of machine operatives, who account for about 40 percent of all manufacturing employees. The next largest section of blue-collar workers is the craft group, amounting to about 20 percent of the total workers. Clerical workers (about 12 percent of the total) make up the largest group of the white-collar workers, followed by the professional and technical workers, who fill about 10 percent of the jobs.

Transportation, communications, and public utilities provide quite different services and products, but they are often grouped together because they are considered to be public service activities and are either owned or regulated by governmental agencies. This sector is about the same size as the construction sector, including slightly more than 5.5 million workers in 1982. In addition to the obvious transportation systems of railroads, local and interurban buses, trucks, and air and water transportation, this category includes pipeline transportation and supporting services for each network. The communications area includes radio and television broadcasting and all other communications, the largest part being telephone systems. Utilities include electric, gas, and water and sewer systems. Among these components, the largest is motor freight transportation and warehousing, employing about 1.5 million workers. The communications area includes about 1.2 million workers, and the public utility area has about 800,000. Within transportation, the largest group of employees are operatives, followed by craft and clerical workers. In the communications area the largest group are clerical workers, and in the utilities most employees are craft workers.

Wholesale and retail trade is another very large sector, including approximately 22.5 million workers in 1982, about three-fourths of them in the retail area. The wholesalers assemble materials from the producers, sometimes recombine them in variously sized lots, and distribute them to retail stores or large users such as schools, hospitals, and industrial firms. The retailers sell goods or services directly to consumers in stores, by mail and telephone, or through door-to-door contact. Although the customer ordinarily is most likely to have contact with a sales worker, sales jobs account for only about one-fifth of the jobs in this sector. Only slightly smaller numbers are employed as managers and administrators, service workers, and clerical workers.

Finance, insurance, and real estate employ almost six million people, most of whom are clerical workers. The finance area, including banking, credit agencies, and financial brokers, employs about 2.3 million employees. Insurance has about 1.8 million workers, and real estate slightly over one million. The clerical workers are heavily concentrated in the finance and insurance areas, while sales workers predominate in real estate. In the 1980s, finance and insurance are expected to grow more rapidly than real estate.

The services sector includes a wide array of activities scattered across seventeen industries and is approached in size only by trade and manufacturing. In fact, if government workers are classified in this sector (where most of them, such as teachers, fit), this sector would include almost 32 million workers, or nearly a third of the entire labor force. Under this heading one finds hotels and lodging places, barber and beauty shops, advertising agencies, automobile repair shops, amusements, doctor and dental services, and educational and other services.

One-third of service workers are professional and technical, the highest proportion in all the sectors. Other large groups include service workers and clerical workers. Less than one-tenth of the employees are blue-collar workers. During the 1980s growth is expected to be greater, both in percentage and in actual numbers, in the service sector than in any other area.

The Standard Industrial Classification System (SICS) has been developed to provide a method for tabulating and comparing data collected on an industry base. Industries are classified according to the type of activity in which they engage. The SICS is described in detail in the *Standard Industrial Classification Manual* published by the Office of Management and Budget and, like other government publications, printed by the U.S. Government Printing Office.

The SICS divides industries into ten major divisions that correspond to the nine areas we have just discussed except that wholesale and retail trade are considered as separate divisions and also an eleventh group, "nonclassifiable establishments," is added. The ten major divisions are divided into eighty-four major groups, each of which is further divided into closely related industries. A coding system of two, three, and four digits is used to identify the grouping level. Figure 8–2 includes a sample page from the *Manual* showing how industries are grouped in this system.

FIGURE 8–2 Sample page from *Standard Industrial Classification Manual.*

Major Group 50.—WHOLESALE TRADE—DURABLE GOODS

The major group includes establishments primarily engaged in the wholesale distribution of durable goods.

Group   Industry
No.   No.

501   **MOTOR VEHICLES AND AUTOMOTIVE PARTS AND SUPPLIES**

    5012   **Automobiles and Other Motor Vehicles**

Establishments primarily engaged in the wholesale distribution of new and used passenger automobiles, trucks, and other motor vehicles. Automotive distributors primarily engaged in selling at retail to individual consumers for personal use, and also selling a limited amount of new and used passenger automobiles and trucks at wholesale to dealers, are classified in Retail Trade, Industry 5511.

Automobile auctions—wholesale
Automobiles—wholesale
Bodies, truck—wholesale
Buses—wholesale
Campers (pickup coaches) for mounting on trucks—wholesale
Motor scooters—wholesale
Motor vehicles, commercial—wholesale
Motorcycles—wholesale
Pop-up campers—wholesale
Taxicabs—wholesale
Trailers for passenger automobiles—wholesale
Truck tractors—wholesale
Truck trailers—wholesale
Trucks—wholesale

    5013   **Automotive Parts and Supplies**

Establishments primarily engaged in the wholesale distribution of automotive parts, supplies, accessories, tools and equipment.

Automobile engine testing equipment, electrical—wholesale
Automobile glass, wholesale
Automotive accessories—wholesale
Automotive parts, new and used—wholesale
Automotive supplies—wholesale
Batteries, automotive—wholesale
Hardware, automotive—wholesale
Seat belts, automotive—wholesale
Seat covers, automotive—wholesale
Testing equipment, electrical: automotive—wholesale
Tools and equipment, automotive—wholesale
Wheels, motor vehicle—wholesale

FIGURE 8–2 continued

5014   **Tires and Tubes**

Establishments primarily engaged in the wholesale distribution of rubber tires and tubes for passenger and commercial vehicles.

Motor vehicle tires and tubes —wholesale	Tires and tubes—wholesale
Repair materials, tire and tube—wholesale	Tires, used—wholesale

502   **FURNITURE AND HOME FURNISHINGS**

5021   **Furniture**

Establishments primarily engaged in the wholesale distribution of furniture, including bedsprings, mattresses, and other household furniture; office furniture; and furniture for public parks, buildings, etc.

Bedsprings—wholesale	Furniture, juvenile—wholesale
Chairs: household, office, and public building—wholesale	Mattresses—wholesale
Furniture: household, office, restaurant, public building —wholesale	

Occupational groupings

The previous section focused on the world of work in terms of *where* the worker performs his or her tasks—the industrial sectors and the various industries. When we think of the various tasks performed by the worker regardless of where they are accomplished we think in terms of occupations. Technically, we use the term occupation to represent a set of tasks widely recognized as usually performed by a single worker, for example, a physician, secretary, tile-setter, short-order cook, or bus driver.

Because we live in a very complex, technical society we now have a very large number of occupations—so many, in fact, that it would be difficult to specify precisely how many there are. The number would depend upon how very closely related sets of tasks are grouped or divided. For example, should one consider "high school teacher" as one occupation or English teacher, foreign language teacher, biology teacher, chemistry teacher, mathematics teacher, physical education teacher, social studies teacher, and speech teacher as eight occupations? In some cases it is advan-

tageous to group broadly and in other situations specificity is best. Printed
materials describing the world of work, occupational data, and other information about occupations use various grouping systems, often dependent
upon the source of the data. Therefore, it is essential that the career counselor be knowledgeable about each of these systems to help a client use
information about alternatives in the decision-making process.

Two of the systems are closely related and can be considered together.
Both are used by the Department of Labor, probably the primary source of
most printed information about occupations. One system, used by the
Bureau of Labor Statistics, is based directly upon systems developed for the
1960 and 1970 Decennial Census. The second system, developed by the
Employment and Training Division, is used in the *Dictionary of Occupational Titles (DOT)* (U.S. Department of Labor, 1977), the most widely
used classification and coding system for occupations. The two groupings
are presented side by side so that the reader can easily see the high degree of
similarity. The *DOT* system has been rearranged in order to demonstrate
the comparability of the two groupings.

	Bureau of Labor Statistics and 1960, 1970 Census	*Dictionary of Occupational Titles*
White-collar	Professional and technical	Professional, technical, managerial occupations
	Manager and administrator	
	Sales workers	Clerical and sales occupations
	Clerical workers	
Blue-collar	Craft workers	Processing occupations
	Operatives	Machine trade occupations
	Transport operatives	Benchwork occupations
	Nonfarm laborers	Structural work occupations
		Miscellaneous occupations
	Private household service	Service occupations
	Other service occupations	
	Farm workers	Agricultural, fishery, forestry occupations

Figure 8–3 shows the expected distribution of workers in 1990 according to the Bureau of Labor Statistics grouping.

Professional and technical workers are concerned with the theoretical
and practical aspects of such fields as architecture, engineering, the sciences,
medicine, education, law, theology, art, and entertainment. Most of these
occupations require lengthy educational preparation at college or other
advanced levels. During the 1980s this group is expected to grow by nearly
20 percent, from slightly over 14.2 to about 16.9 million workers.

Managers and administrators are involved in the operation and direction of organizations such as businesses. Examples of occupations include

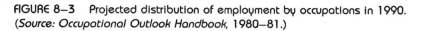

FIGURE 8—3 Projected distribution of employment by occupations in 1990. (*Source: Occupational Outlook Handbook*, 1980—81.)

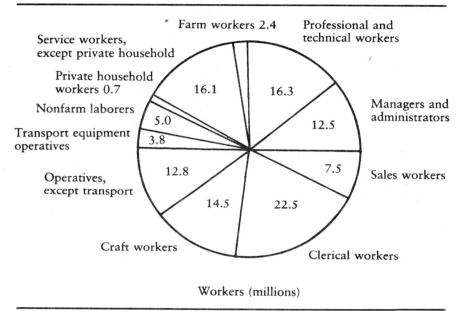

Workers (millions)

bank officers, buyers, credit managers, and managers of fast-food restaurants. This group is expected to increase by slightly more than 21 percent during the 1980s, from about 10.1 to 12.2 million workers.

Sales workers include those individuals concerned with influencing customers in favor of a commodity or service and those workers closely related to this process. Workers are primarily employed in wholesale and retail trade and by manufacturing, insurance, or real-estate companies. Employment is expected to increase by about 27 percent by 1990 to approximately 7.6 million workers.

Clerical workers are those employees who prepare, transcribe, systematize, or preserve written communications and records, or distribute information, or collect accounts. These include bank tellers, bookkeepers, secretaries, typists, and cashiers. Although technological developments are expected to influence most occupations in this group during the next decade, the field is still expected to increase more than any other. By 1990, it is anticipated there will be 21.7 million clerical workers, an increase of about 28 percent.

Private household service workers and other service workers are treated separately by the Bureau of Labor Statistics, but grouped together by the *DOT*. The first group of workers performs duties in private households such as cleaning, making beds, caring for children, planning meals, marketing, and cooking. The second group includes those who are involved in preparing and serving food and drink in commercial or institutional establishments, providing lodging and related services, providing grooming, cosmetics, and other personal and health care services, maintaining and cleaning clothing, providing protection for people and property, and cleaning or maintenance services to interiors of buildings. Private household workers are expected to decline in number still further in the 1980s to about 890,000 workers, a loss of about 26 percent. Other service workers make up the fastest growing group and are expected to increase by about 35 percent to approximately 15.8 million.

Farm workers are concerned with propagating, growing, caring for, and harvesting plant- and animal-life products. Increased technological efficiency has required a decreasing number of workers. Employment in this field is expected to decrease by about 14 percent to approximately 2.4 million by 1990.

The remaining categories of craft workers, operatives, and laborers roughly correspond to the skilled, semiskilled, and unskilled levels used in the first two editions of the *DOT*. Beginning with the third edition of the *DOT*, these workers are regrouped according to the type of work rather than the level of skill. Consequently, there is now no direct comparison between the labels used in the two systems. We will look at the *Bureau of Labor Statistics* titles first and then define the *DOT* categories.

Craft workers are highly skilled workers such as carpenters, tool-and-die makers, machinists, electricians, and mechanics. Long periods of apprenticeship or on-the-job training are usually required to develop the level of skill demanded by these occupations. These workers are expected to increase in number by about 20 percent to approximately 14.9 million by 1990.

Operatives run various machines or processes used primarily in the production of goods. Typical occupations include assemblers, production painters, and welders. The field is expected to increase by about 15 percent to nearly 12.5 million workers by 1990.

Transport operatives are involved in driving various types of vehicles and equipment. This group includes bus drivers, truckers, forklift operators, and taxi drivers. The number of transport operatives will increase by about 17 percent to 4.1 million by 1990.

Nonfarm laborers are involved in occupations that can be learned fairly rapidly, from a short demonstration only or from not more than thirty days of on-the-job training. Examples of these occupations include garbage collectors, construction laborers, and freight handlers. The group will increase by about nine percent to approximately 5.1 million by 1990.

Processing occupations are defined by the *DOT* as those concerned with refining, mixing, compounding, chemically treating, heat treating, or similarly working materials in solid, fluid, semifluid, or gaseous states to prepare them for use as basic materials, stock for further manufacturing treatment, or for sale as finished products to commercial users. Knowledge of a process and adherence to formulas or other specifications are required to some degree. Vats, stills, ovens, furnaces, mixing machines, crushers, grinders, and related machines and equipment usually are involved. The group includes occupations involved in processing metal, ore, food, tobacco, paper, petroleum, chemicals, wood, stone, leather, and other materials.

Machine trades occupations include those concerned with the operation of machines that cut, bore, mill, abrade, print, and similarly work with such materials as metal, paper, wood, plastics, and stone. A worker's relationship to the machine is of primary importance. The more complicated jobs require an understanding of machine functions, blueprint reading, making mathematical computations, and exercising judgment to attain conformance to specifications. In other jobs, eye and hand coordination may be the most significant factor. Installation, repair, and maintenance of machines and mechanical equipment, and weaving, knitting, spinning, and similarly working textiles are included. Typical jobs in this group include machinists, grinders, punch press operators, automobile mechanics, typesetters, and cabinetmakers.

Benchwork occupations are those concerned with using body members, hand tools, and bench machines to fabricate, inspect, or repair relatively small products such as jewelry, phonographs, lightbulbs, musical instruments, tires, footwear, pottery, and garments. The work is usually performed at a set position or station in a mill, plant, or shop, at a bench, worktable, or conveyor. Workers in more complex jobs may be required to read blueprints, follow patterns, use a variety of hand tools, and assume responsibility for meeting standards. Other jobs may only require workers to follow standardized procedures. Some occupations included in this group are jeweler, silversmith, watch repairer, television and radio repairer, piano tuner, assembler, stone cutter, glassblower, tailor, and shoemaker.

Structural work occupations include those occupations involved with fabricating, erecting, installing, paving, painting, and repairing structures and structural parts such as bridges, buildings, roads, motor vehicles, cables, internal combustion engines, girders, plates, and frames. Generally, work is done outdoors, except for factory production-line occupations. The worker's relationship to hand tools and power tools is more important than that to stationary machines, which are also used. Knowledge of the properties (stress, strain, durability, resistance) of the materials used (wood, metal, concrete, glass, clay) is often a requirement. Representative occupations include riveter, structural-steel worker, sheet-metal worker, boilermaker, rigger, test driver, electrician, paperhanger, bulldozer operator, carpenter, plumber, and chimney sweep.

Miscellaneous occupations are concerned with the transportation of people and cargo from one geographical location to another by various methods; packaging of materials and moving of materials in and around establishments; extraction of minerals from the earth; production and distribution of utilities; modeling for painters, sculptors, and photographers; providing various production services in motion pictures and radio and television broadcasting; production of graphic art work; and other miscellaneous activities. Occupations included are truck driver, barge captain, automobile service-station attendant, packager, hoist operator, stevedore, jackhammer operator, miner, motion-picture projectionist, sign painter, photoengraver, bookbinder, and print-shop helper.

The *Dictionary of Occupational Titles* is not only the most widely used classification system but also the most comprehensive. It includes a nine-digit coding system consisting of three separate parts, detailed definitions of occupations based on extensive on-site job analyses, definitions of special terms used in the occupational definitions, an alphabetical index of occupational titles, and a grouping of occupations according to the industrial designation system used within the *DOT*.

Each of the major categories, listed and described above, is identified by a single digit except for the first one—professional, technical, managerial occupations—which is assigned both 0 and 1. These nine broad categories are divided into 82 divisions that are further subdivided into 559 groups. In addition to this system of differentiation within the first three digits of the code, each occupation is described numerically by the second group of three digits according to the occupation's involvement with data, people, and things. Finally, the last three digits in each *DOT* code number provide a specific identifier for each occupation sharing the same first six digits.

Figure 8–4 includes a sample of the category and division coding and Figure 8–5 shows a sample of the division and group coding from pages XXXIV and XXXIX of the *DOT*.

The second group of three digits are the worker functions ratings and describe numerically the degree of involvement the occupation has with data, people, and things. This part of the *DOT* code is based on the assumption that every occupation involves some degree of relationship to each of these three functions. This degree of relationship is then expressed by one of the digits. Prediger (1981), who has long worked with the American College Test World of Work Map, argues very convincingly that the data function should be divided into data and ideas. At present, in the fourth edition, worker functions are reflected as follows:

DATA (4th Digit)	PEOPLE (5th Digit)	THINGS (6th Digit)
0 Synthesizing	0 Mentoring	0 Setting Up
1 Coordinating	1 Negotiating	1 Precision Working
2 Analyzing	2 Instructing	2 Operating–Controlling
3 Compiling	3 Supervising	3 Driving–Operating
4 Computing	4 Diverting	4 Manipulating
5 Copying	5 Persuading	5 Tending
6 Comparing	6 Speaking–Signalling	6 Feeding–Offbearing
	7 Serving	7 Handling
	8 Taking Instruction–Helping	

FIGURE 8—4   Sample of category and division listings in *Dictionary of Occupational Titles* (p. xxxiv).

SUMMARY LISTING OF OCCUPATIONAL CATEGORIES, DIVISIONS, AND GROUPS

OCCUPATIONAL CATEGORIES

0/1	Professional, technical, and managerial occupations
2	Clerical and sales occupations
3	Service occupations
4	Agricultural, fishery, forestry, and related occupations
5	Processing occupations
6	Machine trades occupations
7	Benchwork occupations
8	Structural work occupations
9	Miscellaneous occupations

TWO-DIGIT OCCUPATIONAL DIVISIONS

PROFESSIONAL, TECHNICAL, AND MANAGERIAL OCCUPATIONS

00/01	Occupations in architecture, engineering, and surveying
02	Occupations in mathematics and physical sciences
04	Occupations in life sciences
05	Occupations in social sciences
07	Occupations in medicine and health
09	Occupations in education
10	Occupations in museum, library, and archival sciences
11	Occupations in law and jurisprudence
12	Occupations in religion and theology
13	Occupations in writing
14	Occupations in art
15	Occupations in entertainment and recreation
16	Occupations in administrative specializations
18	Managers and officials, n.e.c.
19	Miscellaneous professional, technical, and managerial occupations

CLERICAL AND SALES OCCUPATIONS

20	Stenography, typing, filing, and related occupations
21	Computing and account-recording occupations
22	Production and stock clerks and related occupations
23	Information and message distribution occupations
24	Miscellaneous clerical occupations
25	Sales occupations, services
26	Sales occupations, consumable commodities
27	Sales occupations, commodities, n.e.c.
29	Miscellaneous sales occupations

SERVICE OCCUPATIONS

30	Domestic service occupations
31	Food and beverage preparation and service occupations
32	Lodging and related service occupations
33	Barbering, cosmetology, and related service occupations
34	Amusement and recreation service occupations
35	Miscellaneous personal service occupations
36	Apparel and furnishings service occupations
37	Protective service occupations
38	Building and related service occupations

AGRICULTURAL, FISHERY, FORESTRY, AND RELATED OCCUPATIONS

40	Plant farming occupations

FIGURE 8-5 Sample of division and group listings in *Dictionary of Occupational Titles* (p. xxxix).

58	Occupations in processing of leather, textiles, and related products		shaving, and napping occupations
580	Shaping, blocking, stretching, and tentering occupations	586	Felting and fulling occupations
581	Separating, filtering, and drying occupations	587	Brushing and shrinking occupations
582	Washing, steaming, and saturating occupations	589	Occupations in processing of leather, textiles, and related products, n.e.c.
583	Ironing, pressing, glazing, staking, calendering, and embossing occupations	59	Processing occupations, n.e.c.
584	Mercerizing, coating, and laminating occupations	590	Occupations in processing products from assorted materials
585	Singeing, cutting, shearing,	599	Miscellaneous processing occupations, n.e.c.

MACHINE TRADES OCCUPATIONS

60	**Metal machining occupations**	617	Forming occupations, n.e.c.
600	Machinists and related occupations	619	Miscellaneous metalworking occupations, n.e.c.
601	Toolmakers and related occupations		
602	Gear machining occupations	**62/63**	**Mechanics and machinery repairers**
603	Abrading occupations	620	Motorized vehicle and engineering equipment mechanics and repairers
604	Turning occupations		
605	Milling, shaping, and planing occupations	621	Aircraft mechanics and repairers
606	Boring occupations		
607	Sawing occupations	622	Rail equipment mechanics and repairers
609	Metal machining occupations, n.e.c.		
		623	Marine mechanics and repairers
61	**Metalworking occupations, n.e.c.**	624	Farm mechanics and repairers
		625	Engine, power transmission, and related mechanics
610	Hammer forging occupations		
611	Press forging occupations	626	Metalworking machinery mechanics
612	Forging occupations, n.e.c.		
613	Sheet and bar rolling occupations	627	Printing and publishing mechanics and repairers
614	Extruding and drawing occupations	628	Textile machinery and equipment mechanics and repairers
615	Punching and shearing occupations	629	Special industry machinery mechanics
616	Fabricating machine occupations	630	General industry mechanics and repairers

FIGURE 8–5 continued

631 Powerplant mechanics and re-pairers
632 Ordnance and accessories mechanics and repairers
633 Business and commercial machine repairers
637 Utilities service mechanics and repairers
638 Miscellaneous occupations in machine installation and repair
639 Mechanics and machinery repairers, n.e.c.

64 Paperworking occupations
640 Paper cutting, winding, and related occupations
641 Folding, creasing, scoring, and gluing occupations
649 Paperworking occupations, n.e.c.

65 Printing occupations
650 Typesetters and composers
651 Printing press occupations
652 Printing machine occupations
653 Bookbinding-machine operators and related occupations
654 Typecasters and related occupations
659 Printing occupations, n.e.c.

66 Wood machining occupations
660 Cabinetmakers
661 Patternmakers
662 Sanding occupations
663 Shearing and shaving occupations
664 Turning occupations
665 Milling and planing occupations
666 Boring occupations
667 Sawing occupations
669 Wood machining occupations, n.e.c.

67 Occupations in machining stone, clay, glass, and related materials
670 Stonecutters and related occupations
673 Abrading occupations
674 Turning occupations
675 Planing and shaping occupations, n.e.c.
676 Boring and punching occupations
677 Chipping, cutting, sawing, and related occupations
679 Occupations in machining stone, clay, glass, and related materials, n.e.c.

68 Textile occupations
680 Carding, combing, drawing, and related occupations
681 Twisting, beaming, warping, and related occupations
682 Spinning occupations
683 Weavers and related occupations
684 Hosiery knitting occupations
685 Knitting occupations, except hosiery
686 Punching, cutting, forming, and related occupations
687 Tufting occupations
689 Textile occupations, n.e.c.

69 Machine trades occupations, n.e.c.
690 Plastics, synthetics, rubber, and leather working occupations
691 Occupations in fabrication of insulated wire and cable
692 Occupations in fabrication of products from assorted materials
693 Modelmakers, patternmakers, and related occupations
694 Occupations in fabrication of ordnance, ammunition, and related products, n.e.c.
699 Miscellaneous machine trades occupations, n.e.c.

FIGURE 8—5 continued

BENCHWORK OCCUPATIONS

70	Occupations in fabrication, assembly, and repair of metal products, n.e.c.	
700	Occupations in fabrication, assembly, and repair of jewelry, silverware, and related products	
701	Occupations in fabrication, assembly, and repair of tools, and related products	
703	Occupations in assembly and repair of sheetmetal products, n.e.c.	
704	Engravers, etchers, and related occupations	
705	Filing, grinding, buffing, cleaning, and polishing occupations, n.e.c.	
706	Metal unit assemblers and adjusters, n.e.c.	
709	Miscellaneous occupations in fabrication, assembly, and repair of metal products, n.e.c.	
71	Occupations in fabrication and repair of scientific,	medical, photographic, optical, horological, and related products
710		Occupations in fabrication and repair of instruments for measuring, controlling, and indicating physical characteristics
711		Occupations in fabrication and repair of optical instruments
712		Occupations in fabrication and repair of surgical, medical, and dental instruments and supplies
713		Occupations in fabrication and repair of ophthalmic goods
714		Occupations in fabrication and repair of photographic equipment and supplies
715		Occupations in fabrication and repair of watches, clocks, and parts
716		Occupations in fabrication and repair of engineering and scientific instruments and equipment, n.e.c.

The more complex involvements carry lower numbers and are also assumed to include the capacity to perform the less complex levels. The worker functions code tells us what the worker with a given occupational designation code does in dealing with data, people, and things. A psychiatrist has a *DOT* code number of 070.107-014. The worker functions code tells us that a psychiatrist coordinates data, mentors people, and works with things, the last at the lowest level of significance. Although each also carries the same worker functions code of 107, the lawyer, school counselor, and speech pathologist work with different kinds of data at the coordinating level, with people in differing ways at the mentoring level, and with very little involvement with things. On the other hand, a bakery worker's code number of 929.686-101 shows that a bakery worker compares data, takes instructions or helps, and brings material to a machine or equipment or takes it away.

By examining the worker functions codes, one can see occupations in vastly different fields that require comparable levels of functioning with data, people and things. Figure 8–6 provides an illustration of occupational definitions as found on a typical page of the *DOT*. Our illustration comes from page 537.

As demonstrated above, many classification systems have been developed by various governmental agencies to meet the needs of that agency or its constituency. In recent years, an effort has been made to develop a system that would satisfy the needs of those diverse agencies and also maximize the comparison and analysis of data available from various sources. This effort led to the development of the *Standard Occupational Classification* (SOC) in 1977. The classification plan was revised in 1980 so that it could be used in the publication of the 1980 Decennial Census. Subsequently, it has been used in the *Occupational Outlook Handbook* (OOH) and other publications. One can expect increased use of this system in occupational data information and reports obtained from governmental offices. With widespread governmental usage, it is likely that the system will gain general application elsewhere.

The *Standard Occupational Classification* is designed to cover all occupations in which work is performed for pay or profit. It uses a four-level system consisting of divisions, major groups, minor groups, and unit groups. Each level provides increasingly greater specification.

The twenty-two divisions included in the 1980 revision of the *SOC* are the following:

Executive, Administrative and Managerial Occupations
Engineers, Surveyors and Architects
Natural Scientists and Mathematicians
Social Scientists, Social Workers, Religious Workers, and Lawyers
Teachers, Librarians, and Counselors
Health Diagnosing and Treating Practitioners
Registered Nurses, Pharmacists, Dietitians, Therapists, and Physician's Assistants
Writers, Artists, Entertainers, and Athletes
Health Technologists and Technicians
Technologists and Technicians, Except Health
Marketing and Sales Occupations
Administrative Support Occupations, including Clerical
Service Occupations
Agricultural, Forestry, and Fishing Occupations
Mechanics and Repairers
Construction and Extractive Occupations
Precision Production Occupations
Production Working Occupations
Transportation and Material Moving Occupations

welding equipment. Rewires ignition system, lights, and instrument panel. Relines and adjusts brakes, alines front end, repairs or replaces shock absorbers, and solders leaks in radiator. Mends damaged body and fenders by hammering out or filling in dents and welding broken parts. Replaces and adjusts headlights, and installs and repairs accessories, such as radios, heaters, mirrors, and windshield wipers. May be designated according to specialty as AUTOMOBILE MECHANIC, MOTOR (auto. ser.); BUS MECHANIC (auto. ser.); DIFFERENTIAL REPAIRER (auto. ser.); ENGINE-REPAIR MECHANIC, BUS (auto. ser.); FOREIGN-CAR MECHANIC (auto. ser.); TRUCK MECHANIC (auto. ser.). When working in service station may be designated AUTOMOBILE-SERVICE-STATION MECHANIC (auto. ser.). Additional titles: COMPRESSOR MECHANIC, BUS (auto. ser.); DRIVESHAFT-AND-STEERING-POST REPAIRER (auto. ser.); ENGINE-HEAD REPAIRER (auto. ser.); MOTOR ASSEMBLER (auto. ser.).

620.261-012 AUTOMOBILE-MECHANIC APPRENTICE (auto. ser.) automobile-and-truck-mechanic apprentice.
Performs duties as described under APPRENTICE (any ind.).

620.261-014 AUTOMOBILE TESTER (auto. ser.)
Tests and examines automotive vehicles, such as automobiles, buses, and trucks, to determine repairs required: Starts engine of automotive vehicle and listens for sounds indicative of malfunctions. Drives vehicle, noting performance of parts, such as clutch, gears, and brakes. Tests motor timing, cylinder compression, fuel consumption, wheel alinement, and steering, using testing devices. Examines body and fenders of vehicle for scratches and dents. Reports findings to supervisor or customer and recommends repairs required. May examine disassembled engine, differential, or other parts during repair. May be designated according to specialty as MOTOR ANALYST (auto. ser.).

620.261-018 AUTOMOBILE-REPAIR-SERVICE ESTIMATOR (auto. ser.) automobile inspector; collision estimator; manager; service; mechanic, trouble-shooting; sales associate, garage service; service writer.
Inspects and tests automobiles and trucks to determine need for and cost of repairs: Determines need for repairs by road test [AUTOMOBILE TESTER (auto. ser.)], by use of mechanical testing devices [BRAKE TESTER (auto. ser.); FRONT-END MECHANIC (auto. ser.)], by questioning customer about vehicle's performance, or by visual inspection of vehicle. Estimates cost of repair and prepares itemized work order, listing costs of parts and labor. May make minor adjustments or repairs, such as brake adjustment, battery cable replacement, or hinge lubrication. May supervise AUTOMOBILE-BODY REPAIRER (auto. ser.); AUTOMOBILE MECHANIC (auto. ser.); PAINTER, AUTOMOTIVE (auto. mfg.; auto. ser.); and other garage workers. May be designated according to specialty as TRUCK-REPAIR-SERVICE ESTIMATOR (auto. ser.).

620.261-022 CONSTRUCTION-EQUIPMENT MECHANIC (const.) heavy-equipment mechanic.
Analyzes malfunctions and repairs, rebuilds, and maintains construction equipment, such as cranes, power shovels, scrapers, paving machines, motor graders, trench-digging machines, conveyors, bulldozers, dredges, pumps, compressors and pneumatic tools: Operates and inspects machines or equipment to diagnose defects. Dismantles and reassembles equipment, using hoists and handtools. Examines parts for damage or excessive wear, using micrometers and gages. Replaces defective engines and subassemblies, such as transmissions. Tests overhauled equipment to insure operating efficiency. Welds broken parts and structural members. May direct workers engaged in cleaning parts and assisting with assembly and disassembly of equipment. May repair, adjust, and maintain mining machinery, such as stripping and loading shovels, drilling and cutting machines, and continuous mining machines and be designated MINE-MACHINERY MECHANIC (mining & quarrying).

620.261-026 ELECTRIC-GOLF-CART REPAIRER (amuse. & rec.; auto. ser.) golf-cart mechanic.
Repairs and maintains electric golf carts at golf course or in automotive repair shop, using handtools and electrical testing devices: Determines type of repairs required by reading work orders, talking to cart operator, or test-driving cart. Tests operational performance of motor, using voltmeter, ammeter, and wattmeter. Dismantles motor and repairs or replaces defective parts, such as brushes, armatures, and commutator, using wrenches, pliers, and screwdrivers. Rewires electrical systems, and repairs or replaces electrical accessories, such as horn and

headlights. Tests and recharges or replaces batteries. Lubricates moving crankshaft. Places fan belt on pulleys, adjusts tension, and tightens bolts. Bolts evaporator unit under dashboard or in trunk. Welds or bolts mounting brackets to automobile frame. Drills holes through interior panels, threads hoses through holes and connects hoses to compressor, evaporator, and cool-air outlet. Fills compressor with refrigerant and starts unit. Measures compressor pressure to determine efficiency of compressor, using gage. Listens to operating unit for indications of malfunction. Removes faulty units from vehicles, disassembles them, and replaces worn and broken parts and fluid in unit. Makes electrical connections as required. May specialize in installation of automotive air-conditioning units and be designated AUTOMOTIVE AIR-CONDITIONER INSTALLER (auto. ser.).

620.281-014 AUTOMOTIVE TECHNICIAN, EXHAUST EMISSIONS (gov. ser.) power equipment mechanic.

Conducts and evaluates tests on vehicles to check exhaust emissions: Reviews instructions to determine details of test to be performed. Drives vehicle over dynamometer. Records identifying data. Performs dwell, timing and idle speed tests using gages, evaluates performance and adjusts performance to manufacturer's specifications. Adjusts dynamometer settings to vehicle specifications and connects instrument sensors to exhaust system. Starts and operates vehicle according to test program, compares performance with specifications and records results. Calibrates, cleans and maintains test equipment and recording devices. May diagnose and repair vehicle malfunctions. May install smog-control device on tested vehicle.

620.281-018 AUTOMOTIVE-MAINTENANCE-EQUIPMENT SERVICER (any ind.) automotive-maintenance-equipment repairer; equipment-service engineer; pump-and-tank servicer.

Adjusts and repairs automotive repairing, servicing, and testing equipment, using handtools and power tools: Disassembles defective equipment, such as gasoline pumps, air compressors, and dynamometers. Replaces defective parts, using pipe fitting and welding tools. Reassembles, adjusts, and tests repaired equipment. May be required to register with government agency to adjust meters and gages of fuel and oil pumps serving public. May install new equipment. May specialize in repairing gasoline pumps, lubrication equipment, air compressors, or other type of automotive service equipment.

620.281-026 BRAKE REPAIRER (auto. ser.) brake mechanic; brake-repair mechanic; brakeshoe repairer.

Repairs and overhauls brake systems in automobiles, buses, trucks, and other automotive vehicles: Pushes handle of hydraulic jack or pushes hoist control to raise vehicle axle. Removes wheels, using wrenches, wheel puller, and sledge hammer. Replaces defective brakeshoe units or attaches new linings to brakeshoes. Measures brakedrum to determine amount of wear, using feeler gage. Inserts vacuum gage into power-brake cylinder, starts engine, and reads gage to detect brake-line leaks. Repairs or replaces leaky brake cylinders. Repairs or replaces defective air compressor in airbrake systems. Replaces wheel on axle and adjusts drumshoe clearance, using wrench. Fills master brake cylinder with brake fluid, pumps brake pedal, or uses pressure tank, and opens valves on hydraulic brake system to bleed air from brake lines. Closes valves and refills master brake cylinder. May be designated according to specialty as BRAKE REPAIRER, AIR (auto. ser.); BRAKE REPAIRER, HYDRAULIC (auto. ser.); BRAKE REPAIRER, BUS (auto. ser.).

620.281-030 BUS INSPECTOR (auto. ser.) motor-inspection mechanic.

Examines and adjusts or repairs engines, chassis, electrical systems, and interior furnishings of buses: Starts engine and listens for indications of malfunctions. Tests engine components, such as carburetors, distributors, radiators, and fuel pumps, to determine causes of malfunctions, using timers, gages, and other testing devices. Inspects chassis for defects in parts, such as universal joints, drive shaft, and air-suspension units. Inspects electrical systems and equipment [ELECTRICIAN, AUTOMOTIVE (auto. ser.)] and interior furnishings. May be designated according to specialty as CHASSIS INSPECTOR (auto. ser.); ELECTRICAL INSPECTOR (auto. ser.); ENGINE INSPECTOR (auto. ser.).

620.281-034 CARBURETOR MECHANIC (auto. ser.) carburetor repairer.

Repairs and adjusts motor vehicle carburetors: Disassembles carburetors and gasoline filter units, using handtools. Examines parts for defects and tests needle valves with wire gages and *flowmeter*. Cleans parts in solvents to remove dirt and gum deposits. Repairs or replaces defective parts. Reassembles carburetor and gasoline filter, and installs . . .

FIGURE 8–7   Sample page from *Standard Occupational Classification Manual* (p. 98).

37 ENGINEERING AND RELATED TECHNOLOGISTS AND TECHNICIANS

371 ENGINEERING TECHNOLOGISTS AND TECHNICIANS

This minor group includes occupations concerned with assisting engineers in both laboratory and production activities. Performs technical tasks under the general supervision of an engineer, utilizing basic knowledge of specific engineering, scientific, mathematical and drafting design, principles, and techniques. May perform technical procedures and related activities independently.

3711 Electrical and Electronic Engineering Technologists and Technicians

This unit group includes occupations involving constructing, repairing, testing, installing, modifying, operating, or designing a variety of production or experimental types of complex electrical or electronic equipment, utilizing knowledge of electrical or electronic theory, physical sciences, and mathematics.

Electrical technician	705	003161010
Electronics technician	705	003161014
Semiconductor-development technician	705	003161018
Instrumentation technician	705	003261010
Calibration laboratory technician	123-343	019281010
Superintendent, meters	532	184167194
Technical testing engineer	589	194381010

3712 Industrial Engineering Technologists and Technicians

This unit group includes occupations involving studying and recording time, motion, method, and speed involving performance of maintenance, production, clerical, and other worker operations to establish standard production rate and to improve efficiency.

Industrial engineering technician	705	012267010

3713 Mechanical Engineering Technologists and Technicians

This unit group includes occupations involving developing and testing machinery and equipment under direction of engineering staff and physical scientists, utilizing theory and principles of mechanical engineering.

Mechanical-engineering technician	705	007161026
Optomechanical technician	648-683	007161030
Heat-transfer technician	705	007181010
Auto-design checker	151	017261010

FIGURE 8–7 continued

3719 Engineering Technologists and Technicians, Not Elsewhere Classified

This unit group includes occupations involving assisting engineers in both laboratory and production activities, not elsewhere classified.

Research mechanic	123	002280010
Flight-test-data transcriber	123	002281010
Scientific glass blower	415	006261010
Chemical-engineering technician	705	008261010
Field engineer, specialist	677	010261010
Test-engine evaluator	679	010261026
Metallurgical technician	705	011261010
Welding technician	705	011261014
Laboratory assistant, metallurgical	475	011281010
Spectroscopist	705	011281014
Tester	705	011361010
Agricultural-engineering technician	705	013161010

Handlers, Equipment Cleaners, Helpers and Laborers
Military Occupations
Miscellaneous Occupations

Each of the divisions is subdivided into more specific categories with major groups identified with two-digit code numbers, minor groups with three-digit numbers, and unit groups with four-digit numbers. Each of the four levels is illustrated in the sample page included in Figure 8–7.

Each *Dictionary of Occupational Titles*, fourth edition, base title is included in the *SOC* and each title is assigned to only one unit group. *DOT* code numbers are listed in the *SOC* as a nine-digit number without the decimal and dash used in the *DOT*. Master titles, terms, titles, and Roman numerals for occupations with the same name and *DOT* industrial designation are used in the same manner as in the *DOT*.

The Employment and Training Administration of the Department of Labor has published the *Guide for Occupational Exploration (GOE)*, a companion volume to be used with the *Dictionary of Occupational Titles*. It includes an occupational grouping system based on extensive research with various well-known interest inventories, including several of those discussed in the previous chapter. It is particularly important to career counselors because it provides a useful bridge between interest inventory results and the *DOT*, as will be seen in the next chapter. A second edition, edited by Harrington and O'Shea (1984) is published by the National Forum Foundation and distributed by American Guidance Service.

The *GOE* grouping is based on twelve interest factors or very broad occupational clusters. Each of these is divided into variable numbers of work groups consisting of closely related activities. The work groups also are divided further into subgroups that include actual DOT codes clustered by industry.

The *GOE* interest factors, briefly defined are as follows:

1. *Artistic*—Interest in creative expression of feelings or ideas.
2. *Scientific*—Interest in discovering, collecting, and analyzing information about the natural world and in applying scientific research findings to problems in medicine, life sciences, and natural sciences.
3. *Plants and Animals*—Interest in activities involving plants and animals, usually in an outdoor setting.
4. *Protective*—Interest in the use of authority to protect people and property.
5. *Mechanical*—Interest in applying mechanical principles to practical situations, using machines, handtools, or techniques.
6. *Industrial*—Interest in repetitive, concrete, organized activities in a factory setting.
7. *Business Detail*—Interest in organized, clearly defined activities requiring accuracy and attention to detail, primarily in an office setting.
8. *Selling*—Interest in bringing others to a point of view through personal persuasion, using sales and promotion techniques.
9. *Accommodating*—Interest in catering to the wishes of others, usually on a one-to-one basis.
10. *Humanitarian*—Interest in helping others with their mental, spiritual, social, physical, or vocational needs.
11. *Leading-Influencing*—Interest in leading and influencing others through activities involving high-level verbal or numerical abilities.
12. *Physical Performing*—Interest in physical activities performed before an audience. (p. 8)

The twelve interest areas are divided into sixty-six work groups that are further subdivided into 348 subgroups. The coding system uses a six-digit arrangement, with the first two digits representing interest area, the first four digits identifying the work group, and all six digits designating the subgroup. Each subgroup lists actual *DOT* occupational titles and code numbers so that *DOT* information can be used when specific occupations are being considered.

The interest areas and work groups included in the *Guide for Occupational Exploration* are as follows:

01 *Artistic*
01.01 Literary arts
01.02 Visual arts
01.03 Performing arts: Drama
01.04 Performing arts: Music
01.05 Performing arts: Dance
01.06 Craft arts

01.07 Elemental arts
01.08 Modeling
02 *Scientific*
02.01 Physical sciences
02.02 Life sciences
02.03 Medical sciences
02.04 Laboratory technology

03 *Plants and Animals*
03.01 Managerial work: Plants and animals
03.02 General supervision: plants and animals
03.03 Animal training and service
03.04 Elemental work: plants and animals
04 *Protective*
04.01 Safety and law enforcement
04.02 Security services
05 *Mechanical*
05.01 Engineering
05.02 Managerial work: mechanical
05.03 Engineering technology
05.04 Air and water vehicle operation
05.05 Craft technology
05.06 Systems operations
05.07 Quality control
05.08 Land and water vehicle operation
05.09 Material control
05.10 Crafts
05.11 Equipment operation
05.12 Elemental work: mechanical
06 *Industrial*
06.01 Production technology
06.02 Production work
06.03 Quality control
06.04 Elemental work: industrial
07 *Business Detail*
07.01 Administrative detail
07.02 Mathematical detail

07.03 Finance detail
07.04 Oral communications
07.05 Records processing
07.06 Clerical machine operations
07.07 Clerical handling
08 *Selling*
08.01 Sales technology
08.02 General sales
08.03 Vending
09 *Accommodating*
09.01 Hospitality services
09.02 Barber and beauty services
10 *Humanitarian*
10.01 Social services
10.02 Nursing, therapy, and specialized teaching services
10.03 Child and adult care
11 *Leading–influencing*
11.01 Mathematics and statistics
11.02 Educational and library services
11.03 Social research
11.04 Law
11.05 Business administration
11.06 Finance
11.07 Services administration
11.08 Communications
11.09 Promotion
11.10 Regulations enforcement
11.11 Business management
11.12 Contracts and claims
12 *Physical Performing*
12.01 Sports
12.02 Physical feats

Each work group area includes a general description of what workers in the group do and where the jobs exist. Figure 8–8 shows an example from the first edition of the brief explanations given in answer to each of the following questions for each work group:

What kind of work would you do?
What skills and abilities do you need for this kind of work?
How do you know if you would like or could learn to do this kind of work?
How can you prepare for and enter this kind of work?
What else should you consider about these jobs?

In addition to the above (or comparable) headings several other pieces of information are included in work group descriptions in the second edition. Two further headings are entitled "licenses and certificates usually

FIGURE 8–8 Sample of work group information in *Guide for Occupational Exploration* (p. 232).

07.02 Mathematical Detail

Workers in this group use clerical and math skills to gather, organize, compute, and record, with or without machines, the numerical information used in business or in financial transactions. Jobs in this group are found wherever numerical record-keeping is important. Banks, finance companies, accounting firms, or the payroll and inventory control departments in business and government are typical of places where this work is done.

—use a calculator to compute wages for payroll records.
—compute the cost of labor and materials for production records of a factory.
—compute freight charges and prepare bills for a truck company.
—compute or verify credit card data to keep customer accounts.
—supervise statistical clerks or insurance underwriting clerks.

What skills and abilities do you need for this kind of work?

To do this kind of work, you must be able to:
—compute and record numbers correctly.
—follow procedures for keeping records.
—use eyes, hands, and fingers at the same time to enter figures in books and forms, or to operate a calculating machine.
—perform work that is routine and detailed.
—read and copy large amounts of numbers without error.
The above statements may not apply to every job in this group.

How do you know if you would like or could learn to do this kind of work?

The following questions may give you clues about yourself as you consider this group of jobs.
—Have you had courses in arithmetic or business math? Are you accurate?

What kind of work would you do?

Your work activities would depend upon your specific job. For example, you might

—Have you taken bookkeeping or accounting? Do you like working with numbers?
—Have you balanced a checking account or figured interest rates? Do you spot errors quickly?
—Have you had experience working with numbers while in the armed forces? Do you like routine work of this kind?

How can you prepare for and enter this kind of work?

Occupations in this group usually require education and/or training extending from thirty days to over two years, depending upon the specific kind of work. People with basic math skills can enter many of the jobs in this group. They receive on-the-job training for specific tasks. To enter some jobs, training in bookkeeping or other business subjects is required. Business training is offered by high schools and business schools.

What else should you consider about these jobs?

Workers in small offices may do a variety of tasks. Some may keep all records for a business or agency. Usually, experience is needed for such positions.

In large offices, workers may have only certain tasks to do, and may repeat these tasks every day. Most jobs of this nature are entry jobs requiring little or no experience.

If you think you would like to do this kind of work, look at the job titles listed on the following pages. Select those that interest you, and read their definitions in the Dictionary of Occupational Titles.

needed" and "organizations and agencies to contact for additional information." Information about specialized training for various subgroups of occupations in each work group is provided, such as the type of education or training usually required and where that preparation can be obtained. Information about the occupations in the subgroups is supplied in tabular form under the following headings: DOT Title and Industry, DOT Code, Strength Factor, and Training associated with the occupation reported as M-L-SVP. The Strength Factor and Training Codes use the codes listed in *Selected Characteristics of Occupations Defined in the Dictionary of Occupational Titles*, a publication that will be discussed later. Strength, or the exertional requirement of an occupation, is defined in terms of the weight that must be lifted or carried in the work and ranges from sedentary to very heavy. Training can be either general or specific. General education is described in six levels of mathematical (M) and language (L) competency ranging from quite simple to very complex. Specific vocational preparation (SVP) is classified in nine levels reflecting the length of time required to gain competency in the occupation, ranging from brief demonstration only to as much as ten years of skill training.

The second edition also supplies the reader with information that relates school subjects, work values, and military occupational specialties to the various work areas. Checklists are also provided to assist a reader in identifying personal characteristics that can be related to corresponding work groups, such as interest areas, leisure activities, home activities, school subjects, and military specialties. Both editions are available. The first edition can be obtained from the Government Printing Office and the second edition from American Guidance Service.

The *GOE* has great potential value for the career counselor because its foundation of interest areas provides a most useful device for helping clients translate assessment of their interests into relevant occupational fields. Further, information in each work-group description about skills and abilities required and preparation programs also provides a base for relating the client's evaluation of aptitudes or general educational plans to appropriate occupational groups at the work-group level. Those work groups that appear to be related to either client interests, aptitudes, or educational plans can be explored further at the subgroup level where the client is referred to specific *DOT* code numbers. See Figure 8–9 for an illustration of the information provided at the subgroup level. This in turn permits the client to use that volume for occupational descriptions and direct access to occupations closely related to the original title. We will consider this application in detail in the next chapter.

The United States Office of Education developed an occupational cluster system in the early 1970s, as public attention began to focus on career education. Because of widespread interest in career education, many publishers of printed and other media career information prepared materials based on this grouping for sale to schools and other organizations. Each cluster includes occupations that have some obvious relationship, often based on an industrial, site-oriented, or activity focus. Most clusters include occupations that vary widely in amount of education or training required, status, rewards, and similar factors. The fifteen clusters that are included in the system are:

1. Consumer and homemaking occupations
2. Health occupations
3. Public service occupations
4. Construction occupations
5. Personal service occupations
6. Transportation occupations
7. Fine arts and humanities occupations
8. Manufacturing occupations
9. Marketing and distribution occupations
10. Agribusiness and natural resources occupations
11. Environmental occupations
12. Marine science occupations
13. Communications and media occupations
14. Business and office occupations
15. Hospitality and recreation occupations

Many different factors, singly or in combination, can be used as a basis for grouping occupations. Over two decades ago, Hatt (1962) compiled a list of more than a dozen basic criteria that can be applied. In some settings, or with certain clients, one or more of these special groupings may be ideally suited for the problem at hand. In the next section we will look briefly at some systems that use factors other than industrial locus or task grouping to combine occupations.

OTHER CLASSIFICATION SYSTEMS

More extensive discussion of classification systems can be found elsewhere (see Herr and Cramer [1984] or Isaacson [1977]). We will consider briefly a sample of widely used groupings.

Roe (1956) prepared a two-dimensional system that combines a horizontal grouping according to primary focus of activity and a vertical grouping based on level of function. The primary focus used for the horizontal axis includes eight groups clustered according to kinds of activities. These categories are largely based on earlier interest measurement research. The reader will readily note aspects of the antecedents of both the *Strong-Campbell Interest Inventory* and the *Kuder General Interest Survey*. The eight groups make up the outer circle in the series of concentric circles that we considered in the discussion of Roe's theory of career choice in Chapter 3. The eight areas comprising the horizontal axis are:

FIGURE 8–9   Sample of subgroup information in *Guide for Occupational Exploration* (p. 233).

07.02

Mathematical Detail

07.02.01   Bookkeeping and Auditing
Audit Clerk (clerical) 210.382-010
Balance Clerk (clerical) 216.382-018
Bookkeeper (clerical) I 210.382-014
Bookkeeper (clerical) II 210.382-018
Bookkeeping-Machine Operator (clerical) I 210.382-022
Bookkeeping-Machine Operator (clerical) II 210.382-026
Classification-Control Clerk (clerical) 210.382-030
General-Ledger Bookkeeper (clerical) 210.382-046
Supervisor, Audit Clerks (clerical) 210.132-010

Clearing-House Clerk (finan. inst.) 216.382-026
Foreign-Exchange-Position Clerk (finan. inst.) 210.367-014
Reconcilement Clerk (finan. inst.) 210.382-058
Reserves Clerk (finan. inst.) 216.362-034

07.02.02   Accounting
Supervisor, Money-Room (amuse. & rec.) 211.137-018

Accounting Clerk (clerical) 216.482-010
Accounting Clerk, Data Processing (clerical) 216.382-010
Calculating-Machine Operator (clerical) 216.482-022
Cost Clerk (clerical) 216.382-034
Mortgage-Accounting Clerk (clerical) 216.362-026
Posting Clerk (clerical) 216.587-014
Rate Supervisor (clerical) 214.137-018
Supervisor, Accounting Clerks (clerical) 216.132-010

Field Cashier (const.) 219.137-010

Account Analyst (finan. inst.) 214.382-010
Advice Clerk (finan. inst.) 216.382-014
Brokerage Clerk (finan. inst.) I 219.482-010
Brokerage Clerk (finan. inst.) II 219.362-018
Check-Processing Clerk (finan. inst.) I 216.387-010
Check-Processing Clerk (finan. inst.) II 216.367-010
Collection Clerk (finan. inst.) 216.362-014
Coupon Clerk (finan. inst.) 219.462-010
Exchange Clerk (finan. inst.) 216.362-018
Fee Clerk (finan. inst.) 214.362-018
Interest Clerk (finan. inst.) 216.382-038
Margin Clerk (finan. inst.) I 216.382-042
Margin Clerk (finan. inst.) II 216.382-046
Probate Clerk (finan. inst.) 216.362-030
Returned-Item Clerk (finan. inst.) 216.382-058
Statement Clerk (finan. inst.) 219.362-058
Stock-Transfer Clerk (finan. inst.) 216.382-070
Supervisor, Securities Vault (finan. inst.) 216.132-014
Supervisor, Trust Accounts (finan. inst.) 219.132-014
Teller, Collection and Exchange (finan. inst.) 211.362-022
Trust-Savings-Account Clerk (finan. inst.) 216.382-074
Trust-Securities Clerk (finan. inst.) 219.362-062
Trust-Vault Clerk (finan. inst.) 216.367-014

FIGURE 8–9 continued

Credit-Card Clerk (hotel & rest.) 210.382-038
Food-and-Beverage Controller (hotel & rest.) 216.362-022
Night Auditor (hotel & rest.) 210.382-054

Cancellation Clerk (insurance) 203.382-014
Dividend-Deposit-Voucher Clerk (insurance) 216.482-026

Distribution-Accounting Clerk (light, heat, & power) 210.362-010
Fixed-Capital Clerk (light, heat, & power) 210.382-042
Supervisor, Accounts Receivable (light, heat, & power; waterworks) 214.137-022

Drivers'-Cash Clerk (motor trans.) 211.462-030

Cashier, Tube Room (ret. tr.) 211.482-010
Contract Clerk, Automobile (ret. tr.) 219.362-026

Clerk, Telegraph Service (tel. & tel.) 219.362-022

07.02.03   Statistical Reporting and Analysis
Flight-Test-Data Transcriber (aircraft-aerospace mfg.) 002.281-010

Chart Clerk (clerical) 221.382-010
Fuel-Oil Clerk (clerical) 222.387-018
Securities Clerk (clerical) 210.382-062
Statistical Clerk (clerical) 216.382-062
Supervisor, Credit and Loan Collections (clerical) 241.137-010
Supervisor, Production Clerks (clerical) 221.137-014

Grading Clerk (education) 219.467-010

Supervisor, Trust Evaluation (finan. inst.) 219.132-018

Claim Examiner (insurance) 168.267-014
Policy-Value Calculator (insurance) 216.382-050

Account-Information Clerk (light, heat, & power) 210.367-010
Cost-and-Sales-Record Supervisor (light, heat, & power) 216.137-010

Chief Clerk, Measurement Department (petrol. production; pipe lines) 221.132-010

Weight Analyst (profess. & kin.) 020.187-018

Statistical Clerk, Advertising (ret. tr.) 216.382-066

Paper-Control Clerk (water trans.) 219.367-022
Receipt-and-Report Clerk (water trans.) 216.382-054

07.02.04   Billing and Rate Computation
Documentation-Billing Clerk (air trans.; motor trans.; r.r. trans.; water trans.) 214.362-014
Ticketing Clerk (air trans.) 248.382-010

Advertising Clerk (bus. ser.) 247.387-010
Media Clerk (bus. ser.) 247.382-010

Billing Typist (clerical) 214.382-014
C.o.d. Clerk (clerical) 214.382-018
Foreign Clerk (clerical) 214.467-010
Invoice-Control Clerk (clerical) 214.362-026
Tax Clerk (clerical) I 219.487-010

I. Service
II. Business
III. Organization
IV. Technology
V. Outdoor
VI. Science
VII. General culture
VIII. Arts and entertainment

The vertical axis is labeled "level of function," which includes the degree of responsibility, capacity, and skill. When these three components do not correlate closely, the first (degree of responsibility) is given basic emphasis. The six levels of function include the following:

1. Professional and managerial—independent responsibility.
2. Professional and managerial—other.
3. Semiprofessional and small business.
4. Skilled.
5. Semiskilled.
6. Unskilled.

Table 8–7 shows how Roe has categorized typical occupations using these two dimensions. Although the table includes only representative occupations, one can easily fit most occupations into the appropriate cell.

In Chapter 3 we discussed Holland's (1973) theory of vocational choice. One will recall that he postulated that there are six working environments, each of which attracts like-minded individuals. Further, since not all work settings are purely one type or another, various combinations of these six can be made with any one category considered primary and different types having secondary and tertiary impact. Holland thus suggests that the various occupations can then be represented by three-letter codes arranged in the order of influence exerted by the six environmental types. The *Self-Directed Search*, discussed in the previous chapter, demonstrates a relationship between an interest-type measurement instrument and an occupational classification system. The *Occupations Finder*, used in conjunction with the *Self-Directed Search*, lists the three-letter codes assigned by Holland to an array of occupations. The six types include Realistic, Investigative, Artistic, Social, Enterprising, and Conventional, arranged clockwise in that sequence around a hexagon. The Holland code for counselor, for example, is SEA. This would be translated to mean that the typical counselor's work is most similar to social occupations, with a secondary component involving enterprising aspects, and a lesser, third component of artistic characteristics.

The World of Work Map for Job Families (Hanson, 1974) presents another two-dimensional approach to classifying occupations, based on

TABLE 8–7   Roe's two-way classification of occupations

Level	I Service	II Business contact	III Organization	IV Technology	V Outdoor	VI Science	VII General cultural	VIII Arts and entertainment
1 Professional & managerial (ind. responsibility)	Personal therapists Social work supervisors Counselors	Promoters	U.S. President & cabinet officers Industrial tycoons International bankers	Inventive geniuses Consulting or chief engineers Ship's commanders	Consulting specialists	Research scientists Univ., col. faculties Medical specialists Museum curators	Supreme Court justices Univ., col. faculties Prophets Scholars	Creative artists Performers, great Teachers, university equivalent Museum curators
2 Professional & managerial	Social workers Occupational therapists Probation truant officers (with training)	Promoters Public relations counselors	C.P.A.'s Business and government executives Union officials	Applied scientists Factory managers Ships' officers	Applied scientists Land owners and operators, large Landscape architects	Scientists, semi-independent Nurses Pharmacists Veterinarians	Editors Teachers, high school and elementary	Athletes Art critics Designers Music arrangers
3 Semiprofessional and small business	YMCA officials Detectives, police sergeants Welfare workers City inspectors	Salesmen; auto, bond, insurance Dealers, retail & wholesale Confidence men	Accountants, average Employment managers Owners, catering, dry-cleaning, etc.	Aviators Contractors Foremen (DOT I) Radio operators	County agents Farm owners Forest rangers Fish, game wardens	Technicians, medical, X-ray, museum Weather observers Chiropractors	Justices of the peace Radio announcers Reporters Librarians	Ad writers Designers Interior decorators Showmen

(continued)

TABLE 8–7 continued

Level	I Service	II Business contact	III Organization	IV Technology	V Outdoor	VI Science	VII General cultural	VIII Arts and entertainment
4 Skilled	Barbers Chefs Practical nurses Policemen	Auctioneers Buyers (DOT I) House can-vassers	Cashiers Clerks Foremen, warehouse Salesclerks	Blacksmiths Electricians Foremen (DOT II) Mechanics	Laboratory testers, dairy products, etc. Miners	Technical assistants	Law clerks	Advertising artists Decorators, window, etc. Photographers
5 Semiskilled	Taxi drivers General house-workers City firemen	Peddlers	Clerks, file, stock, etc. Notaries Runners	Bulldozer operators Truck drivers	Gardeners Farm tenants Teamsters	Veterinary hospital attendants		Illustrators, greeting cards Showcard writers Stagehands
6 Unskilled	Chambermaids Hospital attendants Watchmen		Messengers	Helpers Laborers Wrappers Yardmen	Dairy hands Farm laborers Lumberjacks	Nontechnical helpers in scientific organization		

Source: Roe, A. *The psychology of occupations.* New York: John Wiley and Sons, Inc., 1956, p. 151.

research completed by the staff at American College Testing Program. This research suggests that most occupations relate to two fairly independent bipolar dimensions. One of these, the horizontal continuum, is a people-things relationship and the other, the vertical continuum, is a data-ideas dimension. Further, ACT research postulates that as an occupation's involvement with one of these factors places it nearer one extreme of these two continua, its relationship to the other extreme diminishes. Expressed in another way, one might suggest that New York and San Francisco represent the two ends of a similar continuum, so the nearer one is to New York, the farther one is from San Francisco. Similarly, we might picture another continuum running from Winnipeg to Monterey, intersecting the first at approximately Omaha. The four quadrants thus produced show relationships between the extremes of each continuum. Each quadrant can then be divided into three regions to represent the two areas where one or the other relevant extreme is the more influential and the middle region reflects equal influence. Similarly, an area surrounding the intersection of the two continua can represent a region where the four extreme factors are relatively balanced.

Various job families, or clusters, can then be assigned to appropriate regions according to the relative weights of the pertinent extremes. For example, Education and Social Services is heavily people-oriented and slightly idea-oriented; consequently, it is plotted well to the left on the people-things continuum and slightly below the midpoint on data-ideas (approximately at Las Vegas on our geographic illustration). On the other hand, Natural Sciences and Mathematics is considered to be fairly heavily loaded with ideas and things, so it falls in the mid-area of the lower right quadrant, geographically near Atlanta.

These thirteen areas (twelve sectors and one middle area) accommodate twenty-three different occupational groups called *job families*. The system includes two other families not presently plotted on the map because of the incohesive nature of these two groups.

D'Costa and Winefordner (1969) developed a three-dimensional occupational classification system using the data-people-things concept. Visualizing the world of work as a cube, one can use one factor for each dimension of the cube. If one uses the front left lower corner of the total cube as the starting point, the data continuum can be viewed running from front to back, the people continuum from left to right, and the data continuum from bottom to top.

Because the gradations in each of the three hierarchies are not discrete and precise, they used a three-step division for each—low, average, and high. For convenience, numbers were assigned to each of the three segments, 0 for low, 1 for average, and 2 for high. Further, with each continuum divided into three segments, one now has a three-by-three-by-three matrix of twenty-seven smaller cubes within the total figure, with each smaller cell representing a relationship to data, people, and things. Thus the front left lower cell represents low relationship to all three and can be numerically represented by 0, 0, 0. Similarly, the rear right upper cell reflects high relationship to all three and would be numbered 2, 2, 2. The middle cell, halfway back, halfway right, and halfway up would be average in all relationships, or 1, 1, 1. The rear right lower cell shows high relationship to data and people, but low relationship to things, and is identified as 2, 2, 0. This cell would include the previously mentioned occupations of psychiatrist, counselor, lawyer, and speech pathologist, all of which carry a *DOT* worker function code of .107 (high on data and people, low on things). Similarly, occupations that involve the various combinations of data-people-things relationship can be assigned to the appropriate cell with all other occupations requiring that mix. Only a few occupations require very little or very high involvement with all three; thus 0, 0, 0 and 2, 2, 2 would not be used frequently.

D'Costa et al. (1970) used the Cubistic classification system as a theoretical basis for the *Ohio Vocational Interest Survey* and OVIS II that we discussed in the previous chapter. The scores obtained on the OVIS are related to occupational clusters located in the various cells.

The *General Aptitude Test Battery*, also discussed in the previous chapter, provides a different basis for classifying occupations. Research with the *GATB* has been continuous since the original publication of the test in 1947. Testing large groups of workers in various occupations has identified those aptitudes that are critical for successful performance of that occupation. This has led to the preparation of *Occupational Aptitude Patterns* (OAP) and *Specific Aptitude Test Batteries* (SATB) consisting of those aptitudes that are significantly related to successful performance in a specific occupation, and those portions of the GATB that produce scores for those aptitudes.

The Occupational Aptitude Patterns identify those occupations that require the same array of skills, even though the occupations may be in very different occupational designation families, or industrial sectors, or involve different interest factors. Research has established the links between the OAP's and worker functions, and between OAP's and the work groups used in the *Guide for Occupational Exploration*. Appendix B in the *Guide* lists the occupations by *GOE* work group and subgroup for which Specific Aptitude Test Batteries have been determined. There are now approximately 450 SATB's consisting of combinations of two, three, or four aptitudes with established cutting scores on the appropriate GATB parts for specific occupations. The specific SATB information is provided in the *Manual for the GATB*.

In the next chapter we will refer to many of these classification systems. We also will discuss how some can be used with clients to help them see relationships between their personal characteristics and various occupational requirements.

TRENDS

In the discussion of industrial sectors and occupational groupings, some changes expected to occur among the various fields during the 1980s were also noted. This recognition of variability suggests that the world of work is a dynamic, inconstant, readjusting body. To some extent that is true. However, that does not suggest that the occupational structure is highly fluid, changing drastically by the day or even hour. On the other hand, it is not as immutable as stone. Some aspects of both extremes are sometimes true about most parts of the world of work. Change does occur and to some extent it is constant and persistent. Some portions are more susceptible to frequent and radical change, while other areas change more slowly and within narrower limits.

Consideration of potential change is important for clients for several reasons. Adolescents who are making tentative choices may be several years removed from actual entry into the world of work. They probably should be more concerned about the status of possible occupations at that future date than about today's job market. Individuals at every stage of career development must be able to assess future conditions in their occupation if they are to evaluate correctly and plan effectively for the impact of change or constancy on their lives and lifestyles.

Some changes occur slowly and often can be anticipated or identified long before they exert influence. The transformation that results is usually great—if not permanent, at least long-lasting. Other changes take place more abruptly, and usually are briefer and less drastic in total impact. Some are one-time events and others are cyclical. Prediction of the future is still very inexact; unexpected events sometimes bring dramatic change with great suddenness, and at other times a change that has been widely anticipated and expected fails to occur. Nevertheless, we can be relatively confident that residents in temperate zones will need heavier clothing in the winter, and more ice cream and air conditioning in the summer. Similarly, we can be quite sure that an aging population will require more dentures, medical care, leisure activities, and retirement homes, but a sudden spurt in the birthrate will increase demand for baby food, diapers, and child-care centers.

Long-term trends

Changes that occur gradually, over long periods of time and with great impact, can be classified into at least four broad groups. Some are interrelated, that is, one factor may instigate or retard a different kind of change. Some can be properly classified under more than one heading. For our brief discussion here we will consider long-term trends that can be placed in one of the following groups:

1. Population factors.
2. Sociological factors.
3. Economic factors.
4. Technological factors.

Population factors

The most obvious population factors are those that increase, decrease, or otherwise influence the nature of the population. The impact of the declining birth rate of the last two decades clearly emphasizes the influence of this type of change. Declining school enrollments have caused decreased need for teachers, classroom space and equipment, and school buses. Because fewer babies are being born, the average age of the total population moves upward, focusing the production of goods and services toward an older group.

Improved access to medical care, better nutrition, and other life-extending factors have also changed the death rate so that people tend to live longer than previously. More older people create a different set of demands for goods and services. The two trends of decreased births and increased longevity compound the rate at which the average age of our population increases.

As the average age of the population moves upward, there is an impact on the availability of workers. One of the most difficult employment problems in recent years has been helping the large number of teenagers find beginning jobs. As that pool of prospective workers declines, the number available for beginning jobs decreases and some jobs that are usually filled by this age group may remain unfilled or may necessitate competitive activities to attract potential workers. As the post-World-War-II baby boom moves through the working years, one can expect to see greater competition for desirable positions with fewer opportunities for advancement. Another aspect of the population factor is the average age of workers in a specific occupation. Vacancies occur in occupations because of growth or increased jobs and because of replacement of workers who leave the work because of resignation, retirement, or death. If the average age is high, the replacement rate is also likely to be higher.

Sociological factors

Those influences that derive from the way we live and the values we support or oppose can be considered sociological in nature. Sometimes these aspects are expressed through legislation or by repealing or amending earlier legislation. For example, the efforts to improve the quality of air have increased demand for development, manufacture, and application of pollution-control devices. As those regulations are relaxed the need for the devices will possibly decrease, but the need for different services for those individuals whose health will not tolerate exposure to greater pollution will increase. Shorter working hours and increased emphasis on recreational activities have created demands for camping equipment, boats, travel trailers, and the development of facilities where these items can be used. Increased employment of married women has changed living patterns for many families, affecting housing, transportation, food, and other factors.

Access to training through educational opportunities has a heavy influence on the quality of workers. Many writers have emphasized that those individuals with the least education are usually the least skilled and most frequently unemployed. If access to education is enhanced, the quality and skill of workers is upgraded; if educational opportunities are withdrawn, the process is reversed.

The existence of adequate retirement programs or alternative support systems for older workers influences the number of workers who stay at work. The recent rise in mandatory retirement age from sixty-five to seventy will gradually increase the number of workers who continue beyond the traditional retirement age. Raising the age at which a worker qualifies for full retirement benefits will similarly keep workers on the job, as also will reductions in retirement benefits made available to workers.

Economic factors

In a totally free market, the supply and demand of workers and raw materials would greatly influence the number and nature of available jobs. In most societies, numerous controls have been developed that interfere with the free operation of the market. Many of these came into existence to regulate what had been seen as disruptive surges in that market. Although controls have subdued drastic and sudden fluctuations, there are still discernable trends that suggest upward or downward movements in the marketplace that bear on occupational opportunity.

Changes in capitalization requirements also influence jobs. Undoubtedly, one cause of the consistent decline in employment in agriculture relates to this factor. Farming of almost every type now requires such an extensive investment in land and equipment that efficiency becomes the determining factor between success and failure. In other businesses, the constant search for mergers is often related to economic factors that are fundamentally based on productive efficiency, creating more goods with fewer workers.

Access to new markets or the loss of existing markets may increase or decrease available jobs. Sometimes these factors may involve international relations and may be influenced by national rivalries. Also, access or loss of access to sources of supply are other aspects of the effects of international relations.

Technological factors

The unrelenting search for new and better ways to do things clearly creates entirely new industries and also sometimes wipes out others. One invention often leads to others that change our way of life and the things or services that we use in that life. One startling development in recent years has been the dramatic reduction of the time span between the discovery or invention of something new and the time that its benefits are available to the general public. It would be almost folly to attempt to enumerate here the many devices that we use routinely each day that did not exist a decade or two ago.

Closely related to invention and discovery is access to natural resources. The sudden recognition in the United States of our dependence on outside sources for such crucial items as petroleum has produced and is still producing vast changes in our lives and in occupational opportunities. The automobile industry has undergone a metamorphosis that in turn has affected the production of steel and other supplies. The search for oil has been accelerated, as has the search for alternate sources of energy. There are many other examples.

Short-term trends

Several examples of factors producing short-term trends can be identified. Viewed from an objective perspective, these usually have less effect than long-term trends. Nevertheless, to individuals who are caught in the crunch produced by transitory factors, the impact can be devastating. Some influences have a generalized effect across almost the entire economy, while others may be more specific.

One of the most obvious causes of short-term trends is various types of calamities, either man-made or natural. Natural disasters such as earthquakes, floods, or volcanic eruptions can disrupt and change occupational patterns in the area for extended periods of time. For example, the 1980 eruption of Mt. St. Helens has required considerable occupational readjustment in a very large region.

Man-made disasters can be just as disruptive. War or the threat of war diverts large numbers of workers from civilian occupations to military assignments. It further affects others by switching manufacturing and other sectors to the production of military goods. It may create serious shortages of workers in fields that are considered less essential to the national welfare.

Fads, new directions in fashion, recreation and other activities, or similar caprices can also distort the occupational structure by creating new demands or reducing old ones. Changes in men's hair styles in recent years have eliminated many barber shops. Imitation of movie idols, popular athletes, or television stars can create demands where none previously existed. Some technological developments occasionally start in the area of fads, for example, videodiscs and home computers.

Seasonal variations are also influential. Summer tends to increase demand for goods and services in mountain and seaside resorts, while winter has the same effect on resorts located in warm areas. "Back-to-school" days include buying in retail stores for which manufacturers have previously been preparing. Planting time and harvest time change typical patterns in agricultural areas. The annual Christmas shopping season creates demand for temporary sales workers, letter carriers, transportation workers, and other types of workers.

There also are short-term economic factors that exert influence. Although the general business trend over long periods is either upward or downward, small segments of that larger trend will show considerable variation. Factors that create these short-term zigzags include strikes, unexpected surpluses or shortages of raw materials or processed goods, temporary market disruptions, fluctuations in access to short-term capital caused by changes in interest rates, inflationary pressures, changing tax laws, and sometimes even the anticipation of possible events.

In most situations, the client's consideration of possible career fields includes an expectation of a lengthy involvement. It is necessary, then, to look beyond the immediate job market status and, by evaluating both short-term and long-term trends, help the client make predictions about future circumstances that are as accurately based as possible.

INFORMATION ABOUT OCCUPATIONS

Individuals must have accurate, current, usable information about themselves and about occupations if they are to make wise decisions. As occupations have grown more complex, many also have withdrawn from public view. It is no longer feasible to walk down Main Street with a client and point out examples of all available occupations. We have become dependent upon supplementary sources of information. Only rarely will the client know where and how to obtain the information that will provide an accurate understanding of an occupation. If the client is to be well-served and if career counseling is to be effective, the counselor must know where appropriate information can be acquired and be able to assist the client in obtaining and using that information.

We can review only briefly the types and sources of career information that the counselor must have available. More detailed discussions of this important area can be found in Hoppock (1976), Isaacson (1977), or Norris et al. (1979).

Selecting appropriate materials for a particular client requires understanding of the client as well as knowing what career information is available, and where. One must face such questions as the following: How much information is needed? What kind of information can be most accurately and rapidly integrated into the client's decision-making system? Where is that kind of information readily and economically (in terms of both time and money) accessible? Can the client successfully deal with acquiring and using this type of information?

Sources of information are constantly changing, with new sources and systems appearing and older systems shifting and disappearing. For example, the Department of Labor has recently established a National Occupational Information Coordinating Committee to work with a network of state level committees. This structure is charged with developing a system that will make occupational information more accessible and more usable.

Printed materials

The most abundant type of career information is printed matter. It ranges in scope from a few brief sentences to lengthy volumes. Accuracy and usefulness vary similarly, and there is no apparent correlation among the three factors. A paragraph in the *Dictionary of Occupational Titles* may describe precisely the essence of the tasks performed in a specific occupation, and, at the same time, a monograph of many pages may simply interpret, illustrate, and explain that same paragraph.

Because the educational system has used books so widely, we are accustomed to turning almost automatically to printed sources when we seek new information. Counselors must recognize that not all individuals read well, understand what they read, and are able to apply or use what they read. Sometimes, also, other types of information may fit the needs of a particular client more appropriately.

School media centers, libraries, and career resource centers will often have an extensive collection of printed career information. Often the material will be catalogued and arranged or filed according to one of the frequently used filing systems. The counselor may need to teach the client how the system works if he or she is to use it.

Sources of printed materials include many government agencies, professional organizations, private companies, educational institutions, periodicals, and commercial publishers. *Vocational Guidance Quarterly* includes in each issue a list of recently published career materials. Several commercial publishers of career materials issue an annual index of recently published materials, and at least one book listing current materials appears regularly.

The *Dictionary of Occupational Titles*, the *Guide for Occupational Exploration*, and current issues of the *Occupational Outlook Handbook* are generally considered as basic references.

Valuable additions to this basic group would include *DOT* related publications such as *Supplements to the Dictionary of Occupational Titles* and *Selected Characteristics of Occupations Defined in the Dictionary of Occupational Titles*. State Employment Service offices publish material relevant to the state or regions of the state such as Standard Metropolitan Statistical Areas or Economic Regions that provide locally useful information unavailable from national sources.

Audiovisual materials

The old adage "a picture is worth a thousand words" confirms that audiovisual techniques are useful for counselors. Many films, filmstrips, pictures, audiotapes, and videotapes can be used to assist clients to understand particular occupations. Television and radio series or special presentations, movies, and news broadcasts on either TV or radio may help to build insight or, conversely, may simply reaffirm superficial stereotypes.

High-quality audiovisual (AV) material is more costly to produce than most printed material. Consequently, it is often less accessible than books, monographs, and pamphlets. AV materials are often maintained in centralized locations from which they can be borrowed or rented for short periods. Many school systems are now affiliated with cooperative agencies providing this kind of service.

Both AV and printed materials face a common problem since both may retain their usability longer than their accuracy. The world of work is fluid and, in periods of rapid change, information about salaries, number of openings, and preparatory programs may quickly be seriously dated.

Programmed and mechanized materials

Workbooks or sequenced exercises have been developed to assist individuals in either the entire career-choice process or in certain segments of that process. Typically, these devices provide a logical series of experiences that assist the client to obtain needed information and to process that information in a way that moves him or her toward a decision. The advantages usually include allowing the individual to proceed at a personally determined pace and assuring that specific steps are mastered before advancing to later steps. The disadvantages are that some attention to individual client needs may be lost, and feelings of depersonalization may develop in the client.

Recent examples of programmed material are the *Vocational Exploration and Insight Kit* developed by John Holland and incorporating his *Self-Directed Search*, and two workbooks prepared by the Employment Service entitled *Job Selection Workbook* and *Self-Appraisal Workbook*.

The *VIEW* (*Vocational Information for Education and Work*) system is representative of several mechanized systems that are now in general use. This system, first developed by the San Diego Department of Education, has been adopted and adapted by many state and local agencies over the past fifteen years (Gerstein and Hoover, 1967). *VIEW* incorporates the use of microfilm aperture cards and necessitates the use of a microfilm reader and microfilm printer. The system overcomes many of the disadvantages inherent in much printed and AV material. It provides current and usable national and regional information and retains economy, compactness, and ease of operation. It can be kept updated and also directed toward needs of particular groups.

Further illustrations of mechanized systems include the *Occupational View-Deck* and the *Worker Trait Group Keysort Deck*. Both of these will be discussed in more detail in the next chapter.

Computer-based systems

Computers have been used for a long time to store and retrieve information. Many have been used for career materials. As early as 1974, Harris identified thirty systems in various stages of development or use. Since that time there has been considerable expansion in availability and usage. As computers become even more efficient and simultaneously less expensive, their increased application is assured. Several states have been working in a consortium to explore the use of computers in statewide information delivery systems. The results of this tryout should soon be available for wider application.

Several high school and college systems have adopted the *Computerized Vocational Information System* (*CVIS*) developed by Harris and others at Willowbrook High School. This system is essentially an information-retrieval technology that includes information about the student as well as about occupations, schools, training programs, and so forth. Stored information can be kept current, and the system can be used easily and economically by students wherever it is available.

An example of an advanced level computer system is the *System of Interactive Guidance and Information* (*SIGI*) developed by Katz at Educational Testing Service. *SIGI* incorporates six subsystems that assist the user in assessing values, locating occupations that involve various values, comparing various occupations on assorted criteria, predicting chances for success in local preparatory programs, planning personal preparatory programs, and estimating overall desirability of a specific occupation. Because the system is more complex than *CVIS*, it is also more time-consuming and costly to implement and maintain. Somewhat similar to *SIGI* in level of sophistication is the *DISCOVER* system, also now generally available. Computerized systems will be considered in detail in Chapter 11.

Interviews with experts

One basic source of occupational information has always been the worker. He or she should know more about a job—how it feels, what it demands, how it influences one's life, and the satisfactions it provides—than either the employer or skilled observers, the two other major sources. The worker has at once credibility and authority, "can tell it like it is." Every community is certainly richly endowed with this resource. Elementary school teachers have long capitalized on the use of workers to tell their classes about different jobs and what workers do there. Secondary schools have modified the system slightly but, essentially, the career day or career conference is a device for bringing workers into a conversation with interested students. Many schools maintain a reference file of local individuals who have agreed to talk with students, individually or in groups, about their occupations. Counselors can, of course, locate appropriate workers who are willing to talk with clients as the need arises. A network of local contacts is essential to help identify suitable resource workers.

Some problems can occur with this technique, but most of them can be avoided by carefully selecting workers who are to serve this consulting role. One danger is that the worker's experience is unusual and not characteristic of most individuals in that occupation. Another problem can occur if the selected worker lacks communication skills and is unable to convey feelings, insights, and experiences. An additional problem arises when the worker over-enthusiastically "sells" the occupation with a recruiting approach or else emphasizes only how very difficult or demanding the job can be.

Simulation and synthetic work environments

Simulation involves artificial activities in an artificial setting used to gain insight, understanding, or skill applicable to real activities and in a realistic setting. Teachers have long used this device as a basic tool in classrooms. Role-playing and fire drills are found in every school and typify simulation. Although widely used in teaching, simulation has been used in personal or change counseling more frequently than in career counseling. The *Job Experience Kits* available from Science Research Associates and based on research by Krumboltz illustrate how this approach can be used effectively in career counseling.

Synthetic work environments are one step closer than simulation to reality. Simulation involves artificial activity, whereas synthetic work environments provide realistic activity, although both maintain an artificial setting. This technique is also widely used by teachers and schools. Many vocational education departments teach students construction skills by having the classes actually build a residence that is later sold to provide the land, materials, and equipment for the next year's project. In the process, the student actually performs the various construction jobs under supervision of faculty. Other schools maintain student-operated stores, office practice projects, child-care centers, and similar situations where the student performs the actual work but in a setting where teaching and supervision are available. Where these activities already exist, the counselor can use them to help clients obtain a feel for the "real thing."

Direct observation

Field trips not only help the individual to see what a worker does and how he or she functions, but they also show the worker in his or her "natural habitat." One gains a much better feel for the occupation when one encounters both worker and work setting. Even the casual "walk-through" exposes the individual to sights and sounds and other reactions that cannot be provided by printed statements, pictures, or even interviews with workers. A modified use of the field trip has particular interest for career counselors because they are usually focusing on the needs of a single client. Many counselors report favorable results from an individualized field trip usually, called *shadowing*. In this technique, arrangements are made for the individual to spend a working day with a worker, watching the worker on the job, when time and activity permit listening to the worker explain why things are done a particular way, seeing what happens and how the job relates to the activity of other workers. Sometimes the individual can shadow two or three workers during the day and thereby broaden experiences still further.

Exploratory participation

Career education advocates contend that every student, from early high school onward, should participate in some work experience. *Exploratory work experience* is primarily intended to assist the individual in understanding different types of work, work settings, activities, tools and equipment used, and the general aspects of work and work life. The exploratory experience need not be paid, although there are advantages to the experience of being paid for effort, and it need not be full-time. It does need to be long enough each work day to provide a realistic sample of the work, which probably requires a half-day in most settings. The experience also needs to be continued for enough days and weeks to supply the day-in-day-out variety or lack of variety that is characteristic of the job. Rarely can that be accomplished in less than three or four weeks.

Counselors can use this approach advantageously with many clients who have had very limited exposure to actual work settings. Often the client may be interested in occupations that require lengthy preparatory programs and may be concerned about the appropriateness of a tentative choice. Although direct involvement in the occupation is impossible because of lack of professional knowledge or skill, close contact through exploratory activities may be possible. A client interested in nursing or medicine might find experience as a part time candy-striper or hospital orderly enlightening. Other fields have similar jobs involving lower skill levels that provide some chance for exploratory exposure.

On-the-job tryout

The most realistic experience of all, where it can be arranged, is actual tryout on the job. This is appropriate to positions where requirements for previous training or experience are low, or where clients have completed the necessary preparation and now must make choices among an array of beginning assignments in their professional career. An illustration of the latter is the engineering student who is approaching graduation and is encountering difficulty in choosing among applied, research, sales, and training options.

There are difficulties in creating this type of experience for clients because it requires an actual work situation. Using a position for tryout experiences is costly for the employer, who usually prefers a fully committed, ambitious worker rather than one who may need to be replaced after the tryout period expires. Such personnel changes are expensive, time-consuming, and impose on other workers.

One example of on-the-job tryout that does work successfully is the vocational preparatory work experience program where the participant usually is assigned for a full school year on a half-time basis. The purpose of the program is to teach actual work skills, and participants ordinarily have already made a clear choice. Opportunity to be involved in such an experience would not be available to an undecided client.

In this section we have considered an array of techniques that counselors can use to help clients learn about occupations. Counselors must select those methods that are compatible with client needs and the situation in which counselor and client meet. Often a combination of several approaches will be of greatest help to the client.

REFERENCES

D'Costa, A. G. and Winefordner, D. W. A cubistic model of vocational interests. *Vocational Guidance Quarterly*, 1969, *17*, 242–249.

D'Costa, A. G., Winefordner, D. W., Odgers, J. G., and Koons, P. B., Jr. *Ohio Vocational Interest Survey*. New York: The Psychological Corporation, 1970.

Fredrickson, R. H. *Career information*. Englewood Cliffs, N.J.: Prentice-Hall, Inc., 1982.

Fullerton, H. N., Jr. and Tschetter, J. The 1995 labor force: a second look. *Monthly Labor Review*, 1983, *106*, 11, pp. 3–10.

Gerstein, M. and Hoover, R. VIEW—Vocational Information for Education and Work. *Personnel and Guidance Journal*, 1967, *45*, 593–596.

Hanson, G. *ACT research report 67: Assessing the interests of college youth: Summary of research and applications*. Iowa City, Ia.: American College Testing Program, 1974.

Harrington, T. F. and O'Shea, A. J. (eds.). *Guide for occupational exploration*. 2nd edition. Minneapolis: National Forum Foundation, 1984.

Harris, J. The computer: Guidance tool of the future. *Journal of Counseling Psychology*, 1974, *21*, 331–339.

Hatt, P. K. Occupation and social stratification. In S. Nosow and W. H. Form (eds.). *Man, work and society*. New York: Basic Books, 1962, pp. 238–249.

Herr, E. L. and Cramer, S. H. *Career guidance through the life span*. 2nd edition. Boston: Little, Brown and Company, 1984.

Holland, J. L. *Making vocational choices: A theory of careers*. Englewood Cliffs, N.J.: Prentice-Hall, Inc., 1973.

Hoppock, R. *Occupational information*. 4th edition. New York: McGraw-Hill Book Company, 1976.

Isaacson, L. E. *Career information in counseling and teaching*. 3rd edition. Boston: Allyn and Bacon, Inc., 1977.

Norris, W., Hatch, R. N., Engelkes, J. R., and Winborn, B. B. *The career information service*. 4th edition. Chicago: Rand McNally and Company, 1979.

Personick, V. A. The job outlook through 1995: Industry output and employment projections. *Monthly Labor Review*, 1983, *106*, 11, pp. 24–36.

Prediger, D. J. Getting "ideas" out of the DOT and into vocational guidance. *Vocational Guidance Quarterly*, 1981, *20*, 293–306.

Roe, A. *The psychology of occupations*. New York: John Wiley and Sons, 1956, pp. 143–152.

Silvestri, G. T., Lukarsiewicz, J. M. and Einstein, M. E. Occupational employment projections through 1995. *Monthly Labor Review*, 1983, *106*, 11, pp. 37–49.

United States Department of Commerce, Office of Federal Statistical Policy and Standards. *Standard occupational classification manual*. Washington, D.C.: United States Government Printing Office, 1980.

United States Department of Health, Education and Welfare. *Career education*. HEW Publications No. (OE) 72-39. Washington, D.C.: United States Government Printing Office, 1971.

United States Department of Labor. *Dictionary of occupational titles*. 4th edition. Washington, D.C.: U.S. Government Printing Office, 1977.

———. *Employment projections for the 1980's*. Bulletin 2030. Washington, D.C.: U.S. Government Printing Office, 1979.

———. *Guide for occupational exploration*. Washington, D.C.: U.S. Government Printing Office, 1979.

———. *Occupational outlook handbook, 1980–81*. Washington, D.C.: U.S. Government Printing Office, 1980.

United States Office of Management and Budget. *Standard industrial classification manual*. Washington, D.C.: U.S. Government Printing Office, 1972.

9

Expanding options and narrowing choices

The major purpose of this chapter is to present and discuss techniques the counselor can use to assist the client in translating personal attributes into occupational characteristics. For the typical client—one who is almost totally undecided about career plans—the goal is to identify an array of occupations that capitalize on important client qualities and meet other client specifications already known to both client and counselor. The list should be broad, including representative occupations from many appropriate areas of the world of work. Attempting to compile a comprehensive list is futile and inefficient because there are so many occupations extant. Typical occupations with generic-type titles are more useful initially; for example, physician, carpenter, machine operator are usually more helpful at first than internist, shipwright, or punch-press operator.

The client who has made progress in career choice and now is primarily concerned with establishing priorities among a list of perhaps two or three carefully considered possibilities may not need to spend time expanding options. This is especially the case when the choices have been investigated thoughtfully, appear to fit client characteristics, and the client feels he or she would find the options satisfying. Such a client may be ready to engage in the narrowing phase that we will consider near the end of the chapter. Simply because a client can name two or three possibilities does not assure a counselor that discussion should be limited to that brief list.

The process of translating and matching operates in two directions, as the chapter title suggests. The first goal is to develop a broad array of possible alternatives; the second objective is to reduce the list to a small group of the very best possibilities. Because the counselor's knowledge of the world of work is more comprehensive than the client's, the counselor must assume primary responsibility for the first phase. The client must take major responsibility during the narrowing phase.

In many ways the situation is analogous to what one might encounter when a person decides to go to a large, first-class department store to purchase a major item of clothing. At first, the only limiting factor may be the customer's size; thus he or she may be shown an abundance of choices, often grouped according to quality, designer label, price, type of fabric, and similar criteria. Within each grouping are further subsets based on style, color, pattern, and so on. The efficient and conscientious salesperson attempts to familiarize the customer with each of the broad categories available. The customer then can eliminate this group because better quality is desired, that group because it looks too faddish, another because it's too expensive, and focus on two or three groups that meet his or her general desires. The process continues within this smaller array, with further consideration of additional factors until the final selection is made. Ideally, the salesperson helps the customer see what is available, the advantages and disadvantages of each, and how to compare the available garments. The customer may (and sometimes does) abdicate responsibility and allow the salesperson to sell him or her a particular model, and sometimes the salesperson seizes control and assertively directs the customer to a specific choice, or fails to show several options. Most customers feel that they have been best served when a knowledgeable salesperson has helped them to see and evaluate the available stock and left the decision up to the customer.

The counselor's leadership in the expanding phase is extremely important for several reasons. Most clients can be expected to have quite limited and narrow views of the world of work. After all, what they know about jobs has come from the experiences they have encountered up to this point, and most of the time they were not concerned with learning all they could about every occupation they chanced to meet. Consequently, most have seen only a limited number of occupations and the view they have of those is often superficial. Further, they have rarely, if ever, contemplated the world of work as an organized system or structure, so they will often not understand how occupations interact and fit together in the larger unit. Second, even in those few occupations where they are most knowledgeable, clients may be unable to identify clearly the requirements or characteristics necessary for successful performance. Finally, several professional devices and systems exist that significantly assist this process when properly applied by

FIGURE 9–1   Steps in expanding and narrowing options.

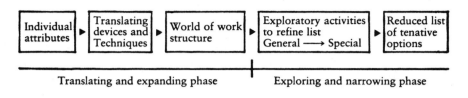

| Individual attributes | ▶ | Translating devices and Techniques | ▶ | World of work structure | ▶ | Exploratory activities to refine list General ⟶ Special | ▶ | Reduced list of tenative options |

Translating and expanding phase | Exploring and narrowing phase

the counselor. This professional knowledge and skill is part of what qualifies a counselor to work with career counseling cases. During this phase the counselor may be involved in both teaching and counseling activities.

The two phases of career counseling that we are considering in this chapter can be described as seen in Figure 9–1. In the first step, the counselor uses various translating tools and techniques to help the client relate important personal attributes to occupations that involve those characteristics. During the second phase, the client explores information about occupations on the list, using data and procedures that the counselor has helped obtain, and reduces the list to a small group of most appropriate options.

Continuing the shopping analogy further, the concern during the *translating phase* of career counseling is to help the client identify a wide array of occupational options that relate to the various personal criteria already identified as important such as personal attributes, attitudinal factors, educational goals, and economic opportunity. During the *narrowing phase* the focus is to help the client properly evaluate and combine in priority fashion those personal criteria and identify the occupational options that appear most likely to match the client's list of priorities and goals. Remer and O'Neill (1980) divide these two phases into seven steps.

TRANSLATING AND EXPANDING PHASE

It is easy to imagine, in our fictitious shopping trip, that one might observe some shoppers whose major concern is price, while others look first for style, color, elegance, quality, or some other factor they have identified as personally most important. Similarly, the counselor must expect that clients approach career counseling with varied sets of priorities. For example, we might envision some client's viewpoint encapsulated by one of the following statements:

> I really like mathematics. I'd want my career to allow me to work with figures.
> I'm pretty good in artistic activities. I'd like to use that skill some way.

TABLE 9–1   Commonly used acronyms included in Chapter 9.

CPI	California Psychological Inventory
DAT	Differential Aptitude Test
D-P-T	Data-People-Things (Worker Functions section of DOT)
DOT	Dictionary of Occupational Titles
EPPS	Edwards Personal Preference Schedule
GATB	General Aptitude Test Battery
GED	General Educational Development
GOE	Guide for Occupational Exploration (also *Guide*)
GZTS	Guilford-Zimmerman Temperament Survey
KOIS	Kuder Occupational Interest Survey
Kuder DD	Kuder Occupational Interest Survey
Kuder E	Kuder General Interest Survey
OAP	Occupational Aptitude Pattern
OVIS	Ohio Vocational Interest Survey
SATB	Specific Aptitude Test Battery
SCII	Strong-Campbell Interest Inventory
SDS	Self-Directed Search
SVP	Specific Vocational Preparation
VEIK	Vocational Exploration and Information Kit

The important thing to me is helping people, I don't care how, as long as I can feel I make their lives better.

I think I'm a very outgoing type of person and I enjoy contact with people. Are there jobs that capitalize on that trait?

My family has always been in agriculture. I want to be involved in that field but I don't want to farm.

I can go to school for two years after high school but that's the limit.

Sometimes I think my deafness stops me from doing anything.

Because each of the above hypothetical statements expresses a different primary focus, they underscore the point that the counselor should start with the attribute that seems most important to the client. In considering these various attributes and the different approaches that capitalize on each, we will look at many devices that are often identified or referred to by acronyms or abbreviations. Most of these have been listed in Table 9–1 to assist the reader in identifying them.

In Chapters 5 and 7 we discussed various ways of helping a client identify and evaluate significant aspects of his or her personal world. We are now ready to help the client relate these individual attributes to the world of work where appropriate occupational options can be identified and later explored. Figure 9–2 confirms that there are several different attributes or personal characteristics that can be used as starting points, and also several different devices or procedures that can be used to identify related occupa-

FIGURE 9–2 The translating and exploring phase.

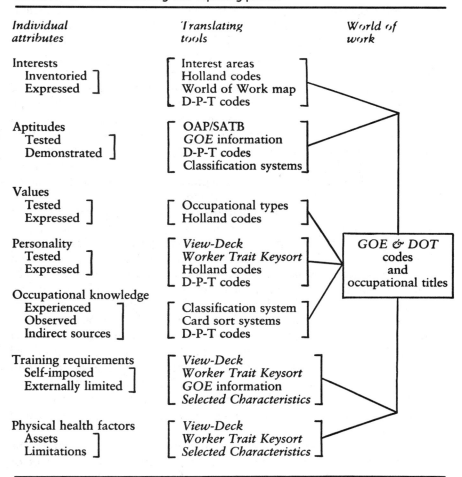

Individual attributes	*Translating tools*	*World of work*

Interests
  Inventoried
  Expressed
	Interest areas
	Holland codes
	World of Work map
	D-P-T codes	

Aptitudes
  Tested
  Demonstrated
	OAP/SATB
	GOE information
	D-P-T codes
	Classification systems	

Values
  Tested
  Expressed
	Occupational types
	Holland codes	

Personality
  Tested
  Expressed
	View-Deck
	Worker Trait Keysort
	Holland codes
	D-P-T codes
		GOE & DOT
		codes
		and
		occupational titles

Occupational knowledge
  Experienced
  Observed
  Indirect sources
	Classification system
	Card sort systems
	D-P-T codes	

Training requirements
  Self-imposed
  Externally limited
	View-Deck
	Worker Trait Keysort
	GOE information
	Selected Characteristics	

Physical health factors
  Assets
  Limitations
	View-Deck
	Worker Trait Keysort
	Selected Characteristics	

tions. Examples in Figure 9–2 are intended only to be illustrative of both personal attributes and translation devices.

Figure 9–2 is essentially a road map for the remainder of our discussion of the translating phase. The primary goal at this point is to help the client match the insights and understanding of self and his or her psychological world, developed in earlier interviews, with potential options in the world of work. Later we will be concerned with focusing or fine-tuning those matches to identify the ones that the client feels will offer the best opportunity of satisfying needs, desires, and goals. We will consider several of the major attributes, such as interests, aptitudes, values, and personality, that counselors frequently use as the starting point in the matching process. With each of these we will describe illustrative devices or techniques that can be applied to facilitate that matching process. We have already taken the position that the best starting point is the attribute on which the client is placing primary attention. The counselor should select the device or approach using that attribute that will be most helpful for the client. The devices included have been selected because they are representative of those that make up the armamentarium of the skilled career counselor.

During this phase of career counseling, the counselor is often involved in both a teaching and a counseling relationship with the client. The teaching aspect, of course, focuses on explaining the attributes being considered and how the various devices relate to these characteristics, as well as their limitations. Counseling, simultaneously, focuses on helping the client continually clarify self-perceptions, relate new information to that self-perception and to identified priorities, and integrate that expanded understanding in ways that will lead to appropriate action.

Rarely will counselor and client use only one, two, or three attributes to build the list of occupational options. Usually, a composite of many of those listed in Figure 9–2, plus others that have special significance for the client, will be used. Using only one or two of the attributes is both inefficient and inappropriate. It is inefficient because the list of occupations that can be related to one factor—interest, for example—is very lengthy and would take a long time to develop. It is inappropriate because it permits occupations to be listed that other personal characteristics show to be inaccessible. Each attribute included in the composite will usually moderate or restrict the list that might be compiled if only the first attribute were considered alone. In other words, the expanding and narrowing phases are not completely exclusive and sequential but rather are simultaneous, with one holding major attention first and the other later. As we shall see shortly, many of the devices used in the expanding phase also can be appropriately used in the narrowing phase.

In addition to the individual attributes listed in Figure 9–2 and to be considered in detail shortly, many clients have special circumstances or characteristics that modify the importance of these relatively universal factors. Examples of these influencing qualities include the attitudes of family members or important others, the presence of unique educational opportunities or experiences, access to influential individuals in educational or occupational settings, and unusual personal experiences, motivations, or competencies. Some may be considered as chance factors, or being in the right place at the right time and able to respond to the situation.

Two widely used systems for explaining the world of work and for organizing various types of occupational information are those used in the *Guide to Occupational Exploration* and the *Dictionary of Occupational Titles*. These two systems will be used as the basis for our consideration of the world of work structure as seen in Figures 9–1 and 9–2. We will consider translating devices in terms of relating personal attributes to occupational codes in those two systems. Because the *GOE* system leads directly to *DOT* code numbers, our focus will ordinarily be on ways to identify first the *GOE* codes.

The repetition of several examples in the "translating tools" column of Figure 9–2 suggests correctly that many of these devices are sufficiently flexible to permit their use with more than one of the personal attributes. In order to simplify our consideration of each device we will discuss each in the same sequence as that listed in Figure 9–2. When an item appears more than once, its major discussion usually will occur the first time we reach that item, and additional later elaboration will be made only in terms of the later personal attributes.

Interests

Many counselors use interest inventory results as the major vehicle for approaching occupational options. There are probably several reasons for this choice, some of them very useful and positive while others, perhaps, less helpful, have sometimes led to the impression that career counseling is a brief "test-and-tell" process. First, several interest inventories are keyed directly to occupational options, for example, the occupational scales of the *Strong-Campbell Interest Inventory* and the *Kuder Occupational Interest Survey—DD*. Second, clients are often inclined to focus attention on interest scores to confirm their subjective evaluations and then move their attention to occupations named by those scores. Third, the counselor's limited skill or the client's unwillingness to spend sufficient time may lead to using a very abbreviated list of occupations either named by the inventory or obviously related to the high scores on the test. Finally, the mistaken impression that if the client has objective information about his or her interests, he or she can fit the rest together without counselor help, leads to insufficient counseling.

Interest areas

Several of the widely used interest inventories produce scores directly reported in terms of general or primary interest areas such as the *Kuder General Interest Survey—Form E,* the *SDS,* and the *SCII* General Occupational Themes. Other scores are reported in group categories that easily translate into primary interest areas, such as the *SCII* Basic Interest Scales and the *Jackson Vocational Interest Survey.* Table 9–2 shows the similarity of other interest area groupings to the twelve interest areas of the *Guide for Occupational Exploration.* The Holland occupational categories and the primary focus area labels of Roe's two-dimensional classification system are included to emphasize the extent to which general labels in these widely used systems correspond. The *Kuder General Interest* scales and the *SCII* General Occupational Themes are listed to demonstrate the compatibility between these two scoring systems and the *GOE* Interest Areas.

TABLE 9–2 A comparison of commonly used interest areas.

USES occupational interest areas (GOE)	Holland occupational categories	Roe's primary focus	Kuder general interest survey-E	SCII basic interest areas
01 Artistic	Artistic	Arts & Entertainment General Culture	Artistic Literary Musical	Art Writing Music/Drama
02 Scientific	Investigative	Science	Scientific Computational	Science Mathematics Medical Science Medical Service
03 Plants & Animals	Realistic	Outdoor	Outdoor	Agriculture, Nature Military Activities
04 Protective 05 Mechanical 06 Industrial		Technological	Mechanical	Mechanical Activities Adventure
07 Business Detail	Conventional	Organization	Clerical	Office Practices
08 Selling	Enterprising	Business Contact	Persuasive	Sales Public Speaking Law/Politics Merchandising Business Management
09 Accommodating 10 Humanitarian 11 Leading-Influencing 12 Physical Participation	Social	Service	Social Service	Domestic Arts Social Service, Religious Activities Teaching Athletics

It is important to recognize that the terms used as labels in various scoring and classification systems are not necessarily synonymous even when the titles use the same word. Consequently, one must be aware that, at best, they are only roughly equivalent and not interchangeable. Since the purpose at this point is to stimulate exploration and consideration of tentative possibilities, that lack of precision need not cause a problem. The *GOE* illustrates the fact that the various categories are less than perfect matches by stating that some of the occupations it lists as "Accommodating" would be listed in Holland's typology under "Enterprising" or "Realistic" and some of the occupations it considers to be "Leading-Influencing" would be classified under the Holland system as "Enterprising" and "Investigative" (*GOE*, p. 325).

Moving from interest-area scores, such as those of *Kuder-E* or *SCII* General Occupational Themes is a very simple process. Table 9–2 shows the *GOE* interest areas that approximate the score areas on the interest inventories, so if one wishes to explore possible occupations related to high *Kuder-E* scores on "Artistic" or "Musical," the entry would be via the *GOE* interest area of "01 Artistic." If one wishes to explore *Kuder-E* "Persuasive" or *SCII* General Occupational Theme "Enterprising," the obvious entry would be the *GOE* area "08 Selling." This latter example demonstrates the lack of perfect fit, because "Persuasive" scores also suggest an entry to *GOE* area "11 Leading-Influencing." Thus, the counselor must help the client to be aware of other tangential areas that warrant some exploration.

Some test scores are reported with occupational titles, for example, the *Kuder Occupational Interest Survey, Form DD,* and the *SCII* Occupational Scales. These titles can be used with the *Dictionary of Occupational Titles* in two ways to identify occupations for further exploration. First, the *DOT* lists closely related titles in the same code area; consequently, a quick scanning of preceding and succeeding titles is often productive. Second, the *DOT* title can be used with Appendix D of the *Guide* to obtain the *GOE* code number that leads to the appropriate section of that book.

Expressed interests are often verbalized most easily in broad categories such as the interest-area labels. Some clients can differentiate their interests using only the single-sentence descriptions of the *GOE* interest areas included in the introductory pages of the *Guide*. Others will find perusing the additional information provided as the lead statement to each of the four-digit code work groups useful in deciding their level of interest. These descriptive statements are found throughout Part V of the *Guide*.

Holland codes

The three-letter Holland codes have become widely recognized because of their use with the *Self-Directed Search* and the *Strong-Campbell Interest Inventory. The Occupations Finder* that accompanies the *SDS* lists illustrative occupations that fit most of the Holland codes, and includes *DOT* code numbers for each. These *DOT* codes and titles can be used in the two ways listed above to help a client develop a list of options. First, the *DOT* codes facilitate direct entry to the *DOT* where the individual will usually find other closely related titles adjacent to the listed number. The definitions available there often provide sufficient information for the preliminary decision of adding or deleting titles.

As indicated above, the *DOT* titles from either the *DOT* or *Occupations Finder* can be used in Appendix D of the *GOE* to identify the related six-digit *GOE* code for each occupation. These *GOE* codes then can be used to locate the appropriate pages in Part V of the *GOE* where the descriptive information for all occupations carrying the same four-digit *GOE* code is placed.

Jones (1980) has developed a table that can be used in identifying the Holland code that best fits each of the sixty-six work groups of the *GOE*. He has also suggested and illustrated the preparation of a list of additional occupations developed from the *GOE* that relate to Holland codes. Both of these activities are representative of the process involved in the expanding phase.

Holland codes obtained from the *SCII* can be used in the same way, if *The Occupations Finder* is available to the counselor. When the publication is not conveniently at hand, one can use the primary single-letter code and translate to *GOE* interest areas as indicated in Table 1 or as listed in Appendix A of the *GOE*. Most of the Occupational Scales of the *SCII* use names that are listed in Appendix D of the *GOE* and also can be used to reach the *GOE* four-digit data.

World of work map

The World of Work Map plots twenty-five occupational groupings or clusters on a two-dimensional map with a People-Things continuum for the horizontal axis and a Data-Ideas continuum forming the vertical axis. The relationship to the appropriate extreme of these intersecting continua determines the location of the cluster. Thus "Management and Planning" is approximately midway between "People" and "Data," while "Clerical and Secretarial Work" is clearly "Data" oriented but only slightly over the midpoint toward "Things." This type of distribution scatters occupations in a way that is actually very similar to both Roe's primary focus and Holland's six typologies as listed in Table 9–2. The *GOE* interest area most closely related to each World of Work Cluster is quite obvious, so one can easily move from *GOE* information to the map or vice versa.

D-P-T codes

The *Ohio Vocational Interest Survey* uses the cubistic classification system as its basis for occupational grouping. This employs the Data-People-Things portion of the *DOT* code structure, called Worker Traits in the third edition and Worker Functions in the fourth edition of the *DOT*. Each of the three components is viewed as one dimension of the cube, and each in turn is divided into low, average, and high, with the low starting point being the front, left, lower corner. Inspection of the twenty-three scales included in the *OVIS* II and the brief description of each provided on the profile sheet reveals that most scales translate quite easily to the *GOE* interest areas. For example, *OVIS* II Machine Operation, Skilled Personal Service, and Communication translates to *GOE* Mechanical or Industrial, Accommodating, Leading-Influencing.

Aptitudes

Clients often will have formed fairly clear ideas of their aptitudes from previous experience in school, extracurricular activities, informal work encounters, or numerous other parts of everyday life. The accuracy of these self-evaluations may range from a high level of precision to total error and, like other data, will require confirmation. Relevant experiences in other aspects of the client's life will frequently provide sufficient confirmation. When the evidence is sketchy or contradictory, additional data may be needed from tests or other sources.

Often, aptitude has been demonstrated quite clearly in various experiences to an extent that objective evidence is available. Obviously, high grades in advanced mathematics or science classes demonstrate ability in these areas as well as or better than test scores. Similarly, winning essay contests or consistently publishing feature stories in the school newspaper may demonstrate writing aptitude of superior quality. Clients sometimes fail to recognize or to give full credence to demonstrated aptitudes; in other situations these aspects of daily life may be over-valued. Counselor and client should try to establish realistic standards for evaluating the criteria being used as well as the performance being judged against these criteria.

OAPs and SATBs

Translating aptitude test information into occupational possibilities is easiest with the *General Aptitude Test Battery*. As discussed in Chapter 7, the *GATB* can be used as a total package to assist a client in understanding self or, by selecting appropriate parts, it may be used to answer narrower questions about specific types of skills. The norms available for the *GATB* are based upon successful workers in various occupations.

When the *GATB* is used in its entirety with a client, scores on all parts can be used to identify those Occupational Aptitude Patterns (OAP) that incorporate the client's highest skills. The *GATB* Manual includes lists of occupational titles that fit each OAP. These titles can be used with Appendix D of the *GOE* to obtain the *GOE* code and access to the information listed under that code structure.

Use of selected portions of the *GATB* suggests that the client is seeking answers to specific questions such as "Can I compete successfully with workers who are employed as _____ or _____?" In this situation only those *GATB* parts that directly relate to the tasks performed in the job have relevance, and these parts are called Specific Aptitude Test Batteries (SATB). At present, about 460 combinations of various *GATB* parts have been identified as SATBs, and cutting scores have been established for these combinations. Individuals whose scores fall above the cut are assumed to have sufficient aptitude to compete successfully in the occupation. The occupations represented by these SATBs are listed in Appendix B of the *GOE* under the appropriate *GOE* code number. This list can be used either to gain access to the *GOE* information or, in the other direction, to help the client confirm that he or she has the aptitudes specified for the occupational area he or she has been exploring in the *GOE*.

A recent article by Droege and Boese (1982) reports further research relating the OAPs and SATBs to the sixty-six work groups included in the *GOE*. The described research indicates that forty-two different SATBs have been identified covering fifty-nine of the sixty-six work groups, thus providing data for 97 percent of the nonsupervisory occupations in the fourth edition of the *DOT*. These new OAPs are included in the 1979 edition of the *Manual for the General Aptitude Test Battery*, Section II. Their use permits direct translation of aptitude data to the *GOE* classification system.

GOE information

Scores from other comprehensive or specific aptitude tests do not translate directly to *GOE* or *DOT* codes. The career planning option of the *Differential Aptitude Test* scoring service does provide information that includes occupational titles purportedly related to high scores on various parts of the test. These can be used with Appendix D of the *GOE* to gain access to the information included in the *GOE*. The occupational titles can also be used to enter the *DOT* code structure for information located there.

Counselor familiarity with the general information provided for each *GOE* four-digit code facilitates the indirect translation of aptitude test data into *GOE* codes. For example, the skills and abilities section of the entry for "05.01 Engineering" includes among others the following statements:

> To do this kind of work, you must be able to:
>   use high level mathematics.
>   understand principles of chemistry, geology, physics, and related sciences.
>   solve problems, using facts and personal judgment.

Obviously, high scores on the numerical, mechanical reasoning, and abstract reasoning sections of the *DAT* are related to these stated required aptitudes.

D-P-T codes

The Worker Trait Arrangement in the third edition of the *DOT* is an example of the use of D-P-T codes with aptitude scores. Each of the Worker Trait Groups in each of the twenty-two Areas of Work includes a Qualifications Profile. This profile suggests appropriate quintile scores on each *GATB* aptitude for the given Worker Trait Group. Where the Worker Trait Group encompasses occupations at different aptitude levels, those differences are recognized by alternative quintile scores. The Qualifications Profile also includes suggested appropriate ranges of General Educational Level, Specific Vocational Preparation, Interest Areas, and Temperament Characteristics for each three-digit Worker Trait Arrangement.

The publication of the fourth edition of the *DOT* implies that at least some of the above third edition information is now outdated. Much of the information included in the Worker Trait Arrangement has been revised and incorporated in the *GOE*. However the aptitude requirements have not been included in either *DOT* or *GOE*. As indicated earlier, they can now be found in the *GATB* manual.

Classification systems

Roe's two-dimensional classification system, described in Chapter 8, essentially equates a generalized aptitude estimate with the vertical axis of that system. One will recall that the six categories in that scale range from "professional and managerial, individual responsibility" down to "unskilled." Roe (1956) has described this dimension as based on level of function, including the degree of responsibility, capacity, or skill. Research by Meir (1970) has substantiated statistically that differences in level in most of the horizontal groupings can be demonstrated.

Super (1957) uses a similar vertical dimension primarily based on aptitude in his three-dimensional classification system, in which the three parts are field, level, and enterprise.

Both of these classification systems deal with aptitude in a generalized sense rather than in a differential way. In other words, instead of relating scores from specific sections of the *DAT* or *GATB* to the system, one would use an overall impression of scores in a total or composite sense. When applied in this way, both classification systems include occupational titles that can be translated to *GOE* and *DOT* codes.

holistic ?

Values

Values are often difficult for counselors to incorporate in the expanding phase, probably because they are frequently viewed to be restrictive in nature. Thus, if values enter the career-choice process at all, they usually are applied in the narrowing phase to eliminate occupations that might conflict with client values. A further complication arises from the fact that they are often described in one sense as global and highly influential and in another sense as very specific. An example of the first or broad use of value terminology can be seen in the Allport, Vernon, and Lindzey *Study of Values* that proposes a six-category typology: theoretical, economic, aesthetic, social, political, and religious. An example of the second or specific application can be seen in Super's *Work Values Inventory* that includes, among others, such scales as Intellectual Stimulation, Supervisory Relations, and Associates. Pryor (1979) has suggested that highly specific usages might better be described not as values but as work option preferences and dealt with in a manner similar to interests. This would restrict the use of values to global, underlying views that are more nearly related to personality than to interest.

Like other personal attributes, values are likely to be considered in the career counseling process approximately to the extent that the client expresses concern or appears to assign worth to these characteristics. In these circumstances, the term is most likely to be used in the broad-based sense. These typologies are roughly analogous to the Interest areas listed in the *GOE*. For example, economic values approximate Business Detail and Selling, social values are roughly equal to Accommodating and Humanitarian, and political values correspond to Leading-Influencing.

The global typologies also relate rather closely to the six single-letter Holland codes and to the horizontal axis in both Roe's and Super's classification systems. We have already discussed how these systems can be used to develop *GOE* and *DOT* codes for further exploration.

Personality

Relating personality or temperament characteristics to occupations is more difficult than either interests or aptitudes. One reason for this is that less research exists on the topic, and a second reason is that most occupations tolerate considerable variation on this factor.

Nevertheless, many individuals hold stereotypes of personality characteristics representative of various occupations. For example, the brash, aggressive, dominant used-car salesperson, the quiet, restrained, orderly accountant, the cool, confident, autonomous air-traffic controller, the nurturant, friendly, untiring nurse. Holland's typology of people and work environments suggests that particular personality attributes are more compatible to certain work settings than to others. Super also implies that different kinds of people will fit into different kinds of occupations.

The most extensive effort to relate temperament characteristics to occupations is probably the one included in the *Dictionary of Occupational Titles,* third edition. The Worker Traits section of Volume II suggests temperaments required of a worker to achieve average success in an occupation, as well as such other traits as aptitudes, interests, and general and specific educational preparation. One must be aware that the approach used in the *DOT* is that the specific occupation evaluated requires the worker to have those temperament or personality traits that enable him or her to deal with the situational nature of the work. Usually two or three major temperament situations are suggested for each worker trait group. Both aptitude and temperament requirements are incorporated in the *Guide for Occupational Exploration* in general terms under the heading of "What skills and abilities do you need for this kind of work?"

The *DOT* temperament traits are useful in assisting a client to evaluate this aspect of his or her individual characteristics and to see the relationship between personality and occupation.

The twelve temperaments listed in the third edition of the *DOT,* Volume II, are as follows:

Different types of occupational situations to which workers must adjust.

1. Situations involving a variety of duties often characterized by frequent change.
2. Situations involving repetitive or short cycle operations carried out according to set procedures or sequences.
3. Situations involving doing things only under specific instructions, allowing little or no room for independent action or judgment in working out job problems.
4. Situations involving the direction, control, and planning of an entire activity or the activities of others.
5. Situations involving the necessity of dealing with people in actual job duties beyond giving and receiving instructions.
6. Situations involving working alone and apart in physical isolation from others, although the activity may be integrated with that of others.
7. Situations involving influencing people in their opinions, attitudes, or judgments about ideas or things.
8. Situations involving performing adequately under stress when confronted with the critical or unexpected or when taking risks.
9. Situations involving the evaluation (arriving at generalizations, judgments, or decisions) of information against sensory or judgmental criteria.
0. Situations involving the evaluation (arriving at generalizations, judgments, or decisions) of information against measurable or verifiable criteria.
X. Situations involving the interpretation of feelings, ideas, or facts in terms of personal viewpoint.
Y. Situations involving the precise attainment of set limits, tolerances, or standards. (p. 654)

TABLE 9–3 A comparison of personality variables used in the *DOT* with those in the *Occupational View-Deck* and the *Worker Trait Keysort*.

DOT temperament trait		Occupational view-deck trait		Worker trait keysort work situation	
1	Variety	A	Variable	1	Frequent change
2	Repetition	B	Repetitive	2	Routine tasks
3	Specific instruction	C	Specific instruction		
4	Direction, control	D	Dominant	3	Planning and directing
5	Dealing with people	E	Gregarious	4	Dealing with people
6	Working alone				
7	Influencing people	F	Influencing	5	Influencing people
8	Handling stress	G	Self-control	6	Working under pressure
9	Judgmental evaluation	H	Valuative	7	Personal judgment
O	Objective evaluation	I	Objective	8	Objective decisions
X	Personal interpretation	J	Subjective	9	Interpersonal and expressing feelings
Y	Precise attainment	K	Definitive	10	Precise limits

Those client personality characteristics that are strong enough to have occupational significance often are identifiable from self-evaluation as the client describes preferences, feelings, and attitudes. When the client is unable to describe himself or herself with confidence or expresses uncertainty with self-evaluations, then personality inventories, such as those described in Chapter 7, may be helpful in clarifying those characteristics that may bear upon occupational success and satisfaction. Although few of the scales of such instruments as the *CPI, EPPS,* or the *GZTS* translate directly to the temperament traits listed in the *DOT,* inferences can be drawn that help the client relate self to work requirements. For example, the Dominance scale of *CPI* and *EPPS* and the Ascendance scale of *GZTS* would appear to involve characteristics relevant to Temperament traits 4 and 7.

Two devices that appear to help in relating personal characteristics to occupations are available to counselors. These are the *Occupational View-Deck* and *Worker Trait Keysort*. Both will be discussed below. Because each uses a slightly different ordering of personality traits, one cannot assume that the same number reflects the same characteristic. Table 9–3 indicates how each relates to the twelve traits used in the *DOT*. Even though only key words have been used in Table 9–3 to describe the listed traits, one can readily observe the general similarity of the three lists.

Occupational view-deck

The *Occupational View-Deck* is based on a list of descriptions of commonly encountered occupations. The third edition includes brief profile statements concerning work performed, training standards, qualifications, sources of additional information, and related occupations for each of 610 occupations. These are arranged in alphabetical order and each has been assigned a four-digit number within the system ranging from 0000 to 4046.

The code numbers are arranged sequentially with other numbers in a 32 by 32 square matrix, providing 1024 codes, of which 610 are now being used. It is assumed that the unused numbers, which occur at the end of each letter sequence, are intended for future expansion of the occupational profiles.

The *Occupational View-Deck* provides information on how each of the included occupations relates to various aspects of each of six different characteristics such as the temperament traits listed in Table 9–3. In addition to temperament, the variables presently included are the following: Interests, Education, Training Programs, Physical Demands, and Working Conditions. The various divisions of each of these headings are listed in Table 9–4. A transparent overlay is provided for each of these forty-six variables, revealing on the 32 by 32 matrix the code numbers for all occupations possessing that characteristic. For example, the overlay for "Temperament B—Repetitive" shows ninety-eight code numbers representing such occupations as airhammer operator, automobile service station salesperson, court reporter, groundskeeper, insurance clerk, machine tool operator, operating engineer, proofreader, typist, and welder. The transparent overlay can be used singly to identify additional occupations to consider in the expanding phase. They can also be used in combination to find those occupations that relate to the grouped characteristics. This usage is a common procedure in the narrowing phase.

Each characteristic is defined briefly in the instruction manual. For example, "Temperament B—Repetitive" is defined thus:

> You prefer to work at the same task for long periods of time. You prefer to work at a machine or work at a task another worker tells you to do.

Clients may have sufficient self-understanding to identify readily those temperament traits that are characteristic of themselves. If they desire confirmation of their estimates, this can be done in the counseling sessions or by using personality inventories. The *View-Deck* also includes a brief self-evaluative checklist consisting of ten yes-no items presumably related to each of the eleven temperament traits. The individual is directed to explore the three traits for which the most yes answers have been given. The interest headings approximate those found on the *Kuder General Interest Survey,* with Outdoor being the only scale not included. Like temperament traits, interest factors may be identified by prior self-evaluation, counseling, or inventorying. The remaining factors—Education-Training, Physical Demands, and Working Conditions—are usually identified easily by most clients.

The occupational profiles include the *DOT* three-digit occupational designation codes, so that use of the *DOT* and the *GOE* is facilitated.

TABLE 9–4 Characteristics Included in the *Occupational View-Deck.*

Temperaments	Interests	Education	Physical demands	Working conditions
A Variable	A Mechanical	A No H.S. diploma	A Strength—sedentary	A Inside
B Repetitive	B Computational	B H.S. diploma	B Strength—light	B Outside
C Specific Instruction	C Scientific	C Career education	C Strength—medium	C Both
D Dominant	D Persuasive	D Associates degree	D Strength—heavy	D Extreme cold
E Gregarious	E Artistic	E Bachelor's degree	E Climbing/balancing	E Extreme heat
F Influencing	F Literary	F Graduate study	F Stoop/kneel/etc.	F Wet/humid
G Self-control	G Musical		G Reaching/handling/etc.	G Noise/vibrations
H Valuative	H Social service	*Training Program*	H Talking/hearing	H Hazards
I Objective	I Clerical	A Apprenticeship	I Seeing	I Fumes/odors/etc.
J Subjective		B On-the-job		
K Definitive				

282

Counselors who frequently use the *Occupational View-Deck* with clients will find it helpful to complete the *DOT* code number and to enter the appropriate *GOE* code number for each of the 610 listed occupations. The addition of this information will simplify the translating process for clients and permit them to work more independently. Each profile also suggests sources for further information, often including industrial, governmental, or professional organizations.

Worker trait keysort deck

The *Worker Trait Keysort Deck* is part of a comprehensive system entitled *Career Information System* developed under the direction of David Winefordner at the Appalachia Educational Laboratory. The various components of the system use the interest areas of the *GOE* as the basic structure for career information. Consequently, every part of the system produces data that translate directly to *GOE* codes. The twelve *GOE* interest areas are called *Career Areas* and the sixty-six *GOE* work groups are called *Worker Trait Groups* in this system. Eight factors are related to the various Worker Trait Groups, including the following:

Work Activities (ten types)
Work Situations (ten types)
Worker Functions (Data, six; People, eight; Things, seven)
Physical Demands (six *DOT* factors)
Working Conditions (seven *DOT* factors)
Aptitudes (eleven *GATB* factors)
General Educational Development (six *DOT* levels)
Preparation and Training (two types, five levels)

Among the eight factors listed above, only the first two relate to the area of personality and will be considered here. The other factors clearly relate to other sections of this chapter and will be incorporated at those points.

The types of work activity and work situations included in the Worker Trait Group system are listed in Table 9–5. The work activities are described as preferences and the work situations are described as demands that the work imposes on the worker. Both lists appear to reflect aspects of personality as well as interest. The close relationship of the items in the Work Situations category to those included in the *DOT* Temperament Trait list, as shown in Table 9–3, suggests that these items are intended to emphasize personality characteristics.

Each of the ten work situations is related to Worker Trait Groups (*GOE* four-digit Work Groups) that involve that characteristic. These range from as few as five related to Situation 6—Working Under Pressure, to as many as forty-seven related to Situation 4—Dealing with People, and forty-

TABLE 9–5 Sorting factors included in the *Worker Trait Group Keysort.*

Work activity	Work situation	Other factors
1. Things and objects	1. Frequent change	General educational development
2. Business contact	2. Routine tasks	(6 levels)
3. Routine, organized	3. Planning, directing	Preparation
4. Direct personal contact-help	4. Dealing with people	(7 kinds)
5. Recognition from others	5. Influencing people	Physical demands
6. Communication of ideas and information	6. Working under pressure	(10 items)
7. Scientific/technical	7. Personal judgment	
8. Creative thinking	8. Objective decisions	
9. Processes, methods, machinery	9. Interpersonal and expressing feelings	
10. Work on/produce things	10. Precise limits	

six related to Situation 8—Making Decisions Using Standards That Can Be Measured or Checked.

Work situations are defined briefly. For example, Work Situation 2—Performing Routine Tasks, is defined as follows:

> Workers do the same tasks over and over. They may not change the tasks or the order in which they do them. Work assignments are of short duration and follow a required method or sequence. Very little judgment is required. (p. 410)

In the *Keysort Deck* numerical or letter codes for five sorting factors (work activities, work situations, physical demands, GED, and preparation) are printed around the margins of a series of cards in which one card represents each of the four-digit Worker Trait Groups. Each card includes a brief descriptive paragraph for that Worker Trait Group and a brief list of occupational subgroups associated with that group. Between each numerical or letter code and the edge of the card is a hole that can be notched when that item relates to the Worker Trait Group. For example, card 01.01 Literary Arts has the following codes notched:

Work Activities
- 5 Activities resulting in recognition or appreciation from others
- 6 Activities involving the communication of ideas and information
- 8 Activities involving creative thinking

Work Situations
- 3 Planning and directing an entire activity
- 4 Dealing with people
- 5 Influencing people's opinions, attitudes, and judgments
- 7 Making decisions using personal judgment
- 9 Interpreting and expressing feelings, ideas, or facts

Physical Demands
- S Sedentary work
- 5 Talking and/or hearing
- 6 Seeing

GED Level
- 5 Apply logical thinking and scientific knowledge to define problems, collect data, establish facts, and reach valid conclusions. Understand and follow a wide variety of technical instructions presented in mathematical or diagram form. Deal with such abstract variables as repair techniques. Deal with such concrete variables as testing equipment.

Preparation
- E Entry (open to anyone with the necessary education and training)

A Advancement (open only to those with related work experience)

N No formal training

T Technical programs beyond high school

C College preparation

The use of a sorting needle facilitates using the sixty-six cards. By first aligning all cards in the deck and then inserting the needle in the hole representing a particular characteristic, it is possible to identify all worker trait groups involving that characteristic. Those cards not involving the factor will remain on the needle; those that do relate to the characteristic will have a notched hole, permitting the card to fall out of the deck. The deck can be sorted singly, considering each group that relates to the characteristic of interest, or by combining characteristics and examining only those cards that relate to the two or three characteristics used for the sort.

The system also includes checklists for Work Activities, Work Situations, and Aptitudes. These are intended to assist the client in self-evaluation in each of the three areas and may be useful when the client is uncertain about his or her characteristics in the specific trait.

Since the Worker Trait Groups compare directly to the four-digit Work Areas in the *GOE,* the *Worker Trait Keysort Deck* permits the individual to relate any of the personal characteristics represented in the five sorting factors to information included in the *Guide for Occupational Exploration.* The six-digit codes included there may be appropriate possibilities for further consideration by the client.

Holland codes

Each of Holland's occupational themes reflects a group of personality characteristics and a work environment where that type of individual can be expected to be found. Since Holland usually uses two or three letter codes to represent an individual, one would expect a combination of personality characteristics to be seen in the individual. According to Holland, an individual will seek a work environment that is congruent with his or her personality.

The descriptors used for each occupational theme appear to have reasonable face validity, but they have not been verified by matching them against the widely used personality inventories. It would seem that they are certainly as useful as self-descriptive terms used on checklists or inventories. They can be compared to the "skills and abilities" statements in the *GOE* where temperament factors are included.

D-P-T codes

Many personality characteristics, either self-identified or inventoried, can be expressed in terms that reveal both amount and complexity of relationships to data, people, or things. Because generalizations are usually applied in such instances, the low-average-high categories used in the cubistic classification system are more likely to be appropriate. Remarks such as "I'm really a people type of person—I enjoy bargaining with people, trying to work out a deal that satisfies both of us," can lead to consideration of those levels of involvement included in the average and high categories of "people" in the Worker Functions classification. Once the general level that matches the individual has been agreed, the client can browse in the Worker Trait section of the third edition of the *Dictionary of Occupational Titles* for possible occupations to be added to the list. One can also use the Worker Trait descriptions in the third edition to approximate the *GOE* grouping so that occupational suggestions from that source can also be considered.

Occupational knowledge

Almost every person, in the process of growing up, has acquired some information about many different occupations. Often that information is sketchy, superficial, perhaps inaccurate; sometimes it is thorough and comprehensive; almost always it has provided the basis for a stereotyped view of an array of jobs.

The individual's information has accumulated from previous experiences involving differing degrees of contact, as well as many other variable factors such as awareness of occupational activity, typicality of the situation, and precision of observation. Some perceptions are the result of direct experience with the occupation, many more are the product of observation, and most are derived from indirect sources such as print media or comments of parents, peers, and others. Obviously, the most trustworthy of these sources, as far as accuracy is concerned, is the direct experience of the individual. This also is likely to be the most restricted source because the typical client often seeks career counseling because of a limited exposure to occupational possibilities. Thus, most of what the usual client knows about occupations comes from observation, often shallow and brief, what lawyers would describe as hearsay.

Even though the quality and quantity of knowledge possessed about many occupations may be suspect, many clients will still have formed opinions and attitudes based on whatever information they have. That framework can be used to help the client develop a broader perspective of ultimate possibilities. Of greatest help are those occupations toward which the client is favorably inclined, although negative comments about jobs also provide insight.

Many counselors ask questions during an intake interview about occupations the client may have considered as possibilities. Such questions may be couched in a fantasy-like approach: "If you could do anything you wanted to, what would you choose?" Sometimes the question is asked in a realistic vein: "If you had to go to work tomorrow, what would you do?" At other times, a self-evaluation query is used: "Tell me what occupations you've considered and why you picked them." Although such questions are occasionally unproductive, most of the time several occupations will be named, and sometimes this area of knowledge provides the logical starting point for expanding horizons. We will consider three techniques for translating named occupations into *GOE* and *DOT* codes in addition to the possibility of taking those identified occupations directly to both volumes. We will discuss classification systems, card sorts, and D-P-T codes.

Classification systems

Several classification systems permit generalizing from a specific occupation because of the way in which occupations are grouped within the system. Since our immediate purpose is to help the client consider a broad range of possibilities, these are particularly useful.

Simple classification systems, such as the Career Education cluster system proposed by the U.S. Office of Education (1971), use very broad categories that often approximate the *GOE* areas. For example, the health, personal service, fine arts, and manufacturing occupations in the cluster system translate easily to the science, accommodating, artistic, and industrial areas of the *GOE* where additional comparable titles can be found.

Two-dimensional classification systems, such as Roe's Primary Focus system or the World of Work map, also expedite access to the *GOE*. Occupations named by a client can be plotted readily on Roe's chart, where the horizontal axis, or primary focus, provides the general grouping and the vertical axis suggests the general educational level and degree of responsibility involved in the occupation. Roe's primary focus labels translate easily into *GOE* areas. The World of Work map is comparably based on six job clusters that encompass twenty-five job families. The proper job family for a named occupation is easily identifiable, and this leads to the names of other jobs within the job family as well as those in other families within the same job cluster. All of these translate easily to the *GOE* for additional possibilities.

Card sort systems

The idea of assisting individuals to make career choices by sorting cards bearing the names of occupations has been around for a long time. Tyler (1961) was one of the first to suggest and use this method. Dewey (1974) developed a card sort system of nonsexist titles that was found to be helpful in assisting college women. Cooper (1976) added a structured workbook to Dewey's card system. Many inventories, for example the *Vocational Preference Inventory* and the *Strong-Campbell Interest Inventory,* include lists of occupational titles that are treated in essentially the same way as a card sort system.

Two card sort systems will be described as examples of several similar devices.

The *Vocational Exploration and Insight Kit* (Holland, 1980) includes a card sort system and a workbook that are used in conjunction with the *Self-Directed Search,* discussed in Chapter 7. The card sort includes eighty-four cards, each bearing the name of an occupation representative of Holland's six types, that the client sorts into three groups—"Might choose," "In question," and "Would not choose." After sorting the eighty-four cards, clients are asked to search for common themes or relationships within each of the broad sortings that influenced their decision to consider or reject the various occupations. After identifying influential factors and eliciting other possibilities not included in the deck of eighty-four options, clients are asked to compare factors that lead to acceptance or rejection and to identify ways in which those "Might choose" occupations relate to their talents, needs, and hopes. Clients assign three-letter Holland codes to the "Might choose" occupations, then complete the *Self-Directed Search* and compare the results with those obtained with the card sort. Clients are finally led through further steps of self-evaluation.

The card sort portion of the *Vocational Exploration and Insight Kit* provides a means of identifying occupations that hold potential interest for the client. Those occupations in the "Might choose" stack can be used immediately or, more usefully, after the client has sorted these according to common themes, to identify *GOE* areas for further exploration.

Another example of a card sort system is called *Occu-sort* and was developed by Jones (1977). *Occu-sort* consists of three different sets of cards, permitting the selection of a set that appropriately matches the client's educational ambitions. The three sets are entitled "plus 3," "plus 4," and "plus 5." Each set of cards includes the names of sixty occupations.

Each of the three levels is based on the general educational level (GED) of occupations as described in the *DOT.* The "plus 3" set has the broadest general application and includes representative occupations covering the 3, 4, 5, and 6 GED levels. Approximately 15 percent of the included occupations require less than high school graduation, 58 percent require between high school graduation and three years of college, and approximately 27 percent require four years or more of college. The "plus 4" set includes occupations with a GED level of 4 or more and is intended for use with college preparatory high school students, community college students, or adults with a high school education. The "plus 5" set includes occupations with a GED level of 5 or 6 and is intended for use with those individuals who are focusing on occupations that require at least graduation from college.

The occupations included in each of the three sets of sixty cards were selected so that each of Holland's six types is represented by ten cards. Further, occupations were selected to represent the appropriate GED level. Occupations with sex-role stereotypes were avoided and neutral gender titles were used. *Occu-sort* includes an eight-page self-guided booklet intended to lead the client through the stages involved in sorting cards, identifying a Holland code, using Holland's *Occupations Finder,* and further steps.

Both *VEIK* and *Occu-sort* are designed to provide a logical system through which a client can progress with maximum independence. Except for the referral to *Occupations Finder,* little consideration is given to helping the client expand consideration of alternative choices. Both card sort systems can be used effectively to widen choices if the "Might choose" pile is used as the basis for translating to the *GOE* areas. The *Occu-sort* cards already include the *DOT* code number, and the *DOT* codes for the *VEIK* cards are listed in the *Occupations Finder.* Both sets of cards could easily be modified to include *GOE* codes, thus simplifying the client's use of the *GOE* independently where he or she is exposed to other related titles, and the general information provided for each work group.

D-P-T codes

Occupations named by a client as those that he or she has considered can be viewed in terms of relationship to data, people, and things. When several are identified, for example, from a list of common occupations or from a card sort deck, clients may be asked to group them according to similar D-P-T involvement. Although such sorting may well lead to increased client insight into personal interests, values, and personality characteristics, the major purpose is to provide a base for expanding occupational options. Once the major level of preference for D-P-T involvement has been identified, additional occupational possibilities compatible to those preferences can be identified by using the cubistic classification system or by reviewing *DOT* code numbers, focusing on the D-P-T digits. As stated above, it is also possible to move from D-P-T levels to appropriate *GOE* interest areas and work groups where additional occupational possibilities can be found.

Educational or training requirements

Clients may have predetermined levels of education or training in mind either as desired goals or as accepted limits. Self-imposed standards may originate from many antecedents including desire for attainment, prestige, or other perquisites that go with higher educational preparation. Similarly, lower limits may be the product of disillusionment with school, a belief that one's abilities are not compatible with formal education, or a strong desire to move into the "real world" and start "making it," and other reasons. External factors can also emphasize specific educational levels. For example, many college counselors have frequently encountered clients who say "My parents don't care what field I choose, just as long as I complete by bachelor's degree" or "No one in my family has yet attended college and they all insist that I must." Often maximum limits are imposed because of family attitudes, limited financial resources, or time constraints.

Primary attention will usually be given to other attributes in the expanding phase unless the client has indicated that he or she considers educational or training level to be a very significant aspect of the choice process. If the rationale is well thought out and accepted by the client, the counselor must recognize those aspects of the client's world; however, if the client's view is not well-founded, appears to contradict abilities or values, or does not provide an adequate basis for future planning, the counselor may want to consider the need for change counseling. At least, when disparity appears to exist between stated educational preferences and personal and psychological characteristics, the counselor must help the client consider and evaluate these discrepancies.

When attention is given to educational or training level, either self-imposed or externally prescribed, it often is handled in a limiting or narrowing way. This need not necessarily be the case, since even at the lowest levels of education, perhaps illustrated by the school dropout, there are numerous occupations that can be satisfactorily performed. For this reason we will consider the topic as a legitimate factor in the expanding process. Several of the tools previously considered can be applied to this area as well, and one new one will also be discussed.

Occupational view-deck

Information on educational or training requirements for each of the 610 occupations presently included in the *Occupational View-Deck* is a basic part of that system. Table 9–4 indicates that educational and training requirements are classified into the following levels:

Educational levels
- A   No High School Diploma
- B   High School Diploma
- C   Career Education
- D   Associate Degree
- E   Bachelor's Degree
- F   Graduate Study

Training programs
- A   Apprenticeship
- B   On-the-Job Training

The various levels or types of programs are self-explanatory and are ordinarily easily understood by clients. Each is represented by a fairly wide range of occupational possibilities. The client can use the appropriate transparency to identify the codes of listed occupations that fit the educational level. The occupations represented by those code numbers can then be found in the Profile Statement booklet. The descriptive statements include the *DOT* Occupational Designation code which, in turn, can be used to obtain the *GOE* code that leads the person to *GOE* descriptions. As previously stated, the counselor can facilitate independent use of the *View-Deck* and the *GOE* or *DOT* by completing the *DOT* code number and adding the *GOE* code to each profile statement.

Worker trait keysort

Table 9–5 indicates that the *Worker Trait Keysort* includes information covering six levels of general educational development and seven levels of preparation. Because the *Keysort* is related directly to *GOE* information, it is a particularly useful device when used in conjunction with the *Guide*. The six levels of general educational development used in the *Keysort* have been adopted from the *Dictionary of Occupational Titles,* third edition. These are arranged from level 6, which is most complex, to level 1, the simplest. Level 6 (as described in the *DOT*, third edition, Volume II) consists of a reasoning level able to:

> Apply principles of logical or scientific thinking to a wide range of intellectual and practical problems. Deal with non-verbal symbolism (formulas, scientific equations, graphs, musical notes, etc.) in its most difficult phases. Deal with a variety of abstract and concrete variables. Apprehend the most abstruse classes of concepts. (p. 652)

Level 1 (as described in the *DOT*) consists of a reasoning level able to:

> Apply common sense understanding to carry out simple one- or two-step instructions. Deal with standardized situations with occasional or no variables in or from these situations encountered on the job. (p. 652)

The concept of general educational development deals with those aspects of the individual's formal or informal education that has taught him or her reasoning skills and tool knowledge such as language and mathematical skills. Although the *DOT* describes levels of competency in reasoning, mathematical and language development, the *Worker Trait Keysort* considers only the first area but includes illustrations of both abstract and concrete variables dealt with at each of the six levels. The keysort cards include information for each four-digit group indicating the GED level required by occupations in that group.

Information about preparation and training is divided into two parts. The first part, consisting of two categories, indicates whether the four-digit group includes "entry" occupations that would be open to anyone with the necessary education and training, and whether the group includes occupations that are open only to those who have related work experience as well as the necessary education and training. The second part consists of the following five levels:

G—Requires college study at graduate level.
C—Requires study leading to baccalaureate degree.
T—Requires technical program beyond high school.
V—Requires high school level vocational training.
NFT—Requires no formal training other than general education.

Individuals for whom a stated educational level is a significant aspect of career choice can use the *Keysort* to identify those *GOE* groups that match the preferred level. Although GED levels can be acquired from informal experiences outside the formal educational structure, for most individuals one can expect a rough correlation to exist between level and quality of schooling and general educational development.

Guide for occupational exploration
Each work group statement within the *GOE* includes a brief description of the type and quantity of preparation required for the occupations that belong to the group. Two examples of the information in such descriptions are included here.

The Life Sciences (02.02) statement includes the following paragraph:

> Occupations in this group usually require education and/or training extending from four years to over ten years, depending upon the specific kind of work. Important academic courses include algebra, geometry, advanced math, chemistry, biological sciences. Technical writing or composition courses are helpful. A bachelor's degree with a major in biology or another life science is generally required. Graduate degrees are needed for most research work or for college teaching. A master's degree may qualify an individual for laboratory teaching. Advanced studies or a Ph.D. are usually required for work in basic research. (p. 41)

Elemental Work: Mechanical (05.12) includes the following descriptions of training requirements:

> Occupations in this group usually require education and/or training extending from a short demonstration to over three months, depending upon a specific kind of work. This kind of work requires only a brief explanation of job duties. The most important hiring consideration is usually the physical ability of the applicant. Many of these jobs are available through union hiring halls. (p. 128)

Selected characteristics of occupations defined in the DOT

The U.S. Department of Labor has recently published a supplementary volume to the *DOT* and the *GOE* entitled *Selected Characteristics of Occupations Defined in the Dictionary of Occupational Titles*. This book provides additional information about training time required in various occupations and identifies physical demands and environmental conditions.

Occupations are listed in Part A according to *GOE* Work Subgroups (six-digit codes). Within each subgroup they are further arranged by *DOT* code number within exertional level demands. Mathematical development, language development, and specific vocational preparation requirements are listed for each occupation. In Part B, occupations are listed sequentially according to *DOT* code number and the *GOE* code, strength factor, *DOT* title, and *DOT* industrial designation are also included.

Examples of entries in both Parts A and B are listed in Table 9–6. As indicated above, Part A provides five pieces of information for each occupation classified in each *GOE* Work Subgroup. The *DOT* code, title, and industrial designation are self-explanatory. Physical demands for each occupation are rated according to standard *DOT* classifications with letters S, L, M, H, and V representing lifting and carrying strength factors. The numbers represent the following demands:

2—Climb and balance
3—Stoop, kneel, crouch, crawl
4—Reach, handle, finger, feel
5—Talk, hear
6—See (acuity, depth perception, field of vision, accommodation) (p. 479)

Environmental conditions are those factors previously labeled as working conditions, and represent the usual *DOT* definitions for those conditions as follows:

I—Inside (75 percent or more)
O—Outside (75 percent or more)
B—Both
2—Extremes of cold plus temperature changes
3—Extremes of heat plus temperature changes
4—Wet and humid
5—Noise and vibration
6—Hazards
7—Fumes, odors, toxic conditions, dust, poor ventilation (p. 479)

The fifth column includes information on the training time required for the occupation. This is provided under three headings. The M and L represent Mathematical Development and Language Development, and SVP is the usual *DOT* factor of Specific Vocational Preparation. M and L are refinements of the General Educational Development aspects originally included in Volume II of the third edition of the *DOT*. The original material included Reasoning Development (see descriptions of these traits included in the penultimate preceding section entitled Worker Trait Keysort), Mathematical Development, and Language Development. The *Selected Characteristics* material for tool knowledges has been rewritten to provide more helpful information for each of the levels ranging from Level 6 (most complex) to Level 1 (simplest). The more complex levels of M are described in terms of three applications as follows:

> Level 6—Advanced Calculus, Modern Algebra, Statistics
> Level 5—Algebra, Calculus, Statistics
> Level 4—Algebra, Geometry, Shop Math (p. 469)

Lower levels of M are described in terms of practical applied arithmetic functions. All levels of L are described as skill requirements in Reading, Writing, and Speaking.

Specific Vocational Preparation represents the amount of time required to learn the techniques, acquire information, and develop the facility needed for average performance in a specific job-worker situation. SVP may include training acquired through vocational education, apprenticeship, inplant training, on-the-job training, or experience in other jobs. Nine levels are recognized, corresponding to those used in the Third Edition of the *DOT*, as follows:

> 1—Short demonstration.
> 2—Anything beyond short demonstration up to 30 days.
> 3—Over 30 days up to and including 3 months.
> 4—Over 3 months up to and including 6 months.
> 5—Over 6 months up to and including 1 year.
> 6—Over 1 year up to and including 2 years.
> 7—Over 2 years up to and including 4 years.
> 8—Over 4 years up to and including 10 years.
> 9—Over 10 years. (p. 479)

Part B includes material that is self-explanatory, as indicated in Table 9–6. Part B is often helpful in finding the Part A information. If the client or counselor has an occupational title, the alphabetical index in the *DOT* can be used to obtain the *DOT* code; then Part B will provide the *GOE* Work Subgroup code under which the occupation can be found in Part A. Similarly, given the occupational title, one can look in Appendix D (Alphabetical Arrangement of Occupations) in the *GOE* where both *DOT* and *GOE* codes are listed, then in Part A of *Selected Characteristics* for information located there.

Physical and health factors

Occasionally, a client will want to expand career options to capitalize on a particular physical asset or characteristic. Most of the time, however, if physical factors are considered in the choice process, this occurs in a nar-

TABLE 9–6 Examples of data included in *Selected Characteristics of Occupations Defined in the DOT* (p. 53).

Part A

Titles arranged by guide for occupational exploration group and physical demands
05.05 Craft technology

Occupations in this group involve performing highly skilled hand or machine operations, utilizing special techniques, training, and experience. Work settings largely include construction sites, machine shops, manufacturing establishments, and processing plants. Skills and abilities required include: Knowledge of tools, machines, materials, and methods used in trade or craft specialty; reading scale drawing or blue prints to visualize objects; using shop math to calculate object dimensions, material amounts needed, and material costs; coordinating eyes, hands, and fingers to use handtools or machines in constructing, making or repairing objects; and adhering to object specifications or standards.

05.05.01 Masonry, stone, and brick work

DOT code	DOT title and industry designation	Physical demands	Environmental conditions	M	L	SVP
775.131-010	SUPERVISOR, CONCRETE-STONE FINISHING (conc. prod.)	L 4 5 6	B 5	3	3	7
801.131-010	SUPERVISOR, CHIMNEY CONSTRUCTION (const.)	L 2 3 4 5 6	O 6	3	2	8
861.131-018	STONEMASON SUPERVISOR (const.)	L 2 3 4 6	O 6	3	3	8
861.361-010	COMPOSITION-STONE APPLICATOR (const.)	L 2 3 4	O 4 6	2	2	7
861.381-034	SOFT-TILE SETTER (const.; ret. tr.)	L 2 3 4 6	I	2	3	7
869.131-014	CONCRETING SUPERVISOR (const.)	L 3 4 5 6	O 5 6	3	3	7
575.131-014	SUPERVISOR, PRECAST AND PRESTRESSED CONCRETE (conc. prod.)	M 4 5 6	B	3	3	7
629.261-014	MILLER, HEAD, WET PROCESS (corn prod.)	M 2 4	1 4 5 6 7	3	3	7
679.130-010	SUPERVISOR (stonework)	M 3 4 5 6	1 5 6 7	3	4	7
771.381-010	STONECUTTER APPRENTICE, HAND (stonework)	M 4 6	I 5 7	3	3	7
771.381-014	STONECUTTER, HAND (stonework)	M 4 6	B 5 6 7	3	3	7
775.281-010	SURFACE-PLATE FINISHER (stonework)	M 4 6	I	4	3	7
844.364-010	CEMENT MASON (const.)	M 2 3 4 6	B 4 6	3	3	7

DOT code	DOT title and industry designation	Physical demands	Environmental conditions	M	L	SVP
844.364-014	CEMENT-MASON APPRENTICE (const.)	M2346	B46	3	3	7
844.461-010	CONCRETE-STONE FINISHER (conc. prod.)	M346	B4	3	3	7
861.131-010	BRICKLAYER SUPERVISOR (const.)	M23456	B57	3	3	8
861.131-014	CHIMNEY SUPERVISOR, BRICK (const.)	M23456	O6	3	3	8
861.131-026	SUPERVISOR, TERRAZZO (const.)	M3456	B	3	3	8
861.381-010	ACID-TANK LINER (const.)	M2346	I5	3	3	7
861.381-014	BRICKLAYER (brick & tile)	M346	B3	2	2	8
861.381-018	BRICKLAYER (const.)	M2346	B6	3	3	8
861.381-022	BRICKLAYER APPRENTICE (const.)	M346	B3	3	3	8
861.381-026	BRICKLAYER, FIREBRICK AND REFRACTORY TILE (const.)	M2346	B34567	3	3	8
861.381-038	STONEMASON (const.)	M2346	O56	3	3	7
861.381-042	STONEMASON APPRENTICE (const.)	M2346	O56	3	3	7
861.381-046	TERRAZZO WORKER (const.)	M346	B45	2	3	7
861.381-050	TERRAZZO-WORKER APPRENTICE (const.)	M346	B45	2	3	7
861.381-054	TILE SETTER (const.)	M346	I	3	3	7
861.684-010	CUPOLA PATCHER (found.)	M2346	I	1	1	4
861.131-022	SUPERVISOR, MARBLE (const.)	H23456	B57	3	3	8
861.361-014	MONUMENT SETTER (const.)	H23456	O	2	3	7
861.381-030	MARBLE SETTER (const.)	H2346	B57	2	3	7
869.681-010	CONCRETE-FENCE BUILDER (const.)	H346	O5	2	2	6

05.05.02 Construction and maintenance

DOT code	DOT title and industry designation	Physical demands	Environmental conditions	M	L	SVP
761.281-014	EXPERIMENTAL-BOX TESTER (wood. box)	L46	I	3	4	7
860.131-014	SUPERVISOR, BOATBUILDERS, WOOD (ship & boat bldg. & rep.)	L23456	B5	4	3	8
860.131-022	SUPERVISOR, JOINERS (ship & boat bldg. & rep.)	L3456	I5	4	3	8
807.361-014	BOAT REPAIRER (ship & boat bldg. & rep.)	M23456	I6	3	3	7

rowing or restrictive sense because of the client's desire to avoid certain physical requirements or environmental conditions, or because of physical or health limitations.

Rehabilitation counselors often encounter individuals with physical disabilities who generalize a physical restriction in one activity to inability to perform any type of activity. Devices that identify those jobs that require only physical activities they are still able to perform may help to develop a more positive approach to the world of work. Obviously, the person who cannot stoop, kneel, crouch, or crawl can compete on an equal basis with other workers if these abilities are not required in the occupation.

Several of the devices described in earlier pages of this chapter include consideration of physical factors. Three of them will be reviewed briefly here.

The *Occupational View-Deck,* as described in Table 9–4, includes individual overlay stencils for the standard *DOT* physical demands. Thus, the physical demands for each of the 610 occupations included in *View-Deck* can be identified singly or in any combination. Similarly, there are nine stencils for the standard *DOT* working conditions.

The *Worker Trait Keysort* also includes the standard *DOT* physical demands and working conditions. Cards for each of the four-digit *GOE* work groups have been notched to indicate the relationship of appropriate physical demands or working conditions to that work group.

Part A of *Selected Characteristics* includes information about both physical demands and environmental conditions, as indicated in Table 9–6. One particular advantage in using *Selected Characteristics* derives from the fact that both factors are identified for every *DOT* occupation. Since the occupations are grouped according to *GOE* work subgroups, one can immediately see which other closely related occupations in that or adjacent subgroups possess the same or different physical demands or environmental conditions.

Occupational definitions in the *1982 Supplement to the Dictionary of Occupational Titles* include listings of physical demands, environmental conditions, general educational development requirements, and specific vocational preparation requirements. Also included are the *GOE* code numbers and the Standard Occupational Classification code number. The inclusion of this information in the *Supplement* suggests that these data will be incorporated in all definitions when the fifth edition of the *DOT* is published. Access to that information within the *DOT* definition will greatly facilitate simultaneous use of *DOT* and *GOE* in the expanding phase.

NARROWING CHOICES

So far in this chapter, we have been considering ways that help a client relate personal attributes to occupations and to view the world of work as broadly as possible in order to develop a wide range of relatively appropriate possibilities. The rationale for this expanding phase is based on the idea that better choices can be made and ultimately greater satisfaction is likely to accrue if the client considers all, or at least most, of the options that are possible. Restrictive impacts such as sex-role stereotypes, limited knowledge of occupations, undue emphasis on some single personal characteristic, and other pressures are likely to be reduced if the client is helped to view the broad picture before focusing on specific choices. Counselors who rely entirely on client suggestions for occupations to be considered in the choice process assume that the client has a far broader view of the world of work than is typically true. Having reviewed several ways that help the client see that broader view, we are now ready to consider procedures for narrowing the range of choices.

As previously stated, the expanding and narrowing phases are not totally dichotomous activities. Some narrowing inevitably occurs in the early phase when the client rejects an occupation encountered in the preliminary stage. If the client's rationale for discarding it appears reasonable there is little advantage to pursuing it further. If, however, the response appears hasty, based on inadequate or biased information, or as an outgrowth of lack of self-understanding, some discussion at that point may be useful to retain the option for further consideration. Similarly, a client well along in the narrowing phase may encounter information or insight relative to an option being considered that leads to recognition of an entirely new group of occupations not already being investigated. Nevertheless, it is usually advantageous to think of the two-step sequence of first building a broadly based list related to those criteria identified by the client as most important in his or her choice process, and then, second, examining that list more critically by matching the listed items against the set of personal criteria as grouped and weighted by the client.

If the first phase involves a heavy teaching role for the counselor because of the use of various translating devices, the second phase turns to major emphasis on counseling. During this phase it is essential for the client to have a clear enough picture of self, motivations and goals, and his or her situation to be able to set priorities consistent with that total picture. Further, it is crucial for the client to have sufficient self-confidence in that evaluation to use it to reject occupational options. The counselor is likely to find the client often needs help in balancing the necessary contradiction between flexibility and commitment, in searching for further clues to support his or her present self-concept, and in accepting new insights of self that may open new opportunities or close ones previously considered. It is the counselor's task to facilitate the process, not by directing, selling, or entreating, but rather by providing support, enhancing self-understanding, and helping gain access to the necessary information.

The narrowing phase usually starts with rejection of those alternatives that are clearly incongruous with the client's self-image. As the process moves forward, the client focuses more sharply on the comparison of his or her view of self with the mental image he or she has of each occupation on the list.

It is readily apparent that many of the procedures described above can also be used just as easily and properly in the narrowing phase. We will avoid duplicating discussion of application of those devices, since the use in this phase remains constant and only the purpose has changed. There are also other aspects to consider in the narrowing phase and our discussion here will focus on those. We will look at four broad topics in this section, namely, self-oriented factors, externally oriented factors, career information, and the choice process. The reader must keep in mind that the client has now developed a fairly extensive list of occupations, each of which has positive relevance to one or more of his or her personal attributes. The client and counselor are now concerned with reducing that list, after appropriate exploration and discussion, to a few occupations that can be described as "best fit," "apparently appropriate," "best bets," or similar terms and from which tentative choices can be made. In general, our purpose is to help the client identify those occupations that reflect the area in which the client's most valued personal attributes and other relevant factors interact. Successfully completing this task requires the client to match his or her assessment of self and environment against credible information about the occupations on the extended list.

Self-oriented factors

Previous counseling sessions with the client, while aimed primarily at identifying the nature of the problem, have also provided considerable opportunity for the client to clarify the depth and breadth of self-understanding. In situations where that has been thoroughly covered, this portion of the narrowing phase can be completed rapidly and provides a basis for client and counselor to check on the extent to which the client is aware of the impact of these factors on career planning and has resolved or is ready to resolve the effect of that impact. In those situations where the client has not dealt with these matters, consideration is now necessary before the narrowing of options can be undertaken.

Attitudinal propensities

This heading includes a group of personal characteristics that bear on the individual's likelihood of making and completing plans. Many of these are abstract and difficult to measure precisely, yet each is an important component of the individual. Terms like "idiosyncrasy" and "quirk" suggest an aspect of peculiarity that distorts the nature of these factors, and words like "trait" or "characteristic" fall short of the particularity that really applies to the individual. Each is a product of the previous interaction between individual and environment and can be modified over time. The items discussed here are intended to be representative, rather than to constitute a comprehensive list.

The amount of drive or motivation possessed by the individual is important to evaluate early because this factor will bear on retaining or eliminating occupations on the list according to their location on the easy-difficult continuum. Individuals with high desire for achievement may be able to cope successfully with occupational challenges that lie beyond the range where average drive would be expected to succeed. Similarly, highly able individuals with low motivation may prefer to consider occupations that demand less than their abilities might suggest.

Another factor that must be considered is the client's ability and willingness to accept delayed gratification. Individuals with short fuses—those with low tolerance for delayed gratification—are unlikely to persist through lengthy training programs or situations where the payoff is likely to be slow.

Similarly, another important attitudinal propensity is the client's definition of acceptable risk. Some occupations, for example, medicine, require outstanding achievement in a lengthy preliminary preparatory program before individuals are selected for the specific training program. Consideration of such an occupation requires acceptance of high risk because several difficult obstacles, each involving considerable hazard, must be overcome in the process of gaining admission to the field. The person who cannot live with a high degree of uncertainty over an extended period may feel that the pressure is greater than he or she wishes to sustain.

The client may react to perceived attitudes and viewpoints of family members or important others. Such reactions can occur in either direction: one in which the client almost automatically acts to please that other person and accepts unquestioningly that person's opinion, or one in which the client sees the view of that other as a challenge and tends to choose the opposite position. Either tendency can distort the individual's ability to evaluate self and occupational options, thus leading to complicating attitudes in the narrowing phase. Consideration of such possibilities before discussion of specific alternatives may help the client to keep such influences in better perspective.

Clients sometimes establish financial and/or time limitations, especially applicable to preparatory programs, or to such intermediate goals as reaching a level of income or independence. If such limitations are held by the client and they appear to be realistic and appropriate, their impact on possible choices must be considered. If, however, the limitations are due to inadequate information, unfamiliarity with potential resources, or similar factors, the client deserves help in evaluating them before they are used to eliminate options that otherwise might be appropriately considered.

The client also needs to consider and verbalize, in generalities, the personal goals that he or she holds. Considering these dreams for certain time points of the future (maybe five, ten, and twenty years from now) in terms of desired achievements, lifestyle, and opportunities may also provide a useful basis for considering occupational options in the narrowing phase.

Multiple personal attributes

Although personal attributes are usually considered singly in the expanding phase, it is simplistic to think that only one factor is important in the narrowing phase. Individuals are composites of many attributes that exist in variable quantities from one person to the next, and these characteristics are valued by each individual in unique ways. It is probably just as simplistic to think that an occupation exists that requires exactly the mix of all attributes that any one individual possesses.

Either during the initial interview or during the discussion of test results, time is often spent helping the client to evaluate his or her attributes and to identify those valued most highly. A review of that earlier discussion, or consideration of the topic at this point, will help the client to establish some priority in viewing those factors. This is important for the client because, almost always, choices among attributes must be made in the narrowing phase. Attempting to place major emphasis upon several different characteristics can result in the elimination of almost every occupation on the expanded list.

The impact of this failure to set priorities can be demonstrated vividly to a client by using a random array of the overlay transparencies in the *Occupational View-Deck*. Almost any mix of five or six of these variables will exclude all code numbers. Some clients will emphasize attributes that conflict with each other, for example, a strong desire to work in a people-oriented and in a things-oriented situation. Holland (1973) describes such preferences as incongruent. The result is a drastic reduction in the number of occupations that can fit such an inversion, sometimes necessitating an either-or choice.

Establishing some priority among the personal attributes and other factors also assists the client in understanding the compromise aspect of the narrowing phase. Further, identifying and reviewing those factors most prized by the client will expedite the use of career materials in the narrowing process since it helps the client maintain focus on the job-related characteristics he or she considers most important.

Externally oriented factors

Restrictive externally oriented factors that seriously affect the choice process have been discussed earlier in Chapter 6. Because every individual interacts with the environment, it is useful to review that interaction as the client begins the narrowing phase. Factors to be identified are any matters that may cause some occupations on the list to appear more or less desirable, available, or appropriate to the client. When such influences are found, client and counselor should consider whether there are ways to overcome, minimize, or capitalize on their impact, or if it is wiser to proceed with the narrowing process while accepting the restrictions. Examples of externally oriented influences include access to opportunity, employment trends, or economic conditions.

Access to opportunity includes both the availability of preparatory programs and the possibility of subsequent employment. The individual who is geographically bound for whatever reason cannot realistically consider occupations in which both local training and local employment are not present. Client and counselor need to review such limitations before moving forward. If the identified boundaries of mobility appear to restrict opportunity, it may be useful to explore the availability of alternative programs. For example, a homemaker now contemplating employment outside the home would like to complete her interrupted college degree program but feels that her family responsibilities prevent regular attendance at the nearest degree-granting school. Before limiting consideration to locally available nondegree fields, the client can be helped to explore the existence of external degree programs, intensive courses, extension work for credit, and similar methods for overcoming the barriers she has identified. If suitable alternatives cannot be developed, then realistic consideration can only be given to those occupations that do not require a degree. Similarly, the geographically bound person needs to evaluate the chances for later employment and, unless such opportunities exist within the geographic area, preparation may be meaningless. Geographic limitation is only one example of factors that may restrict access to both preparation and later employment. Other restrictive elements might include local attitudes and practices, family attitudes or needs, financial problems, transportation difficulties, care for dependents, and other reasons.

Employment trends may also be an important factor for some individuals. Long-run changes affect some groups of occupations in different ways. Technological changes may cause some occupations to undergo extended periods of readjustment, with some fields declining over a long time while others grow. Sometimes these changes may occur on an industry-wide basis with many different causes interacting. The increased use of robot machines, greater use of components produced in foreign factories, reduced sales because of higher prices, difficult credit terms, and greater competition from foreign manufacturers have all changed employment patterns in the American automobile industry. Many of the changes may be long-lasting or permanent. If the client's list of occupations to be considered includes several that are subject to factors such as these, the client may wish to clarify his or her attitudes toward the pressures exerted by such outside forces and determine the extent to which they are to be included in the evaluation of occupational possibilities.

Economic conditions are often viewed from a national perspective, and long-term cyclical trends clearly have a broad impact on the expansion and contraction of occupational opportunities. In addition to national or regional economic conditions, one must also be aware of the considerable variations that occur within smaller geographic units. For example, two adjacent areas may have sizable differences in both short-term and long-range employment possibilities. This is clearly seen in communities that are dominated by one or two industries with a resulting "boom or bust" economic situation.

Total freedom from externally oriented factors is a mythical state because every individual relates to his or her environment in numerous ways. Some of the ties to family, community, educational background, ethnic group, and other aspects of the world that surround the person affect in significant ways the choices that can be made. The client who sees and understands these influences and who decides to deal with them is clearly in a better position to make appropriate choices than the person who either is unaware of these factors or decides to ignore them.

Career information

The previous pages have emphasized the importance of the individual understanding self and the setting, or environment, in which that self operates. Equally important in the career-choice process is the necessity for the individual to know enough about occupations and the world of work to narrow the list to those few possibilities that truly are the most appropriate. Just as the misunderstanding or misinterpretation of personal attributes such as aptitude, interest, motivation, or opportunity can lead to poor choices that result in serious consequences, so too can the lack of accurate career information result in poor choices that lead to disaster, disappointment, or discontent.

Counselors, teachers, parents, and individual clients, too, sometimes assume that, because an individual has lived for several years in an environment surrounded by people at work, he or she has absorbed a fairly comprehensive picture of what many different occupations involve. Common sense should be sufficient to recognize the fallacy of this assumption. Most occupations are not generally performed in the public view. Among those jobs that are easily and widely observed, there are many aspects of the work that are not so easy to see. Further, most individuals, as they have contact with workers on the job directly or vicariously via television or movies, are not seeking specific insight into the components of the occupation, and hence form only vague stereotypes of what, how, and why the worker does whatever he or she does. Even well-developed insight into a few occupations that may come from various sources (such as family involvement or incidental but frequent contact) may be distorted and inaccurate because the specific worker observed was not representative of the occupation generally.

Recognition of the need for increased effort to assist students in gaining a broader and deeper understanding of the world of work and their ultimate involvement in it, has led to the increased emphasis on career education programs in elementary and secondary schools.

Brief consideration of the world of work and how the counselor acquires and organizes such information has been reviewed in Chapter 8. Most counselor preparatory programs include more thorough study of this area in courses with such titles as "Career Theory," "Career Development," or "Occupational Information." Typical references that treat this subject from a counselor's viewpoint include books by Hoppock (1976), Isaacson (1977), and Norris et al. (1979).

In Chapters 5 and 6 we discussed the amount of information about self that the client needs to have in order to proceed with the career-choice process. The position arrived at was that the client needs to have sufficient self-awareness and self-understanding so that distortion and misunderstanding can be avoided and individual strengths and weaknesses can be properly related to demands made by various occupations. Although a great deal less than the exhaustive and comprehensive result of prolonged psychoanalysis, it is sufficiently extensive for the person to make appropriate and satisfying choices. Similarly, our concern in the area of career information is not for the client to become encyclopedic, but instead to have a sufficient amount of accurate and dependable information about occupations so that he or she neither erroneously discards options worthy of further study nor retains items that are not appropriate for additional consideration. This fundamental approach assumes that the individual may need only broad, general information during the early part of the exploring and narrowing phase, but as the process continues there will be a need for more comprehensive information. Thus the client will usually move through the three types of career information shown in Figure 9–3 as he or she progresses toward a choice.

FIGURE 9–3   Career materials in the exploring and narrowing phase.

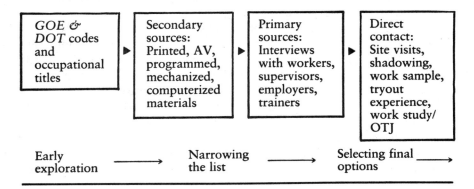

Secondary sources of career information
As the client begins the narrowing phase, he or she may often have sufficient information about some occupations on the list to make the first sort. However, there are likely to be many titles for which present information is entirely too scanty for an informed decision. Since the first sort is frequently based on such factors as a combination of two or more important personal attributes, or such self-oriented items as self-imposed training time limits or geographic preferences, the client often needs only a little additional information to complete the first review. Fortunately, a wide array of information is available that provides enough information to facilitate the first elimination. We will look briefly at a few examples of the various kinds of information. Our primary purpose is to emphasize the existence of many categories of information so that the counselor can select or suggest that type most useful for a specific client.

The most obvious type of career information is printed matter. Since the educational system and many other aspects of society rely primarily on printed materials, it is entirely logical to think first of this way of learning more about jobs. Those clients who read well and understand what they read can use this approach effectively; others may have difficulty. Most career information libraries and resource centers use printed material as their basic source and supplement this with the other kinds of material we will consider briefly in the rest of this section. At first, the client will usually find brief general descriptions most useful. Later in the process, more detailed information may be desired such as monographs or even books. Typical examples of the materials useful at the beginning of the narrowing phase include the *Occupational Outlook Handbook,* the *Guide for Occupational Exploration* and the *Dictionary of Occupational Titles,* all published by the U.S. Department of Labor. Other examples of helpful beginning materials are the brief occupational descriptions published by commercial companies such as Chronicle Guidance Publications and Science Research Associates. Appropriate materials that are useful at this stage are available from many different sources, including government agencies, commercial companies, schools and universities, professional or industrial societies, and other sources.

A second type of career information that is helpful in the early part of the exploring and narrowing phase is available through use of audiovisual media. An old proverb states that one picture is worth a thousand words, and this is often validated in learning about occupations. The recent emphasis on career education in the public schools has increased the amount and quality of AV materials related to occupations. Although most of the items were developed for use with groups, they are equally appropriate for individual clients. Well-stocked career resource centers or AV centers will offer many options that range from general overviews to specific and detailed presentations of single occupations. Materials include films, filmstrips, slides, slide sets, audiotapes, and videotapes. The major advantage of AV media is that the client can see and/or hear "reality" and thus more is usually learned than can be acquired from the printed page. The primary disadvantage accrues from the picture that is seen, since it may be dated, atypical, or incomplete. Further, AV materials usually require special equipment, so accessibility may be limited. In addition to media developed for educational purposes, there are many entertainment-oriented AV materials that provide information about occupations. These include radio and television programs and movies. The likelihood of distortion or misinformation is greater, but entertainment media can still be used advantageously.

Programmed materials constitute a third type of career material that can be used by clients in the narrowing process. Typical examples include workbooks, prepared exercises or assignments, and sequenced materials. Numerous workbooks related to career planning are presently available. Most of these deal with the whole process of career choice and many give major attention to the self-evaluation phase. There are some workbooks now on the market that have been prepared for career-awareness activities in career education programs. These are most likely to be useful for the individual client who needs to develop a broader view of the occupational world.

Mechanized systems of career information have become quite common in the last decade. Probably the most common example of this material is the VIEW system that has been adopted by about three-fourths of the states. This program has evolved from the Vocational Information for Education and Work system originally developed by the Department of Education in San Diego, California. In that evolutionary process the system has acquired a variety of names, most of them using the original VIEW acronym. Basically the system uses a set of microfilm aperture cards that include national and also regional or local information about occupations that are found in the geographic area. The cards are prepared, revised as needed, and distributed by a central state office, often in the state office of public instruction. It is an inexpensive system that provides regional and local data that often are difficult to acquire otherwise, and this system maintains the currency of those data. The *Occupational View-Deck* and the *Worker Trait Keysort* can also be considered examples of this type of career information.

A final illustration of secondary source information is seen in the several computerized systems that have gained wide usage in recent years; many of these will be discussed in Chapter 11. One of the first of these was the *Computerized Vocational Information Service (CVIS)* developed at Willowbrook High School and described by Harris (1968). Several states now have statewide systems that serve high schools, postsecondary schools, hospitals, and other state institutions. Most of these programs are essentially information retrieval programs that also permit the user to incorporate various restrictors, often including the kinds of factors we have considered earlier such as interest, ability level, amount of education, and lifestyle. Two more advanced computerized systems are now in use; both permit a more complex transaction between user and machine. These systems include *Project Discover* and *System of Interactive Guidance and Information (SIGI)*.

The various types of career information identified in this section are all used extensively in career-development activities at all educational levels, in classroom and group activities as well as in individual counseling. When they are used in teaching and guidance activities, the focus is usually on helping individuals acquire a general knowledge of many occupations during the awareness and exploration stages of career education. Each type of information is equally applicable in an individual counseling relationship where the focus is on the narrowing phase.

Primary sources of career information

The first screening of the expanded list is intended to remove those options that relate to one or more personal attributes but nevertheless clearly are contradictory to other significant attributes, goals, or values. That sorting process is usually completed rather quickly because the conflicts are often apparent. Subsequent screenings are intended to remove from the list those titles not so obviously in conflict but that offer less likelihood of goal satisfaction than others on the list. The objective, ultimately, is to reduce the list to a small number of titles, all of which have high possibilities of meeting the criteria established by the client. During the early reviews, the client needs sufficient information to make informed decisions, but usually does not need extensive knowledge about any of the items. Most of what is needed during this early part of the narrowing phase can come from secondary sources such as those described just above. As the process continues, however, the client generally needs more information than can be acquired easily from secondary sources. At this point the client may want counselor help in identifying individuals who can answer many of the specific questions being considered by the client. Conversations or interviews with workers, supervisors, employers, or those who prepare workers may provide a dimension not easily obtained from the most extensive reading lists. Each of these may view the occupation from a slightly different perspective and may have special information not generally perceived by the others.

The worker can help the client understand the occupation from the viewpoint of the actual job holder. This includes what the task is really like, what one does, and why and how each step is completed. The worker is in the best position to describe what the work setting is like, what the work actually requires of the worker, how workers feel about themselves, and the rewards and satisfactions that workers receive from the work. They can also describe the negative aspects of the occupation—what they don't like, what worries or displeases them, and the dangers that are inherent in the job or work setting.

Supervisors and employers often view occupations from a wider perspective than the individual worker. They are in a better position to see the different ways in which similarly prepared workers are used and to make comparisons between these subsets within the same occupation. They may have a clearer picture of the opportunities for advancement and the different tracks followed by workers to gain advancement and the options available to workers after such promotions are won. Often they are in a better position to assess the rewards that are available to workers, or likely to be available in the future. They also may be able to describe future conditions in the occupation, including the impact of technology, anticipated changes, long-run opportunities, and likely future requirements for admission, retention, and advancement.

Those who prepare workers, either in formal educational programs or other settings, have a perspective that also provides useful information. They are likely to be most knowledgeable about the levels of ability or preparation needed for admission to employment, differential standards in various settings, the numbers of potential workers available or in the process of being prepared, and the characteristics of that group. They can best describe the various training or preparatory programs, the requirements for admission to those programs, and the placement opportunities related to each.

Counselors, especially those who are related to counseling centers in secondary educational institutions, have found it advantageous to develop and maintain a community resources file that includes the names of individuals from the above groups who can and are willing to talk to those who would like such help. Although one can never anticipate all of the fields about which questions will be asked, one can predict a great many of those for which inquiries are sure to arise. Advance identification of possible resource persons enables the counselor to help the client more effectively.

Direct contact sources

Those opportunities that put the client in direct touch with the work itself are likely to be the most enlightening experiences. Because they also involve the greatest amount of time and effort, they can be justified most easily if they are used primarily in the final screenings of the narrowing phase.

Site visits permit the individual to observe the worker in his or her actual setting. One can see what the worker does, how the activity is related to the efforts of other workers, and through the senses of sight, hearing, smelling, and feeling acquire a deeper insight into the total nature of the occupation. The advantage of developing a better understanding is clear. There are also some possible disadvantages in using this technique. One of the more serious is the chance that the site visited and the workers observed are not typical of the occupation generally. Another disadvantage may occur even when a representative setting is visited, if the visitor does not observe accurately, or fails to understand what he or she has observed.

Recent attention has been given to a special type of extended site visit often referred to as shadowing. There are several variants of this technique. However, the most common pattern assigns the client to an individual worker for an extended period, typically a full workday. During that time, the individual remains with or near that worker, following him or her in all activities and going in and out like a shadow. Although the observer does not usually participate in any of the activities conducted by the worker, it is possible to watch closely, to question the worker and fellow workers, to see all the tasks performed in that time period, and to form impressions of processes, skills, and other components of the job. In general, the advantages and disadvantages listed above for the site visit also apply to shadowing.

Work samples are most likely to be available for those skilled occupations and crafts for which workers are prepared in vocational or technical schools. Counselors who work in other settings will usually encounter difficulty in finding opportunities for clients to use this technique.

Tryout experiences are difficult to obtain for those occupations that require lengthy educational or training programs, complex skills, or judgment and responsibility. This restriction eliminates essentially all of the professions and many of the skilled occupations. For example, there is no way that someone interested in law, medicine, structural steel erection, or law enforcement can be given an opportunity to try out the real thing. Nevertheless, in almost every case one can find other occupations with lower skill levels within the same work setting where work participation will put the individual in close proximity to the occupation being explored. Many secondary and postsecondary schools have developed work experience or cooperative programs in which the individual can be employed in closely related occupations while completing preparation for a more advanced one. Opportunities for informal experience of this type are limited, for the most part, only by the degree of occupational diversity within the geographic area.

MAKING THE CHOICE

Essentially, the choice process is simply the end product of the continuation of what we have called the narrowing phase. The individual starts with the list of occupations developed by him- or herself and the counselor, and gradually narrows the list through the process of eliminating less suitable possibilities. Throughout this stage the client is using a very complex set of criteria as the basis for keeping or discarding titles on the list. These criteria include his or her perception of self, including all of the personal attributes and propensities that we have discussed above, and his or her perception of what we have called external factors that emanate from the client's present or anticipated future environment. Early eliminations are usually based on relatively gross estimates of these factors, but as the process continues finer and finer evaluations must be used.

When the client has narrowed the list to the final few possibilities, it is usually appropriate to stop again, review carefully perceptions of self and situation, match them with the priorities for self identified earlier, and determine if any further adjustment or revision is necessary. The client is then ready to consider the advantages and disadvantages that might result from each of the items remaining on the list.

Once the pro and con points for each remaining possibility have been reviewed, the client should consider whether there are existing or latent factors that might enhance opportunities in any of the tentative fields. In other words, the client should address the question "Do I have anything extra going for me or can I start something going for me in any of these occupations?" The "something extra" can cover the entire gamut of possibilities, but typical examples would be unusual personal characteristics, special skills, personal or family contacts or acquaintances, and economic or social factors. If such bonus points can be obtained, their value should be included in the final evaluation.

In the next step the client is asked to rank the final list, keeping in mind the major factors that have so far been considered. Although this task is seldom easy, the client has at hand the data needed to establish priorities.

It is helpful to clients to label the highest-ranked item as "tentative" and to suggest that they think about their rankings for a few days before proceeding further. This provides an opportunity for "breathing space" and a chance to test the choice a little more before feeling committed. Further, using a label such as "tentative" may help clients keep in perspective that career choices are exactly that. As individuals and conditions change, later revision and adjustment will undoubtedly be necessary and should be considered a likely event.

After clients have had a few days to "try on," "live with," or "adjust to" the tentative choice, they usually will have begun to integrate the choice into their self-concepts. The result is a more positive view of themselves, a feeling of satisfaction, and eagerness to move ahead. Many clients are inclined to feel that the career counseling process has been completed, and there is some risk that clients may terminate prematurely at this point. There is an important next step in the process to be considered: how to implement the choice. We will discuss that topic in Chapter 10.

REFERENCES

Appalachia Educational Laboratory, Inc. *Worker trait group guide.* Bloomington, Ill.: McKnight Publishing Company, 1978.

————. *Worker trait keysort.* Bloomington, Ill.: McKnight Publishing Company, 1978.

Cooper, J. F. Comparative impact of the SCII and the Vocational Card Sort on career salience and career exploration of women. *Journal of Counseling Psychology,* 1976, *23,* 348–351.

Dewey, C. R. Exploring interests: A non-sexist method. *Personnel and Guidance Journal,* 1974, *52,* 311–315.

Droege, R. C. and Boese, R. Development of a new occupational aptitude pattern structure with comprehensive occupational coverage. *Vocational Guidance Quarterly,* 1982, *30,* 219–229.

Harris, J. The computerization of vocational information. *Vocational Guidance Quarterly,* 1968, *17,* 12–20.

Holland, J. L. *Making vocational choices: A theory of careers.* Englewood Cliffs, N.J.: Prentice-Hall, Inc., 1973.

————. *Vocational exploration and insight kit.* Palo Alto, Cal.: Consulting Psychologists Press, Inc., 1980.

Hoppock, R. *Occupational information.* 4th edition. New York: McGraw-Hill Book Company, 1976.

Isaacson, L. E. *Career information in counseling and teaching.* 3rd edition. Boston: Allyn and Bacon, Inc., 1977.

Jones, L. K. *Occu-sort: A self-guided career exploration system.* Raleigh, N.C.: North Carolina State University, School of Education, Office of Publications, 1977.

————. Holland's typology and the new *Guide for Occupational Exploration:* Bridging the gap. *Vocational Guidance Quarterly,* 1980, *29,* 70–76.

Meir, E. I. Empirical test of Roe's structure of occupations and an alternative structure. *Journal of Counseling Psychology,* 1970, *17,* 41–48.

Norris, W., Hatch, R. N., Engelkes, J. R., and Winborn, B. B. *The career information service.* 4th edition. Chicago: Rand McNally and Company, 1979.

Occupational view-deck. 3rd edition. Moravia, N.Y.: Chronicle Guidance Publications, Inc., 1978.

Pryor, R. In search of a concept: Work values. *Vocational Guidance Quarterly,* 1979, *27,* 250–258.

Remer, P. and O'Neill, C. Clients as change agents: What color could my parachute be? *Personnel and Guidance Journal,* 1980, *58,* 425–429.

Roe, A. *The psychology of occupations.* New York: John Wiley and Sons, 1956.

Super, D. E. *The psychology of careers.* New York: Harper & Row, Publishers, 1957, p. 48.

Tyler, L. E. Research explorations in the realm of choice. *Journal of Counseling Psychology,* 1961, *8,* 195–202.

U.S. Department of Labor. *Dictionary of occupational titles.* Volume II. 3rd edition. Washington, D.C.: U.S. Government Printing Office, 1965.

————. *Guide for occupational exploration.* Washington, D.C.: U.S. Government Printing Office, 1979.

————. *Selected characteristics of occupations defined in the Dictionary of Occupational Titles.* Washington, D.C.: U.S. Government Printing Office, 1981.

U.S. Office of Education, Department of Health, Education, and Welfare. *Career education.* HEW Publication No. (OE) 72-39. Washington, D.C.: U.S. Government Printing Office, 1971.

10

Making plans

Everyone who has traveled can confirm that deciding where to go is only the first in a long sequence of decisions that must be made if the trip is to be completed successfully. Questions must be answered about when to go, how long to stay, how to travel, what and whom to take along, what to see and do while there, what to read in preparation, what documents to obtain, and so forth. So, too, in career counseling, selecting a tentative career objective is only the first decision in a series. The previous chapter focused on selecting the objective, and this chapter will consider the subsequent decisions that are a consequence of that preceding choice.

The comprehensive question for the client is "How should I plan to implement the choice I have made so that I best enhance my opportunities for the satisfactions I hope to attain?" Because we deal with individuals whose experiences and present circumstances are unique, we must assume that each will have particular problems and concerns. Some matters that are troublesome to many clients will be of little concern to others, and what one finds vexatious may be routine to others. Therefore, some of the topics discussed in this chapter may require great or little attention by a specific client.

Healy (1982) emphasizes the need for more research on the effectiveness of career plans developed by clients as part of the career counseling process. It is clear that little information exists in the literature about this important step in the total process. He further emphasizes that plans must be individualized to deal with specific needs and characteristics of the specific client. Although some counselors use packaged or prescribed plans arranged according to a standard set of elements, Healy suggests that plans focusing on the particular demands of a target environment will be more viable.

The topics included here are representative of those frequently considered by clients as they attempt to develop plans. Any one client very well may have other significant items that need attention as much as any of these. Obviously, they should be incorporated at the appropriate point in the planning process. Similarly, those items that are inconsequential for a particular client should be passed over.

PRESENT LOCATION AND FUTURE GOAL

One of the first questions to be faced in the planning process is "Where am I now relative to where I want to go?" In terms of our earlier travel analogy, one cannot make plans to go to a certain destination without first ascertaining one's present location.

For the most part, the items of concern here were discussed with the client during the initial interview, as described in Chapter 5. It is now only necessary to review those pertinent facts that were obtained in that earlier interview, evaluating each major item in relation to the tentative choice.

Major attention should be given to those matters that bear most directly on implementing the choice. This includes such items as educational background, work experience, and client characteristics. There may be important considerations in the areas of family, health and physical status, significant experiences, and the client's view of self. Other details that are sometimes important include age, financial resources, and items that restrict flexibility and independence. Sometimes the individual wants to emphasize where he or she wants to live, a desired lifestyle, access to or avoidance of certain conditions or resources such as urban areas, ski slopes, the beach, and the like. All personal characteristics that are clearly relevant to the desired goal should be reviewed, whether they are assets or liabilities.

MEETING REQUIREMENTS

Once a tentative choice has been made, one can identify what is necessary for successful participation in that field, how one demonstrates that one possesses those prerequisites, and how entry is obtained.

The most evident requirement for entry into most occupations, other than beginning-level unskilled positions, is possession of specific skill or knowledge. The particular skill needed may range from very simple and concrete (such as making change for small purchases) to very complex and abstract (such as calculating location by celestial navigation). The number of skills required may range from few to many. Specified skills and knowledge will usually involve some combination of tool knowledge, such as mathematical and language development, and also specific vocational preparation.

The amount of required training time, both general and specific, can usually be identified easily in publications such as *Selected Characteristics of Occupations Defined in the Dictionary of Occupational Titles*. The particular content of that training time—the general and special skills and knowledge needed to perform the task—is somewhat harder to identify. Some clues are available from the *DOT*, employer job descriptions or program descriptions available from training institutions.

For some occupations the requirements are well known, highly standardized, and uniformly enforced. For others, particularly occupations with low general educational requirements and relatively brief specific vocational preparation, there may be considerable variation and flexibility. In these latter cases, local or regional hiring requirements may be the best index of common practice.

For many occupations, especially the professions and other highly skilled fields, the required skills and knowledge are translated into specialized training programs, and successful completion of the preparatory program is considered *prima facie* evidence that the skills and knowledge are possessed. In other cases, completion of a specified preparatory program followed by an examination, an internship, or similar practical experience demonstrates competence.

In many of the occupations that require formal training and/or examination programs, competence is established by acquiring some type of official permission such as licensure or certification. Standards for qualifying for this type of recognition may be set by either an occupational group or a governmental unit. Examples of this method of demonstrating that one has the requisite skills and knowledge include the teacher's certificate, an accountant's license, or a journeyman machinist's card. Although there may be some variation from state to state or across other political boundaries, in most cases there will be considerable similarity from unit to unit.

Among occupations where formal standards have not been established, one may find great variability. In some cases one may establish competence in a short, informal, on-the-job demonstration observed by a supervisor. There are many levels between the simplest and most complex methods and sometimes variation within a specific occupation.

Methods of demonstrating competence differ greatly across the various occupations. So, too, there is considerable divergence in how one gains admission to different occupations. At the simplest level this may consist only of identifying an employer who is willing to employ the applicant. At the most complex level this may involve not only acquiring the necessary certificate or license but also demonstrating, in some approved manner, greater skill than any other applicant. This may be accomplished through formal preparation, examinations, or hours of seniority at an appropriate lower-level related occupation. Many occupations have a typical admission or placement procedure that is common across the occupation.

The general purpose of this section has been to emphasize the importance of helping the client identify clearly what skills and knowledge are required for admission to the desired field, and how he or she can demonstrate possession of those skills and knowledge. At that point the client is able to establish the difference between present status and the desired status. This intervening span (skill, knowledge, training, experience) is what must be traversed if the client is to qualify for admission. The remainder of this chapter considers matters involved in crossing that intervening area.

POSSIBLE PATHS

Once the client has determined his or her present status and identified the deficiencies that must be satisfied to qualify for what he or she wants to do, the next step is to ascertain the alternative ways for acquiring the needed skills and knowledge. In some cases the route is clear cut and specific; however, in many occupations several options may be possible. For example, the high school student who decides he or she wants to become a registered nurse has a choice of three paths after completing high school: (1) enrollment in a hospital-based nursing preparation program, (2) enrollment in an associate degree program, or (3) enrollment in a bachelor's degree program. Similarly, most crafts and skilled trades can be entered via on-the-job experience or a formal apprenticeship.

Information about the types of preparatory routes leading to various occupations can be found in such publications as *Guide for Occupational Exploration* and *Occupational Outlook Handbook*. Information is also included in the *Occupational View-Deck* and the *Worker Trait Keysort* (both described in Chapter 9), and in printed career materials and most computerized information systems.

Additional questions are encountered when the tentative choice is an occupation for which the customary preparatory path is formal education. The concerns to be addressed include all of those faced by any individual considering some formal type of postsecondary education. The specific questions are almost endless, ranging across such broad topics as the following:

> What schools offer preparation for this occupation?
> Are the programs in most schools similar or diverse?
> > What special features accompany different emphases?
> > What advantages and disadvantages are recognizable?

How can one evaluate the quality of programs?
>What about supporting or adjunct areas?
Are there special demands or requirements in some programs?
Are there special opportunities or payoffs in some programs?
How much time is required?
>What is the minimum program available?
>What is the usual pattern followed?
>What is ideal?
What cost-benefit ratios can be estimated?
Do certain kinds of programs fit my needs better than others?

In addition to the wide variety of program-specific questions, the client must also consider such broad, general institutional characteristics as size, type of school, location, environment, general admission requirements, type of student body, faculty data, student life, campus and community facilities and resources, and the like. This kind of information is easily obtained from the many general educational directories in common use and from many of the computerized information systems. Detailed information relative to particular preparatory programs is harder to obtain from general sources, although professional organizations in the chosen field may prove useful. Both the *GOE* and the *OOH* also list some sources for such data. Further, local practitioners in the occupation and local employers are additional resources for information about preparatory programs that are regionally or locally favored.

Except for the professional and technical areas, where the customary preparatory path is formal education to at least the baccalaureate level, most occupations can be entered through paths that require considerably less classroom involvement. Some of the educational options that are available include the following:

Full-time

1. A two-year program in a technical school or community college leading to an associate degree.
2. A one-year program in a technical school or community college leading to an occupational certificate.
3. A one-year-or-less program in a trade or vocational school.

Part-time

4. Any of the above programs extended over a longer period because of the individual's involvement in work.
5. Continuous, related classroom experience associated with an apprenticeship program.
6. Supplementary classroom involvement related to an on-the-job training program.

7.   Incidental short courses, intensive or extension courses or work-
      shops occasionally available and relevant to the work expe-
      rience.

Entry lines that are primarily work-oriented and where classroom
preparation is less emphasized include formal apprenticeships, formally
structured on-the-job training programs, and informal on-the-job employment where the individual starts in an entry position as helper or assistant
and expects to move into the occupation as a result of observation and
incidental participation. Some occupations can also be approached through
related fields (for example, civilian counterparts of military jobs).

CHOOSING A PATH AND SETTING A SCHEDULE

Although the task now confronting the client can be described easily in
decision-making terms, its resolution may be nearly as complicated as the
occupational choice process through which the client has recently jour-
neyed. The fundamental issue for the client can be stated simply with the
question "What plan is best for me?" Personal attributes, both self-oriented
and externally oriented, are likely to influence decisions about preparatory
programs just as they swayed occupational choices.

The process to be followed at this stage is essentially the same as
before: self-evaluation, acquisition of information about alternatives, evaluation of available alternatives in terms of all pertinent personal factors, and
deciding which alternative is best. Fortunately, at least two factors usually
make this decision easier and quicker than earlier ones. First, the client has
learned something about the decision-making process and, second, he or she
has already dealt with most of the significant personal data in selecting the
tentative occupational choice. The major differences are that some new data
may be pertinent to this decision and the data are being matched against
different criteria at this point. The personal attributes identified in Chapter
5 and applied in Chapters 7 and 9 are relevant to this decision. Those characteristics that were recognized earlier as particularly significant probably
also warrant attention with this choice.

Questions about the time frame in which the preparatory path is to be
completed can be considered only after the preferred path has been identified. Although one might assume that a client who has decided where he or
she wants to go and how he or she plans to reach that objective would
automatically proceed with all reasonable haste, there may be several factors that require consideration and that may interfere with that automatic
assumption. Some of the more apparent items that might delay immediately
beginning a training program include the existence of waiting lists for entry,
the need to acquire financial support or assistance, infrequent starting dates,
complex selection and entry procedures, and a host of personal factors that
we will consider in the following section.

Similarly, clients occasionally will seek ways to speed up the process in order to reach the destination in less than the usual time. This reaction is not limited to those who have been delayed in the usual schedule, for example by military service or family responsibility, but it is likely to occur more frequently with this group. Where skill acquisition is based on a time frame of hours or weeks of experience, little can be done to juggle the established patterns. However, where the basic unit is credit hours or similar educational units, many opportunities exist for shortening the time. Examples of ways to accomplish this include testing out of basic courses, carrying a heavy course load, and year-round schooling.

IDENTIFYING EXPECTED ADJUSTMENTS

Sooner or later, the client must personalize the effect that decisions and choices will produce once the process of implementation is initiated. As much as possible, that impact should be anticipated so that it occurs as a natural, expected result of moving ahead with a deliberate plan and not as a sudden, nasty, unforeseen surprise. Although one cannot predetermine every eventuality, it certainly is possible to identify many of the major factors.

One area likely to be influenced by the development of plans is the client's present lifestyle. The young high school graduate who proceeds directly to further formal education probably experiences minimal conflict in this area. For the most part, this person has adjusted his or her life to the cycles, pressures, and other characteristics of academic life. The areas where adjustments may cause the greatest disruption may be related to increased self-responsibility and "out of school" life. For example, college students often report problems adjusting to group life in the dormitory or other housing unit, accepting responsibility for their own time schedule, handling routine matters such as laundry and checking accounts, and dealing with absence of family and long-time friends. On the other hand, students who return to formal study after a lengthy interval describe problems related to academic aspects of their new situation—coping with extensive reading assignments, developing study skills, learning new techniques and using new equipment, or preparing for examinations. They also frequently emphasize time conflicts, with classes and study time encroaching on other activities that have previously filled their lives.

Lifestyle can be affected in financial ways if the preparatory program necessitates diverting funds from other purposes to pay for the education, or if time previously used in income-producing activities is now used in the preparation program. This impact is more likely to be significant for the individual returning to school after a lengthy interruption, for example, the midlife changer or the homemaker returning to paid employment. Budgeting both time and funds may be necessary to accomplish desired goals.

Another aspect of lifestyle that may be influenced by planning for career change or development includes current time commitments. Again, ongoing students moving to postsecondary educational programs are already accustomed to allocating large blocks of time to classwork and study. The returning student, however, may underestimate the time required for school-related activities. Also, many such individuals may have assumed various responsibilities or involvements that they are reluctant to relinquish. Examples of these are almost unlimited: community responsibilities such as committees, church or other organizational assignments, recreational or leisure activities such as team memberships, sponsoring or coaching time or regular attendance at events, even personal activities such as reading, hobbies, traveling, and conversation. The important point for counselor and client to consider is the provision of a realistic plan for whatever time is required for the new undertaking. Because most people have already filled their schedules with various activities, this new commitment probably requires elimination or drastic reduction of previous time-consuming involvements. One serious error for many clients is to assume that the new endeavor can simply be an "add on."

Some individuals must also consider the impact on others produced by the proposed change. The housewife or mother who decides to initiate a preparatory program leading to away-from-home employment is, perhaps, most representative of individuals who must resolve many problems in this area. The reallocation of housekeeping activities to other family members, provision of child care, accessibility when needed by children or spouse, time management, and establishing priorities are representative of the kinds of dilemmas included in this topic. Because people exist in social settings, the impact of plans and behavior on others is almost a universal concern. Many of these problems are easily solved, particularly if they are considered in advance and acceptable answers are identified.

Significant others play a vital role in the life of everyone. Consideration of impact on others is clearly a two-way street. Not only must the client review how his or her plans impinge on the lives of those important other individuals, he or she must also evaluate how the lives and activities of those other people restrict or enhance the likelihood of succeeding with the plan that is being developed. One must recognize the individuals who surround the client, and the client's interactions with those people, not only as sources that limit, restrict, or impede client plans, but also as sources of succorance, encouragement, support, and assistance.

JOB SEARCH STRATEGIES

Some clients will choose to seek employment immediately rather than elect to acquire additional preparation. Several reasons for such action are immediately obvious. Some individuals will have identified salable skills in the self-study process, others will see that they prefer the immediate gratification of holding a job rather than accepting the delay that comes with a preparatory program, and still others will feel that financial pressures, the need for independence, a desire for accomplishment, or other compelling reasons necessitate going to work as soon as possible.

Occasional periods of high economic activity with accompanying demand for workers tend to mislead many people into believing that the job-getting process is a very simple one of announcing one's availability and then sorting through the numerous offers to select that perfect position. Such situations make nice fairy tales, but rarely reflect reality. Even in periods that economists label as "full employment" millions are unemployed, most of whom are seeking a job. Periods of technological change and industrial readjustment produce additional stress by both reducing the number of job opportunities and increasing the number of competitors for each position.

Much attention has been given in recent years to the increased pressure encountered in the job-search process. Several books have appeared that specifically address the problems encountered in this search and how one can deal with those difficulties; representative of such publications are those by Bolles (1978), Crystal and Bolles (1974), Figler (1979), Irish (1978), Kiesel (1980), and Klingner and Davis (1980). The last two use a workbook format that assists the user step-by-step in preparing for and conducting a job-search campaign. Each of the books listed, as well as many others, provides a great deal of specific information and advice including what to do, how to do it, when to do it, and how to follow up. In general, these volumes are directed toward individuals who have postsecondary education and/or some previous work experience. Several publishers of high school textbooks have similar volumes that are designed for upper high school students who are not contemplating further education. Typical of this type of booklet are those by Blackledge, Blackledge and Keily (1975), Kushner and Keily (1975), and Zedlitz (1981).

Counselors working with individual clients may find that an appropriate self-help book such as one of the above can provide a useful basis for encouraging and developing client initiative. When the counselor, or counseling center, has several clients who are approaching or in the job-seeking stage, a group approach offers many advantages to both clients and counselors. One useful reference for organizing and operating an effective job club is the handbook by Azrin and Besadel (1979). This volume describes techniques for helping job-seeking clients help themselves and fellow club members in the process.

The job-search process, like career counseling generally, starts with developing and clarifying self-understanding. Many of the self-help books start with some form of self-inventory that typically includes identification of personal skills, prior work experience, job-related training or education, personal characteristics and preferences, values, desired lifestyle, goals, degree of mobility, and similar factors. These are basic components of the client's psychological world discussed in Chapters 5 and 7 and earlier in this chapter.

Zunker (1981), for example, discusses skill identification using client self-estimates. He suggests that work skills can be classified as functional, adaptive, or technical. Functional skills include those general work-related skills that may be applicable to a number of different positions, such as administrative, analytical, judgmental, planning, and writing skills. Adaptive skills reflect ability to relate to the work environment or work associates, tolerate stress, or work compatibly with others, including such personal traits as being aggressive, courteous, imaginative, and persistent. Technical skills are specific job- or task-oriented competencies and are generalizable or transferable only to other jobs requiring the same specific skill. Bolles (1978) proposes a "Quick Job-Hunting Map" based on Holland's typology that an individual can use to identify functional skills. Often clients, particularly those with little or no significant work experience, overlook many functional skills they may have developed in nonwork settings such as the classroom, the home, or leisure and volunteer activities. Similarly, they often overlook the adaptive or interpersonal skills in which they may be highly proficient.

The second phase of the job-search process, according to several of the above-listed authors, is identification of the individual's own "job market." This usually incorporates consideration of such general factors as geographic items, size and type of community, mobility factors, kind of employer preferred, and kind of work preferred/able/willing to perform. In addition, this stage includes efforts to help the client broaden his or her scope of what is available by teaching how to use resources that previously may have been overlooked, such as recognizing existing contacts or establishing new ones, using a networking system, evaluating special resources for which one may qualify, using agencies and advertisements, and learning about the hidden job market of unlisted vacancies that can be created for the client.

The third phase focuses on helping the client to sell himself or herself to prospective employers. Major attention is usually given to building skill in writing job-search letters, preparing resumes, conducting interviews, asking appropriate questions, answering the interviewer's questions, and following up on postinterview actions. The appropriateness of these various activities depends largely on the type of position being sought. Professional, technical, and administrative positions may involve all of these steps while production, retail sales, and service positions are likely to require only a brief application form and a brief interview.

Preparing useful resumes is often a worrisome task for job applicants. The client who reports difficulty in accomplishing this task can be helped by using one of the job-search handbooks mentioned earlier. Bolles (1978) and Irish (1978) include very specific suggestions on structure and content, while emphasizing the limited usefulness of the resume. Bolles, for example, states that there are only four functions served by a resume, namely: a self-inventory, an extended calling card, an agenda for an interview, and, its most useful purpose, a "memory jogger" for the employer after the interview. Similarly, Irish distinguishes between the functional resume that describes what the applicant wants in a position and has in the way of skills and the descriptive resume that elaborates on the applicant's chronology of experiences.

Many clients are equally uncertain about preparing for an interview. The content of the interview varies according to the type of position involved, particularly in relation to the degree of responsibility, amount of initiative or independent judgment, and level of complexity involved in the position. Zunker (1981) includes a list of fifty questions frequently asked by employers interviewing college seniors and another list of negative factors often looked for in an interview. Both lists can be helpful in preparing nervous applicants for their first interviews.

Bolles (1978) also puts the situation in perspective by emphasizing that the purpose of the interview is to answer the questions of the applicant and of the employer, and that both parties have three basic questions or concerns. The applicant wants to make three proposals:

1. Help me understand the job completely and thoroughly.
2. Then, let me tell you if I think my skills truly match the job.
3. If they do, I will try to persuade you to hire me. (p. 165)

The employer has three questions in mind, namely:

1. Why are you here?
2. Precisely what can you do for me?
3. How much is it going to cost me? (p. 165)

Bolles emphasizes that the applicant should be sure that both sets of questions are satisfactorily addressed during the interview. He also points out the importance of personal appearance, including appropriate dress and hair care and personal deportment.

The job-search process is a nerve-wracking experience for many individuals, filled with uncertainties, periods of self-doubt, discouragement, and depression. The counselor can help the client to build and use support systems like those described by Azrin and Besadel (1979) or consisting of friends and family. The counselor, almost inevitably, becomes a key part of the client's support system.

PLANNING FOR CHANGE

Clients sometimes ask "What if, after all this careful study and planning, this proposal has to be changed?" The obvious answer is "Of course, it's almost inevitable that you will have to make some changes." Although the likelihood of further adjustment is disconcerting to many clients, reality necessitates an honest answer. A little reflection usually leads the client to recognize that he or she is constantly encountering change, even on short-term plans. Whether the question is verbalized or not, clients deserve an opportunity to explore alternative or fall-back options.

Remer and O'Neill (1980) recognize with the following statement the overwhelming likelihood of change after a tentative plan has been developed:

> The counselor, emphasizing the tentative nature of the choice, stresses that the person and the environment will change. The emphasis is on clients becoming committed to the "best" alternatives for them right now. (p. 428)

Because planning an alternative for every eventuality would be a futile process, the counselor's concern is primarily to help the client accept the unavoidable likelihood of some modification, recognize appropriate ways of accommodating to that necessity, and have confidence in his or her ability to deal intelligently with that need as it arises. Often a brief discussion will suffice to determine the degree of flexibility possessed by the client. The total time needed for consideration of this topic is probably roughly related inversely to the amount of self-confidence and flexibility demonstrated by the client.

Within a short time frame after tentative choices have been made, realignment of plans should be relatively easy because logical alternatives should be apparent within the range of options that existed in the final phases of the narrowing process. Certainly those two to four finalists would be worthy of review if the factors necessitating reconsideration are basically related to the original final choice—for example, all available training programs are closed for a longer time than the client feels he or she can wait or available preparatory programs are too costly in time and funds for the client.

The value of unchosen final alternatives as second-round choices, if the first preference becomes inoperative, diminishes with time and changing circumstances. It is very unlikely that those other options will still be viable a year or two after a decision is made. Similarly, any major change in important self-oriented or externally oriented factors may also invalidate secondary alternatives because their appropriateness was based on conditions existing before the major change occurred. Clients who have considered, during the counseling process, the possible impact of changing circumstances are usually prepared to deal with such contingencies when they occur and to do so without panic or anxiety.

TAKING THE FIRST STEP

So far in this chapter we have been discussing those matters that must be dealt with in the interval between making a choice and beginning to implement that choice. The client has identified the space (measured in terms of preparation, skills and knowledge, experience, time, effort, and money) between his or her present situation and the desired goal. He or she has determined what is needed to traverse that distance in those same terms and has chosen the most suitable alternative among the various options available. He or she has also evaluated the influence of this choice on self and others and has considered how to deal with minor and major adjustments that can be expected. Finally, he or she has modified the developing plan to provide the best fit to his or her individual circumstances as they appear to exist.

One of the products of this planning period can be the development of a time chart consisting of the sequential steps necessary to reach the goal. The degree of specificity will vary according to the complexity of the task facing the client. The objective is simply one of determining what must be done first and, within the client's time frame, when that step should be accomplished. At least two advantages accrue from actually setting down a tentative time schedule; first, important steps are less likely to be overlooked or missed and, second, many clients are less likely to procrastinate or postpone action if they have developed a time chart for which they feel responsible.

Primary responsibility for developing and using the time chart rests with the client. The counselor can help the client to see the advantage of such a simple device and to accept it as a demonstration of his or her responsibility for planning and organizing paths that lead to accepted goals. Often, first steps can be taken immediately. The counselor, after evaluating client self-responsibility, self-confidence, and independence can determine whether any monitoring of these early steps is necessary before terminating counseling.

EVALUATING AND GENERALIZING

The final step in the career counseling process is to assist the client in understanding how to evaluate the appropriateness of the selected goal and his or her progress toward it, and how to generalize the skills acquired in the career counseling process to the solution of other problems. Although the actual application of these activities lies in the future, consideration of both is appropriate within the counseling process and logically occurs just prior to termination of the counseling relationship.

In the penultimate section of this chapter we discussed the inevitability of change. Because decisions are made on the basis of the best available data—sometimes imprecise and always incomplete—they must be subject to review and modification as new data become available to the client. That continuous or intermittent review is the evaluation with which we are concerned. Recognizing the tentativeness of all decisions related to career, the client should expect regularly to ask him- or herself, "Is this goal still appropriate and desirable?" An affirmative response, either total or general, should result in a continuing commitment to the adopted plan. An uncertain or negative response should lead the client to review carefully the plan with the intent of either making some adjustment or completely replacing it. Unfortunately, clients are sometimes inclined unnecessarily to feel guilt, frustration, or failure when new information or changing conditions make previous plans obsolete. Recognition of this possibility of change, and confidence in one's ability to make necessary adjustments, should lead to greater acceptance when change is encountered.

The primary goal of career counseling, obviously, is to assist the client to identify an appropriate, attainable, and satisfying career goal and develop plans for preparing for and entering that field. Another product of the process should be to teach the client the decision-making process so that he or she can use that technique with future problems, both career-related and non-career-related. Clients sometimes are so involved in the various steps that they fail to grasp the overall sequence in the total process. The counselor can resolve this myopic view by helping the client review the system step-by-step and relate it to hypothetical problems that are likely to be encountered in the near and distant future.

REFERENCES

Azrin, N. H. and Besadel, V. B. *Job club counselor's manual: A behavioral approach to vocational counseling.* Baltimore: University Park Press, 1979.

Blackledge, W. L., Blackledge, E. H. and Keily, H. J. *The job you want—How to get it.* 2nd edition. Cincinnati, Ohio: South-Western Publishing Co., 1975.

Bolles, R. N. *A practical manual for job-hunters and career changers: What color is your parachute?* Berkeley, Cal.: Ten Speed Press, 1978.

Crystal, J. C. and Bolles, R. N. *Where do I go from here with my life?* New York: The Seabury Press, 1974.

Figler, H. *The complete job-search handbook.* New York: Holt, Rinehart and Winston, 1979.

Healy, C. C. *Career development: Counseling through the life stages.* Boston: Allyn and Bacon, Inc., 1982, pp. 470–472.

Irish, R. K. *Go hire yourself an employer.* Garden City, N.Y.: Anchor Books, 1978.

Kisiel, M. *Design for change: A guide to new careers.* New York: New Viewpoints/Vision Books, 1980.

Klingner, D. E. and Davis, A. J. *The job-seekers guide.* New York: Human Sciences Press, 1980.

Kushner, J. A. and Keily, H. J. *How to find and apply for a job.* 3rd edition. Cincinnati, Ohio: South-Western Publishing Co., 1975.

Remer, P. and O'Neill, C. Clients as change agents: What color could my parachute be? *Personnel and Guidance Journal,* 1980, *58,* 425–429.

Zedlitz, R. *Getting a job.* Cincinnati, Ohio: South-Western Publishing Co., 1981.

Zunker, V. G. *Career counseling: Applied concepts of life planning.* Monterey, Cal.: Brooks/Cole Publishing Company, 1981.

11

Computer systems in career counseling

Technological advancement was identified in an earlier chapter as one of the factors producing significant change in occupations. Certainly one of the most widespread technological developments occurring today is the rapid expansion of the application of computers to many occupations. The rapid growth of more powerful computers in smaller, less expensive packages and the development of relevant software to use with these amazing machines foretells the time within the near future when a computer terminal will be a routine part of each counselor's office equipment. Turkington (1982) points to estimates that predict that by the turn of the century as many as 75 percent of the workforce will need computer skills for their jobs. Counselors need those skills today to use effectively any of the existing computer-assisted career-guidance systems.

If the present rate of development continues, one can expect even better systems to be available soon. The issue is no longer "Should we use computers in career counseling?" Instead it has become "How can we best apply computers to our setting and clientele?"

It is impossible to provide the reader with a comprehensive, up-to-date review of a topic in which changes occur with great frequency. Technological improvements of computers can occur several times each year. These changes are followed shortly by the introduction of new software and proposals for better systems of application. Clearly, the state-of-the-art is still unfolding and many surprises lie ahead. Because of inevitable delays in publication, every book and journal discussion of computers must be viewed as describing "where we were" rather than "where we are." Accordingly, two publications are available that describe that status in 1983. One of these is *Microcomputers and the School Counselor*, edited by Cynthia Johnson, published by American School Counselor Association. The other is a journal issue, Volume II, Number 4, of *The Counseling Psychologist* including major contributions by J. Harris-Bowlsbey, M. R. Katz and L. Shatkin, D. V. Tiedeman, and others. The reader will find each of these to be useful supplements to this chapter.

HISTORICAL BACKGROUND

Serious efforts were undertaken as early as the mid-1960s to relate computer technology to career counseling. Some of the early attempts are still operational today, although modernized and expanded. Jo Ann Harris-Bowlsbey, at that time director of guidance at Willowbrook High School, was instrumental in the planning that led to the *Computerized Vocational Information System* (*CVIS*), placed in operation in 1968. At the same time, Donald Super and Roger Myers of Columbia University were working with Frank Minor of IBM to create the *Education and Career Exploration System* (*ECES*), and David Tiedeman of Harvard and his colleagues were developing a system called *Information System for Vocational Decisions* (*ISVD*). *CVIS* provided a method for storing information about approximately 400 occupations arranged in the classification system originally developed by Roe and discussed briefly in Chapter 8. The information file also included certain items of individual information for each student user such as class rank, composite achievement and ability test scores, and interest inventory scores, thus permitting some comparison of prior data with requirements for entry and success in occupations. The system was primarily online information retrieval, and it effectively capitalized on the technology available at that time. It continued as a pilot program until 1972 and was then established as a demonstration center leading to widespread adoption of the system.

Both *ECES* and *ISVD* were more extensive efforts to computerize larger portions of the counseling process. Both provided for development and storage of self-descriptive information that would assist the client in better self-understanding, extensive data about future possibilities (in *ECES* this included occupations and educational files; in *ISVD* these two areas were supplemented by files on military service and family), and procedures for clarifying and developing plans. Both reached the operational stage in the 1969–1970 period. The elaborate program incorporated in each system was theoretically sound, useful to the client, and technologically possible. Both, however, required heavy usage of computer time so were ahead of reality in terms of cost-effectiveness, considering the developmental stage of computers, and consequently neither has been widely adopted. Several of Tiedeman's colleagues on the *ISVD* project later turned to the development of a simpler system that has become the *Guidance Information System* (*GIS*) in extensive use today.

Other early pioneers in applying computers to career counseling included Joseph Impellitteri at Pennsylvania State University, Martin Katz at Educational Testing Service, and Bruce McKinlay at the University of Oregon. Impellitteri's system incorporated an information retrieval system based on a limited number of occupations keyed to the *General Aptitude Test Battery* (*GATB*) but supplemented by computer-controlled audiovisual equipment that provided the user with slides of actual workers on the job and tapes of recorded comments by workers and narration about the occupation. Impellitteri's unexpected death interrupted development of the system. In the meantime, Katz was researching ways to relate work values to the decision-making process via a computer-assisted system. His efforts led to the *System of Interactive Guidance Information* (*SIGI*), which became operational in 1972. McKinlay and his associates developed a statewide system for Oregon called *Career Information System* (*CIS*), now used in several other states as well.

In the mid-1970s, the Department of Labor provided funding to eight states to develop statewide information systems. Four of these states (Colorado, Massachusetts, Minnesota, and Washington) used the Oregon *CIS* system as a basis for developing their plans. Three states (Alabama, Ohio, and Wisconsin) adopted the *GIS* system. Michigan elected to create its system using parts of both *CIS* and *GIS*. Most of the participating states have continued their systems under state funding. After the project ended in 1978, the director of the Michigan system relocated and marketed that system as *Coordinated Occupational Information Network* (*COIN*). It is in general use today.

The National Occupational Information Coordinating Committee (NOICC) was established in 1976 to enhance cooperation among federal agencies using occupational data. At the same time, similar committees often referred to as State Occupational Information Coordinating Committees (SOICC) were established at the state level. The primary goal at both federal and state levels has been to facilitate cooperation in the collection, dissemination, and use of occupational data. One outcome has been the continued development of state and regional computer-assisted programs. Maze and Cummings (1982) report that by March 1982, there were seventeen localized systems based on *CIS*, eighteen others were using *GIS*, four were using *COIN*, four were using *CHOICES* (a Canadian system), and two were using *DISCOVER* (a descendant of *CVIS*). It appears highly probable that these networks will continue to increase in number.

It is not the purpose of this chapter to discuss the technical aspects of computer science. After all, many of us drive thousands of miles each year with only a rudimentary understanding of the theory of internal combustion engines and possibly no idea at all of the workings of catalytic converters, transaxles, or voltmeter gauges. Nevertheless, just as one must know certain basic automobile terms in order to explain to the mechanic why the whatchamacallit sounds strange, so too one must know a few basic terms to discuss computers and their application. Table 11–1 includes a brief, infor-

TABLE 11–1   A list of commonly used computer terms (a phrasebook for computerese).

Access Strategy—The approach used to obtain the desired information from the computer files. In computer-assisted career guidance systems this is often a combination of client characteristics.

Acoustic Coupler—A mechanical device (*modem*) that permits a computer terminal to be connected to a computer by using telephone lines.

BAUD—An acronym relating to the speed of transmitting data; for example, 300 *BAUD* represents approximately 30 characters per second.

Bit—The smallest unit of information stored in the computer.

Byte—A piece of information consisting of eight bits.

CRT—Cathode ray tube, the part of some terminals that looks like a television screen on which the computer displays the requested information.

Data Bank—The information stored in the computer.

Disk—A thin disk of magnetic material, somewhat similar to a phonograph record, on which the information is stored for later retrieval.

File—A set of data used in a program; for example, all stored information about occupations makes up the occupations file.

Hardware—A general term that refers to the mechanical equipment that processes data, the terminals, and central processing unit.

Interactive—A computer system that can ask the user questions and respond appropriately according to the answer given. Retrieval systems, on the other hand, can only recall specific answers to specific commands.

Local—A setting on a terminal marked "Local" or "Loc" that prevents the terminal from sending information or commands to the computer.

Log-In—Sometimes referred to as "log-on." The method by which the user demonstrates to the computer that he or she is a valid user, usually requiring a code word or account number presented in a fixed sequence. Similar to the way one validates use of one's access card at a bank's automatic teller machine.

Log-Off—The method by which the user properly terminates use of the program and exits from the system.

Mainframe—A large central processing unit, usually operating many pieces of peripheral equipment such as terminals. The largest of the three groups of computers. See *microcomputer* and *minicomputer*.

TABLE 11–1 continued

Memory—The sum of data and instructions stored in the computer. The size of the memory is sometimes used to indicate the capability of the computer.

Microcomputer—The smallest group of computers, sometimes referred to as *personal computers*. They consist of a microprocessor and a keyboard in a single unit. Recent technological advances enable microcomputers to perform functions that until recently could be done only on mainframes.

Minicomputer—The intermediate-sized computers, originally developed to capitalize on the time-share concept that the speed of computer processing actually permits the computer to serve a number of different users apparently simultaneously. Technological progress has also enhanced the power and capability of these machines.

Modem—Also called acoustic coupler, a device that enables connecting a terminal and a computer by using telephone lines.

Module—A self-contained unit of computer-assisted activity, usually including instructions for completing the unit. It may consist of simulation, game-board activities, various exercises, and/or problems.

On-Line—The period when direct communication with the computer is possible; the time between log-in and log-off.

Password—An identifier that is used to gain access to the computer system. Its intent is to restrict use of the system to authorized individuals.

Print-out—A printed copy of some or all interactions with the computer. A printer terminal records all transactions. A CRT terminal usually has a printer attached as auxiliary equipment so that the user can make a copy of data he or she wishes to keep.

Program—The specific instructions used to enable the computer to perform a particular task.

Software—The various programs that can be performed by the computer.

Terminal—The part of the equipment used to communicate with the computer. Terminals usually consist of two parts: a keyboard similar to a typewriter and either a video screen or a printer.

Time-Sharing—A system by which several users have access to the computer at approximately the same time. The very high speed processing of data by the computer allows the machine to respond to each user one at a time but so rapidly that each user feels he or she has the complete attention of the computer.

mal definition of several terms commonly encountered in descriptions of computers and computer-assisted systems.

RELATING COMPUTERS TO CAREER COUNSELING

In the preceding chapters we have considered in detail the steps involved in the career-counseling process. Broadly described, that process can be divided into four phases, including the following:

1. Knowing and understanding self and one's psychological world.
2. Knowing about the world of work.
3. Expanding options/narrowing choices, making decisions.
4. Making plans.

Computers can be employed in each of these four aspects although, at present, they are more useful and efficient in some steps than in others. In this section we will examine briefly the present (1984) applications that are practical with existing systems and programs. In a later section we will consider in more specific detail how some of the major systems accomplish the functions that we will mention only briefly here. The reader must be aware that new developments may facilitate extensive application in areas that now are not feasible.

Knowing and understanding self

In general, computers have quite limited value at present in this phase. Considering the many components of each individual's psychological world, the experiences and events that have made that world unique, and the interaction between the individual and that world, one can see at once that attempts to establish categories or ranks must result either in superficial groupings or innumerable, and impractical, combinations.

Small sections of this area—for example specific personal attributes such as interests, aptitudes and abilities, personality, and values—lend themselves to computer applications. These attributes can be measured on-line, at least in part, either by the kinds of assessment instruments discussed in Chapter 7 or by programmed exercises that are quite similar in function to tests. Obviously, most of the so-called paper-and-pencil tests can be incorporated into a computerized presentation so that the client answers test items presented using the computer instead of in the customary manner. This approach, however, has little advantage (possibly the only one would be almost instantly available test results) and some serious disadvantage, particularly the inefficient use of terminal time, since the test-taking client would prevent the use of the equipment by others for the time periods involved in the various tests. No additional information ordinarily would be available, and most test data warrant some discussion with the counselor to prevent misunderstanding and even error if instructions have not been followed. Several software systems for computerized administration of many commonly used interest and personality tests are now available. Ordinarily, they are used separately from a computer-assisted career-counseling program. Also, there are several companies that provide computerized scoring service for tests on either a batch or single-copy basis.

Among the current major computer-assisted systems, very little effort is made within the system to help the client review and understand his or her personal attributes, attitudes, ambitions, and psychological world generally. The *CIS* software includes a brief group of eight questions about temperaments and another eight questions about abilities. The *GIS* system assumes that review and evaluation will precede use of the system. Both *SIGI* and *DISCOVER* include modules that aim at value clarification. *DISCOVER* also includes a module that incorporates Holland's *Self-Directed Search*.

Knowing about the world of work

From their first application to career counseling, computers have been most useful in the storage and retrieval of career information. Myers (1978) describes this step as the "opportunities realm" and as the most dazzling of the computer's capability. Except for the smallest of the microcomputers, storage space in most systems is sufficient to provide detailed information on a thousand or more occupations. The occupations included can be arranged in multiple combinations or clusters using such variables as occupational family, related personal attributes, educational or training requirements, geographic location, and a great many others.

Two very important advantages accrue from maintaining a computerized bank of career information. One of these advantages is the ability to maintain currency. Unlike print material, where revision is slow and cumbersome and, worse, may result in continued usage of outdated information, computer-stored information can be readily revised by replacing present information with new data, much like erasing a chalkboard and then writing a new statement. Second, the greater degree of flexibility permits maintaining all of the data that might be found in the usual print-media file, plus regional or state information that may contrast significantly with national information. Most computer-assisted programs can capitalize on the existing array of clustering and grouping systems to permit users to survey occupational information at various levels of detail according to user needs, or to use data on a regional or national level, or adjust the system in terms of any one or several variables of concern to the user.

One word of caution must be emphasized relative to the occupational information data bank. The world of work is amazingly complex and, as indicated in Chapter 8, there are numerous levels of specificity in classifying occupations. The more specific and precise the classification system, the greater the number of categories included in the system. If one were to use all of the coded titles included in the *Dictionary of Occupational Titles* the demand for memory storage would greatly exceed all but the largest of the mainframe computers. For example, we can compare the generic title "high school teacher" with the specific titles that represent each particular kind of high school teacher—probably twenty or more, depending on how precisely we wish to make distinctions (teacher, social studies teacher, history teacher, world history teacher, and so on). For most of these more exact titles the data in the memory bank would be practically identical. Therefore, systems are continually caught in a conflict between exact information versus expediency. Although memory bank capacity is growing rapidly, most systems must still use titles that can best be described as generic or broad. Most systems with approximately one thousand occupational titles have sufficient specificity to claim that they include the occupations pursued by 90 to 95 percent of the working population.

At present, stored occupational information is delivered to the user ordinarily as a *print-out* either on the terminal CRT or via the terminal printer. As previously mentioned, Impellitteri was refining a system that incorporated computer-controlled slide projectors. Others have also pursued the possibility of supplementing print information with visual or audio information. Undoubtedly, further technological improvements will permit use of such varied delivery systems in the near future.

Expanding options/narrowing choices—making decisions

Computerized systems are unequaled in their ability to assist clients rapidly in identifying occupations that relate to specified personal attributes, both singly and in various combinations. It is almost standard practice in computer-assisted systems to include in occupational descriptions such data as relevant interest and ability patterns, physical requirements, and working conditions. It is a very simple response for the computer to list all occupations (of those in the data bank) that relate to a preference for mechanical kinds of activities, or those that involve a high level of manual dexterity, or those that are performed entirely indoors.

As indicated above, the list drawn from the memory bank is restricted by the degree of detail in that memory. If the total list of occupations is seriously restricted, the occupations identified with each personal attribute will also be restricted. Even with the best present system there has been considerable compacting of occupational titles. Most clients who use the computer to obtain a list of occupations that relate to certain specified personal attributes will need to be alerted to the fact that the print-out includes representative titles only and should not be viewed as comprehensive. Clients may need counselor help in identifying additional titles that are closely related to those on the print-out. Although some systems are moving toward providing access to related titles, the client may very well need to turn to such supplementary sources as the *Dictionary of Occupational Titles*, the *Guide for Occupational Exploration, Selected Characteristics*, or *Occupational Outlook Handbook* in order to see titles that are more specific than the "teacher" that was used in the illustration above.

The computer is equally skillful in the narrowing process, in which the client is ordinarily focusing on identifying those occupational options that relate most closely to a combination of personal attributes that he or she feels is most reflective of self. It is a simple step to move from asking the computer "What occupations in the memory bank involve mechanical activities?" to asking "What occupations in the memory bank that involve mechanical activities also involve high manual dexterity, work that is performed entirely indoors, don't require shift work, pay at least a specified annual income, and exist in this geographic region?" The combination of personal attributes and other factors can be manipulated in many ways, including most desired factors, excluding factors the person wishes to avoid, taking any one factor from a group of several, readjusting an earlier command to a more or less demanding level, and so forth.

At some point in the narrowing process, the list will have been reduced to the point where the client can be helped best by turning to sources with more data than can be included in the memory bank. When the client reaches this point, he or she is ready to use the types of resources discussed in the last half of Chapter 9. Clients often will need to be cautioned against accepting too literally a brief list of generic titles as the perimeters of their occupational possibilities. The computer can do a superb job of delivering its available information in innumerable combinations, but it cannot provide information not in the data bank, nor can it be sure that the client is asking the question in the same exact sense in which the programmer considered it when data were entered.

Making plans

Many parts of the planning phase can be incorporated in computer-assisted systems in ways that are very helpful to the client. Most obvious of these parts are those that deal with training and educational programs and those that relate to job-search procedures. Caution again is necessary to recognize that standardization of response is an inevitable aspect of computer usage. It is easy to overlook or disregard the individual's unique needs that always should be a major concern for the counselor. While most people can fit into the range of categories included in standardization systems, one should always be sensitive to the fact that the systems do not fit all people equally well.

Many computer-assisted systems handle information about educational and training programs in a fashion parallel to occupational information. This often means that files exist according to type and level of education, for example, apprenticeship programs, two-year schools, four-year schools, and graduate and professional schools. A user can readily identify schools at the appropriate level that offer desired programs and then, by using personally important other variables, narrow the list as far as he or she wishes.

Job-search procedures vary considerably among systems. Many include at least basic information on how one prepares for specific occupations and the types of work settings in which those occupational members are found. The best statewide systems are incorporating information from the State Employment Service including such data as actual vacancies, expected hiring numbers, and salary and wage data. Because such information is so volatile, currency and comprehensiveness are still difficult to acquire and maintain.

In summary, the present state of the art suggests that computer-assisted programs have limited value in identifying, assessing, and helping the client understand his or her psychological world and personal attributes. However, the systems are both efficient and helpful in assisting the client acquire occupational information and match it against various combinations of personal attributes during the expanding and narrowing phases. Similarly, the systems are highly useful in relating educational and training opportunities to personal plans and characteristics. Finally, the systems provide only limited help in job-seeking and placement activities. Computer-assisted systems are useful supplements to counselors, particularly in the middle sections of the career counseling process; even in those areas, constant counselor monitoring and surveillance is advantageous.

EVALUATIVE CONSIDERATIONS

Making a decision about using a computer-assisted career guidance system, like other important decisions in life, requires careful study of many factors. Thoughtful reflection on the best available information and consideration of all appropriate alternatives are more likely to lead to satisfying choices than hasty judgments based on inadequate information. Often, there is a chasm between the ideal solution and what is realistically possible, so that we must look for ways to bring the two sides as close together as possible and find ways to bridge the remaining gap. In this section we will discuss briefly some of the major questions to be considered in preparing for such a decision. Each local situation will include other factors that warrant major attention in the decision-making process.

What clientele will be served?

The starting point is to identify the various populations to be served by the system. If the site is a high school, or includes a group of high schools, the population is clearly different from that encountered in a community college, university, or local agency serving out-of-school adults. What are their needs, both as seen by themselves and by the counseling staff? What age range is likely to be included in the user population? What educational, reading ability, and general ability ranges exist? What range of career goals do they have, and what educational attainments are likely to be most representative?

If data have not already been obtained that adequately describe the user population, a carefully developed needs survey will be required to provide this basic information. Very few programs presently incorporate sufficient flexibility to serve broadly diverse populations equally well. Thus it is likely, if the variation is great, that some members will be less well-served than others. A crucial question then arises regarding which section of the continuum should receive major attention, or how much depth and specificity can be sacrificed to obtain broader applicability.

User clientele is a broad term that certainly includes those individuals for whom the programs and information systems have direct applicability. The term is not restricted just to that group, however, because there are other users in most settings whose needs also warrant consideration. Counseling center staff, administrative personnel, cooperating agencies or office staffs, and, in educational settings, such added groups as instructional faculty, placement officers, and others may also have needs or involvement that must not be overlooked.

What is the staff's basic philosophy?

Some systems primarily provide excellent programs of educational and occupational information, some focus primarily on teaching the decision-making process, and others emphasize certain counseling functions. The counselor, or counseling staff, must determine the role of computerized equipment in the people-helping process of career counseling. Clearly, the computer-assisted system must be compatible with the viewpoint of those individuals who are in positions that enable or retard user access to equipment.

What do we want the system to do?

Probably one of the most frequent errors committed by individuals making some major purchase is to go shopping to see what is available before first deciding as clearly as possible what is needed and wanted. The result is that the shopper is much more vulnerable to glib salestalk, impressive and showy "features," bargain prices, and similar distracting and often irrelevant factors.

One necessary early decision is that of choosing between buying a computer or a computer-assisted system. The major argument for focusing on hardware only would be that the purchase cost is less and one is then free to program the computer entirely according to local needs. The often unspoken disadvantage of such a choice is that, while programming is relatively simple, it is time-consuming, and requires regular and periodic updating by someone who likes and can do programming. Most counselors are probably too busy to devote the time needed to acquire the necessary skill and to commit the regular time required for updating memory files. The major advantage of a computer-assisted program is that the software has been developed by professionals to do what the specifications describe, and usually there is provision for either periodic updating of files or distribution of replacement files to assure a relative degree of currency.

Some counselors who develop an interest in a computer or computer-assisted program may discover that their work site already owns or has access to computer services for other functions. For example, school systems may use computers for scheduling, business office records, and other uses. If time is available on their equipment the counselor may face an additional dilemma: Can the existing equipment perform the services identified by user needs, or should an effort be made to obtain additional free-standing hardware that may partially duplicate what already exists?

Many benefits can be derived from equipment that is already in place. Student records can be maintained in a computer file that can be easily updated, readily recalled, and duplicated. Student files can be classified in various ways so that students with a wide variety of special needs can be easily identified. Student progress can be monitored as additional information is incorporated into the file. Computer time can also be made available to supplement instruction in those classes where such benefits are readily evident.

Participation in one of the national systems offers tremendous advantage for most counselors. The system usually will be well established and its usefulness and viability will have been clearly demonstrated. The software has been prepared by knowledgeable professionals who are adept at maximizing delivery. The system usually incorporates a regular plan for maintaining currency and often for using special files or programs that have local significance.

Another issue to be faced is whether the computerized program is to be used primarily to supplement counselor services or whether it is to be used primarily in lieu of a counselor. If the plan is to supplement a counselor, the system can be narrower in range, for example, delivering services primarily within the middle phases of career counseling while the counselor helps clients prepare for computer use and follows through on previous computer use. If the computer is to serve as a counselor substitute, a much wider program will be needed to help clients identify personal attributes as well as make plans for career development. The issue basically is whether the computer system is to be an information system or a guidance system.

Schenk, Murphy, and Shelton (1980) describe the development of a low-cost computerized system designed to serve primarily as a supplementary outreach program on a single college campus. The system uses hardware existing on campus and software that has been locally developed through collaboration of counseling center staff and computer center staff. Additional software providing national data has been purchased from national consortia.

Finally, another decision must be made concerning operational plans: Is it expected that the equipment will be operated by clients, by peer helpers or nonprofessional aides, or by the counselor? If clients are to be responsible for operation, the system must be relatively simple or "user friendly," and must include modules that explain clearly how one proceeds.

Are attitudes of administrators and staff positive?

Adding a computerized system to an ongoing counseling program involves major changes in procedures, responsibilities, and activities if the system is to be used cost-effectively. Even though equipment costs have dropped precipitously in recent years, a computerized system still represents a major investment for most organizations. Budgetary questions inevitably arise: Can we afford it? What must we forgo if we proceed? Will it pay off in terms of increased or more effective service? How about upkeep, operational, and replacement costs? Will prices come down if we wait another year or two? Suppose we buy all their stuff and it becomes obsolete in a few months? Are we ready and able to make the changes that will permit us to capitalize on computer usage? Clearly, administrators and staff must evaluate the impact on all aspects of the existing program as the decision is considered.

Do we have special needs or circumstances to consider?

When an unusually tall individual shops for a new car, he or she pays special attention to the amount of head room available to the driver, but shoppers of average height disregard this factor entirely. If this characteristic is overlooked, the very tall driver will be reminded of the error every time he or she drives, either by bumping against the roof or by uncomfortably hunching forward to avoid that bump. Similarly, one must look for those distinguishing characteristics that are unique to a particular setting, clientele, or staff. Once those special features are identified, their possible impact on the selection of a computer system can be evaluated. In some cases they take on overriding importance, at other times they are likely to be irrelevant, but they must be considered. The variety of possibilities is so great that it is almost impossible to set parameters. Some possibilities include the existence of equipment within the organization that can be accessed easily and inexpensively, the opportunity to use equipment cooperatively with other organizations, an unusually homogeneous clientele, or local circumstances that moderate or limit client access to educational and occupational opportunities, to name a few.

The above questions are only suggestive of the many that must be clarified before considering the various available systems. Once the staff is ready to consider the various options, it is time to consult with other organizations who have already installed systems, gather printed material on each system that might warrant consideration, participate in demonstrations, and talk to representatives of the available systems. Riesenberg (1983) provides a summary of factors to consider when evaluating computerized systems and includes a brief checklist and rating system to help identify the program that best meets local needs. Maze and Cummings (1982) suggest a helpful formula that permits useful comparisons for determining user costs of various programs. Jacobson and Grabowski (1982) present a criteria tree that identifies the various evaluative factors considered in developing recommendations for a statewide system in Illinois.

TYPICAL PROGRAMS IN OPERATION

In this section we will compare briefly the major characteristics of some of the more widely used programs currently in service. In the next section we will look in more detail at how a system actually operates. Again, the reader is reminded that systems that are now in the developmental stage may shortly become operational and gain widespread adoption, and that currently operational systems may modify present programs as a result of technological advances that cause these descriptions to appear obsolete.

Jacobson and Grabowski (1982) describe existing systems as belonging to one of three categories: batch-process, online career information systems, and online career guidance systems. *Batch-process systems* are described as those where the user has no direct access to the computer, prepares personal data or information requests on a form that is forwarded to a Central Processing Unit, and receives back a print-out of occupations or schools related to the characteristics submitted earlier. *Online career information systems* are essentially storage-and-retrieval systems that permit the user direct computer access, a variety of access systems with immediate feedback on the impact of each input, and an opportunity to adjust or erase each choice as it is made. *Online career guidance systems* provide the same help as online career information systems plus the capability of online instruction, simulation, and practice in values clarification and/or decision making, along with assessment of present level of career development and/or online use of assessment instruments.

As stated earlier, Maze and Cummings (1982) report that both *CIS* and *GIS* are each presently used as the basic system in almost twenty regional or statewide programs. Both of these are examples of online career information systems. Although *DISCOVER* and *SIGI* have been adopted primarily on an individual institutional basis, they warrant consideration as representative of broader-based online career guidance programs.

The reader who desires more comparative information will find several sources helpful. Maze and Cummings (1982) devote a chapter to each of the four systems we will consider only briefly here; further, they include a chart that provides basic comparisons for eleven operational systems. Shatkin (in C. Johnson, ed., 1983) describes the scope and content of seven operational systems based on information collected for an extensive comparison prepared by Katz and Shatkin (1980). Zunker (1981) briefly describes ten programs, including two that are essentially historical (*ISVD* and *ECES*) and two that are still mainly in the developmental stage (*INQUIRY* and *FUTURE I*) but which show the direction that development is taking. Because change is always likely, the most current information is probably directly available from the systems.

Career information system (CIS)

The *CIS* program was developed as the Oregon state system under one of the early Department of Labor grants in 1969, directed by Dr. Bruce McKinlay. A separate organization, National CIS, now exists to coordinate the application of *CIS* elsewhere and to provide additional services in the development of software, provision of training, and the like. From the beginning, *CIS* has emphasized the use of local or regional information; as a result, each local *CIS* system has modified and adjusted the basic plan to fit the needs in that user area. The system has also incorporated specific training and preparation for those individuals such as counselors, librarians, and teachers who are involved in helping clients use the system. The system is currently used in educational settings such as high schools and colleges, and in employment service agencies, prisons, rehabilitation agencies, and training programs.

The system includes several components. The access strategy, called QUEST, is a brief twenty-five-item questionnaire related to self-estimates of physical limitations, geographic preferences, anticipated educational level, aptitudes, interests, and desired beginning wage. Several QUEST items are based on occupational factors identified by Department of Labor analysis of occupations. QUEST is available online or in a needle sort format (notched cards that can be sorted with a needle-like device). The user is provided a print-out of occupations related to his or her combined QUEST responses. The occupational descriptions are brief 300-word summaries of between 250 and 550 occupations, including duties, pay, aptitudes, work setting, hiring practice, outlook, and current employment. Information is local, state, and nationally based, and regularly updated.

In addition to QUEST and the Occupational Description file, most *CIS* systems include a Preparation file and a Bibliography file in the occupational information section and a Program file and School file in the educational information section. The Preparation file identifies ways to prepare for an occupation and includes information on skills needed, licensing, and a cross-reference to related postsecondary training. The Bibliography file lists the most pertinent published sources for further information on each occupation. The Program file includes information on postsecondary educational programs in the *CIS* site area; for example, *Oregon CIS* lists all postsecondary programs in the state. The information includes a description of degrees offered, specialties, program objectives, courses, and lists of schools that offer the program. The School file contains information on all the two- and four-year colleges and proprietary schools in the area. Institutions in the School file can be compared simultaneously, three at a time, on sixty-five different information topics. In addition to the above files, *Oregon CIS* includes six files, some of which are used in other *CIS* programs. These additional files include an Attribute file showing QUEST responses related to each occupation, an Employment file that aids in job search, a Visit file that includes names of individuals working in each occupation who are willing to discuss the occupations with *CIS* users, a Clubs file that identifies career-exploratory clubs in the state, a National School file listing 1700 four-year colleges in other states, and a Financial Aid file that helps a prospective student determine the amount of aid he or she might expect while attending particular schools.

The *User's Handbook* includes instructions for operating the system as well as the QUEST items, and users are expected to complete QUEST and read the instructions before using the system. Additional help is included in the system. Most users find the system easy to use, interesting, and helpful. The average online time is thirty minutes per use, and many users return for further information at least once within the year. The information files can be accessed directly, but if a user wants to include QUEST information he or she must start over if he or she returns at a later time.

Maze and Cummings (1982) report that *CIS* has been adapted to more than ten models of computers to meet the needs of various regional and state users. Per-user cost is reduced by the relatively brief time needed on the terminal, but increased by the somewhat higher cost of obtaining and maintaining local data. Because *CIS* is used in several different settings, there is likely to be considerable variation in charges by participating agencies.

Factors that might be considered as limitations by some evaluators could well be counted as assets by others. No attempt is made by the system to provide guidance for the user beyond the items in QUEST that are used to narrow the list of occupations considered by the user. *CIS* does not incorporate any online assessment, so clients may be uncertain of personal attributes or characteristics they could profitably identify in the interaction with the computer. Counselor help will often be needed before the user is ready to use the system. Didactic modules that teach the client how to use *CIS*, or that explain the available system, do not exist online. This information is available to the client in the *User's Handbook*. A further limitation can also arise from the basic concept on which *CIS* has been developed, that is, the flexibility that allows the system to emphasize local information and adjust to local clientele needs can result in variable quality of information between

CIS franchises. The local quality is primarily dependent on the regularity of updating and the thoroughness and precision used in acquiring the basic data used in updating.

Guidance information system (GIS)

The Guidance Information System is probably the most widely used of existing systems, with reported use in the fall of 1982 at more than 4000 locations. Nationally, GIS is operated by Time Share Corporation, a part of Houghton Mifflin Company. GIS provides access to national data in six files: occupations, four-year colleges, two-year colleges, graduate schools, financial aid information, and armed services occupations. The occupations file contains over 1000 primary occupational listings with reference to another 2500 related jobs; the armed services file contains information on over 100 military occupations; the two- and four-year college files include information on over 3400 educational institutions; and the graduate school file has information on 1500 such schools. In addition to these national files, local or regional information files can be developed covering such topics as vocational schools, local financial aid, and local human services. Local occupational information can now be incorporated with the national file so that the user obtains both national and local information in those occupations where local information has been developed, often about half of the occupations in the national file. The overall aim of GIS is to deliver to the user information that is useful in the career decision-making process.

Information in the files is arranged according to groups of characteristics or attributes. For example, the occupations file includes data on interests (11 characteristics), aptitudes (10 characteristics), physical demands (12 characteristics), work conditions (9 characteristics), lifestyle (16 characteristics), salary (12 characteristics), employment potential (5 characteristics), education and training (21 characteristics), and other qualifications (5 characteristics). The four-year college file is arranged according to academic program (approximately 450 characteristics), location (68 characteristics), type of institution (14 characteristics), undergraduate enrollment (11 characteristics), control (2 characteristics), religious affiliation (5 characteristics), accreditation (5 characteristics), faculty (2 characteristics), admissions information (13 characteristics), academic characteristics of freshmen (22 characteristics), admissions policies (15 characteristics), calendar plan (6 characteristics), degree requirements (3 characteristics), student body data (5 characteristics), annual costs (24 characteristics), residence policies (11 characteristics), financial aid (13 characteristics), special programs (27 characteristics), ROTC (4 characteristics), campus life (25 characteristics), athletic programs (129 characteristics), and athletic scholarships (86 characteristics).

Efficient use of terminal time requires the user to give prior consideration to those characteristics that are important to him or her. This can be done either independently or with the counselor, and many *GIS* sites have locally developed worksheets that facilitate identifying the characteristics the user wants to include. As the various characteristics are entered, the computer immediately responds with the number of occupations or schools remaining on the list, so that the user can see at once the impact of that particular characteristic. If the user previously has identified the characteristics he or she is most interested in, the required terminal time is usually not more than ten or fifteen minutes.

The user can obtain general or detailed information about occupations or schools in which he or she is interested. The PRINT command can be used to obtain general information about a specific occupation or school or about several occupations or schools. The ITEMIZE command can be used similarly to obtain detailed information about either a single occupation or school or about several. If desired, detailed information about specific sets of characteristics can be obtained without itemizing all of the information in the file. This request for general or detailed information about one or more occupations or schools is labeled the *direct method*. Obviously, it is most useful when the client has an occupation or school in mind and wants to obtain information about it. The armed services file works only with this method; all other files can also be approached in this way.

The *search method* is probably more frequently used. This approach is designed to help the user who wants to know what occupations or schools would meet characteristics or requirements he or she might have in mind. Local worksheets for the various files are usually arranged so that they list brief identifiers for each of the characteristics included in the file. The user is asked first to identify those characteristics to be included, those to be excluded, and those that can be combined on an either/or basis. Next, the user is asked to arrange these marked items in a hierarchy with the most important item, either inclusion or exclusion, listed first. Summary sheets are often provided for this ranking. The ADD command is used to enter those characteristics to be included and the SUBTRACT command is used for excluded items. If combined items exist on the list, the EITHER/OR command tells the computer to include any occupation or college that has at least one of the listed characteristics. Starting with all occupations or schools in the file being searched, the system reports after each entry the number that remain. As each ADD or SUBTRACT is made, the number qualifying dwindles. When those occupations or schools remaining in the list number twenty-five or fewer the user can ask for the names of those remaining. This list can then be used with the PRINT or ITEMIZE commands described above. If the user enters a command that reduces the list too drastically, or changes his or her mind about the characteristics, the DELETE command can be used to eliminate that characteristic from the search. The user has great flexibility in organizing the search and can capitalize on personal preferences and change directions during the search. He or she can also move from one file to another easily, for example, from the occupation file where possible jobs were identified to one of the school files to explore information about relevant preparatory programs.

The *GIS Guide* is a user handbook that explains how the system operates and includes a description of each characteristic included in the national files. The *Guide* is revised regularly and distributed to centers using *GIS*. In addition to the *GIS Guide* there are *Indices* for each of the national files. Each *Index* is most useful for the user who wishes to apply the direct method. For example, the *Occupations Index* arranges occupations according to a cluster system, the *Dictionary of Occupational Titles* code number, and alphabetically. Additional supplementary materials are available.

Most clients will want and/or need counselor help both before and after terminal use. Although the various characteristics included in the various files are clear and easily understood, their relationship to the client's psychological world becomes more apparent in a counseling session. Similarly, the final print-out of the narrowed list of occupations or schools may well leave the user with a sense of lack of closure. The counselor can help the user consider exploratory steps that can be taken next to acquire the additional information on the listed items that will lead to decision making and subsequent planning.

Discover

The development of *DISCOVER* has been largely the work of Jo Ann Harris-Bowlsbey and, in part, is an outgrowth of her earlier effort on *CVIS* (*Computerized Vocational Information Service*), one of the early retrieval systems that gained widespread usage. If the early batch-processed systems are considered to be first generation, and the online information retrieval systems such as *CIS*, *CVIS*, and *GIS* are labeled as second generation, then *DISCOVER* and *SIGI* (to be discussed later) are clearly third-generation systems. Rayman and Bowlsbey (1977) describe the development and content of the various components. Much of this information is now incorporated in *DISCOVER* and IBM promotional literature. Rayman, Bryson, and Bowlsbey (1978) describe the procedures used to field-test the system in two Baltimore schools.

DISCOVER was developed as a systematic career-guidance program to assist in career development activities at the secondary school level. The career-development process is viewed by Rayman and Bowlsbey (1977) as consisting of the five following components:

1. Self-information, including values, interests, and competencies.
2. Exploration of occupations in a systematic way.

3. Teaching and low-risk practice of decision making.
4. Relationship of self-information to occupational alternatives.
5. Informational assistance with implementation of choice.

The system incorporates a series of modules that provide assistance in those five activities.

Because of the numerous modules included in the system, *DISCOVER* is designed to operate on an IBM mainframe computer, either the IBM System/370 or IBM 4300 series. The system includes a memory bank that maintains information on what modules had been used earlier and the results of that usage, so that clients may use the system over a period of months or even years, readily review previous action, and move ahead to new modules or rework previously completed sections. The computer system usually includes a CRT terminal so the user operates it with a light pen rather than using the usual typewriter-style terminal. The system includes a printer so the user can have a print-out if desired. The mainframe computer permits multiple terminals to operate simultaneously. Seven large data banks provide the basis for user activity. These include occupations, four-year colleges, two-year colleges, technical and specialized schools, apprentice programs, military programs, and graduate/professional schools.

The system consists of several modules, an explanatory package, and twenty others that fall into three groups. All modules provide interaction with the user. Some modules incorporate materials developed by others, but most are original in nature. The modules and a brief description of each are as follows:

> *00 Entry*   This module teaches the terminal to the user and explains the system. It also monitors each individual's use of the system and stores the entry and exit points for later reference. It also includes an online survey of career development, the results of which serve as a basis for the computer to suggest the most appropriate modules.

> *Values and decision-making education*

> *1A Understanding My Values*   This module contains experiences designed to help the user to define values, analyze personal values, and decide on actions to implement those values. The nine occupationally related values are similar to those included in *SIGI* except for interest field, and are based on the work of Katz.

> *1B Playing a Values Game*   This module teaches the user the nine work-related values in a board-game approach. The user can also relate the individual values to occupations at various levels and can combine various values to search for occupations that

relate to the given combinations. The user ultimately identifies his or her personal weight for each value, and this rating is retained for later use.

2A *Learning to Make Decisions* This module uses an example and flowchart method to teach the decision-making process. Several exercises are included to provide practice in the sequence of steps.

2B *Practicing Career Decisions* This module uses Super's career-decision tree to demonstrate how decisions affect occupational choice. Each of twenty branches represents a group of occupations. Key decisions that lead to entry into each group are illustrated, and the user can plot a course along one or several branches. Simulation is used to permit exploration of the impact of various decisions.

Relating and exploring occupations

3A *Learning How Occupations Can Be Grouped* This module introduces the user to two classification systems—the American College Testing Program plan of data-people-things-ideas used in the World of Work map, and Holland's typology. Exercises are provided to help the user develop skill in using these systems, and responses are monitored to determine if more practice is needed.

3B *Browsing Occupations* Using Holland's two-letter codes, the user can explore up to 300 occupations represented by those two-letter codes. Lists of relevant occupations are provided, from which the user can select titles and receive a brief description of the work setting and work tasks for each.

4 *Reviewing My Interests and Strengths* This module delivers Holland's *Self-Directed Search* online. The results are interpreted online.

5 *Making a List of Occupations to Explore* This module provides the user with five ways to develop a list of personal vocational options. These include using personal work values, using SDS results, selecting titles from a terminal-provided list, combining selected occupational characteristics, and relating school subjects to occupations.

6 *Getting Information About Occupations* This module provides twenty-one questions that the user can select to obtain information about an occupation. These include questions about duties, potential benefits, future outlook, and additional sources of information. It is expected that the user will leave this module with a list of occupations in which he or she has serious interest.

7 *Narrowing My List of Occupations*   This module is designed to help the user narrow his or her list still further and ultimately to arrange the remaining items in priority order. Emphasis is placed on additional information, identified work values, desired level of training, interests, and competencies.

Career planning

8 *Exploring Specific Career Plans*   The user starts with one specific occupation in mind, and this module identifies the possible paths of preparation leading to the occupation. The user chooses a path to explore in depth and branches to the appropriate module of the remaining nine modules.

8A *Local Jobs*   This module provides information on how to seek a job. It may also provide a search strategy for finding a job in the local area if the local site has developed a job data bank.

8B *Financial Aid*   This module provides a definition of standard financial-aid terms, information on how to obtain financial aid including an online assessment of needs based on ACT's Family Financial Statement, and information about available sources of financial aid.

8C *Apprenticeships*   This module provides general information about apprenticeship programs and also search strategies for locating apprenticeship occupations. Local companies can be included if the data are developed.

8D *Four-Year College Information and Search*   This module includes information about college admissions and selection and about search strategy. The data file is based on information obtained from the American College Testing Program and includes the customary basic data about included institutions The user obtains a list of schools that have the characteristics identified by the user as important.

8E *Community and Junior Colleges*   Like the four-year college module, this unit provides information about two-year schools and a search strategy.

8F *Graduate and Professional Schools*   This module includes information and search strategies for graduate and professional schools.

8G *Technical and Specialized Schools*   This module has the same structure as the preceding modules, focusing on technical and specialized schools.

8H *Continuing Education*   General information about adult and continuing education and how to find such opportunities locally is included in this module. Local data can be added to the file if those data are developed.

8I Military Information and Search This module answers questions about the military and provides a search strategy to find those military programs that provide training needed for entry into specific civilian occupations. The data are based on the Department of Defense's *Military-Civilian Occupational Source Book*.

The long list of modules clearly demonstrates that *DISCOVER* is far more comprehensive than the online retrieval systems such as *CIS* and *GIS*. The system is designed to assist in each step of the career-counseling process and assumes that counselors will not have sufficient time to provide the individual help that clients need. There are at present two versions of *DISCOVER*, a secondary school form and a college/adult form. The modules are identical in nature and content, but labels and word usage have been adjusted for the two groups.

An important part of each module is the didactic material. This teaching material provides both basic information on the subject of the module and information on how to operate the module. The inclusion of assessment material such as Holland's *Self-Directed Search* makes it possible for a user to clarify his or her interests while online. Including both didactic and assessment materials relieves the counselor of some time-consuming tasks and also implies that the included material is the most appropriate for all users. The fact that it is primarily a self-contained career-guidance system makes it highly attractive to those settings where counseling services are staffed inadequately.

The national files are updated regularly. In the occupations file such information as salary, outlook, and training are checked yearly. The two- and four-year college files are checked annually also. Other materials are checked on a two- or three-year cycle. Local information will depend on the local plan for updating.

Because of the scope of materials included in the modules, using *DISCOVER* is a time-consuming task. Jacobson and Grabowski (1982) estimate that seven hours are required to complete the entire process; Maze and Cummings (1982) report that as many as twelve hours can be required. All of this time is computer-connected time and therefore relatively costly per client. Further, since each user monopolizes a terminal for that time period, a relatively large number of terminals is required to operate the system, necessitating a larger capital investment. It is possible to use only selected portions of the system and thus shorten the process time. Maze and Cummings (1982) report average user time of three to four hours at one site.

Operation of *DISCOVER* requires access to a mainframe IBM computer. The DISCOVER Foundation has developed two programs designed for micro- and minicomputers. These are called *DISCOVER II* and *EXPLORE*. Both maintain the general form of *DISCOVER*, but the first includes only four modules and the second only eight.

System of interactive guidance and information (SIGI)

SIGI is the outgrowth of nearly a decade of developmental effort by a research group led by Martin Katz at Educational Testing Service. It was originally intended for use by students in or about to enter two-year colleges. It is now applied more broadly, including usage in four-year schools and with out-of-school adults in a variety of settings.

The philosophical basis for *SIGI* proposes that values identification and clarification are basic to an effective career-decision process, involving evaluation of the rewards and risks that accompany each option. The *SIGI* system is a straightforward attempt to lead the user through six modules, called *subsystems* in *SIGI*, that teach that concept. The user is required to proceed in order through the sequence; however, after he or she has completed the entire process it is then possible to use any subsystem singly or in any order.

The series of subsystems is preceded by an introductory module that teaches the basic concepts used by the system and familiarizes the user with the subsystems he or she will encounter. Each system will be described very briefly, including the questions answered by that subsystem, then described in more detail. The subsystems include the following:

1. *Values.* In this subsystem the user examines ten occupational values and establishes his or her weighting for each value. Questions addressed include "What satisfactions do you want in an occupation?" and "What are you willing to give up?"

2. *Locate.* In this subsystem the user can select varying levels of five values at a time and obtain lists of occupations that meet that combination. Questions considered include "Where can you find what you want?" and "What occupations should you consider?"

3. *Compare.* The user can contrast any three occupations at a time on a long list of informational questions in this subsystem. Questions answered include "What would you like to know about occupations?" and "Should you reduce your list?"

4. *Prediction.* The user can determine probabilities of obtaining specified grades in key courses for the preparatory programs for selected occupations based on locally developed data. The questions addressed are "Can you make the grade?" "What are your chances of successfully completing the preparatory program?"

5. *Planning.* The user can obtain information about the preparation paths for selected occupations, including courses to be completed and licensing or certification requirements. Questions considered include "How do you get from here to there?" "What steps do you take to enter this occupation?"

6. *Strategy.* This subsystem evaluates occupations being considered in terms of rewards offered and risks involved. Questions answered include "Which occupations fit your values best?" "How

do you choose between risky highly desirable occupations and those that are safer but less desirable?"

In the VALUES subsystem the user encounters the fundamental philosophy of *SIGI*—the idea that one's values are the overriding and major factor in career choice. The user is asked to consider ten values (income, prestige, independence, helping others, security, variety, leadership, interest field, leisure, and early entry) and to assign a weight to each one according to the importance to the user. After each value has been weighted, the user is then tested by considering combinations of hypothetical jobs, each of which stresses one particular value. If the user selects choices that conflict with earlier weighting, he or she is warned of the discrepancy. After thorough testing, the system reports to the user how he or she has operationally responded to the values. Finally he or she is asked to reconsider the weights originally assigned and force the sum of the weights to a fixed total, so that he or she can assign more than average weight to one item only by assigning another item below-average weight. The overall goal of this subsystem is to acquaint the user with a clear understanding of his or her personal values and their relative strengths.

Once the user is well aware of personal values, he or she is ready to proceed to the LOCATE subsystem. In this module the user may use any five of the values simultaneously. Ordinarily these will be the five most highly weighted, but the user is not restricted to that choice and can make substitutions as he or she progresses in the system. Within each value selected the user may assign any one of four, five, or six levels or types. High income includes five levels ranging from less than $13,000 annually to more than $32,000, field of interest includes six types, and all other values are assigned four levels. The computer presents lists of occupations that meet the combinations of value levels specified by the user. If the list exceeds forty entries, the user is encouraged to increase the level on some or all of the values included. If the list is nonexistent, he or she is encouraged to reduce the level on one or more of the included values. The user may change the values and the specified levels as much as desired; each change, of course, revises the list of occupations presented. Because *SIGI* was developed for use with community college students, its occupational file lacks the depth possessed by most systems. Fewer than 200 occupations are included and about two-thirds of these require more than a year of postsecondary education. All of the occupational file is based on national data.

The list of occupations identified for further exploration is carried forward to the COMPARE subsystem. Here the user may ask any of twenty-eight specific questions about such items as work activities, entry requirements, income, personal satisfactions, working conditions, and outlook, and compare any three occupations simultaneously. The occupations selected for comparison may include others than those identified in the previous module.

The PREDICTION subsystem can be used only if the local institution has developed the data on which this module functions. If the subsystem is operational, the user can enter personal data such as earlier academic performance, test scores, and estimates of possible grades, and receives probability statements predicting the grade that would be earned in key courses in various preparatory programs being considered. The predictions are based on grades of previous students. The quality and usefulness of this subsystem is highly dependent on the care used in developing the data as well as such variables as stable faculty, well-established course content, uniform evaluation procedures, and significance of the course in the overall program.

The user next proceeds to PLANNING, or goes directly to this subsystem if the local site has not developed the PREDICTION module. In this section the user is shown the requirements for entry in the occupation(s) being considered. He or she is assisted in judging personal willingness to meet the requirements. If the user is uncertain, he or she is shown the rewards and risks involved in trying the preparatory program for a semester versus switching to another program. As the client proceeds in the subsystem, he or she is shown the preparation recommended for the occupation. The local site can incorporate local information, if desired, such as specific course titles and numbers. A semester-by-semester program is usually included. Information about financial aid is also in the PLANNING subsystem.

The STRATEGY subsystem focuses on the decision-making process. Three occupations at a time can be matched against the earlier weighted values, the occupational questions considered, and the previous predictions. The display shows a rating of the likelihood of each of the three occupations providing the satisfaction or reward related to each value. The weight of each value is multiplied by the degree of opportunity offered by the occupation to produce an overall index of the occupation's desirability for the user. This desirability is then matched against probability of successful entry and the relative risks and rewards. The user can compare as many different occupational options as desired.

Both *SIGI* and *DISCOVER* use terminals with CRT screens. This system is easier for most users because the computer response is generally more readable than that of the hard-copy printer. The disadvantage encountered is that the user has no record of previous decisions as he or she proceeds through the module.

Each subsystem includes some didactic material related to that specific module, and since each piece is an essential part of *SIGI*'s view of the career-decision process, the didactic material teaches that total process. Assessment focuses almost entirely on personal value structure. Although other personal attributes are incorporated, there is no online procedure for directly considering or evaluating these factors. The information included relates directly to the goals and expected clientele of *SIGI*, consequently less occupational information is included and preparatory information tends to focus on local-site resources. Information not in *SIGI* includes such topics as search procedures for jobs or schools and military information. The materials that are in the subsystems are updated annually.

Maze and Cummings (1982) report that the average user spends three-and-one-half hours to complete the process. This time is all computer connect time and terminal use time and therefore is relatively costly under present conditions. *SIGI* software has been developed for use with a variety of computers of all three sizes. Use of mini- and microcomputers requires some adjustment to the program, but the essentials remain constant. As microcomputers decrease in cost and increase in usability, one can expect wider applications of systems like *SIGI*.

Like other systems, *SIGI*'s strengths and weaknesses depend upon how those characteristics are valued by user sites. *SIGI* is forthrightly based on a clearly conceived theoretical position. By emphasizing the importance of values, it will be seen by some as underplaying other important attributes. By focusing on an educationally related clientele, it will be seen as serving other groups less adequately. By requiring the user to progress methodically through its conception of the career-decision process, it will be seen as more rigid and less flexible than systems that do not adhere to a clear philosophic position. Research studies by Cochran et al. (1977) with students at Illinois State Normal, by Pyle and Stripling (1976) at Santa Fe Community College in Florida, and by Dewees (1983) with adults in Ohio learning centers report high acceptance by users and generally higher levels of career maturity after completing the *SIGI* program.

HOW ONE SYSTEM WORKS

In this section we will consider in more detail how a typical system operates. Our purpose is to illustrate the kinds of services that can be provided in typical situations at reasonable cost. As previously stated, Maze and Cummings (1982) report that in March 1982 over forty localized regions were using systems such as those described in the previous section. Any one of those forty programs could have served effectively as the basis for this section. Each of the systems has some unique features as well as many commonly held characteristics. It is important to keep in mind that the system described here is not proposed as a prototype or ideal model, or as a reflection of what may develop in the future; rather, this is a program that serves a broad range of clientele through several diverse participating agencies, widely scattered geographically, and does so effectively and economically. Like the other systems now in operation, this one is evolving as technology improves and as user needs become more apparent. That process of change will undoubtedly continue for several years.

The Training and Educational Data Service, Inc. (TEDS) was formed in Indiana in 1981 as a private not-for-profit corporation. It was, and is, a cooperative venture of five state agencies (Indiana Office of Occupational

Development, Department of Public Instruction, State Board of Vocational and Technical Education, Commission for Higher Education, and Indiana Rehabilitation Services). Three years (1978–1981) were devoted to determining existing needs in various clientele populations and developing plans to meet those needs. Early in the process the study group determined that sufficient information existed but that the major need was for a comprehensive delivery system that would provide accurate, current career information quickly and easily.

Prospective users also indicated early a need for localized or regional information more specific than statewide or national data. A cooperative agreement was soon formed with the State Occupational Information Coordinating Committee (INDOICC) so that the agency responsible for coordinating occupational data could work closely with the agency (TEDS) responsible for coordinating educational and training data. The dimensions of the information to be included in the system soon became extensive, with the scope stretching across occupations and all the types of training and education used to prepare for those occupations, and the depth covering regional, state, and national levels of that information. The *Guidance Information System* was adopted as the national base of occupational and educational information, and these files were supplemented by state and regional information developed by INDOICC, TEDS, and the State Division of Employment Security.

The mass of data to be used in the system compelled adopting a computerized system. The variety and scattered locations of user agencies, however, necessitated providing alternative types of access because computer hardware costs were beyond the budgets for several user agencies. By late 1983, six ways to access the data bank had been developed. These include the following:

1. A telephone service by which the user agency employs a toll-free number to reach a centrally located terminal operator who instantly conducts the search, reports the obtained information orally, and mails the print-out to the agency.

2. A direct, dial-up terminal connection between a local terminal and the centrally located computer, using either a wide-area telephone service or regular telephone lines.

3. The installation of the TEDS data base in a local mainframe computer to serve local clients and local agency customers.

4. Access to a local or nearby distribution center that has the TEDS data base in a mainframe computer.

5. Installation of the TEDS data base in a local Apple III Microprocessor.

6. An arrangement by which a TEDS representative brings a terminal to a local site for short-term (usually half- or full-day) usage via wide-area telephone lines.

The data base, reviewed and updated twice yearly, is arranged in nine files, including the following:

INOC**—the occupational file contains 1025 occupations including local and regional data for about 500.

ASOC—information on approximately 100 armed-services occupations.

INVT*—information about 235 institutions offering nondegree job-training programs.

COL2—two-year college file.

COL4—four-year college file (about 3200 institutions are included in the COL2, COL4, and GRAD files).

GRAD—graduate school information.

AIDS—information on 400 national sources of financial aid.

INFA*—information on 340 sources of in-state financial aid.

INSE*—information on 320 agencies providing services to the handicapped.

Files marked with one asterisk consist of statewide information developed by TEDS. The INOC file, marked with two asterisks, includes national *GIS* data as well as state and regional data developed by cooperating state agencies.

Like *GIS* programs in other user sites, an individual may use the files to obtain general or specific information about an occupation or training/ educational program applying the Direct method, as previously described. The user also may use the system using the Search method to obtain lists of occupations or training/education programs that meet user-identified characteristics. The first of these two methods is a straightforward acquisition of current information parallel to effective use of a comprehensive reference library. The second method is a useful component in the career-counseling process; therefore, we will focus our attention on its application.

GIS does not incorporate either a method for self-appraisal or any assessment instruments. If the client is to make effective use of search procedures with either occupational or training/educational data, he or she must complete this step before log-in. TEDS does make available the *Self-Directed Search*, the *EUREKA Skills Assessment,* and the *SAT Verbal Familiarization* online to users, but computer charge-time makes this costly and inefficient except when the user is accessing via the Micro-TEDS system with a local microprocessor or using a local mainframe data bank.

Ordinarily, client and counselor will discuss, clarify, and rank order significant client characteristics before employing the computer. If the career-counseling process described in Chapters 5, 6, and 7 has been followed, using a computer assisted system occurs logically when the client and counselor are ready to turn to the expanding/narrowing phase. If a client expects to use the system without counselor assistance, he or she must have sufficient understanding of self to be able to identify important characteristics, both for inclusion and exclusion. Although users can proceed experimentally by adding and subtracting a wide array of characteristics, and deleting commands whenever a prior command wipes out the list, they are likely to find this approach generally unsatisfactory. In other words, most users will find it advantageous to discuss their psychological world with a counselor so that they have a fairly clear idea of themselves before they approach the terminal.

The *GIS Guide* provides an identifier code number for each characteristic included in the national file. A similar system is applied by TEDS to characteristics included in the locally developed files. Local user agencies often develop a worksheet for their clients that facilitates the identification of those characteristics that are important to the individual user. Such worksheets customarily abbreviate the descriptions included in the *Guide* so the user may need to refer frequently to that publication for more information about the characteristics. Table 11–2 contains a typical worksheet for identifying and ranking the characteristics in an occupations search. Table 11–3 contains a similar worksheet for use in a four-year college search.

Clients often need help in understanding that they should mark only those characteristics that are important to them. One common mistake is to view the worksheet like a test and attempt to respond to each characteristic. They also often need help in avoiding self-defeating contradictory choices, for example, choosing scientific and technical interests and less than high school diploma, or operating machines and equipment and subtracting the dexterity and coordination characteristics. The user also needs to understand that the EITHER/OR command keeps the options wider than a single ADD command.

The major reason for urging the client to arrange characteristics, both ADD and SUBTRACT commands, in priority order is to help the client deal first with those characteristics that are truly most important personally. Because some commands can produce very restrictive results, the client may prefer to keep that command only when it is very important. If such a restriction occurs well down the client's list, he or she may elect to delete the command and consider an EITHER/OR option or drop it entirely. On the other hand, if the factor is important, the client needs to be aware of how restricting that choice becomes.

When the client has completed the summary section of the worksheet and is satisfied that the rank order developed there is most representative of self, he or she is ready to initiate the search. The actual use of the computer is a relatively simple process. It can be done by the client alone or, depending on local agency policy or the needs of the individual client, may be completed with the help of the counselor or a peer assistant. A typical instruction sheet is included in Table 11–4. This form assumes that either the telephone service or the terminal connection service is available to the user. Instructions might be slightly different in those settings that use a local computer or microprocessor.

TABLE 11-2 Sample occupations worksheet of a TEDS—occupations search worksheet.

A. Circle the numbers of each characteristic important to you.
B. Bracket those characteristics to be entered as EITHER/OR.
C. Put an "X" on the number of each characteristic to be subtracted or avoided.
D. Rank order all marked items in the Summary Section.

Interests

_____ 2 Scientific, Technical
_____ 3 Creative, Develop Own Ideas
_____ 4 Evaluating Information, Making Decisions
_____ 5 Business Contact With People
_____ 6 Influencing Opinions, Decisions
_____ 7 Working Closely As A Helper

_____ 8 Working Alone, Independent
_____ 9 Operating Machines, Equipment
_____ 10 Working With Things, Objects
_____ 11 Set Routine, Organized
_____ 12 Working With Plants, Animals

Aptitudes

_____ 16 Verbal
_____ 17 Numerical
_____ 18 Spatial
_____ 19 Form Perception
_____ 20 Clerical Perception

_____ 21 Motor Coordination
_____ 22 Finger Dexterity
_____ 23 Manual Dexterity
_____ 24 Eye-Hand-Foot Coordination
_____ 25 Color Discrimination

Physical demands

_____ 31 Sed. Lift to 10#, Little Walking
_____ 32 Light, Lift to 20#, Carry 10#
_____ 33 Med. Lift to 50#, Carry 25#
_____ 34 Heavy, Lift 100#+, Carry 50#
_____ 35 Climb, Balance, Stoop, Kneel, Crawl
_____ 36 Reach, Handle, Feel

_____ 37 Talk/Hear
_____ 38 See Clearly
_____ 39 Mostly Stand
_____ 40 Mostly Sit
_____ 41 Both Stand/Sit
_____ 42 Considerable Walking

Working conditions

_____ 46 Mostly Outside
_____ 47 Mostly Inside

_____ 48 Both Inside/Outside
_____ 49 Extreme Cold/Temperature Change

357

TABLE 11–2 continued

_____ 50 Extreme Heat/Temperature Change
_____ 51 Wet and Humid
_____ 52 Noise/Vibration

Lifestyle

_____ 61 Weekday Work
_____ 62 35–40 Hour Work Week
_____ 63 40–48 Hour Work Week
_____ 64 Occasional Overtime
_____ 65 Overtime Normal
_____ 66 Overtime, Seasonal/Sporadic
_____ 67 Shiftwork Usual
_____ 68 Occasional Night Work

Salary ranges

_____ 81 Under $8000
_____ 82 $8000 or more
_____ 83 $10,000 or more
_____ 84 $12,000 or more
_____ 85 $15,000 or more

Special earnings conditions

_____ 96 Earnings may be seasonal/sporadic

Employment potential

_____ 101 Very high employment potential
_____ 102 Good employment potential
_____ 103 Stable employment potential

Education and training (Required or Preferred)
High school

_____ 122 No H.S. Diploma Required

_____ 53 Hazardous Conditions
_____ 54 Dirt, Dust, Odor, Fumes

_____ 69 Frequent Night Work
_____ 70 Occasional Weekend/Holiday Work
_____ 71 Frequent Weekend/Holiday Work
_____ 72 Being "On Call"
_____ 73 Work Seasonal/Sporadic
_____ 74 Occasional Travel
_____ 75 Frequent Travel
_____ 76 Irregular Hours

_____ 86 $18,000 or more
_____ 87 $21,000 or more
_____ 88 $25,000 or more
_____ 89 $30,000 or more
_____ 94 No salary info. available

_____ 97 Earnings on a commission gains

_____ 104 Limited employment potential
_____ 105 Special conditions (not clearly related to economic factors)

_____ 123 H.S. Diploma Required or Preferred

Vocational technological training
_____ 124 Voc Tech: 1–2 years
_____ 125 Voc Tech: 3–5 years

Business school
_____ 126 Business School 1–2 years

College or university
_____ 127 Some College Training
_____ 128 Associate Degree
_____ 129 Bachelor's Degree
_____ 130 Masters or Equivalent
_____ 131 Doctorate

Apprenticeship
_____ 136 Apprenticeship: 2–3 years
_____ 137 Apprenticeship 3 + years

On the job training
_____ 138 Short Demonstration Only
_____ 139 1–3 months
_____ 140 4–6 months
_____ 141 Over 6 months
_____ 142 Unspecified Length

Other training routes
_____ 143 In Plant, Usually Classroom
_____ 144 Correspondence
_____ 145 Private Instruction
_____ 146 Training available through military

Summary section:
List below in order of their importance to you the characteristics to be entered (circled and bracketed numbers go in the *desirable* column and "X" numbers go in the *undesirable* column). It is suggested that you show your priority ranking for "subtract" characteristics by drawing an arrow from "subtract" items to the appropriate space(s) in the "add" column.

DESIRABLE
ADD (A)

UNDESIRABLE
SUBTRACT (S)

359

TABLE 11–3 Sample college worksheet of a TEDS—4-year college search worksheet.

1. Circle the number of each characteristic important to you.
2. Bracket those characteristics to be entered as EITHER/OR.
3. Put an "X" on the number of each characteristic to be subtracted or avoided.
4. Rank order all circled numbers in space provided. Most important = 1, Next = 2, etc.

Program of study

	1st choice	2nd choice	3rd choice

Use GIS Guide to determine
program number, insert here:

Location

	1st choice	2nd choice	3rd choice

Use GIS Guide to determine
state or region no., insert here:

Size of city/town

____ 65 In or near Large City
____ 66 In Large City
____ 67 Medium City (50–500,000)
____ 68 Small City (10–49,000)
____ 69 Small Town (less than 10,000)

Type of institution

____ 72 University
____ 73 Liberal Arts College
____ 74 Jr./Comm. College
____ 75 Technical School
____ 76 Teachers College
____ 77 Fine Arts College
____ 78 Religious College/Seminary
____ 79 Business College
____ 80 Military Academy
____ 81 Other Special School
____ 82 Also Offers Assoc. Degree
____ 84 Has Branches Elsewhere
____ 85 Mainly 4 yr, some 2 yr prog.
____ 86 Mainly 2 yr, some 4 yr prog.

Undergraduate enrollment

___ 88 Under 500
___ 89 500–999
___ 90 1000–1499
___ 91 1500–2999
___ 92 3000–4999
___ 93 5000–9999
___ 94 10,000–15,000
___ 95 Over 15,000
___ 96 All Women
___ 97 Co-educational
___ 98 All Men

Control

___ 100 Public Control
___ 101 Private Control

Religious affiliation

___ 103 No Affiliation
___ 104 Jewish
___ 105 Protestant
___ 106 Roman Catholic
___ 107 Other

Accreditation

___ 109 Regional Accreditation
___ 110 American Assoc. Bible Coll.
___ 111 Assoc. Ind. Coll. & Schools
___ 112 Candidate for Accreditation
___ 113 Correspondent for Accreditation

Faculty

___ 115 50% Hold Doctorate
___ 116 75% Hold M.S. or Doctorate

Admissions information

___ 118 No Test Required
___ 119 Either SAT/ACT
___ 120 SAT
___ 121 ACT
___ 122 TOEFL (Intntl Stu)
___ 123 Michigan Test
___ 124 Other Special Tests
___ 125 Prev. Coll. Work Required
___ 126 Qualified Stu Admit After 11 gr.
___ 127 Adv Stg Coll. Level H.S. Work
___ 128 Transfer Credit Granted
___ 129 CLEP Exam
___ 130 Credit for Life Experience

TABLE 1–3 continued

Academic characteristics

MDN-V	*SAT*		*MDN-M*		*ACT Composite*
——	132 Data Not Reported		——	138	—— 144 Data Not Reported
——	133 Under 400		——	139	—— 145 Under 12
——	134 400–499		——	140	—— 146 12–16
——	135 500–599		——	141	—— 147 17–20
——	136 600–699		——	142	—— 148 21–25
——	137 650+		——	143	—— 149 26+

Time of admission

—— 150 Fr Admitted Other Times	—— 155 Open Adm/in District
—— 151 Transfer Student Admitted	—— 156 Open Adm/in State
—— 152 Tr. Stu. Adm. Other Times	—— 157 Geograph. Diverse
—— 153 Early Dec. Plan Available	—— 158 Ethnically Diverse
—— 154 Rolling Admissions	—— 159 High % Minority

H.S. Class standing

—— 160 0–25% Top 10%	—— 162 Over 50% Top 10%
—— 161 26–50% Top 10%	—— 163 Data Not Available

Application deadline

—— 171 Prior to Feb. 2	—— 174 After Aug. 1
—— 172 Feb. 2–May 1	—— 175 No deadline
—— 173 May 2–Aug. 1	

Calendar plan

—— 177 Semester	—— 180 4–1–4
—— 178 Trimester	—— 181 Summer Session Available
—— 179 Quarter	—— 182 Other Calendar Plan

362

Degree requirements
____ 184 Bach. Degree in less than 4
____ 185 Some Eve. Class Credit
____ 186 All Eve. Class Credit Poss.

Freshmen attrition
____ 187 70% Frosh. Returned
____ 188 90% Frosh. Returned
____ 189 No data reported

Graduates
____ 191 Half of Men to Higher Ed.
____ 192 Half of Women to Higher Ed.

Costs—Tuition and Fees (Annual)
____ 193 In-State up to $1500
____ 194 In-State up to $2500
____ 195 In-State up to $3500
____ 196 In-State up to $4500
____ 197 In-State up to $5500
____ 198 In-State over $5500
____ 199 Out-of-State up to $1500
____ 200 Out-of-State up to $2500
____ 201 Out-of-State up to $3500
____ 202 Out-of-State up to $4500
____ 203 Out-of-State up to $5500
____ 204 Out-of-State over $5500

Costs—Tuition, Fees, Room and Board (Annual)
____ 205 In-State up to $2000
____ 206 In-State up to $3000
____ 207 In-State up to $4000
____ 208 In-State up to $5000
____ 209 In-State up to $6000
____ 210 In-State over $6000
____ 211 Out-of-State up to $2000
____ 212 Out-of-State up to $3000
____ 213 Out-of-State up to $4000
____ 214 Out-of-State up to $5000
____ 215 Out-of-State up to $6000
____ 216 Out-of-State over $6000

Residence policies
____ 218 Majority Live on Campus
____ 219 Res. for Men Available
____ 220 Res. for Women Available
____ 224 Kosher Food Available
____ 225 Vegetarian Meals Available
____ 226 Public Transportation Available

TABLE 11–3 continued

_____ 221 Co-ed Dorms Available
_____ 222 Frosh. Required on Campus
_____ 223 Frosh Allowed Cars

_____ 227 Off-Campus Housing Available
_____ 228 Day Care Facilities on/near camp.

Financial aid

_____ 230 Fed. Coll. Work Study
_____ 231 BEO (Pell) Grants
_____ 232 Supp. Ed. Opp. Grants
_____ 233 Guaranteed Loan Program
_____ 234 Natl. Dir. Student Loan
_____ 235 Coop. Educ. Plan
_____ 236 Vets Training (Title 38)

_____ 237 Scholarships for Blacks
_____ 238 No Athletic Scholarships
_____ 239 Ath. Scholarships—Men
_____ 240 Ath. Scholarships—Women
_____ 241 Off-Campus Employment Available
_____ 242 Other Financial Aid Available

Special programs/services

_____ 244 Pre-Med Program
_____ 245 Pre-Dental Program
_____ 246 Pre-Law Program
_____ 247 Pre-Veterinary Program
_____ 248 Dept. Honors Program
_____ 249 Independent Study Courses
_____ 250 Interdisciplinary Courses
_____ 251 Can Include Other Coll.
_____ 252 Pass/Fail
_____ 253 Basic Studies Available
_____ 254 Remedial/Tutorial (Engl/Math)
_____ 255 Indiv. Instr. Available
_____ 256 Continuing Ed—Enrichment
_____ 257 Counseling Services

_____ 258 Foreign Lang. Res. on Campus
_____ 259 Study Abroad Program
_____ 260 Foreign Student Advisors
_____ 261 English as a Foreign Lang.
_____ 262 Rem/Tutorial, Foreign Stu.
_____ 263 Prog. for Hearing Impaired
_____ 264 Services for Deaf
_____ 265 Sign Lang. Interp.
_____ 266 Services for Blind
_____ 267 Braille Matrls Available
_____ 268 Services for Learning Disabled
_____ 269 Services for Mobility Impaired
_____ 270 Facilities for Mobility Impaired

ROTC

_____ 272 ROTC Required
_____ 273 Air Force ROTC Available

_____ 274 Army ROTC Available
_____ 275 Navy ROTC Available

Campus life

_____ 277 Stu. Share in Dc. Making
_____ 278 Cult. Center on Campus
_____ 279 Cult. Center off Campus

Religious services

_____ 283 Prot. Serv. on/near Campus
_____ 284 R.C. Serv. on/near Campus

Campus activities

_____ 288 Band
_____ 289 Publications
_____ 290 Cheerleading
_____ 291 Choral Groups
_____ 292 Debating
_____ 293 Drama

_____ 294 Modern Dance
_____ 295 Orchestra
_____ 296 Outing Club
_____ 297 Political Org.
_____ 298 Radio Station

Fraternities/Sororities

_____ 280 Social Fraternities Available
_____ 281 Social Sororities Available

_____ 285 Jewish Serv. on/near Campus
_____ 286 Att. at Rel. Serv. Required

_____ 299 Religious Org.
_____ 300 Soc. Serv. Org.
_____ 301 Student Govt.
_____ 302 TV Station
_____ 303 Other Campus Act. Avail.

Athletic programs

See page 54 in GIS Guide, Edition 13 for details of intramural and intercollegiate athletic programs for men and women and athletic scholarships.

Summary section

List below in order of their importance to you the characteristics to be entered (circled and bracketed numbers go in the Add column, and "X" numbers go in the undesirable column). It is suggested that you show your priority ranking for "subtract" characteristics by drawing an arrow from each "subtract" item to its priority place in the "add" column.

DESIRABLE
ADD (A)

UNDESIRABLE
SUBTRACT (S)

TABLE 11–4   Sample user instruction sheet

Search method

1. Complete appropriate worksheet for the file you plan to use. Use GIS or ISIF Guide for additional explanation of items if you are uncertain about meaning.
2. Transfer your worksheet data to a summary sheet. Be sure to arrange your data according to your personal ranking of priority—both the *add* characteristics you want to include and the *subtract* characteristics you prefer to exclude.
3. Arrange with your counselor or TEDS representative to access the file. (Some local offices use a telephone connection to an Indianapolis-based terminal, some use a direct terminal connection.)

Telephone connection	*Terminal connection*
4. After the connection is completed the operator will ask "Which file?" Identify the file you want to use.	4. After the "sign-on" the computer asks "Which file?" Identify the file you want to use, then press the *Return Key*.
5. Tell the operator the characteristic number you want to add and those you want to subtract in priority order. Put in those characteristics that are most important adds or subtracts first.	5. Type in your commands and appropriate characteristic numbers in order of your priority ranking. Put in the most important adds and subtracts first. Press *Return Key* after you complete typing a command.
6. The operator will tell you how many occupations or schools meet your requirements.	6. The computer will tell you how many occupations or schools meet your requirements.
7. Continue to narrow your search by listing the number of the other characteristics in your priority list if the operator reports more than 25 occupations or schools still meet your requirements. You may add, subtract, or change commands.	7. Continue to narrow your search by entering commands for the other characteristics on your priority list if the computer indicates further reduction is possible. Use *add, subtract, either/or,* or *delete* commands to adjust your requests. Always press *Return Key* when you complete a command.
8. When your list has 25 or fewer entries, you may ask for the names.	8. When you have reduced your search to 25 or fewer occupations or schools, you can type "N" to obtain their names and GIS code numbers. Press *Return Key*.
9. If you want general information about specific items or all the items on your list, the print-out will be mailed to the office where you are using TEDS.	9. If you want general information about specific items on your list, type "P" followed by the code number of the specific item. If you want general information about *all* items, type only "P." Press *Return Key*.

TABLE 11–4 continued

Telephone connection	*Terminal connection*
	10. If you want itemized information about a specific item, type "I" followed by the code number of the item. If you want some itemized information, use the "FT" command. Type "I" followed by the code number of the occupation or school, then type "F" followed by the code number where itemizing is to start, then type "T" followed by the code number of the last itemized entry. Press *Return Key*.
	11. If you wish to see all commands presently operating, type "L." If you wish to check why a particular occupation or school does not appear on your list, type "C" followed by the code number of that occupation or school. Press *Return Key*.
	12. Use "Q" to tell the computer that you no longer wish to use the present file. The computer will respond "Which file?" If you want to change to a different file, type its four letter name. If you wish to stop using the system type "NONE" and sign off. Return telephone to its cradle. Disconnect terminal and modem.

Case study: Terry*

The following data briefly describe a hypothetical client who is seeking help in identifying appropriate occupations for exploration:

> Terry enjoys machine shop where he is able to work alone with machines and equipment. This is, in part, due to his exceptional manual dexterity. His favorite academic classes were those that involved evaluating information and making decisions. Terry's teachers view him as a likeable, cooperative student in spite of the disruption he causes because "he just can't seem to sit still."
>
> Terry would be willing to continue his education beyond high school, but for no more than two years. Due to his personal situation, he will need a steady income of at least $15,000 per year.

*This case study uses material developed by S. A. Horowitz, Director of TEDS and is printed here with permission.

After Terry and his counselor reviewed the occupations search worksheet (Table 11–2), the summary section showed the following:

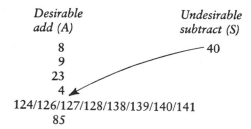

Desirable add (A)	Undesirable subtract (S)
8	40
9	
23	
4	

124/126/127/128/138/139/140/141
85

Terry used a printer terminal to search the *TEDS* file. His print-out appeared as follows:

```
Indiana Occupational Information Ready
1025 occupations qualify

?a8a9a23a4s40e124/126/127/128/138/139/140/141 a85
Add 8  Occupation involves working alone much of the
time
412 occupations qualify

Add 9  Occupation deals with machines/equipment much
of the time
327 occupations qualify

Add 23  Ability to move hands easily/skillfully
76 occupations qualify

Add 4  Occupation requires evaluating and making
decisions
46 occupations qualify

Subtract 40  Leave out Involves mostly sitting
43 occupations qualify

Add
  Either 124  Vocational/technical training: 1-2
              years
      or 126  Business school: 1-2 years
      or 127  Some college training required or
              preferred
      or 128  Associate's degree required or
              preferred
      or 138  OJT: short demonstration only (up to 30
              days)
      or 139  OJT: 1-3 months
      or 140  OJT: 4-6 months
      or 141  OJT: over 6 months
  35 occupations qualify
```

```
Add 85  National average salary at least $15,000
9 occupations qualify
?n
238
CYTOTECHNOLOGIST
264
DIE MAKER, BENCH, STAMPING
491
INSTRUMENT MAKER (ANY IND.)
542
MACHINIST
576
MECHANIC, AIRFRAME-AND-POWER-PLANT
580
MECHANIC, DIESEL
793
REPAIRER, CENTRAL-OFFICE (TEL. & TEL.)
798
REPAIRER, ELECTRICAL-INSTRUMENT
962
TOOL-AND-DIE MAKER
?
```

At this point Terry states that he would like to know more about diesel mechanic. The counselor uses the Direct inquiry method and asks the computer for general and specific information by using the command B580. The print-out obtained was as follows:

```
580
MECHANIC, DIESEL

JOB DESCRIPTION:
Repairs and services diesel engines for buses, ships,
railroad trains, trucks, electric generators and
construction machinery. Locates problem and takes
engine apart. Examines parts for wear and damage.
Reconditions and replaces parts such as pistons,
bearings, gears, valves and bushings. Requires manual
dexterity, independent judgment and ability to learn
and apply craft techniques.

School courses in mathematics and machine shop
helpful. High school or vocational school graduates
preferred. Training is available on the job and
through apprenticeship. Vo-tech schools offer
programs in diesel engine repair which are helpful.
```

Training for this occupation is also available
through the military. Diesel mechanics may be
employed by the manufacturers, distributors, dealers
or users of diesel-powered vehicles. Others are
employed by diesel repair shops. Some may become shop
supervisors.

Indications are that through 1990, employment
potential for this occupation will be good in AK, AZ,
CO, FL, NE and NV.

The national average starting salary is at least
$18,954.

Indications are that through 1984, employment
potential for this occupation will remain stable
throughout the state. Demand for workers will be
highest in Regions 1, 3, 5, 6, 8, 10, 11, 12 and 13.
Regions 2, 4 and 7 show a moderate demand. The supply
of trained workers may be inadequate in Regions 2, 3,
4, 6 and 8. High school students may receive training
at local area vocational schools.

RELATED JOBS:

OCCU No.	DOT No.	JOB TITLE
858	625.281-022	Fuel-Injection Servicer
	625.281-014	Diesel-Mechanic Apprentice
	625.281-026	Gas-Engine Repairer
	625.281-034	Small-Engine Mechanic

RELATED INFORMATION IN GIS FILES:
ASOC Occupation No. 34

RELATED INFORMATION IN GIS STATE FILES:
INVT characteristic 100,114

RELATED INFORMATION FROM OTHER SOURCES:
Occupational Outlook Handbook: DOT No. 625.281-010
Standard Occupational Classification No. 6112

RELATED INFORMATION FROM OTHER STATE SOURCES:
For further information see your local Employment
Office.
For further information see your local JTPA center.

International Association of Machinists & Aerospace
Workers
1300 Connecticut Avenue
Washington, DC 20036

1   INTERESTS RELATED TO THE OCCUPATION
2   Occupation deals with scientific/technical
          areas

4   Occupation requires evaluating and making
    decisions
8   Occupation involves working alone much of the
    time
9   Occupation deals with machines/equipment much
    of the time
10 Occupation often involves working with
    things/objects
15 APTITUDES RELATED TO THE OCCUPATION
23   Ability to move hands easily/skillfully
30 PHYSICAL DEMANDS OF THE OCCUPATION
34   Heavy/Very heavy: lifting more than one hundred
      pounds
35   Involves climbing, balancing, kneeling,
      stooping, crawling
36   Involves reaching, handling, feeling
37   Involves talking and hearing
38   Involves ability to see clearly
39   Involves mostly standing
45 WORK CONDITIONS
47   Mostly inside
52   Exposure to noise and vibrations
60 LIFESTYLE
63   40-48 hour work-week normal
65   Overtime normal
68   Occasional night work
70   Occasional weekend/holiday work
72   Occupation involves being ``on call''
74   Occasional travel
100 EMPLOYMENT POTENTIAL
103   Stable employment potential
120 EDUCATION AND TRAINING
123   High school diploma required or preferred
124   Vocational/technical training: 1-2 years
137   Apprenticeship: over 3 years
141   OJT: over 6 months
144   Correspondence school
146   Training available through the military
150 OTHER QUALIFICATIONS
154   Union membership
160 OCCUPATIONAL CLUSTERS
170   Manufacturing.
175   Transportation
179 DOT OCCUPATIONAL CATEGORIES AND DIVISIONS
230 MACHINE TRADE OCCUPATIONS
233   Mechanics and machinery repairers
270 INTEREST AREAS
275   Mechanical

```
290  STANDARD OCCUPATIONAL CLASSIFICATION GROUPS
342  MECHANICS AND REPAIRERS
344     Mechanics and Repairers (61)
374  INDIANA STATE INFORMATION
375  SALARY INFORMATION
382     $12,500-14,999
390  OTHER QUALIFICATIONS OR REQUIREMENTS
394     Driver's license may be required
396  PROJECTED EMPLOYMENT OUTLOOK
399     Statewide:   Stable
404     Region 1:    Stable
409     Region 2:    Stable
414     Region 3:    Stable
419     Region 4:    Stable
424     Region 5:    Stable
429     Region 6:    Stable
434     Region 7:    Stable
439     Region 8:    Stable
444     Region 9:    Stable
449     Region 10:   Stable
454     Region 11:   Stable
459     Region 12:   Stable
464     Region 13:   Stable
469     Region 14:   Stable
```

Terry then stated that he wondered why "Farm Equipment Mechanic" wasn't on the list. The counselor entered the check command (C584) and received the following print-out:

```
C 584

584
MECHANIC, FARM-EQUIPMENT I is not on the list
A8    Occupation involves working alone much of the
        time    fails
A9    Occupation deals with machines/equipment much
        of the time    is OK
A23   Ability to move hands easily/skillfully    is OK
A4    Occupation requires evaluating and making
        decisions    is OK
S40   Leave out Involves mostly sitting    is OK
E124  Vocational/technical training: 1-2 years    is OK
/126  Business school: 1-2 years    fails
/127  Some college training required or
        preferred    fails
/128  Associate's degree required or preferred    is OK
/138  OJT: short demonstration only (up to 30
        days)    fails
/139  OJT: 1-3 months    fails
/140  OJT: 4-6 months    fails
```

```
/141   OJT: over 6 months     is OK
A85    National average salary at least $15,000     fails
```

Terry said that he had heard that the national employment outlook for diesel mechanics is not very good and he wondered if that were also true in the state of Indiana. The counselor reminded Terry that state and regional information was included in the occupations file for many occupations and suggested that they look again at the print-out. The counselor checked the index and reported that projected employment outlook is listed in the 396 to 471 area. Referring to the print-out they confirmed that the final sixteen lines included the data Terry was seeking.

Terry has obtained a list of occupations that meet the characteristics he feels are most important, and at least one appears attractive, but before he moves too rapidly he should be encouraged to explore all titles on the list. Appropriate steps at this point would include interviews with individuals employed in several of these occupations, visits to work sites and training programs, and perhaps a "shadowing" experience with one or more workers, followed by further sessions with the counselor. Later he may wish to return to the computer for information about training programs or, perhaps, to consider a different set of characteristics that might lead in another direction to a new list of occupational possibilities.

Case study: Linda*

The following data briefly describe a hypothetical client who desires information about possible colleges she might attend:

Linda has expressed an interest in majoring in international relations at a four-year college. She wants to attend a college in either Indiana, Michigan, or Ohio, but she does not want to go to a college with an enrollment over 5000. If possible, she would like to continue her drama activities as well as participate in intercollegiate cross-country skiing.

After reviewing the 4-year college search worksheet (Table 11–3), Linda and her counselor agree that she should start her search with a summary section that appears as follows:

Desirable add (A)	Undesirable subtract (S)
948	93
18/19/20	94
293	95
401	

* This case study uses material developed by S. A. Horowitz, Director of TEDS and is printed here with permission.

Linda's print-out appeared as follows:

```
Four Year College Information Ready
1775 colleges qualify

? a 948 e18/19/20 s93s94s95a293a401
Add 948   International relations
214 colleges qualify

Add
 Either  18  Indiana
     or  19  Michigan
     or  20  Ohio
 29 colleges qualify

Subtract 93  Leave out Enrollment 5,000-9,999
26 colleges qualify

Subtract 94  Leave out Enrollment 10,000-15,000
22 colleges qualify

Subtract 95  Leave out Enrollment over 15,000
18 colleges qualify

Add 293  Drama
18 colleges qualify

Add 401   Intercollegiate cross-country skiing for
  women
No colleges qualify
```

At this point Linda decides to change her mind about intercollegiate competition since she can pursue this interest on her own and elects to delete her last command. The computer returns to the previous entry with 18 colleges qualifying. Linda then uses the N command, asking for the names of the schools and receives the following print-out:

```
n
444
Butler University
447
Earlham College
465
Manchester College
475
St. Joseph's College
481
University of Evansville
484
Valparaiso University
722
Alma College
```

```
724
Aquinas College
739
Hope College
1181
Ashland College
1182
Baldwin-Wallace College
1197
College of Wooster
1210
Lake Erie College
1217
Muskingum College
1230
Ohio Wesleyan University
1243
Walsh College
1246
Wittenberg University
1248
Xavier University
?
```

Although Linda has several options for obtaining more information about these institutions, either collectively or individually, on those items listed in the search worksheet, she elects to discontinue the search. At this time, she may wish to confer with her parents, talk to friends or relatives who are familiar with some of the schools, look at college catalogs or college directories in the school library, and similar activities before returning to the computer file for more information. As she narrows the list she will probably talk further with the counselor, request more specific itemized data from the file, and ultimately visit some of the campuses.

SUMMARY

Perhaps the most unsettling thought encountered during the preparation of a chapter on computer usage in career counseling is the idea that technological advances may make all that is said about computers out of date by the time the chapter appears in print. The reader must also be aware of this possibility and recognize that newer, better procedures may well justify disregarding portions of the chapter just read.

Computers and computer-assisted career guidance programs appear destined to play an increased role in the career counseling process. As this transition occurs it will be important for counselors, and for their clients as well, to maintain a high degree of flexibility, balanced with a reasonable amount of skepticism. Many new software products and applications will neither survive nor be worthy of survival. At the same time, some developments may be historic in their impact on the profession. Forward movement requires judicious separation of these two categories attained by fair appraisal of new equipment and procedures and a willingness to reject those that do not improve counseling services.

Presently existing systems suffer from a rigidity that requires all users to be treated essentially in the same way, even though their needs, level of maturity, and personal attributes vary widely. It seems reasonable to expect that this problem will be resolved as technological development continues, and we can look forward to systems that offer the same degree of individual adjustment presently possessed by the counselor and described in Chapter 9.

The complexity of the world of work creates similar difficulties for computer-assisted systems. Although the use of generic titles gives some systems the ability to include most of the commonly held occupations, the systems will be much more useful when the coverage is comprehensive. The discrepancy between several thousand titles in the *Dictionary of Occupational Titles* and the 200, 400, or 1000 titles included in most systems is apparent to even unsophisticated users and often results in a depreciation of the usefulness of the system. The fact that the number of educational institutions included in most systems far exceeds the number of occupational titles suggests that present capacity may already exist to include many more titles. As storage capacity expands in the systems, it should be possible to increase the amount of cross-referencing and thereby expand the lists of occupational titles to a comprehensive level.

The opportunity to develop special systems for particular groups will be enhanced as the capability of the microprocessor expands and its cost declines. Myers (1978) describes one of the forerunners of such specialized programs, called the Officer Career Information and Planning System. Rehabilitation agencies and other offices that need much greater detail about physical requirements, working conditions, job modification, and so on can look forward to access via the microcomputer in the near future. At least two kinds of situations are likely to be helped with this type of development: those settings that serve a clientele with special kinds of needs and those settings where clientele requires access to much greater detailed information than is customarily the case.

Both Maze and Cummings (1982) and Harris-Bowlsbey (1983) see similar developments in the near future. Both suggest that microcomputers will facilitate greater usage for small and specialized programs. Both also predict that the increasing usefulness of the microcomputer will permit more varied programs to large populations as well. In addition, they anticipate that technical developments will soon permit expanded use of audio and visual materials to supplement the present dependence on print data. Maze and Cummings state that at the same time that this expansion occurs, the application of communications networks via regular lines, microwave transmitters, and satellites, will expand the usage of large systems by simultaneously reducing costs and enhancing currency of available information. Harris-Bowlsbey believes that there will be increasing usage of broader based guidance systems rather than information systems.

The degree to which new applications can effectively serve counselors and their clients depends to a large extent on the willingness and ability of counselors to identify needs and transmit those needs to computer specialists in understandable terms. If counselors succeed in communicating, the situation can best be described by that old ungrammatical exclamation "We ain't seen nothing yet!"

REFERENCES

Cochran, D. J., Hoffman, S. D., Strand, K. H. and Warren, P. M. Effects of client/ computer interaction on career decision-making processes. *Journal of Counseling Psychology*, 1977, 24, 308–312.

Dewees, P. A survey of adults' response to the SIGI system as part of career development programs in Ohio Learning Centers. Paper presented at American Personnel and Guidance Association Convention, Washington, D.C., March 1983.

GIS Guide. Hanover, N.H.: TSC/Houghton Mifflin Company, 1983.

Harris-Bowlsbey, J. A historical perspective. In C. Johnson (ed.), *Microcomputers and the school counselor*. Alexandria, Va.: American School Counselor Association, 1983.

Jacobson, M. D. and Grabowski, B. T. Computerized systems of career information and guidance: A state-of-the-art. *Journal of Educational Technology Systems*, 1982, 10, 3, 235–255.

Katz, M. R. and Shatkin, L. *Computer-assisted guidance: Concepts and practices.* Research Report RR-80-1. Princeton, N.J.: Educational Testing Service, 1980.

Maze, M. and Cummings, R. *How to select a computer-assisted career guidance system*. Madison, Wisc.: Wisconsin Vocational Studies Center, 1982.

Myers, R. A. Exploration with the computer. *The Counseling Psychologist*, 1978, 7, 3, 51–55.

Pyle, K. O. and Stripling, R. O. The counselor, the computer, and career development. *Vocational Guidance Quarterly*, 1976, 25, 71–75.

Rayman, J. R. and Bowlsbey, J. H. DISCOVER: A model for a systematic career guidance program. *Vocational Guidance Quarterly*, 1977, 26, 3–12.

Rayman, J. R., Bryson, D. L. and Bowlsbey, J. H. The field trial of DISCOVER: A new computerized interactive guidance system. *Vocational Guidance Quarterly*, 1978, 26, 349–360.

Riesenberg, B. Considerations in the selection of a computerized guidance system. In C. Johnson (ed.), *Microcomputers and the school counselor*. Alexandria, Va.: American School Counselor Association, 1983.

Schenk, G. E., Murphy, P. P., and Shelton, R. L. Computerized career information systems on the college campus: A low-cost, do-it-yourself approach. *Personnel and Guidance Journal*, 1980, *58*, 516–520.

Shatkin, L. The state of the art in software. In C. Johnson (ed.), *Microcomputers and the school counselor*. Alexandria, Va.: American School Counselor Association, 1983.

Turkington, C. Computers in class: Who gets to learn? *APA Monitor*, 1982, *13*, p. 6.

Zunker, V. G. *Career counseling: Applied concepts of life planning*. Monterey, Cal.: Brooks/Cole Publishing Company, 1981.

12

Counseling special populations

A basic assumption throughout the previous chapters has been that each individual is a unique combination of personal attributes and characteristics such as physique, personality, abilities, attitudes, interests, motivations, and values, derived from the interactions of the individual's genetic endowment, biological and mental traits, and a lifetime of experiences. Because of this uniqueness, one might assume that career counseling necessitates individualization so that the person can capitalize on particular strengths and minimize those areas of inability or disinterest. The evidence supporting individual differences is so overwhelming that no one can contend successfully against it. Nevertheless, the recognition that each of us is a unique individual does not preclude the further recognition that each of us has much in common with other individuals.

This chapter is concerned with recognizing some of those commonalities shared by groups of individuals that may influence career counseling in somewhat similar ways. Although the ways in which individuals can be grouped to consider such impact are almost limitless, we will consider five broad groups with which counselors frequently have contact. These five groups include young women, individuals who for various reasons enter the world of work at a later time than most others, those who face transition or change during their occupational lives, those whose personal attributes include characteristics that can be described as special problems, and those who have different cultural backgrounds.

YOUNG WOMEN

Until quite recently general social attitudes toward the role of women seriously restricted the opportunities of women to participate in the world of work. While those attitudes have not yet been completely reversed, there is definite evidence that change is under way. Clearly, the young women graduating from high school today have wider occupational options than did their mothers.

For the most part, early career theorists developed hypotheses within the framework of prevalent social attitudes. Super (1957) did give attention to career development patterns of women and, within the common social standards of the late 1950s, identified seven different patterns; only one provided for lifetime commitment to "career" and the other six placed primary emphasis on the role of wife, mother, and homemaker. Ginzberg (1966) showed awareness of the changes occurring in the 1960s by describing three ways or roles women used to relate to work: these include the traditional homemaker role, the transitional role that encompasses some participation in work outside the home, and the innovative role that allots equal time to outside work and to homemaking.

Reports from the Census Bureau and from the Department of Labor show that women who work outside the home have long been concentrated in a small number of occupations. About half of the women employed for pay work in service occupations or as machine operatives, nearly one-third work as clerical or sales workers, and about one-seventh are professional or technical workers. Even within these areas there is a concentration into specific occupations; for example, in the area of professional and technical occupations, where the overall percentages of men and women are nearly equal, the men are widely scattered across the spectrum while most of the women are in teaching and nursing. The injustice of such discrimination was made illegal by the passage of the Civil Rights Act of 1964 and the Educational Amendments of 1972. The first law prohibits discrimination on the basis of sex and other factors in employment and in pay received for work. The second act guarantees equal access to educational opportunity. The passage of such legislation is clear recognition of changing social attitudes and provides the basis for wider opportunity in the future. It does not, however, immediately wipe out the imbalances that have developed over the years such as concentration in restricted areas and lower income.

Attitudes of both young men and women toward involvement in the world of work are heavily influenced by the attitudes expressed within the family. Probably these family viewpoints are even more influential for young women because child-rearing practices have usually put more stress on obedience, dependency, and respect for girls and more stress on independence and self-reliance for boys. Family attitudes generally have long assumed that Dick would work when he grew up, and if any issue arose it usually focused on what Dick would do. On the other hand, many families expected Jane to marry as soon as she grew up and devote her attentions to husband, children, and home, with "work" as an alternative or supplement only if a husband weren't available or if he died, or if he proved unable to support his wife and family adequately. To the extent that families assert the view that "a woman's place is in the home," daughters will be caught in a bind as they consider how they want to relate to the world of work.

Many factors have caused the traditional family-oriented viewpoint to change. Technological developments have reduced the time required to handle the usual homemaking chores and also created many jobs outside the home. Family planning has reduced average family size and permitted scheduling of births. The development of nursery schools and child-care centers has provided out-of-home care for preschool children and extended-day programs have furnished care for school-age youngsters. Inflation and other economic pressures have increased the need for additional income in order to maintain or improve family lifestyle. Perhaps more important than all of the other reasons is the increasing recognition that work plays a crucial role in the lives of both men and women in providing a sense of self-worth, satisfaction, and personal identification. One can anticipate that before the end of this century the general mores will accept without question the equal participation of men and women in work.

During the intervening decade or two, many young women will face conflicts in identifying and developing personal attitudes and values toward their individual relationship to work and family. One major task for counselors may be to assist in the resolution of that conflict.

Mead (1982), in a recent study of types of stress encountered by two-worker couples, identified three working roles assumed by the women she studied. The first group, labeled *traditional,* included those women who followed the family-oriented pattern and devoted the major share of their time and energy to home and family. The second group, labeled *dual earner,* included those women who spent a large portion of their time at work, either full-time or part-time, and worked for a variety of reasons including economic, social, self-fulfillment or other, but felt no commitment to career advancement. The third group, labeled *dual career,* devoted either full-time or part-time to their positions, expressed a commitment to work as a significant part of their lives, and expected and sought opportunities for career advancement in responsibility, pay, and satisfaction.

Although this study focused on women with partners, the three categories may be useful in counseling young women who are without partners. That is, some young women, probably a decreasing group, will view their future plans in terms of the traditional model of home-and-family orientation in which work outside the home plays no significant part. Another group of young women (earners) will expect to make work a significant part of their lives but will view work participation as a means of acquiring income, a socially enjoyable and desirable experience, a self-satisfying activity, or some similar purpose. Within this framework, change of position to another employer or different activities is easy if the change maintains or enhances the individual's rationale for working. Finally, there is a third group of young women (careerists) who express a commitment to work because of their desire to progress in a selected field and to accrue the opportunities for advancement, increased pay and responsibility, recognition, and self-actualization that come with that dedication to work.

A further advantage of this system is that both family and work are components in each of the three categories. This possibility of viewing family *and* work with variable independent degrees of emphasis on each may help young women to plan more effectively and to overcome the frequent obstacle of trying to decide between family *or* work. In other words, involvement and commitment to one does not necessarily exclude the other. In the study mentioned above, Mead found that women in earner and career roles encountered more stress in the area of time-management, while traditional women reported more stress in economic matters.

The attitude toward women's roles held by significant others, including parents, other family members, peer groups, close friends, role models, and later spouses as well, has great influence in shaping the attitude espoused by the young woman. When these groups hold similar views, it is unlikely that she will develop a contradictory position. Much more frequently, however, is the likelihood that differing views will be held by various significant individuals, and indecisiveness may develop because the young woman is reluctant to appear to reject or snub someone whom she holds in high regard. The counselor's task may become one of helping the individual identify the attitudes and values that she holds personally most important. She may also need help in developing the self-confidence and assertiveness necessary to choose a position and to maintain it.

Another closely related topic that bears upon the young woman's relationship to work is the attitude and viewpoint of future significant others. Miller (1978) has shown that as early as mid-high-school the attitudes of boyfriends and boys in the peer group have considerable influence on the actions and expressed attitudes of girls. When one considers that the attitudes of young men have also been heavily influenced by viewpoints held by their families and other significant individuals and that, for the most part, those attitudes have provided greater advantage to the male role, one can anticipate a tendency for boys and young men to expect their future spouse to assume a role similar to the one they saw their mother portray Other studies have confirmed that college males generally agree that their future spouse should have the opportunity to work if she wants to do so. but most of them expect her to assume all the homemaking activities of the traditional woman. Most fail to recognize, or prefer to disregard, the likelihood that a spouse's involvement in both work and home life necessitates the male's similar involvement and sharing in both.

In addition to the career-choice process discussed in the previous chapters, the counselor may have further responsibilities when the client is a young woman. One of these responsibilities is to help her to see and understand the three broad relationships that exist between women and work—traditionalist, earner, and careerist. In helping her to evaluate these roles for her life, consideration must be given not only to attitudes but also to personal life values. If she considers independence, achievement, intellectual stimulation, security, and similar factors of greater importance, she is tilting toward the earner-careerist end of the continuum. If she gives highest status to affiliation, nurturance, and affection she is moving in the traditionalist-earner direction. If she wants to balance these two sets of values, she is less likely to satisfy herself at either end of the continuum. The counselor also should help her to consider the place of work and family and how she hopes to relate these two areas in her future years.

In the career-counseling process with young women clients, special care must be given to the use of interest inventories. The very process of widening opportunities so that women participate in many fields where they previously were scarce or nonexistent, calls into question the validity of occupational interest scores based on gender groupings. The previously developed norms may no longer permit useful comparisons, and test items may also include sex bias. Interest inventory experts are still uncertain as to whether separate gender norms or composite norms are more useful. The counselor's responsibility requires that he or she be certain that the client is not using inaccurate or inappropriate information as a basis for decisions and restricting career options on the basis of gender.

DELAYED ENTRANTS

The customary pattern followed by most workers in our society is to enter employment directly from whatever preparatory educational program they choose to follow. That normal progression may be interrupted or delayed by a number of factors. Probably the largest group that has digressed from this typical pattern are viewed as having followed a regular developmental scheme. This group consists of women who interrupted their preparatory programs to marry, or who married at the point where that program was completed or shortly later before acquiring significant work experience, and who then assumed the traditional role of homemaker. At least two other sizable groups, primarily males, are also representative of delayed entrants These two groups include military personnel who have served varying lengths of time (typically three to six years) in the armed forces before acquiring significant civilian work experience. The other group is often described as prior offenders and includes those individuals who were incarcerated before acquiring significant work experience. Many other causes produce delay in pursuing a career pattern. However, we will consider only these three.

Displaced homemakers

Previously, the term *displaced homemaker* was applied to the middle-aged or older woman whose children are either grown or nearly so, and who suddenly, because of widowhood or divorce, finds that she is no longer able to continue in her traditional role of homemaker. The escalating divorce rate in the United States suggests that the term should be extended to include younger women who sometimes have dependent children and who are unable to continue their homemaker role. It also seems appropriate to include a third group consisting of traditional homemakers who decide that they wish to assume earner or careerist roles. Although the three subsets face slightly different problems, they have much in common, especially if they have neither specific vocational preparation nor significant work experience. Some members of this group of displaced homemakers face situations similar to those encountered by midcareer changers, a group that we will consider in a subsequent section.

Because of the drastic, sudden, and often traumatic changes that have recently occurred in their lives, many displaced homemakers are "change" clients as discussed in Chapter 6. They will need help in many areas before they can effectively concentrate on career decisions. Sometimes the individual may feel that total immersion in a job or training program will help to resolve the myriad problems they face. Unfortunately, those problems must be faced, and at least partially resolved, before any realistic career planning can occur because the client's ability to deal with those issues and to clear them out of the way largely determines her opportunity to make and implement useful career plans.

Obviously, one major problem consists of modifying and restructuring self-concept so that the individual can accept responsibility for decisions that may previously have been made jointly or by the absent partner. This may involve not only building self-confidence, but in many situations necessitates acquiring information and knowledge upon which decisions can be made. Typical examples that might fall in this category include those items often assumed by the male partner such as property maintenance, automobile purchase and care, legal and financial matters, and other responsibilities. None of these is gender-oriented; however, lack of familiarity with the subject produces uncertainty and doubt. The counselor may be able to suggest workshops, exercises, or group participation that will assist in building the needed self-confidence and assertiveness.

Displaced homemakers are sometimes confronted with serious financial problems that can be either short-term or long-term or both. Although the counselor may not feel competent to deal with difficult matters of financial planning, he or she has responsibility to assist the client in finding sources where that kind of help is available. Included in this general topic are such items as need or appropriateness of disposing of property or acquiring it, relocation of residence, and other financial dealings.

A further common problem is the need to identify and cultivate support systems to replace those lost in the displacement process. Again, the counselor may best help by serving a referral role and helping the client consider and explore ways in which support systems can be developed. This includes helping her evaluate ways of meeting new friends through mutual interest activities, hobbies, organizations, or other groups.

Many topics considered in the previous section about counseling the young woman apply equally well to counseling her older sister or mother. One fundamental problem to be faced is whether the woman is considering immediate employment only, or if she is also considering entry into an educational or training program prior to actual employment. If the latter is a possibility, additional attention must be given to such costs as time, effort, money, and whether the anticipated payback justifies those expenditures. Decisions about earner versus careerist roles in this situation are heavily related to attributes such as age, access to resources, motivation, and opportunity. If the client is thinking primarily of getting a job, the counselor must help identify the presence and level of reliable skills (many relevant skills are possessed by individuals who report they have "just been a housewife") and develop adequate job-search skills. If the client has little or no previous recent contact with paid work, she may need to acquire occupational information so that she has a realistic picture of existing opportunities and competition.

The third group of women included under this general heading, those present homemakers who decide voluntarily to replace their traditionalist role with that of earner or careerist, do not confront all of the problems encountered by the truly displaced individual. First of all, the decision is a voluntary one, although she will often feel that either economic factors or the desire for self-fulfillment compels her toward paid work. Second, the problems of readjusting lifestyle are often easier because she has not confronted the bereavement or loss that accompanies death or divorce; however, the change she is considering will probably require more revision in lifestyle than she anticipates. Although her support systems of partner, family, and neighbors remain intact, the new role she is contemplating will cause readjustment in each of these relationships. Because she anticipates a different role, she faces many of the same problems as the widowed or divorced woman in terms of self-concept, assertiveness, development of independence, occupational information, and job-search skills.

former military personnel

Individuals who return to civilian life after a period of military service can be divided into three distinct groups: those who have fulfilled twenty to thirty years of service and are now retiring; those who have incurred a disability that prevents continuing in military service; and those who are leaving after a brief period, often three to six years, of either volunteer or obligated service. The first two groups will be discussed later in this chapter under the headings of midcareer changers and special need clients respectively.

In addition to the customary reasons of patriotism and long-range career plans, many young people volunteer for military service for quite different purposes. Probably the majority of voluntary enlistees are recent high school graduates or pregraduation dropouts. Some, recognizing that they have no clear-cut educational or occupational plan, decide to enlist in order to give themselves time to decide what they want to do. Some, unable to obtain acceptable civilian employment because of either economic factors or the lack of salable skills, enlist as an alternative course of action. Others may volunteer to escape an array of problems—difficult family situations, unsatisfactory living conditions, a desire for affiliation and belonging, sometimes even to resolve encounters with the court system. Still others may have very clearly formed long-range civilian goals in mind and enlist to acquire specialized training that they expect to use in a civilian position, or to accrue educational benefits that will permit later completion of civilian college programs.

Many military occupations have equivalent civilian counterparts, and individuals who have acquired these skills in military service can transfer with little difficulty from one to the other just as other workers move from one employer to another. There are, however, a great many military occupations for which transferability of learned job-skills is impossible.

Service personnel who elect not to sign up again, or who are not eligible to do so, and who have had military assignments where no transferable skill was acquired are most likely to need counselor assistance. Like the displaced homemaker, many in this group will view themselves as disadvantaged because they are competing against younger individuals for entry-level jobs. Similarly, they may also have only vague ideas about work values and occupational goals and often fail to see that, while they lack transferable specific skills, they may have generalized skills that are highly valued by employers. Further, as a result of having lived in a tightly structured and directed environment, some will need help in assuming responsibility for decision-making.

Whenever the counselor identifies the existence of problems involving self-concept, values, interpersonal relations, attitudes toward work and society, or similar personal attitudes or viewpoints, he or she must help the client focus on these factors first as a change client (see Chapter 6) before proceeding to career choice. Added complications are sometimes encountered in the former service personnel because they often feel that they are in a hurry to catch up with their age cohorts who have been in civilian jobs while they were in service, or because some fail to realize the extent of differences between life in military and civilian settings. Further, many of those who enlisted because of vocational uncertainty, or for various personal problem reasons, find those difficulties are still unresolved.

Those individuals who have completed periods of obligated service have usually incurred the obligation by accepting financial support from military sources for some portion of advanced educational training—for example, scholarship support for Advanced ROTC at the undergraduate level or a stipend or scholarship for completion of a professional school graduate program. Few of these people will need career counseling because the acquired preparation is ordinarily highly transferable. Those who have participated in such programs usually did so because they anticipated military careers or originally planned to transfer to civilian activity after satisfying the obligated period of service. Occasionally, a client who has followed this path may decide that the original choice of field was inappropriate or is no longer desirable, and may wish to move to some other kind of work.

Many governmental agencies maintain special programs of assistance for former military personnel. Clients are sometimes unaware of the help that is available to them through various community resources. Among the best known of these programs are State Service Officers, State Employment Service Agencies, state and federal Civil Service and Personnel agencies, and Veterans Administration.

Prior offenders

Delayed entrance to the world of work is sometimes the result of incarceration for acts of criminality or delinquency. Although there are some similarities between reentry problems encountered by these individuals and the problems faced by the former military personnel, there are also very significant differences.

State and federal penal institutions vary widely in fundamental philosophy relative to their purposes of rehabilitation versus custodial care. Probably the range of variation is even greater when one examines the services actually provided in these two areas. Many prison officials confirm that even in those institutions that emphasize rehabilitation programs, the primary attention is still placed on security and custody. One must conclude that very few inmates acquire significant occupational training during their imprisonment. Critics of the existing penal system often contend that the only skills learned in prison are criminal.

Most prior offenders will need extensive personal counseling before effective career counseling can be initiated. In many cases, the factors that originally led the person into difficulty may still exist. These have often been compounded by the experiences of confinement, producing an explosive mixture of hostility, anger, and frustration.

The former inmate is faced with new challenges and difficulties on release. Few communities provide any type of reentry assistance such as half-way houses or other organized social services. Prospective employers or educational institutions often react negatively to the individual on learning about the prior record. Probation and parole officers are usually overloaded and can often provide only cursory assistance. The resources available to assist in this difficult transition are generally very few, frequently of limited quality, and rarely able to overcome the opposing pressures.

In many ways, prior offenders can be described as the most disadvantaged of the disadvantaged. C. D. Miller and Oetting (1977) classified the barriers to employment faced by disadvantaged individuals into four categories, including poor job qualifications, social and interpersonal conflicts, legal and financial problems, and emotional problems. Each of these clusters is likely to be significant in counseling the prior offender. Zunker (1981) has suggested that counselors who work with disadvantaged clients should help clients set short-term goals, identify appropriate role models, and establish increased feelings of self-directedness. These activities appear to be particularly suitable to this group.

MIDLIFE CHANGERS

A recent phenomenon has been seen in increasing numbers of men making significant changes in their career plans during the midlife period. Most of the theorists whose positions we considered in Chapter 3 view career choice as occurring relatively early in life and then remaining quite firmly fixed for the remainder of the individual's working life. More recently, Super and Kidd (1979) have recognized the increased number of midlife changers by stating that role changes occurring in middle age and old age present many developmental tasks that require the individual to be ready to cope with change.

Murphy and Burck (1976) have suggested that the frequency of midlife career change will likely increase in the future. They suggest that most men reach a point between ages thirty-five and forty-five where reflection on personal and career development in recent years and consideration of what they want to accomplish in future years, causes them to choose between rededication to previously set plans or a decision to consider other options. They propose that Super's life stages be modified by inserting a "renewal" stage between the "establishment" and "maintenance" stages as recognition that change in midlife is increasingly frequent.

Thomas (1977) discusses the idea of reconfirmation versus change and proposes a two-by-two classification scheme that shows an interaction between career change and life structure change. Those men who alter both are viewed as *changers* and those who maintain both aspects are seen as *persisters*. Men who change career but retain the same life structure are labeled as *pseudochangers,* and those men who reverse this pattern by keeping the same career pattern but changing life structure are labeled *cryptochangers.*

In this section we will consider two broad groups of midlife career changers: those who change voluntarily and those who change for other reasons. Isaacson (1981) has discussed these two dimensions of career change elsewhere.

Voluntary changers

Hoppock (1976) states that individuals will change their occupational choice when they believe that the change will meet their needs in a better way. Snyder, Howard, and Hammer (1978) reinforce this statement with the view that midlife career change occurs when the combination of the attractiveness of the new opportunity plus the expectancy of successful entry exceeds the force to remain in the current position.

One factor contributing to the consideration of midlife career change is a perceived discrepancy between the individual's career dreams and aspirations and the observed realities of the present and expected future work situation. Most workers probably enter a position recognizing a disparity between their dream and reality, but also with the hope or expectation that they will be able to bring the two factors into alignment. Some readjustment is possible in most jobs, but many do not have sufficient flexibility to accommodate the change desired by some workers. When this gap cannot be closed, the worker may become frustrated, particularly if the aspiration is especially important and the chance for attaining it appears remote. Thomas (1979) found that 76 percent of a sample of men changing from high-status careers said they changed careers in order to find more meaningful work. Sixty-nine percent of that same group said they wanted to have a better fit between their values and work, but only 11 percent wanted a better salary, and 13 percent wanted more security.

Occasionally a worker suddenly discovers or gradually becomes aware of an opportunity that appears to offer the possibility of fulfilling long-held dreams. The perceived break may be new, or perhaps only the awareness of its existence is new. Either way, the worker may now look at the present job and those aspirations in a new context.

Some workers will recognize internal changes in interests and needs, and will see self as a different person from earlier times, sometimes so different that the old dreams are replaced by new ones. Those changes in aspiration may lead to career change to provide an opportunity to pursue and satisfy the new goal. Similarly, changes in family pressures or circumstances can contribute to career change. Anticipated expenditures for a large house, educational fees, or dependent parents can motivate one toward opportunities that offer higher income. Reductions in those pressures resulting from paying off the mortgage or graduation of the last child may produce the reverse desire.

Increases in the number of dual-earner and dual-career families have permitted more workers to consider the possibility of midlife career changes. The existence of another income within the family permits more room to risk change. A spouse who finds fulfillment and satisfaction in work may cause the partner to seek activities that are similarly satisfying rather than only income-producing.

Conditions related to the work setting may also produce voluntary midlife change. For example, the relocation of the work site, revision of tasks included in the job, purchase by or merger with another company, new awareness of potential dangers, even the unexpected promotion of a colleague may cause the worker to initiate a change. Similarly, technological change in either process or product may upgrade or downgrade demands made on the worker and produce dissatisfaction and uncertainty that lead to voluntary change. Other factors that instigate voluntary change include distrust of supervisors, dislike of fellow workers, inadequate pay or working conditions, or conflict with company philosophy. Often these reasons are rationalizations for deeper feelings of discontent.

Voluntary change may occur as the result of increased maturity, greater insight and self-understanding, clearer conceptualization of one's values and goals, or changing needs and new opportunities. These would appear to be worthy motives leading the worker toward situations that enhance opportunity for self-actualization.

The possibility of underlying, less positive motivators must also be considered. Vaitenas and Wiener (1977) report a significant study comparing career changers with nonchangers. They matched a group of young changers (median age of 29.4) with a group of older changers (median age of 43.0) and compared both groups to two similarly aged control groups of nonchangers. Comparisons were made on measures of personal background, aptitude, interest, emotional adjustment, and personality. They found clear differences between changers and nonchangers but little difference attributable to age. The changers were lower in congruity and consistency of interests and higher on emotional problems and fear of failure. The results suggest that at least some midlife changers and younger counterparts may be reacting to aspects of interest, emotional problems, and fear of failure that are possibly of long duration.

Voluntary midlife career changers often require more than career counseling in order to maximize opportunity in a new position. The counselor may need to help the client increase self-understanding in many areas, including those identified by Vaitenas and Wiener—consistency and congruence of interests, presence and extent of emotional problems that affect the worker in the job, and fear of failure. Such personal and motivational aspects must be evaluated and understood before considering abilities, values, life goals, and expectancies. Like younger clients, midlife career changers must first deal with self-knowledge and understanding before considering career information and job opportunities.

Involuntary changers

Some midlife career changes originate from other sources than the worker's desire to capitalize on opportunity or pursue new or old aspirations. Sometimes the worker is confronted with the necessity of making an involuntary change that may be undesired, unexpected, and often disadvantageous.

A frequent example of an involuntary changer is the recently discharged worker. Whether the worker is released because of unsatisfactory work, inability to get along with a supervisor, or dissolution of the company, the result is the same: the worker is suddenly separated from work that has been an important aspect of life. Closely related to the discharged worker is the forced-out worker—the individual who foresees imminent dismissal and resigns or quits before the boss can act.

Technological change can wipe out production processes and even entire plants, making many jobs obsolete. Similarly, company decisions to discontinue production, relocate or combine plants, develop a substitute process or product, or mechanize or automate manual processes lead to the obsolescence of workers.

Although most involuntary change happens unexpectedly, there are some situations in which the event can be anticipated, often far in advance. The most typical examples of this kind of change occur in those occupations that have "early leaver" characteristics, for example, professional athletics where one is an "old timer" by the mid-thirties. Another illustration of anticipated involuntary change can be seen in those occupations involving high physical risk and possibly early compulsory retirement, for example, firefighter, police officer, and military personnel. While some positions of this type do not carry age restrictions, the stress of heavy physical demand or the attractiveness of the pension plan essentially forces the worker to abandon the job once the minimum years of service have been fulfilled.

Jones (1979) has succinctly described the dilemma of the involuntary changer thus:

> Involuntary career loss is often a traumatic and devastating experience for an individual. The necessity of identifying and beginning a new career, when the

needs for security, self-direction, purpose, and future were being fulfilled in the former, may result in considerable turmoil. It is often accentuated by a grief reaction not easily understood by the individual involved. (p. 196)

Even though the worker may have viewed the job with little enthusiasm, its loss is still traumatic. The effect on the individual is not unlike the grief experienced with the loss of a family member. Jones states that the individual's vulnerability to grief in job or career loss will be determined by the person's understanding of why the loss occurred, the effectiveness of available support systems, and the ability to cope with stress. Until the grief aspect can be resolved, little can be done profitably in career planning. Once the person has worked through the grief, he or she can begin to focus on new opportunities or on establishing a new work life.

Involuntary changers such as forced-out workers or those who anticipated the change may have little grief involvement because they could foresee the separation and developed some accommodations before the event transpired. Although they are likely to recall good old days that now seem better than they were, readjustment is likely to be easier for them than for those for whom change was unexpected.

The counselor working with an involuntary changer must be alert for the possible presence of the grief syndrome. As in all career counseling, the counselor should first ascertain if there are particular obstacles or problems likely to interfere with effective career counseling. Where such factors appear to exist, they must be attended before proceeding to career considerations.

SPECIAL NEEDS CLIENTS

Two groups represent special needs clients. These include individuals who have a handicap as a result of physical or mental disability and individuals who are disadvantaged because of education, language, or economic factors. In one sense, every client has characteristics that might identify him or her as a special needs client because almost everyone has some physical, mental, educational, economic, or cultural limitation that impinges upon career considerations. For practical purposes, however, we will restrict our application of these two terms to those individuals where the handicap or disadvantage clearly intrudes on the career development process to a degree that demands special attention to that characteristic.

Handicapped clients

Although many people have physical or mental disabilities, not all of them are considered to be handicapped by that disability. Technically, any physical or mental anomaly that limits the individual's everyday activities is considered a disability. A disability is thought to be a vocational handicap if it is sufficiently severe or extreme enough to limit the individual's employment opportunities. A simple illustration of physical disability can be observed in most individuals who use eyeglasses. Except for those who wear glasses for cosmetic reasons, most individuals resort to wearing glasses because imperfect vision interferes with their everyday activities. The use of eyeglasses usually improves vision to such a level that most people have no problem in their occupation, so the disability is not a vocational hardship. If the person develops, through accident or illness, an uncorrectable visual deficiency so severe that he or she cannot perform his or her previous work or some other work, the person's disability is a handicap. Similarly, a congenital disability that interferes with the acquisition of salable skills would also be considered a handicap.

Disability can appear at birth or anytime thereafter. The disability can be physical such as orthopedic or sensory, mental such as retardation or cerebral palsied, or emotional in nature. One can expect that within almost every school there are youngsters who have disabilities sufficiently severe to be considered handicaps. Also within almost every community one can expect to find adults with similar problems.

Many public and private rehabilitation agencies exist at local, state, and national levels to provide special services to handicapped individuals. Unfortunately, the range of services is uneven and their quality varies considerably in different geographic areas. Further, few agencies have effective outreach programs that attempt to find those individuals who might qualify for available assistance. Thus, many handicapped individuals are unaware of services that could help them.

The counselor of a handicapped client may find it necessary to extend the counseling role to a teaching role in order to familiarize the client with the variety of assistance programs available in the locality. It is also likely that the counselor may have to assume an advocacy role to help the client obtain services to which he or she is entitled. Having a disability often makes people reticent and reluctant to assert themselves, even when they may know of available services. The counselor also may assume the role of advocate in other situations facing the handicapped client besides obtaining agency services. Examples of other situations are likely to be found when the client seeks admission to training programs or placement in a work setting. The client may also need an advocate in establishing independent living arrangements, or in other situations where he or she attempts to establish suitable living or working arrangements. Governing bodies have declared through many laws and legal decisions that handicapped individuals have the right to participate fully in society.

The goal of counseling with a vocationally handicapped person, as with a nonhandicapped individual, is to assist that person to maximize opportunities to be a self-directing, independent, functioning individual who can take responsibility for his or her life, make appropriate career decisions, and implement those decisions in a way that brings satisfaction and benefit to the individual and to society. The presence of a physical or mental handicap often produces two opposite types of reactions in others that are equally disadvantageous to the handicapped. Some people project a person's disability to all aspects of that individual's life, and conclude erroneously that because the person can't walk easily he or she can't do anything else either. This often results in that other person doing for the handicapped many things they can do for themselves, thus forcing handicapped persons into positions of dependency. Others are made uncomfortable by another's handicap and behave as though the disability were nonexistent, expecting the handicapped to do everything that everyone else does, leading to frustration and failure for the handicapped person. Somewhere between these extremes is a more realistic position. In many cases handicapped individuals can and do compete successfully with the nonhandicapped and lead lives that are just as fulfilling.

A matter for early consideration by counselor and client is the individual's attitude and feeling toward the disability and how he or she deals with that reality. Most desirable, of course, is an honest acceptance of the condition, recognizing clearly the scope of limitations produced by the disability but accompanied also by an equally clear understanding of what can still be done. Such clarity of self-understanding requires an unusual degree of maturity and insight. Consequently, the counselor will usually need to help the client explore his or her feelings and develop a better understanding of how he or she views the situation. Because the apparent disability is restrictive, it is necessary for the client to capitalize on a narrower range of activities and skills than the nonhandicapped person. Before that can be approached effectively, the client must view self realistically and positively.

Closely related to the client's self-concept is the perception held by significant others in the client's life. This group can include parents and siblings in cases where the handicapped person is a younger individual, or peers, spouse, or children if the person is an adult. Because there is a clear interaction between the views held by self and others, it is especially important for those others to react to the individual in ways that reinforce and support positive efforts toward self-sufficiency. It is entirely possible for a handicapped person to find the attitudes of significant others to be as disabling as the physical condition faced. When those significant individuals are helped to deal with attitudes and feelings toward their loved one's disability, the handicapped person finds it easier to deal with the disability. Occasionally, the counselor can help the client to recognize and correct the attitudes or feelings of those important others. More often, the counselor may become involved in family or group counseling to help build the attitudes of understanding, acceptance, and support that the client needs for successful career planning. Until the counselor is certain that the attitudes and feelings of the client towards self are positive, and the attitudes and feelings of those significant others are either positive and supportive or at least clearly understood by the client, there is little hope for success in any career-counseling efforts.

The handicapped client also needs to understand clearly the nature of the disability and its implications for his or her life both vocationally and away from the job. Misunderstanding of explanations by physicians and others can occur and can result in needless self-restriction or reckless risk taking. If there appears to be any discrepancy between the apparent disability and the client's understanding of it, the counselor must explore the reasons for this misalignment. Often the client's physician can help counselor and client acquire a more precise understanding of the existing medical information. It is especially helpful if the physician can explain the situation in terms of residual physical capacities, including the extent to which the client can meet the commonly recognized physical demands. These factors can later be used directly in considering future occupational possibilities.

Historically, handicapped individuals have been restricted to very narrow segments of the world of work. Typical of such limiting views is the widely held idea that the only suitable occupations for a blind person are vendor in a government building, piano tuning, or making and selling brooms. In actuality, the range of occupations suitable for handicapped people is very wide indeed. Cook, Dahl, and Gale (1978) report a survey in which they found seriously handicapped workers in sixty-four of the eighty-two two-digit DOT Occupational Divisions and in every one of the nine one-digit DOT Occupational Categories. Dahl (1982) emphasizes that this does not imply that every handicapped individual can qualify for every job, nor can every nonhandicapped person. Dahl further asserts that vocational counselors working with handicapped clients must consider two basic questions: (1) What occupations present realistic opportunities for disabled clients? and (2) What barriers exist to realizing such opportunities and how can these barriers be removed?

In general, career counseling with handicapped clients follows the same format as career counseling with nonhandicapped clients. Obviously, the disability introduces an additional factor that requires the counselor to have and use a wider range of knowledge and expertise. The initial stage of establishing a basis for a counseling relationship requires the counselor to recognize immediately the impact that the disability may have had on the client and the way he or she deals with self, others, and everyday life. This influence is often revealed through an anticipation of failure and hesitancy to attempt new activities or develop plans, low self-esteem, inadequate communication skills, and often a narrower range of experiences in "the real world."

As in all counseling cases, decisions about the use of typical assessment instruments depend on the need for the information they can provide and the appropriateness of their use with the specific client. Careful assessment of client attributes is often extremely important because of the need to plan more precisely with handicapped clients. Zunker (1981, 1982) has described and evaluated a number of assessment instruments that are particularly appropriate for use with handicapped clients. An important part of the evaluation process, when suitable arrangements can be made with a rehabilitation agency, is the work sample. Typical agencies will usually be able to provide work sample settings for bench work, light machine operations, clerical jobs, and sometimes more complex tasks such as woodwork, machine shop, or drafting. Assessment through the use of work samples permits some appraisal of existing work skills and habits, the potential for acquiring training, and an estimate of physical capabilities. Using work-sample tryouts may also have therapeutic values for the client, who may change attitudes toward self and his or her potential as a result of such experience. Further, he or she may acquire a more realistic understanding of what other workers expect on the job.

The expanding and narrowing of options in the decision-making process provide an opportunity to consider carefully those occupations that hold realistic opportunities for this specific client. Some occupations that may meet the limitations of the client may have to be discarded for secondary reasons such as local transportation difficulties or inaccessible work stations. Planning for preparation through formal training or education may also necessitate confronting some of the same difficulties that will be encountered in the placement process.

Job placement of handicapped clients may involve the counselor to a greater extent than with most clients. Most employers are highly sympathetic with the desires of handicapped individuals to participate in all aspects of society, including work. Many, however, see real or imaginary problems in using these persons in *their* work site. Some fear that extra expenses might be involved, others are concerned about liability, union rules, seniority, or a host of similar matters. Many communities already include sources of help to resolve problems related to placement, and the counselor should be familiar with these sources before their help is needed.

Finally, handicapped clients who recently have been placed in employment are also in greater need of follow-up during the early period of employment. Often, problems of adjustment to supervisors or fellow workers can be easily resolved when they are identified early. Minor adjustments in the work station may be needed to accommodate the individual. Dahl (1982) has discussed some of the more common barriers to employment faced by seriously handicapped individuals and has suggested strategies that counselors will find most helpful for overcoming those barriers.

The disadvantaged

Those labeled as disadvantaged include individuals with limited education (either in quantity or quality or both), with very limited economic resources (either urban or rural poor), and with geographic dislocation (often rural poor who have moved elsewhere in search of something better). Many individuals fit more than one of these categories, compounding the problems to be resolved.

Unemployment rates among these special groups indicate quite clearly the problems faced by members. According to figures reported in the *Employment and Training Report of the President* (1981), unemployment rates far exceed the rate for the general population. For example, in 1980 the overall unemployment rate for adult men and adult women was approximately six percent. In that same year the unemployment rate for blacks was approximately 15 percent and for Hispanics almost 11 percent. Even those individuals from disadvantaged groups who are employed are often in lower-paying jobs with little permanence, security, or benefits.

J. V. Miller (1982) suggests that some of the major problems related to career planning faced by the disadvantaged include lack of basic skills, unsuccessful vocational adjustment at the early stages of career entry, low income levels, incongruity between self-concept and the low-level jobs previously held, and periods of unemployment. In other words, limited education, income, or language skill has restricted access to most jobs except the most menial and transitory, where wages are minimal and satisfaction from work is even less. Limited education and income often prevent breaking the cycle in which the individual is trapped.

C. D. Miller and Oetting (1977) identified employment barriers faced by a disadvantaged urban group as four types: inadequate job qualifications, social and interpersonal conflicts, legal and financial problems, and emotional problems. They suggested that programs and services of the following kinds would remove many barriers:

1. Programs to assist with child care.
2. Information on using local transportation.
3. Programs that teach how to present qualifications.
4. Assertiveness training that emphasizes differences between aggression and assertiveness.
5. A program to resolve legal and financial problems.
6. Help with emotional and personal problems.
7. Help with drug and alcohol abuse.
8. A program for health care.
9. Language usage and communication skill development. (pp. 90–92)

Adult education and literacy programs have become more available in recent years. These provide one way of overcoming the lack of basic skills and increasing employability. Participation requires motivation on the part of the individual as well as the solution of several related problems such as transportation, scheduling, and child care. Some communities also provide access to skill training programs designed to prepare the person for participation in significant employment. Placement services, job clubs, or other support groups can assist the person in learning how to operate the system—learning how to interview for employment, use the telephone to seek job leads, prepare brief resumes, and meet employer expectations of punctuality, reliability, and cooperation.

Both J. V. Miller (1982) and Zunker (1982) discuss the importance of helping disadvantaged clients to work with both short-range and long-range goals. The counselor can use short-term planning accompanied by frequent rewards and positive reinforcement to help the client gradually move toward longer-range goals. Appropriate role models, with similar background, and confidence-building strategies will help the client to increase self-esteem and plan for longer periods of his or her life. Zunker has also described individual and group counseling procedures that are appropriately used with disadvantaged clients and has identified and described assessment instruments that can be used with such individuals.

CULTURALLY DIFFERENT CLIENTS

The culturally different include both recent legal or illegal immigrants (Vietnamese, Cubans, Mexicans, Haitians) and descendants of former immigrants who have lived in a subculture in which family and community influences, language, ethnic factors, or religious practices have caused isolation and/or alienation from the dominant culture. Also appropriately included in this category are those whose families may have lived in this country for several generations but who, because of geographic isolation, self-imposed or for other reasons, have had limited contact with the general population (for example, the Amish and Appalachian residents). Some culturally different groups may have limited English skills, atypical educational experience, unfamiliarity with socially accepted practices, and a diverse background that has produced what many might consider to be unusual values, viewpoints, and behaviors. Some of these minority groups have been included in the previous section, especially those who are economically disadvantaged.

Counselors in university counseling centers may encounter as clients students from foreign countries studying on that campus. Although most international students come to American campuses with rather firmly fixed career goals in mind, they, like their American counterparts, sometimes find that the goal was not wisely chosen. Helping that client to modify the earlier choice becomes especially difficult for the counselor whose understanding of that client's native culture may be very limited and even inaccurate. This difficulty is further compounded by the absence of any information about the structure of the world of work in that society. A further complicating ramification of this situation is faced when the student has decided that he or she wishes to remain in the United States rather than return home.

D. W. Sue (1978) has proposed a helpful framework for the counselor who works with culturally different clients. He has suggested a two-dimensional concept in which locus of control is the horizontal axis and locus of responsibility is the vertical axis. Using Rotter's social learning theory, he describes internal-control people as those who believe that reinforcement is primarily a product of their own action and external-control people as those that believe that reinforcement is not entirely self-related but can be produced by luck, chance, fate, or powerful others. Similarly, people with high internal locus of responsibility believe that success or failure is primarily attributed to the individual's skills or personal adequacy and people with high external locus of responsibility believe that the environment is more powerful than the individual. The quadrants produced by the intersection of these two axes provide four different ways to view individuals interacting with their environment or, in Sue's words, four kinds of world views.

The internal control/internal responsibility (IC/IR) quadrant, according to Sue, typifies American middle-class culture. People with this view believe they are masters of their fate and responsible for what happens to them. This viewpoint is also fundamental to a philosophy of counseling and held by most counselors. Most minorities, however, subscribe to the views reflected by one of the other quadrants. For example, people in the external control/internal responsibility (EC/IR) sector have felt they have little control over how others define them, and blame themselves or their people for their problems. Those who adhere to the external control/external responsibility (EC/ER) view see their problems of poverty, lack of education, and unemployment as the result of an oppressive social system that they are powerless to change. Thus, the counselor who holds a typical American viewpoint may fail to understand that the client looks at the world in a very different way and the counselor may, then, have expectations for client behavior that are unrealistic. The counselor may focus attention on the individual and expect him or her to initiate change when this approach is contradictory to the client's self-concept and view of the world. Misunderstanding may occur in either direction—the counselor may expect client behavior that is impossible for the client, or the client may misunderstand the counselor or the counseling process. Sue maintains that counselors must become culturally aware so that they understand their own view of the world and also understand and accept the possible legitimacy of the views of others.

One group of studies (S. Sue, Allen, Conaway, 1978; S. Sue and McKinney, 1974; and S. Sue et al., 1974) reported that Asian-American, black, Chicano, and Native American clients terminated counseling after one contact about half of the time while Anglo clients did so less than one-third of the time. The disparity in rate of termination was believed to be due to inappropriateness of interpersonal interactions. Another study (Padilla, Ruiz, and Alvarez, 1975) identified three major factors that interfere with establishing a good counseling relationship, including (a) a language barrier, (b) class-bound values suggesting that counselors work within the middle-class range, and (c) culture-bound values that are used to judge normality and abnormality in clients. Sue and Sue (1977) also suggest that other factors that interfere with communication between counselor and a culturally different client include aspects of nonverbal behavior such as personal space (interpersonal distance during verbal exchange), eye contact, and conventions like hand-shaking or other body contact, silence, loudness of speech, and directness in address.

Sue and Sue recommend that the counselor, recognizing that counseling is a white middle-class activity, guard against possible misinterpretation of behaviors and recognize that many aspects of counseling may be antagonistic to client values. Further, the counselor must evaluate his or her theoretical framework in light of client needs and values and determine the appropriateness of counseling approaches. He or she must be more action-oriented in initiating counseling, structuring the interview, and helping clients cope with problems of immediate concern. D. W. Sue and Associates (1982), in a position paper on the competencies needed for cross-cultural counseling, include the following statement:

> . . . the reality is that in most cases, counseling a person from a culturally different background poses major problems. In a cross-cultural counseling situation, differences between the counselor and client may potentially block, either partially or wholly, a counselor's (a) true understanding of the client's situation, difficulties or strengths; (b) ability to empathize with and understand the world view of the client; and (c) ability to utilize culturally relevant counseling/therapy modes. Cross-cultural counseling problems are most likely to occur when there is a low degree of client-counselor assumed similarity in terms of their respective backgrounds, values, and life-styles. Because cross-cultural counseling has been defined in terms of assumed dissimilarity between the counselor and the client, the importance of sociopolitical interpretations of differences must also be an intimate part of the definition. (p. 48)

They suggest the beliefs and attitudes, knowledge, and skills needed for effective cross-cultural counseling. These include an openness in attitude that permits the counselor to be aware of his or her own cultural heritage and its values and biases, to recognize the differences that exist between counselor and client, and to be sensitive to the needs and feelings of the client. Further, the counselor must be aware of the sociopolitical system in his or her country, knowledgeable about the minority group represented by the client, and conscious of institutional barriers. Finally, he or she must be a skilled counselor, able to generate many verbal and nonverbal responses, to send and receive messages accurately and appropriately, and to intervene on behalf of the client when appropriate.

SUMMARY

In this chapter we have considered several special groups whose characteristics or needs differentiate them from the general population encountered by the counselor. The major reasons for focusing particular attention on these groups is to emphasize that the counselor must always approach each client mindful of the classic figure-ground illustrations from basic psychology. One must be fully aware of both figure *and* ground if one is to understand the picture being presented.

We can group individuals in many ways because of shared or common backgrounds—developmental stage, experiences, handicaps or problems, cultural heritage, and other similarities. That grouping can help identify characteristics that the individual likely has in common with the other members of the group. These commonalities may suggest procedures and techniques that may be helpful with a particular client. To assume automatically that all members of a group should be treated in the same way is a most grievous error; hence, we must continually refocus on the figure as we keep in mind the background.

REFERENCES

Cook, P. F., Dahl, P. R., and Gale, M. A. *Vocational opportunities.* Salt Lake City: Olympus Publishing Company, 1978.

Dahl, P. R. Maximizing vocational opportunities for handicapped clients. *Vocational Guidance Quarterly,* 1982, *31,* 43–52.

Employment and training report of the President. Washington, D.C.: U.S. Government Printing Office, 1981.

Ginzberg, E. *Life styles of educated American women.* New York: Columbia University Press, 1966.

Hoppock, R. *Occupational information.* 4th edition. New York: McGraw-Hill Book Company, 1976.

Isaacson, L. E. Counseling male midlife career changers. *Vocational Guidance Quarterly,* 1981, *29,* 324–331.

Jones, W. H. Grief and involuntary career change: Its implications for counseling. *Vocational Guidance Quarterly,* 1979, *27,* 196–201.

Mead, J. J. A comparison of types and amount of stress encountered by dual career, dual earner, and traditional couples. Unpublished doctoral dissertation, Purdue University, 1982.

Miller, C. B. The impact of group career counseling on career maturity and on stereotypical occupational choice of high school girls. Unpublished doctoral dissertation, Purdue University, 1978.

Miller, C. D. and Oetting, G. Barriers to employment and the disadvantaged. *Personnel and Guidance Journal,* 1977, *56,* 89–93.

Miller, J. V. Lifelong career development for disadvantaged youth and adults. *Vocational Guidance Quarterly,* 1982, *30,* 359–366.

Murphy, P. P. and Burck, H. D. Career development of men at mid-life. *Journal of Vocational Behavior,* 1976, *9,* 337–343.

Padilla, A. M., Ruiz, R. A., and Alvarez, R. Community mental health services for the Spanish-speaking/surnamed population. *American Psychologist,* 1975, *30,* 892–905.

Snyder, R., Howard, A., and Hammer, T. Mid-career change in academia: The decision to become an administrator. *Journal of Vocational Behavior,* 1978, *13,* 229–241.

Sue, D. W. Counseling across cultures. *Personnel and Guidance Journal,* 1978, *56,* 458–462.

Sue, D. W., Bernier, J. E., Durran, A., Feinberg, L., Pedersen, P., Smith, E. J., and Vasquez-Nutall, E. Position paper: Cross-cultural counseling competencies. *The Counseling Psychologist,* 1982, *10,* 2, 45–52.

Sue, D. W. and Sue, D. Barriers to effective cross-cultural counseling. *Journal of Counseling Psychology,* 1977, *24,* 420–429.

Sue, S., Allen, D. B. and Conaway, L. The responsiveness and equality of mental health care to Chicanos and Native Americans. *American Journal of Community Psychology,* 1978, *6,* 137–146.

Sue, S. and McKinney, H. Asian Americans in the community mental health care system. *American Journal of Orthopsychiatry,* 1974, *45,* 111–118.

Sue, S., McKinney, H., Allen, D., and Hall, J. Delivery of community mental health services to black and white clients. *Journal of Consulting and Clinical Psychology,* 1974, *42,* 794–801.

Super, D. E. *The psychology of careers.* New York: Harper & Row, Publishers, 1957.

Super, D. E., and Kidd, J. M. Vocational maturity in adulthood: Toward turning a model into a measure. *Journal of Vocational Behavior,* 1979, *14,* 255–270.

Thomas, L. E. Mid-career changes: Self-selected or externally mandated? *Vocational Guidance Quarterly,* 1977, *25,* 320–328.

———. Causes of mid-career changes from high status careers. *Vocational Guidance Quarterly,* 1979, *27,* 202–208.

Vaitenas, R., and Wiener, Y. Development, emotional, and interest factors in voluntary mid-career change. *Journal of Vocational Behavior,* 1977, *11,* 291–304.

Zunker, V. G. *Career counseling: Applied concepts of life planning.* Monterey, Cal.: Brooks/Cole Publishing Company, 1981.

———. *Using assessment results in career counseling.* Monterey, Cal.: Brooks/Cole Publishing Company, 1982.

Index

SUBJECT INDEX